Jonathan Glover

Causing Death and Saving Lives

Penguin Books

PENGUIN BOOKS

Published by the Penguin Group
Penguin Books Ltd, 27 Wrights Lane, London W8 5TZ, England
Penguin Books USA Inc., 375 Hudson Street, New York, New York 10014, USA
Penguin Books Australia Ltd, Ringwood, Victoria, Australia
Penguin Books Canada Ltd, 10 Alcorn Avenue, Toronto, Ontario, Canada M4V 3B2
Penguin Books (NZ) Ltd, 182–190 Wairau Road, Auckland 10, New Zealand

Penguin Books Ltd, Registered Offices: Harmondsworth, Middlesex, England

First published in Pelican Books 1977
Reprinted in Penguin Books 1990
10 9 8 7 6 5

Copyright © Jonathan Glover, 1977
All rights reserved

Printed in England by Clays Ltd, St Ives plc
Set in Intertype Times

PENGUIN BOOKS

CAUSING DEATH AND SAVING LIVES

Jonathan Glover was born in 1941 and educated at Tonbridge School and Corpus Christi College, Oxford. He is a Fellow and tutor in philosophy at New College, Oxford, and has written *Responsibility* (1970), *What Sort of People Should There Be?* (Penguin, 1977) and *I: The Philosophy and Psychology of Personal Identity* (Penguin, 1989). He is married and has three children.

To A.M.B. and S.G.B.

Contents

CONTENTS

Acknowledgements

Far too many people have influenced this book to be mentioned here. Its topics have been discussed with many graduates and undergraduates studying philosophy, as well as with members of medical groups and with friends having no professional interest in these questions. For several years, Derek Parfit, Jim Griffin and I have given a class in the summer term at Oxford, and there especially I have found the ideas and criticisms put forward helpful and stimulating.

Ted Honderich was a source of most valuable advice and comments. Derek Osborn disapproved in a constructive way of Chapter 7 and the section about Father Zossima's brother is an attempt to accommodate his criticisms, though it is unlikely that we now fully agree. Alan Ryan and Nancy Davis each gave me written comments on an earlier draft, and the present version is better as a result. R.M. Hare has been exceptionally generous in his encouragement of the book. I have also been helped by conversations with Richard Keshen and with Ann Puntis. Peter Skegg has introduced me to a lot of relevant literature I would otherwise have missed. Geoffrey de Ste Croix made interesting comments about the chapter on war. David Owen drew my attention to the passage from Aristotle on pages 51–2. John Havard read the proofs more effectively than I did.

I am grateful to Stephanie Verhoeven for typing most of the chapters. The Warden and Fellows of New College gave me a sabbatical term during which I finished the book.

Derek Parfit has discussed most of these topics with me over the period of writing, and generously wrote many pages of perceptive comments on an earlier draft. I have learnt a great deal from him. Chapter 4 especially makes use of his ideas, but I would like to think that the whole book, because of his influence, is a bit more imaginative than it otherwise would have been.

My wife Vivette has discussed all these questions with me, and has affected this book more than anyone else. Many details have changed as a result of her comments, but, more important, the whole way I see things is different because of our thinking and talking together.

Preface

This book discusses the moral problems involved in killing and saving lives. It is a philosophical book, but is written for anyone interested in these topics and assumes no familiarity with philosophy.

Some of the topics discussed could in certain ways be handled better by those with experience which I lack. Any totally non-medical person is bound to feel some presumption in suggesting what would be the right decision for a doctor to take in a matter of life or death. Some doctors have great experience of these choices and their outcomes. And there are lawyers with greater understanding of complexities which I merely gesture at in suggesting here and there that reform is desirable. There are sociologists who are better informed about suicide, and criminologists better qualified to discuss the effect of capital punishment. And I have discussed the morality of war despite having only an amateurish interest in the thinking of strategists.

But, after noting these limitations, I am less apologetic about them than might seem appropriate. This is because the questions discussed here are related to each other. Attitudes to suicide and euthanasia, or capital punishment and war, cannot rationally be kept totally separate. And what we say about any of these topics has links in one direction with general philosophical views about why it is wrong to kill, and has implications in another direction for social policies involving either saving lives or risking them. No one is qualified to talk about all these problems, but something is lost if, as a result, each is discussed only out of the context of the others.

There are two limitations about which I feel more regret. I had intended to discuss the relative importance of saving lives in the order of social priorities: the sort of issues raised when economists doing cost-benefit studies wonder how to weight the saving of lives or some increased risk to life. I have read and thought about these questions, but they now seem much more difficult than I expected, and my thinking is still too confused and tentative to include here. The second limitation is the absence of any proper treatment of the problems of killing animals. I am inclined towards the conventional view that animal life is much less important than human life, but my reasons for this when written down have a disconcerting air of intellectual dishonesty, as though they were merely constructed to rationalize my non-vegetarianism. So they are not included here.

My original motives for writing this book were the interest of the questions involved and my own lack of any clear and defensible answers. Now, I have two hopes for the book. One of its aims is to persuade people to change opinions which they already hold. This is because some of the views criticized here cause much unnecessary misery, while others lead to loss of life that could and should be avoided. The conventional view that philosophical discussions are quite remote from having any practical upshot, such as prevention of suffering or loss of life, has very little to be said for it.

The second aim does not entirely harmonize with the first. It is to encourage people to work out views opposed to those argued for here. If discussion of these questions is to get beyond mere exchange of intuitive prejudices, it is necessary to work out fairly systematically the implications of different general approaches. Obviously no opinions on these topics will at once gain general support, and perhaps this is especially true of some of those put forward here. But I would be very pleased if this book helped people who disagree to work out their own views more clearly by contrast.

Part One: Problems and Methods

Chapter 1 The Problems

Many of us find moral problems about killing difficult, and most of those who do not should do. It is often said to be always wrong to take human life, but many people find it hard to say this when confronted with questions of killing set in some specific contexts. Very few people are committed to absolute pacifism. Some support capital punishment. There are several different views about abortion.

If we think that there is any act of killing that can be justified, we are confronted with the problem of drawing boundaries between killings that are permissible and those that are not. In what circumstances, if any, is war justified? When, if ever, is abortion justified? Some people say that it is justified where the baby is likely to be born grossly abnormal, as when the mother has German measles early in her pregnancy. But many of the same people would be appalled at the suggestion that we should kill grossly abnormal children or babies who have already been born. Are we morally justified in drawing this kind of line between foetus and baby, and if so why?

Can we formulate any general principles to tell us which acts of killing, if any, are right and which are wrong? This is the central question of this book. But discussion of this problem is less fruitful when carried on in isolation from other related questions. Are there any general principles to tell us when, if ever, it is morally obligatory to save life? Doctors often say that in difficult cases they act on the principle 'Thou shalt not kill, but needs't not strive officiously to keep alive.' But why is there thought to be a moral difference between killing someone and intentionally failing to save his life? When I spend money on my own pleasures instead of giving it to Oxfam, it is likely that I am allowing someone to die whom I might have saved. Is this so much less bad than killing someone, and, if so, why? If there is any kind of moral duty to save lives, how high a priority should this be given? What should we do in situations where there is a choice between the lives of different people? Should we allocate scarce medical resources as nearly randomly as possible, or should we give preference to some people over others? How much weight should we give to the possibility of saving a larger number of lives by departures from randomness?

These questions can be very roughly divided into two classes: problems that arise in medical contexts and those that arise in more general social and political contexts. The medical questions are about abortion, infanticide, euthanasia and the allocation of scarce life-saving resources. The more general social and political questions include those about the morality of war, revolution, assassination and capital punishment. Others are suggested by reflection on some of our society's priorities. In some contexts, lives are saved at great expense while other people die when far less money could have saved them. To what extent should we spend money on a dramatic rescue of a small number of known people, rather than on higher safety standards that will save a larger number of people in the future, but whose identity will never be known to us?

It is obvious that these two groups of questions are not always sharply distinct. Suicide is not less a social problem than assassinations or capital punishment, but may also be thought to raise issues of principle similar to those of the 'medical' problem of voluntary euthanasia. Again, reasons we may give for valuing numbers of lives saved in a medical context are relevant to thinking about revolutions and wars. These questions will be discussed separately here, but they will be discussed in the light of general principles. It will be argued that these principles apply to all situations where the taking or saving of life is in question. We need general principles to show us how to act in specific cases, but the specific cases also act as tests of the adequacy of our principles.

Many people think that a discussion of this kind, arguing about the merits of general moral principles, is either superfluous or else impossible. This is often because they make one of two false assumptions.

20

One of these assumptions is that there is one set of 'true' moral beliefs, which no humane, rational and informed person could reject once he understood them. This view makes moral argument redundant. The other assumption is that moral beliefs are so subjective that no useful discussion can take place between those who differ. (We do not try to argue someone out of his preference for raspberries over strawberries.) This view makes moral argument impossible.

Because discussions of the morality of killing, like those of any moral matter, are so often vitiated by philosophical confusions, the next chapter is about methods of argument. It is necessary to consider the extent to which beliefs about what we ought to do can be supported or undermined by rational argument.

The second part of the book is about some general moral theories. It considers six moral beliefs that dominate discussion about when it is right or wrong to kill:

(i) The doctrine of the sanctity of life: that killing is an intrinsic evil.

(ii) Utilitarianism: the doctrine that an act is right or wrong according to whether or not it maximizes happiness and minimizes misery.

(iii) The view that whether someone lives or dies is normally something that other people cannot decide without an objectionable denial of his autonomy.

(iv) The belief that people have a right to live.

(v) The doctrine of 'double effect', which can crudely be stated as the view that it may be permissible to perform a good act with some foreseeable bad consequences, but that it is wrong to do a bad act for the sake of the good consequences that will follow.

(vi) The belief that there is an important moral difference between acts and omissions, say between killing and 'not striving to keep alive'.

In the light of the discussion of these general moral beliefs, the third part of the book will return to questions of killing and saving lives in particular medical or social contexts.

Chapter 2   The Scope and Limits
of Moral Argument

There are several different scales of values in the world, if not
many: there is a scale for events near at hand and a scale for
events at a distance; there is a scale for old societies and a scale
for young ones; a scale for happy events, a scale for
unfortunate ones. Glaringly, the divisions of the scales fail to
coincide: they dazzle and hurt our eyes, and so that we do not
feel the pain we wave aside all alien scales, judging them to be
folly and delusion, and confidently judge the whole world
according to our own domestic scale.

Alexander Solzhenitsyn: *'One Word of Truth . . .'* London, 1972

1 Preliminaries

There is no general agreement how the word 'morality' should
be used. Some people think of morality as a set of rules laid
down by God. Others think of it as a set of socially imposed
rules with the function of reducing conflict in society. Others
say it is a set of principles about how we ought to live that apply
to everyone impartially, or which can be defended by appealing
to the interests of people in general. These disagreements are a
problem for anyone trying to say what moral beliefs are, but
they will not be discussed here.

The question of what it means to say that a person 'ought' to
do something is also one that will not be raised here. Much
recent moral philosophy is devoted to this difficult problem,
which still has no generally accepted solution. But I shall
assume that we all, at *some* level, understand what is meant by
saying that someone ought to do something. Perhaps that is all
that the arguments of this book require, beyond the ruling out

of one particularly narrow use of the word 'moral'. On this narrow view, morality is divorced from what we ought to do. A soldier may say that part of his morality is the command 'thou shalt not kill', but that moral considerations have to be subordinated to practical ones, such as the need to defend your country. But, as the word 'morality' is to be used here, where the soldier thinks that patriotism *ought* to take priority over not killing, it is not true that his morality forbids all killing.

2 Moral Disagreements

If a pacifist and a non-pacifist argue about the morality of war, it may be that their disagreement is essentially factual. The pacifist may say that wars always cause more misery than they prevent, so that no war is ever justified. The non-pacifist may agree that no war would be justified if all wars caused more misery than they prevented, but he may deny that this is true. Evidence, even if only of an inconclusive kind, can be cited in support of one view or the other.

But sometimes moral differences could survive the answering of all relevant factual questions. A pacifist and a non-pacifist might agree that some particular war was likely to cause less misery than it prevented, but still disagree about its morality. The pacifist might say that the reduction of misery does not justify the deliberate taking of human life. If he is asked why he thinks this, he may reply that the sanctity of life is an ultimate belief of his, capable of no further justification. He may then press the non-pacifist to say why he attaches such weight to reducing misery, and the non-pacifist may similarly have to reply that the undesirability of suffering is one of his ultimate beliefs.

Where two people hold different beliefs at the most fundamental level, it may be that no further argument is possible between them. I can defend my view that the avoidance of war is good, because I regard it as only an instrumental good: it is good as a means to things I regard as intrinsically good, such as the avoidance of suffering. But I cannot defend my view that the avoidance of suffering is good. This is just because I think it good in itself, rather than good because it leads to something else that could be cited in its defence.

But it is possible that, in the argument between the pacifist and the non-pacifist, we have not yet reached the level of ultimate principles. The pacifist may claim that killing is always wrong because God has forbidden it. We may then, if we waive questions about how he knows that God exists or what God has forbidden, ask him why he believes that we ought to obey God. Perhaps it will be at this point that no further justification is forthcoming, and we realize that we have finally reached an ultimate belief: in this case that it is intrinsically good to obey God.

Similarly, the non-pacifist may provide reasons why he believes we ought to reduce suffering as much as possible. He may say that people always want to avoid suffering. We may then, if we waive questions about martyrs and masochists, ask him why we ought to satisfy universally held wants. If he can give no further reason, we have discovered something he believes to be intrinsically good.

We can often supply a chain of reasoning when challenged to defend a moral belief about what ought to be done. Any such chain of argument seems either to involve an infinite regress or else to end with an ultimate moral belief. Such a belief is ultimate in that what it tells us to do is not prescribed because it is instrumental to some further good. These ultimate beliefs are like the axioms of a system of geometry: the other beliefs of a moral system are derivable from the axioms, but the axioms themselves cannot be 'proved'.

Many of those who accept John Stuart Mill's claim that 'Questions of ultimate ends are not amenable to direct proof' think that this is sufficient to establish the futility of argument in moral matters. It may seem that, since nothing could count as 'proving' one set of values to be 'true', it is as pointless to argue about morality as it would be to try to persuade someone by argument to prefer one colour to another.

But this is to take too pessimistic a view. Even leaving aside the extent to which argument about facts can be relevant to questions about what ought to be done, there are various fruitful methods of argument about moral beliefs.

One method of arguing against a moral belief is to show that it depends on concepts that are blurred or incoherent. Someone who believes that homosexual acts are wicked because they are unnatural may be open to this kind of argument. If pressed to define 'unnatural' he may find it hard to provide a definition that includes homosexual acts without also including singing at the opera.

Another method of rational moral argument involves the exposure of logical inadequacies. This may take the form of showing that what are taken to be good reasons for holding a belief are not really so. (It is often said that human suffering matters more than animal suffering because we have rationality of a kind or degree that animals lack. But reflection about feeble-minded children may make us question this as a reason for thinking that animal *suffering* is less important.) Or it may take the form of exposing inconsistencies in someone's principles. If you disapprove of all abortions, I may ask you to give a reason. If you reply that to take human life is always wrong, I will ask if you are a complete pacifist. If you hold some non-pacifist . views about war, you must either abandon or modify your principle that taking life is always wrong or else change your mind about pacifism. This (very crude) example shows how it is possible to apply legitimate pressure to the moral beliefs of anyone sufficiently rational to be disturbed by inconsistency.

And moral argument has a wider scope than the exposing of inconsistencies within someone's formulated principles. It often takes the form of showing someone that his beliefs have unnoticed consequences that he would find unacceptable. Some general principles used in support of abortion provide an equally good justification for infanticide. Someone who holds such a principle, but who cannot accept the consequent rightness of infanticide, is trapped in an inconsistency. The general principle must be abandoned or modified or else the un-palatable consequence must be accepted. The pattern of argument here is similar to that used to link abortion and pacifism in the previous case. The difference is that there the inconsistency was between two beliefs already formulated and accepted, while here inconsistency is between an accepted principle and a moral response to a question not previously considered.

Moral beliefs can be undermined by our responses to their consequences. But our responses are themselves liable to modification, either by experience or by the development of imagination. Someone who accepts with equanimity that his patriotic principles commit him to supporting certain wars may find this consequence less acceptable if he ever experiences war as a soldier. It is a truism that we are able to accept the rightness of actions or policies often only because of a failure of imagination, and experience of their consequences often greatly changes our responses. Sometimes experience may not be needed. It can be enough to use some imagination, and often films or novels can help us to respond in a more sensitive or imaginative way. Someone who thinks that Stalin's labour camps were an acceptable consequence of a morally legitimate policy may not himself be able to experience such a camp, but the novels of Solzhenitsyn may modify his views about what is acceptable.

3 The Interplay Between Responses and General Beliefs

On the view so far outlined, moral principles are 'tested' by our responses that their consequences are acceptable or unacceptable. It may seem that, on such an account, our general moral beliefs do very little work, and exist as mere summaries of our particular responses. But our general beliefs need not be merely derivative from our responses: they can also function to modify and evaluate our responses. In the light of a general morality it is possible to regard a specific response as inadequate, exaggerated or misplaced. If I hear of some painful experiment carried out on an animal, I may feel that all vivisection is unacceptable. But reflection on this in the light of my whole morality may make me regard this response as too squeamish or too hasty. It may be hard to sustain an opposition to medical experiments on animals when I remember my responses to human suffering caused by diseases.

The interplay between our responses and our general moral beliefs is in some ways similar to that between observations and theories in science. A scientific theory can be modified or refuted by the experimental falsification of a prediction derived from it. But when a theory is well established, there is great reluctance to accept that it has been falsified and a tendency to explain away the supposedly falsifying observation as unreliable. There are no formulated general rules of scientific method that tell us how much weight to give a theory and how much weight to give to an observation apparently incompatible with it. In extreme cases, what is rational is fairly clear. When a theory has little supporting evidence, the disconfirming of one of its main predictions by a few reputable experimenters will normally undermine it. On the other hand, very firmly established theories are not rejected because of daily failures to confirm their predictions in school laboratories.

Just as in science there are no general rules to tell us exactly when a certain theory is more likely to be right than a claim about an apparently falsifying observation, so in moral thinking there are no rules to adjudicate between general beliefs and responses to specific cases. But, just as rationality in science involves trying to harmonize theories and observations, so rationality in ethics involves trying to formulate a coherent set of beliefs that does justice to as many of one's responses as possible.

A science which is alive in one historical period can go dead in another. This 'going dead' consists in the abandonment of the interplay between theory and observation. The theory is treated as dogma; no new questions are asked; no experimental tests are carried out. Moralities are sometimes dead in a parallel way. Taught as dogma and left uncriticized, they are no longer modified by experience and imagination in the direction of greater subtlety or sophistication. As a dead morality comes to be seen as rigid and crude, there is a natural temptation no longer to regard it as a morality in the sense under discussion. The word 'morality' comes no longer to be used to denote a set of beliefs abôut what ought to be done. Instead, it is used to denote a set of rules that can often rightly be ignored, like the rules of etiquette. Dead moralities encourage people to think in a way that allows them to say such things as 'I know it is morally wrong, but moral considerations ought to take second place to practical ones.'

A view not based in this way on dead moralities rejects claims of this kind, and thus rules out an important defence mechanism. For when someone, contrasting moral considerations with practical ones, gives priority to the latter, he is defending himself in two ways. He is defending his conduct against the criticism that it is immoral, by implying that it falls outside the scope or jurisdiction of morality. At the same time he is protecting his morality from being modified by his experience. He admits that his morality is impractical, with the insinuation that it is in the nature of a morality to be so. The soldier who thinks that killing is always morally wrong but often right in practice has a 'morality' and a way of life that are comfortably protected from each other.

Just as one kind of scientific integrity consists in submitting one's theories to thorough testing, so one kind of moral integrity consists in refusing to isolate one's morality from one's conduct and experience. There are at least two kinds of bad faith that can arise here. The first, already mentioned, consists in holding 'moral' beliefs that one does not believe ought to be acted on and whose consequences as a result are not often experienced. The second consists in a deliberate filtering or distortion of experience, so that responses incompatible with accepted general beliefs do not arise. An opponent of voluntary euthanasia who refused to visit a geriatric ward out of fear of his beliefs being disrupted would be exhibiting this kind of bad faith, as would a supporter of it who refused to think about or meet the doctor asked to do the killing.

It can sometimes be right to avoid contact with people affected by your own actions, where this might generate a bias in favour of their interests relative to those of other people. (This factor seems to have influenced Mr Roy Jenkins, Home Secretary in 1974, when he had to decide whether to yield to a hunger strike by the Price sisters, I.R.A. members convicted of a violent crime, in support of their demand for transfer to a prison in Northern Ireland. Mr Jenkins said, 'I have not seen them myself. I considered this possibility, but rejected it firmly. I did not see the suffering of their victims in hospital. I do not think it right that I should see their hunger strike in prison. The person on whom the ultimate decision rests must, I am sure, stand back a little.' This seems quite legitimate for someone who has to weigh up the interests of the Price sisters and the interests of potential future victims of acts of violence similar to theirs.)

4 Why Have General Moral Beliefs?

Sometimes it is said that we can do without general moral beliefs and simply be guided by our intuitive responses. (D.H. Lawrence has been influential here.) Discussion of morality in general terms can be seen as something stale and second-hand. On this view, insights as to how we should live arise as we develop experimentally a way of life, and the making of generalizations is a derivative task for lovers of taxonomy and the legalistically inclined.

One argument for formulating general moral beliefs is that the alternative is very likely to involve a tacit inconsistency. To take again a crude example, it is characteristic of many people's responses in a political context that they believe that tax increases are a bad thing, but that more money should be spent on schools, hospitals, roads, defence and pensions. There is at least a surface inconsistency in these responses. Only thinking in general terms about priorities, as well as about how to put them into effect, will either remove the inconsistency or show it to be only apparent. (It is striking how many people mess up their lives by not thinking clearly and coherently about what they really value.)

Another argument appeals, not to consistency, but to autonomy. We do not reach adult life with open minds about morality. Whether or not we accept Freud's claims about the way the pressures of family relationships and sexual adjustment mould the super-ego, or Marx's claims about the crucial role of the economic system in determining the moral consciousness of society, only a naïve person could deny the influence of social and personal pressures on moral responses. Many people's responses are simply the result either of childhood conditioning or of the views currently fashionable in their society. The first step away from being manipulated, and towards a more autonomous outlook, is to stand back from a set of responses and to think.

There is also the argument that there may be cases where intuitive reactions cannot be relied on for guidance. Sometimes we suspect that self-interest or emotional disturbance is distorting our responses. Someone asked by a doctor whether or not further efforts should be made to prolong the life of an old relation, painfully ill in a geriatric ward, may not trust his own responses. It may be hard to tell how much they are distorted by the fact that in the event of survival the relation would be a burden, or by fear of guilt if he agrees that treatment should stop. It is helpful, in deciding whether to trust a response, to see whether or not it fits in with general beliefs worked out when free from such pressures.

Sometimes people do not have a single, clear intuitive response by which to be guided. Some babies with gross abnormalities are allowed to die when their lives could be saved. For someone who accepts that this is justified, it may be hard to know where to draw a line. How serious an abnormality makes it better for a person not to live? Many of us have no clear intuitive answer to such a question. If we were doctors or surgeons having to make such choices we would often be quite uncertain what we ought to do. In such cases, we could only fall back on general beliefs about the sorts of factors that ought to be considered. Such beliefs will not always give clear guidance. But for someone who has neither intuitive answers nor any relevant general beliefs, there is no basis whatever on which to decide.

5 Degrees of Guidance

There are at least two reasons why general moral beliefs may give inadequate guidance in a particular case. It may be that not all the facts are clear: we may not know how senile the old person will be if he lives, or how much the abnormal baby will come to be able to have a relationship with other people. Another reason is that cases vary so much that beliefs formulated in very general terms may not immediately generate a decision in a complicated situation.

Those who doubt the value of such general beliefs often think that moral beliefs must either be crude and inflexible or else of a cumbersome complexity similar to tax law. But these are not the only alternatives. It is possible to have a moral system whose outlines are sketched in, but whose detailed applications were only worked out in advance where often needed. (A surgeon may give more detailed thought in advance to abortion or euthanasia than to moral questions about censorship.) The more detailed guidance a moral system gives, the more complex it is likely to be. On the other hand, the less it is worked out in detail, the more likely it is to entail unnoticed unacceptable consequences.

6 Is It Futile to Propose Moral Beliefs?

It is sometimes said that it is pointless to argue for a set of moral beliefs. It may be claimed that, in morality, any formulated proposal must either reflect a way of life which already has an independent existence or else must be a mere pipe dream. The view that moral proposals must be either superfluous or else powerless seems to underlie some famous remarks made by Hegel. He said:

> One more word about giving instruction as to what the world ought to be. Philosophy in any case always comes on the scene too late to give it. As the thought of the world, it appears only when actuality is already there cut and dried after its process of formation has been completed. The teaching of the concept, which is also history's inescapable lesson, is that it is only when actuality is mature that the ideal first appears over against the real and that the ideal apprehends this same real world in its substance and builds it up for itself into the shape of an intellectual realm. When philosophy paints its grey in grey, then has a shape of life grown old. By philosophy's grey in grey it cannot be rejuvenated but only understood. The owl of Minerva spreads its wings only with the falling of the dusk.[1]

It is no doubt true that a person's moral views are influenced by the historical period and by the society in which he lives. But it is possible to develop new beliefs that are not mere reflections of practices already in existence, perhaps as a result of critical thought about existing beliefs and practices. Hegel himself was sceptical of the value of working out such new beliefs. He said:

> Whatever happens, every individual is a child of his time; so philosophy too is its own time apprehended in thoughts. It is just as absurd to fancy that a philosophy can transcend its contemporary world as it is to fancy that an individual can overleap his own age, jump over Rhodes. If this theory really goes beyond the world as it is and builds an ideal one as it ought to be, that world exists indeed, but only in his own opinions, an insubstantial element where anything you please may, in fancy, be built.

But this scepticism of Hegel's seems to rest on the dubious assumption that new ideas about how the world ought to be cannot influence what in fact happens. And, even if it were true

1. G.W.F. Hegel: *Philosophy of Right*, translated by T.M. Knox, Oxford, 1942, Preface.

that new moral ideas were generally uninfluential, it would be hard to deny their potential in areas of moral confusion. When certain questions about killing arise, there is no generally agreed doctrine about what ought to be done. In this area especially, it seems unduly pessimistic to suppose that systematic thinking must be powerless to shape conduct. This doctrine of the impotence of ideas rests on one of two beliefs. One is that, in matters of morality, people can never be influenced by each other's beliefs. The other is that our moral beliefs and attitudes never determine what we do. The truth of these claims is more often assumed than argued for.

7 Imaginary Cases

We have seen that general beliefs about what ought to be done can be 'tested' by seeing whether or not one finds their consequences acceptable. But sometimes this testing has to rely on responses to hypothetical cases rather than to actual ones. These hypothetical cases are often necessary even to determine what someone's beliefs are. Two people may both oppose capital punishment and may both hold the view that capital punishment does not reduce the murder rate. But their reasons for opposing capital punishment may be fundamentally different. One may think that it is impermissible because there is no evidence that it prevents murders, while the other may hold a view (similar to that of an absolute pacifist) that it would be wrong even if it did substantially reduce the murder rate. The only way to bring out their deeper level difference of belief is to ask the hypothetical question, 'but suppose it did deter potential murderers, what would you believe then?'

For many people, a natural response to a question of this kind is to show a certain impatience. If capital punishment is not a deterrent, what is the point of discussing a non-existent situation in which it did deter people? But this response is too brisk. We are interested in someone's general beliefs. Since, as in the case of capital punishment, people with very different

33

general beliefs may, in the situation that actually exists, support the same policy, we can only bring out their disagreements by asking them to imagine a rather altered situation. And the point of these imaginary cases is not only to make it clear what general beliefs someone holds, but also to provide tests of their acceptability. A man who thinks that capital punishment is wrong because the state never has the right to take a citizen's life may be asked whether he would still think this if ten potential murder victims were saved by each execution. Such a case functions as a test of whether he really finds the consequences of his belief acceptable.

The use of hypothetical cases in this way is not a new method in ethics. Consider this passage from the introduction to the *Republic*.

'That's fair enough, Cephalus,' I said. 'But are we really to say that doing right consists simply and solely in truthfulness and returning anything we have borrowed? Are those not actions that can be sometimes right and sometimes wrong? For instance, if one borrowed a weapon from a friend who subsequently went out of his mind and then asked for it back, surely it would be generally agreed that one ought not to return it, and that it would not be right to do so, or to consent to tell the strict truth to a madman?'

'That is true,' he replied.

'Well then,' I said, 'telling the truth and returning what we have borrowed is not the definition of doing right.'

But of course the antiquity or prestige of those who first used a method of thinking are only of historical interest and in no way count as defences of it. The objection to the use of hypothetical cases in ethics seems to be that there is something 'unreal' or artificial about such a procedure. The legitimate defence against this criticism can take the form of saying that the artificiality involved is one that has been fruitful in other fields. In a scientific experiment, the influence of all factors not being studied is, as far as possible, 'artificially' eliminated. A defence of experimental method has its parallel in the case for arguing about ethics by means of asking for responses to deliberately simplified imaginary situations. The imaginary cases discussed in this book are not ones which are merely conceivable, but satisfy the stronger requirement that our present knowledge does not show them to be factually impossible.

8 The Possibility of Disagreement

Various ways in which rational argument about moral principles resembles scientific inquiry have been stressed here. The purpose has been to make clearer the relatively rarely understood methods of one inquiry by comparing them with the more commonly understood procedures of the other. The aim has not been to borrow the prestige of science. No claim is made that moral argument can establish general principles which any rational and informed person must accept. The testing of a coherent set of moral beliefs comes in one's responses. Since different people often have different responses, not everyone will agree as to when a general belief has been undermined. There is always the possibility, and sometimes the reality, of ultimate disagreement. There would be little point in public discussion and argument if people's responses hardly ever coincided about anything. But, although that state of moral anarchy does not exist, different people's responses do vary more fundamentally and more frequently than is often recognized. It would be possible for someone to accept all the *arguments* put forward in the rest of this book and yet legitimately to reject many of the conclusions because they do not accept the premises.

Sometimes I shall argue against certain beliefs that they are incoherent, or else that reasons thought to support them do not really do so. Such claims can in principle be objectively established or refuted. At other times I shall argue that the consequences of some beliefs are morally unacceptable. I do not want to pretend that this sort of claim has any kind of 'objectivity'.

Part Two: Moral Theory

Chapter 3   The Sanctity of Life

I cannot but have reverence for all that is called life. I cannot avoid compassion for all that is called life. That is the beginning and foundation of morality.

Albert Schweitzer: *Reverence for Life.*

To persons who are not murderers, concentration camp administrators, or dreamers of sadistic fantasies, the inviolability of human life seems to be so self-evident that it might appear pointless to inquire into it. To inquire into it is embarrassing as well because, once raised, the question seems to commit us to beliefs we do not wish to espouse and to confront us with contradictions which seem to deny what is self-evident.

Edward Shils: 'The Sanctity of Life', in D.H. Labby: *Life or Death: Ethics and Options*, 1968

Most of us think it is wrong to kill people. Some think it is wrong in all circumstances, while others think that in special circumstances (say, in a just war or in self-defence) some killing may be justified. But even those who do not think killing is always wrong normally think that a special justification is needed. The assumption is that killing can at best only be justified to avoid a greater evil.

It is not obvious to many people what the answer is to the question *'Why* is killing wrong?' It is not clear whether the wrongness of killing should be treated as a kind of moral axiom, or whether it can be explained by appealing to some more fundamental principle or set of principles. One very common view is that some principle of the sanctity of life has to be included among the ultimate principles of any acceptable moral system.

In order to evaluate the view that life is sacred, it is necessary to distinguish between two different kinds of objection to killing: direct objections and those based on side-effects.

1 Direct Objections and Side-effects

Direct objections to killing are those that relate solely to the person killed. Side-effects of killings are effects on people other than the one killed. Many of the possible reasons for not killing someone appeal to side-effects. (To call them 'side-effects' is not to imply that they must be less important than the direct objections.) When a man dies or is killed, his parents, wife, children or friends may be made sad. His family may always have a less happy atmosphere and very likely less money to spend. The fatherless children may grow up to be less secure and confident than they would have been. The community loses whatever good contribution the man might otherwise have made to it. Also, an act of killing may help weaken the general reluctance to take life or else be thought to do so. Either way, it may do a bit to undermine everyone's sense of security.

Most people would probably give some weight to these side-effects in explaining the wrongness of killing, but would say that they are not the whole story, or even the main part of it. People who say this hold that there are direct objections to killing, independent of effects on others. This view can be brought out by an imaginary case in which an act of killing would have no harmful side-effects.

Suppose I am in prison, and have an incurable disease from which I shall very soon die. The man who shares my cell is bound to stay in prison for the rest of his life, as society thinks he is too dangerous to let out. He has no friends, and all his relations are dead. I have a poison that I could put in his food without him knowing it and that would kill him without being detectable. Everyone else would think he died from natural causes.

In this case, the objections to killing that are based on side-effects collapse. No one will be sad or deprived. The community will not miss his contribution. People will not feel insecure, as no one will know a murder has been committed. And even the possible argument based on one murder possibly weakening my own reluctance to take life in future carries no weight here, since I shall die before having opportunity for further killing. It might even be argued that consideration of side-effects tips the balance positively in favour of killing this man, since the cost of his food and shelter is a net loss to the community.

Those of us who feel that in this case we cannot accept that killing the man would be either morally right or morally neutral must hold that killing is at least sometimes wrong for reasons independent of side-effects. One version of this view that killing is directly wrong is the doctrine of the sanctity of life. To state this doctrine in an acceptable way is harder than it might at first seem.

2 Stating the Principle of the Sanctity of Life

The first difficulty is a minor one. We do not want to state the principle in such a way that it must have overriding authority over other considerations. To say 'taking life is always wrong' commits us to absolute pacifism. But clearly a pacifist and a non-pacifist can share the view that killing is in itself an evil. They need only differ over when, if ever, killing is permissible to avoid other evils. A better approximation is 'taking life is directly wrong', where the word 'directly' simply indicates that the wrongness is independent of effects on other people. But even this will not quite do. For, while someone who believes in the sanctity of life must hold that killing is directly wrong, not everyone who thinks that killing is sometimes or always directly wrong has to hold that life is sacred. (It is possible to believe that killing is directly wrong only where the person does not want to die or where the years of which he is deprived would have been happy ones. These objections to killing have nothing to do with side-effects and yet do not place value on life merely

41

for its own sake.) The best formulation seems to be 'taking life is intrinsically wrong'.

There is another problem about what counts as 'life'. Does this include animals? When we think of higher animals, we may want to say 'yes', even if we want to give animal life less weight than human life. But do we want to count it wrong to tread on an ant or kill a mosquito? And, even if we are prepared to treat all animal life as sacred, there are problems about plant life. Plants are living things. Is weeding the garden wrong? Let us avoid these difficulties for the moment by stating the principle in terms of human life. When we have become clearer about the reasons for thinking it wrong to kill people, we will be better placed to see whether the same reasons should make us respect animal or plant life as well. So, to start with, we have the principle: 'taking human life is intrinsically wrong'.

Can any explanation be given of the belief that taking human life is intrinsically wrong? Someone who simply says that this principle is an axiom of his moral system, and refuses to give any further explanation, cannot be 'refuted' unless his system is made inconsistent by the inclusion of this principle. (And, even then, he might choose to give up other beliefs rather than this one.) The strategy of this chapter will be to try to cast doubt on the acceptability of this principle by looking at the sort of explanation that might be given by a supporter who was prepared to enter into some discussion of it. My aim will be to suggest that the doctrine of the sanctity of life is not acceptable, but that there is embedded in it a moral view we should retain. We should reject the view that taking human life is *intrinsically* wrong, but retain the view that it is normally *directly* wrong: that most acts of killing people would be wrong in the absence of harmful side-effects.

The concept of human life itself raises notorious boundary problems. When does it begin? Is an eight-month foetus already a living human being? How about a newly fertilized egg? These questions need discussing, but it seems preferable to decide first on the central problem of why we value human life, and on that basis to draw its exact boundaries, rather than to stipulate the boundaries arbitrarily in advance. But there is another boundary problem that can be discussed first, as it leads us straight into the central issue about the sanctity of life. This boundary problem is about someone fallen irreversibly into a coma: does he still count as a living human being? (It may be said that what is important is not the status of 'human being', but of 'person'. In this chapter I write as though human beings are automatically persons. In the later discussion of abortion, there will be some attention given to those who say of a foetus that, while it is certainly a member of species *homo sapiens*, it is not yet a person.)

3 The Boundary Between Life and Death

It was once common to decide that someone was dead because, among other things, his heart had stopped beating. But now it is well known that people can sometimes be revived from this state, so some other criterion has to be used. Two candidates sometimes proposed are that 'death' should be defined in terms of the irreversible loss of all electrical activity in the brain or that it should be defined in terms of irreversible loss of consciousness.

Of these two definitions, the one in terms of irreversible loss of consciousness is preferable. There is no point in considering the electrical activity unless one holds the (surely correct) view that it is a necessary condition of the person being conscious. It seems better to define 'death' in terms of irreversible loss of consciousness itself, since it is from this alone that our interest in the electrical activity derives. This is reinforced by the fact that, while loss of all brain activity guarantees loss of consciousness, the converse does not hold. People incurably in a vegetable state normally have some electrical activity in some parts of the brain. To define 'death' in terms of irreversible loss of consciousness is not to deny that our best evidence for this may often be continued absence of electrical activity. And, when we understand more about the neurophysiological basis of consciousness, we may reach the stage of being able to judge conclusively from the state of his brain whether or not someone has irreversibly lost consciousness.

An argument sometimes used in favour of the definition in terms of irreversible loss of consciousness is that it avoids some of the problems that nowadays arise for adherents of more traditional criteria. Glanville Williams[1] has discussed a hypothetical case that might raise legal difficulties. Suppose a man's heart stops beating and, just as the doctor is about to revive him, the man's heir plunges a dagger into his breast. Glanville Williams wonders if this would count as murder or merely as illegal interference with a corpse. If, to avoid complications, we assume that there was a reasonable expectation that the man would otherwise have been revived, the question is one of the boundary between life and death. Making irreversible loss of consciousness the boundary has the advantage, over more traditional criteria, of making the heir's act one of murder.

It may be objected that, in ordinary language, it makes sense to say of someone that he is irreversibly comatose but still alive. This must be admitted. The proposed account of death is a piece of conceptual revision, motivated by the belief that, for such purposes as deciding whether or not to switch off a respirator, the irreversibly comatose and the traditionally 'dead' are on a par. Those who reject this belief will want to reject the 'irreversible loss of consciousness' account of death. And, if they do reject it, they are not forced to revert to traditional views that give a paradoxical answer to the Glanville Williams case. It would be possible to have two tests that must be passed before someone is counted as dead, involving respiratory and circulatory activities stopping *and* brain damage sufficient to make loss of consciousness irreversible. Let us call this the 'double-test' view.

In giving an account of 'death', how should we choose between irreversible loss of consciousness and the double-test view? If we are worried about doctors being wrong in their

1. Glanville Williams: *The Sanctity of Life and the Criminal Law*, London, 1958. Ch. 1.

diagnosis of irreversible loss of consciousness, the double-test view would in practice give an additional safeguard against the respirator being switched off too early. But that is a rather oblique reason, even if of some practical importance. If detecting irreversible loss of consciousness posed no practical problem, how would we then choose between the two views? Appeals to traditional usage are of no value, for what is in question is a proposal for conceptual reform. The only way of choosing is to decide whether or not we attach any value to the preservation of someone irreversibly comatose. Do we value 'life' even if unconscious, or do we value life only as a vehicle for consciousness? Our attitude to the doctrine of the sanctity of life very much depends on our answer to this question.

4 'Being Alive Is Intrinsically Valuable'

Someone who thinks that taking life is intrinsically wrong may explain this by saying that the state of being alive is itself intrinsically valuable. This claim barely rises to the level of an argument for the sanctity of life, for it simply asserts that there is value in what the taking of life takes away.

Against such a view, cases are sometimes cited of people who are either very miserable or in great pain, without any hope of cure. Might such people not be better off dead? But this could be admitted without giving up the view that life is intrinsically valuable. We could say that life has value, but that not being desperately miserable can have even more value.

I have no way of refuting someone who holds that being alive, even though unconscious, is intrinsically valuable. But it is a view that will seem unattractive to those of us who, in our own case, see a life of permanent coma as in no way preferable to death. From the subjective point of view, there is nothing to choose between the two. Schopenhauer saw this clearly when he said of the destruction of the body:

But actually we feel this destruction only in the evils of illness or of old age; on the other hand, for the *subject*, death itself consists merely in the moment when consciousness vanishes, since the activity of the brain ceases. The extension of the stoppage to all the other parts of the organism which follows this is really already an event after death. Therefore, in a subjective respect, death concerns only consciousness.[2]

Those of us who think that the direct objections to killing have to do with death considered from the standpoint of the person killed will find it natural to regard life as being of value only as a necessary condition of consciousness. For permanently comatose existence is subjectively indistinguishable from death, and unlikely often to be thought intrinsically preferable to it by people thinking of their own future.

5 'Being Conscious Is Intrinsically Valuable'

The believer in the sanctity of life may accept that being alive is only of instrumental value and say that it is consciousness that is intrinsically valuable. In making this claim, he still differs from someone who only values consciousness because it is necessary for happiness. Before we can assess this belief in the intrinsic value of being conscious, it is necessary to distinguish between two different ways in which we may talk about consciousness. Sometimes we talk about 'mere' consciousness and sometimes we talk about what might be called 'a high level of consciousness'.

'Mere' consciousness consists simply in awareness or the having of experiences. When I am awake, I am aware of my environment. I have a stream of consciousness that comes abruptly to a halt if I faint or fades out when I go to sleep (until I have dreams). There are large philosophical problems about the meaning of claims of this kind, which need not be discussed here. I shall assume that we all at some level understand what it is to have experiences, or a stream of consciousness.

2. A. Schopenhauer: *The World as Will and Representation*, translated by E.J.F. Payne, New York, 1969, Book 4, section 54.

But this use of 'consciousness' should be distinguished from another, perhaps metaphorical, use of the word. We sometimes say that men are at a higher level of consciousness than animals, or else that few, if any, peasants are likely to have as highly developed a consciousness as Proust. It is not clear exactly what these claims come to, nor that the comparison between men and animals is of the same sort as the comparison between peasants and Proust. But perhaps what underlies such comparisons is an attempt to talk about a person's experiences in terms of the extent to which they are rich, varied, complex or subtle, or the extent to which they involve emotional responses, as well as various kind of awareness. Again, it is not necessary to discuss here the analysis of the meaning of these claims. It is enough if it is clear that to place value on 'mere' consciousness is different from valuing it for its richness and variety. I shall assume that the claim that being conscious is intrinsically good is a claim about 'mere' consciousness, rather than about a high level of consciousness.

If one is sceptical about the intrinsic value of 'mere' consciousness, as against that of a high level of consciousness, it is hard to see what consideration can be mentioned in its favour. The advocate of this view might ask us to perform a thought experiment of a kind that G.E. Moore would perhaps have liked. We might be asked to imagine two universes, identical except that one contained a being aware of its environment and the other did not. It may be suggested that the universe containing the conscious being would be intrinsically better.

But such a thought experiment seems unconvincing. There is the familiar difficulty that, confronted with a choice so abstract and remote, it may be hard to feel any preference at all. And, since we are dealing with 'mere' consciousness rather than with a high level of consciousness, it is necessary to postulate that the conscious being has no emotional responses. It cannot be pleased or sorry or in pain; it cannot be interested or bored; it is merely aware of its environment. Views may well differ here, but, if I could be brought to take part in this thought experiment at all, I should probably express indifference between the two universes. The only grounds I might have for preferring the universe with the conscious being would be some hope that it might evolve into some more interesting level of consciousness. But to choose on these grounds is not to assign any intrinsic value to 'mere' consciousness.

The belief that the sole reason why it is directly wrong to take human life is the intrinsic value of 'mere' consciousness runs into a problem concerning animals. Many of us place a special value on human life as against animal life. Yet animals, or at least the higher ones, seem no less aware of their surroundings than we are. Suppose there is a flood and I am faced with the choice of either saving a man's life or else saving the life of a cow. Even if all side-effects were left out of account, failure to save the man seems worse than failure to save the cow. The person who believes that the sanctity of life rests solely on the value of 'mere' consciousness is faced with a dilemma. Either he must accept that the life of the cow and the life of the man are in themselves of equal value, or he must give reasons for thinking that cows are less conscious than men or else not conscious at all.

It is hard to defend the view that, while I have good grounds for thinking that other people are conscious, I do not have adequate reasons for thinking that animals are conscious. Humans and animals in many ways respond similarly to their surroundings. Humans have abilities that other animals do not, such as the ability to speak or to do highly abstract reasoning, but it is not only in virtue of these abilities that we say people are conscious. And there is no neurophysiological evidence that suggests that humans alone can have experiences.

The alternative claim is that animals are less conscious than we are. The view that 'mere' consciousness is a matter of degree is attractive when considered in relation to animals. The philosophical literature about our knowledge of other minds is strikingly silent and unhelpful about the animal boundaries of consciousness. How far back down the evolutionary scale does consciousness extend? What kind and degree of complexity must a nervous system exhibit to be the vehicle of experiences?

What kind and degree of complexity of behaviour counts as the manifestation of consciousness? At least with our present ignorance of the physiological basis of human consciousness, any clear-cut boundaries of consciousness, drawn between one kind of animal and another, have an air of arbitrariness. For this reason it is attractive to suggest that consciousness is a matter of degree, not stopping abruptly, but fading away slowly as one descends the evolutionary scale.

But the belief that 'mere' consciousness is a matter of degree is obscure as well as attractive. Is it even an intelligible view?

There are two ways in which talk of degrees of consciousness can be made clearer. One is by explaining it in terms of the presence or absence of whole 'dimensions' of consciousness. This is the way in which a blind man is less conscious of his environment than a normal man. (Though, if his other senses have developed unusual acuity, he will in other respects be more conscious than a normal man.) But if a lower degree of consciousness consists either in the absence of a whole dimension such as sight, or in senses with lower acuity than those of men, it is not plausible to say that animals are all less conscious than we are. Dogs seem to have all the dimensions of consciousness that we do. It is true that they often see less well, but on the other hand their sense of smell is better than ours. If the sanctity of life were solely dependent on degree of consciousness interpreted this way, we often could not justify giving human life priority over animal life. We might also be committed to giving the life of a normal dog priority over the life of a blind man.

The other way in which we talk of degrees of 'mere' consciousness comes up in such contexts as waking up and falling asleep. There is a sleepy state in which we can be unaware of words that are softly spoken, but aware of any noise that is loud or sharp. But this again fails to separate men from animals. For animals are often alert in a way that is quite unlike the drowsiness of a man not fully awake.

Whether or not 'mere' consciousness fades away lower down on the evolutionary scale (and the idea of a sharp boundary *does* seem implausible), there seems at least no reason to regard the 'higher' animals as less aware of the environment than ourselves. (It is not being suggested that animals are only at the level of 'mere' consciousness, though no doubt they are less far above it than most of us.) If the whole basis of the ban on killing were the intrinsic value of mere consciousness, killing higher animals would be as bad as killing humans.

It would be possible to continue to hold mere consciousness to be of intrinsic value, and either to supplement this principle with others or else to abandon the priority given to human life. But when the principle is distinguished from different ones that would place a value on higher levels of consciousness, it has so little intuitive appeal that we may suspect its attractiveness to depend on the distinction not being made. If, in your own case, you would opt for a state never rising above mere consciousness, in preference to death, have you purged the illegitimate assumption that you would take an interest in what you would be aware of?

6 'Being Human Is Intrinsically Valuable'

It is worth mentioning that the objection to taking human life should not rest on what is sometimes called 'speciesism': human life being treated as having a special priority over animal life *simply* because it is human. The analogy is with racism, in its purest form, according to which people of a certain race ought to be treated differently *simply* because of their membership of that race, without any argument referring to special features of that race being given. This is objectionable partly because of its moral arbitrariness: unless some relevant empirical characteristics can be cited, there can be no argument for such discrimination. Those concerned to reform our treatment of animals point out that speciesism exhibits the same arbitrariness. It is not in itself sufficient argument for treating a creature less well to say simply that it is not a member of our species. An adequate justification must cite relevant differences between the species. We still have the question of what features of a life are of intrinsic value.

7 The Concept of a 'Life Worth Living'

I have suggested that, in destroying life or mere consciousness, we are not destroying anything intrinsically valuable. These states only matter because they are necessary for other things that matter in themselves. If a list could be made of all the things that are valuable for their own sake, these things would be the ingredients of a 'life worth living'.

One objection to the idea of judging that a life is worth living is that this seems to imply the possibility of comparing being alive and being dead. And, as Wittgenstein said, 'Death is not an event in life: we do not live to experience death.'

But we can have a preference for being alive over being dead, or for being conscious over being unconscious, without needing to make any 'comparisons' between these states. We prefer to be anaesthetized for a painful operation; queuing for a bus in the rain at midnight, we wish we were at home asleep; but for the most part we prefer to be awake and experience our life as it goes by. These preferences do not depend on any view about 'what it is like' being unconscious, and our preference for life does not depend on beliefs about 'what it is like' being dead. It is rather that we treat being dead or unconscious as nothing, and then decide whether a stretch of experience is better or worse than nothing. And this claim, that life of a certain sort is better than nothing, is an expression of our preference.

Any list of the ingredients of a worth-while life would obviously be disputable. Most people might agree on many items, but many others could be endlessly argued over. It might be agreed that a happy life is worth living, but people do not agree on what happiness is. And some things that make life worth living may only debatably be to do with happiness. (Aristotle:[3]

3. *Eudemian Ethics* 1216 a 11.

'And so they tell us that Anaxagoras answered a man who was raising problems of this sort and asking why one should choose rather to be born than not – "for the sake of viewing the heavens and the whole order of the universe".')

A life worth living should not be confused with a morally virtuous life. Moral virtues such as honesty or a sense of fairness can belong to someone whose life is relatively bleak and empty. Music may enrich someone's life, or the death of a friend impoverish it, without him growing more or less virtuous.

I shall not try to say what sorts of things do make life worth living. (Temporary loss of a sense of the absurd led me to try to do so. But, apart from the disputability of any such list, I found that the ideal life suggested always sounded ridiculous.) I shall assume that a life worth living has more to it than mere consciousness. It should be possible to explain the wrongness of killing partly in terms of the destruction of a life worth living, without presupposing more than minimal agreement as to exactly what makes life worth-while.

I shall assume that, where someone's life is worth living, this is a good reason for holding that it would be directly wrong to kill him. This is what can be extracted from the doctrine of the sanctity of life by someone who accepts the criticisms made here of that view. If life is worth preserving only because it is the vehicle for consciousness, and consciousness is of value only because it is necessary for something else, then that 'something else' is the heart of this particular objection to killing. It is what is meant by a 'life worth living' or a 'worth-while life'.

The idea of dividing people's lives into ones that are worth living and ones that are not is likely to seem both presumptuous and dangerous. As well as seeming to indicate an arrogant willingness to pass godlike judgements on other people's lives, it may remind people of the Nazi policy of killing patients in mental hospitals. But there is really nothing godlike in such a judgement. It is not a moral judgement we are making, if we think that someone's life is so empty and unhappy as to be not worth living. It results from an attempt (obviously an extremely fallible one) to see his life from his own point of view and to see what he gets out of it. It must also be stressed that no suggestion is being made that it automatically becomes right to kill people whose lives we think are not worth living. It is only being argued that, if someone's life is worth living, this is *one* reason why it is directly wrong to kill him.

8 Is the Desire to Live the Criterion of a Worth-While Life?

It might be thought that a conclusive test of whether or not someone's life is worth living is whether or not he wants to go on living. The attractiveness of this idea comes partly from the fact that the question whether someone has a worth-while life involves thinking from his point of view, rather than thinking of his contribution to the lives of other people.

This proposal would commit us to believing that a person cannot want to end his life if it is worth living, and that he cannot want to prolong his life where it is not worth living. But these beliefs are both doubtful. In a passing mood of depression, someone who normally gets a lot out of life may want to kill himself. And someone who thinks he will go to hell may wish to prolong his present life, however miserable he is. The frying pan may be worse than nothing but better than the fire. And some people, while not believing in hell, simply fear death. They may wish they had never been born, but still not want to die.

For these reasons, someone's own desire to live or die is not a conclusive indication of whether or not he has a life worth living. And, equally obviously, with people who clearly do have lives worth living, the relative strength of their desires to live is not a reliable indicator of how worth-while they find their lives. Someone whose hopes are often disappointed may cling to life as tenaciously as the happiest person in the world.

If we are to make these judgements, we cannot escape appealing to our own independent beliefs about what sorts of things enrich or impoverish people's lives. But, when this has been said, it should be emphasized that, when the question arises whether someone's life is worth living at all, his own views will normally be evidence of an overwhelmingly powerful kind. Our assessments of what other people get out of their lives are so fallible that only a monster of self-confidence would feel no qualms about correcting the judgement of the person whose life is in question.

9 Length of Life

The upshot of this discussion is that one reason why it is wrong to kill is that it is wrong to destroy a life which is worth living.

This can be seen in a slightly different perspective when we remember that we must all die one day, so that killing and life-saving are interventions that alter length of life by bringing forward or postponing the date of death. An extreme statement of this perspective is to be found in St Augustine's *City of God:*

There is no one, it goes without saying, who is not nearer to death this year than he was last year, nearer tomorrow than today, today than yesterday, who will not by and by be nearer than he is at the moment, or is not nearer at the present time than he was a little while ago. Any space of time that we live through leaves us with so much less time to live, and the remainder decreases with every passing day; so that the whole of our lifetime is nothing but a race towards death, in which no one is allowed the slightest pause or any slackening of the pace. All are driven on at the same speed, and hurried along the same road to the same goal. The man whose life was short passed his days as swiftly as the longer-lived; moments of equal length rushed by for both of them at equal speed, though one was farther than the other from the goal to which both were hastening at the same rate.

The objection to killing made here is that it is wrong to shorten a worth-while life. Why is a longer-lasting worth-while life a better thing than an equally worth-while but briefer life? Some people, thinking about their own lives, consider length of life very desirable, while others consider the number of years they have is of no importance at all, the quality of their lives being all that matters.

There is an argument (echoed in Sartre's short story *Le Mur*) used by Marcus Aurelius in support of the view that length of life is unimportant:

If a god were to tell you 'Tomorrow, or at least the day after, you will be dead', you would not, unless the most abject of men, be greatly solicitous whether it was to be the later day rather than the morrow, for what is the difference between them? In the same way, do not reckon it of great moment whether it will come years and years hence, or tomorrow.[4]

This argument is unconvincing. From the fact that some small differences are below the threshold of mattering to us, it does not follow that all differences are insignificant. If someone steals all your money except either a penny or twopence, you will not mind much which he has left you with. It does not follow that the difference between riches and poverty is trivial.

There are at least two good reasons why a longer life can be thought better than a short one. One is that the quality of life is not altogether independent of its length: many plans and projects would not be worth undertaking without a good chance of time for their fulfilment. The other reason is that, other things being equal, more of a good thing is always better than less of it. This does not entail such absurd consequences as that an enjoyable play gets better as it gets longer, without limit. The point of the phrase 'other things being equal' is to allow for waning of interest and for the claims of other activities. So, unless life begins to pall, it is not in any way unreasonable to want more of it and to place a value on the prolonging of other people's worth-while lives.

This suggests an answer to a traditional scepticism about whether people are harmed by being killed. This scepticism is stated in its most extreme form by Socrates in the *Apology*:

4. Marcus Aurelius: *Meditations*, translated by M. Staniforth, Harmondsworth, 1964.

'Now if there is no consciousness, but only a dreamless sleep, death must be a marvellous gain.' There is clearly some exaggeration here. Death is not a dreamless sleep, but something we can treat as on a par with it. There is the doubtful suggestion that people would normally prefer a dreamless sleep to their waking lives. But, stripped of these exaggerations, there remains the valid point that being dead is not a state we experience, and so cannot be unpleasant. It was this that led Lucretius to think that the fear of death was confused:

If the future holds travail and anguish in store, the self must be in existence, when that time comes, in order to experience it. But from this fate we are redeemed by death, which denies existence to the self that might have suffered these tribulations.

He reinforced this by a comparison with the time before birth:

Look back at the eternity that passed before we were born, and mark how utterly it counts to us as nothing. This is a mirror that nature holds up to us, in which we may see the time that shall be after we are dead. Is there anything terrifying in the sight – anything depressing . . .?[5]

Lucretius is right that being dead is not itself a misfortune, but this does not show that it is irrational to want not to die, nor that killing someone does him no harm. For, while I will not be miserable when dead, I am happy while alive, and it is not confused to want more of a good thing rather than less of it.

Bernard Williams has suggested that a reply to Lucretius of this kind does not commit us to wanting to be immortal.[6] He argues that immortality is either inconceivable or terrible. Either desires and satisfactions change so much that it is not clear that the immortal person will still be *me*, or else they are limited by my character and will start to seem pointlessly boring: 'A man at arms can get cramp from standing too long

5. Lucretius: *The Nature of the Universe*, translated by R.E. Latham, Harmondsworth, 1951.

6. Bernard Williams: 'The Makropulos Case', in *Problems of the Self*, Cambridge, 1973.

at his post, but sentry-duty can after all be necessary. But the threat of monotony in eternal activities could not be dealt with in that way, by regarding immortal boredom as an unavoidable ache derived from standing ceaselessly at one's post.' It is true that the reply to Lucretius does not commit us to desiring immortality. But I am not convinced that someone with a fairly constant character *need* eventually become intolerably bored, so long as they can watch the world continue to unfold and go on asking new questions and thinking, and so long as there are other people to share their feelings and thoughts with. Given the company of the right people, I would be glad of the chance to sample a few million years and see how it went.

10 The 'No Trade-Off' View

In stating the principle of the sanctity of life, it seemed important not to suggest that it always took priority over other values: 'taking human life is intrinsically wrong', not 'taking human life is always wrong'. The same point holds for the acceptable principle that we have tried to extract from the sanctity of life view: 'it is wrong to destroy a life which is worth living'. There is a tacit 'other things being equal' clause. For we can hold this view while thinking that the avoidance of other things even worse may sometimes have to take priority. We can have this objection to killing without being absolute pacifists.

The alternative, which may be called the 'no trade-off' view, gives an infinite value to not killing people (whose lives are worth-while) compared to anything else. This may be because the *act* of killing seems infinitely appalling, which is an implausible view when we think of other horrendous acts, such as torturing. Or it may be because infinite value is set on worthwhile life itself. If this second alternative is chosen, it commits us to giving the saving of life overriding priority over all other social objectives. A piece of life-saving equipment is to be preferred to any amount of better housing, better schools or higher

57

standard of living. Neither of these versions of the no trade-off view seems particularly attractive when the implications are clear.

11 The Social Effects of Abandoning the Sanctity of Life

Sometimes the doctrine of the sanctity of life is defended in an oblique way. The social implications of widespread abandonment of the view that taking human life is intrinsically wrong are said to be so appalling that, whatever its defects, the doctrine should not be criticized.

It must be faced that there is always a real possibility of producing a society where an indifference to the lives of at least some groups of people has terrible results. The sort of attitude is exhibited clearly in some passages from letters sent by the I.G. Farben chemical trust to the camp at Auschwitz.[7]

In contemplation of experiments with a new soporific drug, we would appreciate your procuring for us a number of women ... We received your answer but consider the price of 200 marks a woman excessive. We propose to pay not more than 170 marks a head. If agreeable, we will take possession of the women. We need approximately 150 ... Received the order of 150 women. Despite their emaciated condition, they were found satisfactory. We shall keep you posted on developments concerning this experiment ... The tests were made. All subjects died. We shall contact you shortly on the subject of a new load.

If criticism of the doctrine of the sanctity of life made even a small contribution to developing such attitudes, that would be an overwhelming reason for not making any criticism. But the views to be argued for here in no way give support to these attitudes. (It is the first and most elementary test to be passed by an adequate account of the morality of killing that it should not fail to condemn them.) It is a thesis of this book that con-

7. Bruno Bettelheim: *The Informed Heart*, London, 1961, Ch. 6.

THE SANCTITY OF LIFE

ventional moral views about killing are often intellectually unsatisfactory. The attempt to replace the unsatisfactory parts of
a moral outlook may even result in something less likely to be
eroded.

Chapter 4   Actual and Potential People

BEVIS: How can a society that accepts termination of pregnancy quibble about the giving of life to a foetus? We are not creating life. If we can kill the foetus – and this seems to be expected and accepted – why can we not 'put it together'?

PERUTZ: If you kill a foetus nothing happens, there will be no child, but if you 'put together' a child, you might produce an unhappy individual. The responsibility is of a different kind.

Law and Ethics of A.I.D. and Embryo Transfer, CIBA Foundation, 1973

It has been argued here that one reason for the direct wrongness of most acts of killing is the intrinsic value of a worth-while life, and in particular the greater value of a longer rather than a shorter span of such a life. But to take this view leaves us with some unanswered questions. Should we place any additional value on additional numbers of people having worth-while lives? Either answer seems paradoxical. If we say that a smaller number of worth-while lives is just as good as a larger number, it is hard to see how we can use the intrinsic value of a worth-while life as an argument against killing. But if we say that it is better for more people to have such lives than fewer such people, this seems just as good an argument for conceiving as it is against killing.

Obviously, when we take side-effects into account, killing someone is much worse than deliberately failing to conceive a child. But many of us feel dissatisfied with the thought that side-effects are the whole explanation of the moral difference. If that were so, killing the man in prison mentioned in the last chapter would be morally on a par with using a contraceptive. Those of us who feel dissatisfied with this will want a reason for saying that killing is directly wrong in a way that deliberate non-conception is not.

Three lines of thought suggest themselves. The first is that there may be something intrinsically wrong with the *act* of killing which discriminates it from failing to conceive in a way that is independent of their similar outcomes. This is sometimes believed because there is thought to be an important moral difference between acts and omissions with the same outcome. (The question of whether such a view is plausible will be discussed in a later chapter, where some arguments for it will be rejected.) Or, without appealing to the distinction between acts and omissions, it may be held that some acts, such as killing, are intrinsically bad in a way that has nothing to do with their outcome. But this view seems completely obscure: how are we to identify such bad acts, and what *reasons* (apart from appeals to authority) can be given for thinking them bad? This sort of view is often gestured at, but its supporters have a lot of work to do. There is not merely the problem of justifying it, but the prior task of showing that the view is a coherent one. (What does it mean to say that the act of killing is bad, independent of the loss of life which is its outcome?)

A second line of thought, which will be followed up in the next chapter, is that there may be other direct objections to killing as well as that based on the intrinsic value of a worthwhile life. These might be based on people's rights, or on respect for their autonomy. We do not have to think that there is only one reason why killing is directly wrong.

The third line of thought, to be discussed in this chapter, is that suggested by the remark of Perutz about 'putting together' a foetus. On this view, the important thing about killing is that there is a person who is affected by it, while, when a couple do not conceive, there is no person who can be shown to have lost a life. The debate on this matter has taken place within the utilitarian tradition, and we must now look at the utilitarian theory.

1 Utilitarianism

Utilitarianism is the belief that we ought to live in such a way as to promote the greatest happiness. For a utilitarian, killing is wrong to the extent that it reduces happiness or creates misery. The 'side-effect' objections to killing that have been mentioned would be endorsed by a utilitarian, and his direct objection to killing is that it is wrong to shorten a happy life. To those who think that a life worth living is the same as a happy life, it will be obvious that the utilitarian view and that defended in the previous chapter are identical. Those who think that there is more to a life worth living than happiness will regard the utilitarian view as a narrowed-down version of that argument against killing. I prefer not to take sides on this issue here, but to take advantage of the flexibility of the idea of a life worth living, which can be subscribed to by utilitarians and by others. Since it can hardly be denied that the things valued by a utilitarian are at least aspects of lives worth living, some of the difficulties discussed within the utilitarian framework are of direct relevance here.

The case against utilitarianism is often expressed. There are practical objections about the difficulties of the utilitarian calculation: the difficulties of predicting consequences of actions, the difficulties of comparing the happiness of different people and the difficulties of measuring happiness even in the case of a single person. Then there are the moral objections, based on appeals to other, non-utilitarian, values. It is said that, for the utilitarian, 'the end justifies the means', and that the means may include morally objectionable acts of dishonesty, injustice, cruelty or killing.

In order to allow the discussion of the utilitarian attitude to killing to get off the ground, I shall assume, without argument, that the practical objections are not conclusive. They seem likely to be extremely serious problems for any attempt at a precisely quantified science of utilitarian ethics, but it is far from clear that they are fatal to utilitarianism as an approximate guide to conduct. After all, most of us, whether utilitarians or not, take some account of the likely effects of our actions on people's happiness, and we should all be in a mess if there were no correspondence between trying to make someone happier and succeeding.

Utilitarians are divided over the interpretation they place upon 'happiness'. The traditional version treated happiness as a special mental state. But problems arose about identifying this state. Is it the same as pleasure and the absence of pain, as Bentham thought? Can it vary in quality as well as quantity? If I am happily married for ten years, is this mental state always, or usually, present for that time? What is there in common between the mental state experienced during a happy picnic and that experienced when your child is born? The problems are obvious.

Many utilitarians have been led to abandon the mental-state version, and instead to interpret happiness in terms of getting either what you want or what is in your interests. (And 'interests' are on this view normally explained in terms of present and probable future desires, and perhaps also of desires you would have if you had more knowledge.) But within this version, there are problems about which desires to give weight to. Do we include the predictable desires of people not yet born? Or the desires of dead people? ('After my death I want you to say a silent prayer for me each day.') And should 'desires' include 'backward-looking preferences'? ('I am glad my parents conceived me', 'I am glad I wasn't aborted', etc.) Can it be in someone's interests or against his interests to have been conceived? And, even restricting ourselves to people now alive, there are problems. Should we give weight to someone's desire even where he will not know whether or not we have done so? ('My husband wants me to be faithful to him while he is in prison, but he will never know about this.') And what about a desire whose satisfaction will give no pleasure? (The man who on retirement fulfils his lifetime ambition, and finds that crossing the Sahara by Land Rover is not the sort of thing he enjoys after all. It is tempting to say, in the spirit of the mental-state version, that the only case for lending him a Land Rover is that he will feel frustrated if he does not go.)

Those utilitarians who do not want to give weight to the desires of dead people, or to desires whose fulfilment does not bring any satisfaction, may restrict the desires to be considered and in doing so produce something more like the mental-state version. It may be thought that which version is adopted will make a difference to the morality of killing. The mental-state version may at first sight seem to license the unexpected killing of someone in his sleep, where there are no bad side-effects. This is because the victim will not experience the act of killing, and a dead person is not in a position to feel any regret that his desire to live was disregarded. But this consequence does not follow. For, if he is not killed, he will experience the continuing fulfilment of his desire to live, and, one hopes, of other desires. And these experiences have to be taken into account by supporters of the mental-state version.

Whether or not the two versions give different answers to questions about the value of creating new people depends on whether the desire version includes 'backward-looking preferences', and on whether we think it a good thing to create desires simply in order to satisfy them. The mental-state version, unless modified in various ways to be discussed, can be used to justify conceiving new people. For, when they do exist, they will (we hope) have the mental states in question. The desire version can be used in the same way, if backward-looking preferences are relevant. For, if we conceive someone, he will later (we hope) be glad that we did so. On the other hand, if backward-looking preferences are excluded, the desire version gives no reason (apart from side-effects, such as someone's desire to have a child) for conceiving someone (unless we adopt a version telling us to create extra satisfiable desires, perhaps by creating extra people). For no one has the desire to be conceived.

As the problem is about the links between the morality of killing and conceiving, I shall assume that we are dealing with a mental-state rather than a desire version of utilitarianism. For the problem arises acutely only on some interpretations of the desire version, but arises unambiguously on the mental-state version. If what we value is life of a certain kind, whether described vaguely as life worth living or more narrowly as life containing mental states of various sorts, the simplest objection to killing someone seems to be that it reduces the number of such lives by one. But this suggests that it is *numbers* of such lives which we value or amount of such life lived, which in turn suggest that, apart from side-effects, killing is on a par with using a contraceptive.

A utilitarian who allows that additional happiness may be an argument for creating extra people is in danger of some of the undesirable consequences of a commitment to maximize total happiness (the 'total view'). For total happiness can be increased either by making existing people happier or by making extra happy people. There emerges the disagreeable theoretical possibility that one might be able to produce more happiness by aiming for a larger population than by aiming for a smaller one, even if the average level of happiness was considerably lower in the larger population. This picture of an absolute drop in *level* of happiness being more than compensated for by additional numbers of happy people puts great strain on our working assumption that rough comparisons of happiness are possible. But the tension between level of happiness and numbers of happy people can be a real one: consider either population policy in a moderately prosperous country, or parents with limited money in a slightly crowded house wondering how many children to have. And, as soon as we allow any possibility of a lower level of happiness being outweighed by greater numbers, a horrifying possibility looms for supporters of the total view. So long as the average person has *some* net surplus of happiness, however small, sufficiently many extra people can justify any drop in level of happiness.

Most utilitarians will not be attracted by this consequence of the total view, and will also wish to avoid being committed to saying that killing is no worse (directly) than using a contraceptive. A crude strategy might be to build a time bias into utilitarian morality, according to which the interests of people

65

now alive take priority over those of future people. This would make failing to conceive a future person less bad than killing a present person, and would also act as a check on increasing the population to the detriment of the happiness of those already alive. But the adoption of a time bias is unsatisfactory. In the first place, it does not rule out the bad consequences of the total view when we are making long-term plans not affecting present people. And, more fundamentally, it is hard to defend this kind of bias as part of morality. Why should a bias in favour of people living *now* be any more defensible than a space bias in favour of people living *here*? We do tend to mind less about misery in far-off countries, but few would want to make this a principle of their morality.

A more sophisticated strategy for dealing with these problems is to place a restriction on the utilitarian principle, such that an act is right or wrong only if people are affected by it. Let us examine this restriction.

2 The 'Person-Affecting' Restriction

This restriction says that an act is right or wrong only if there is or will be some person affected by it. Utilitarianism with this restriction rules out killing someone whose life is expected to be on balance happy. This is because he is an identifiable existing person, and killing him counts as affecting him for the worse. The restriction involves no time bias, as the future interests of present people, and the interests of people who will exist in the future, are taken into account.

Jan Narveson[1] has proposed a version of utilitarianism incorporating this restriction, which, if successful, gives a utilitarian a way of avoiding the total view and of explaining why killing is directly worse than non-conception. On his view, we should make people happy, but not feel obliged to make happy people. He thinks we have an obligation to prevent the conception of a person whose life will be miserable, but no obligation to con-

1. Jan Narveson: *Morality and Utility*, Baltimore, 1967, pages 46–50.

ceive someone whose life will be happy. Given the person-affecting restriction, this must depend on the belief that, when we create a miserable person, there is then someone who has been affected for the worse. Can this be combined with the lack of any duty to conceive a happy person? These two beliefs are hard to combine without relying on implausible assumptions. One assumption that would reconcile them would be a kind of negative utilitarianism, saying that what matters is not affecting people for the worse, and giving no positive weight to affecting people for the better. But this is not a moral view that has much to be said for it in other contexts. The other assumption would be that conceiving a miserable person is a way of affecting someone for the worse, while conceiving a happy person is not a way of affecting someone for the better. It is hard to imagine how *this* view could be made at all plausible.

The interpretation of the person-affecting restriction obviously varies according to whether or not conceiving someone counts as affecting him for better or worse. This somewhat metaphysical question requires rather elaborate discussion, which I prefer not to go into here. (Those interested are referred to Derek Parfit's paper.[2]) If conceiving someone is allowed to count as affecting him, the person-affecting restriction then seems less likely either to avoid the total view or to discriminate sharply between killing and non-conception. So I shall assume that the interest of the person-affecting restriction depends on holding that you do not affect people by conceiving them.

It is not simply Narveson's version of the person-affecting restriction which runs into difficulty. An ingenious objection to any such restriction has been made by Derek Parfit.

Suppose there are two medical programmes between which a health authority with limited funds must choose. In the first programme, millions of women would be tested during pregnancy and those found to have an illness which would handicap their children would be cured. In the second programme, millions of women would be tested before becoming pregnant and those found to have an illness which would handicap their

2. 'Overpopulation', *Philosophy and Public Affairs*, forthcoming.

children would be warned to postpone conception. Let us suppose that in each of these programmes the handicap is the same, and is one which is not so severe as to make life not worth living. And also suppose that the two programmes are likely to affect the same number of people; in each case a thousand women who would have had handicapped children will have normal ones.

The difference between the programmes is that failure to adopt the first programme will harm some people (those who will be born handicapped but who would have been normal if it had been adopted) while there is no one who is worse off if the second programme is not adopted. This is because those born handicapped when the second programme is rejected are not worse off than *they* would have been if the programme had been adopted. If it had been adopted, they would not have been born at all, and they do have lives that are worth living. (I am not the same person who would have been born if my mother had conceived in a different month.)

Supporters of the person-affecting restriction have to say that, while there is a case for adopting the first programme (avoiding harm to a thousand people), there is no case for adopting the second programme, since no one is harmed by our rejecting it. Those of us who think that there is as strong a case for adopting the second programme as there is for adopting the first have to abandon the person-affecting restriction.

Parfit's objection seems very powerful, and I shall take it as making implausible any morality consisting only of principles subject to the person-affecting restriction.

Does this mean that the utilitarian must give up the attempt to avoid the total view, or that he cannot do much to discriminate between the direct wrongness of killing and non-conception? This conclusion would be too hasty. There are still two alternative possibilities of success. One is to adopt a form of utilitarianism which does not attach any value to extra people, but which still does not fall foul of the Parfit objection. The other possibility is to adopt a version where extra happy lives are valued, but other restrictions prevent this from sliding into the total view.

The first alternative would be a principle that did not tell us to create extra happy people. One such principle would say that, when we are going to add to the population, where the choice arises we must always prefer to add a happier rather than a less happy person. (A policy of always choosing the best ones when picking apples does not commit us to picking as many as possible.) I shall not develop this alternative, partly because I am unsure what the most satisfactory form of it would be, and partly because I think that there are good reasons for taking a view which does attach some value to the creation of additional people whose lives are worth living. So let us examine the second alternative.

3 Extra Happy People

Should we attach any value to the creation of extra people whose lives are worth living?

One reason for utilitarians, and for all of us whose idea of a life worth living is bound up with some kinds of mental state, to answer 'yes', is that the mental states resulting from an act of conception are very like the mental states that would be eliminated by killing someone. It has been pointed out that the mental-state utilitarian will not license killing on the strength of the argument that dead people will not know that their desire to live has been over-ridden. This is because of the experiences the person will have if not killed, including his experience of the continuing fulfilment of his preference for being alive. But a similar argument can be used to support the creation of a person who will be glad he was born.

Another reason has to do with the continuance of the human race. Suppose we could take a drug which would render us infertile, but make us so happy that we would not mind being childless. Would it be wrong for everyone now alive to take it, ensuring that we would be the last generation? Would it have mattered if the human race had become sterile thousands of years ago? Some people are indifferent to either of these possibilities, and I have no argument to convince them. But other people, including me, think that to end the human race would be about the worst thing it would be possible to do. This is because of a belief in the intrinsic value of there existing in the future at least some people with worth-while lives. And, if we reject any kind of time bias, it is hard to see the case for valuing extra people spread out across future time that would not also place some value on extra people contemporary with us.

These reasons seem to me good ones for thinking that, *other things being equal*, the more people with worth-while lives there are the better. This is likely to arouse feelings of horror in many people, for reasons related to our reluctance to accept the total view. We may think of an exhausted mother of eight children feeling obliged to have still more. Or we may think of starvation, shortages and overcrowding caused by over-population.

In practice, the disastrous side-effects of people feeling obliged to have children they do not want, and of having too large a population for the world's resources, together with the more problematic happiness of children not really wanted, will normally heavily outweigh the view that, if other things were equal, the more happy people there are the better. Even if we adopted the total view, it seems likely that in many cases the addition to the population of extra people with worth-while lives would often not even increase the total happiness.

It may be said that, even if in practice the total view is often innocuous for these reasons, it is still at least theoretically possible that a larger population at a very low level could have greater total happiness than a smaller population at a much higher level. If so, many people, including me, will be very reluctant to adopt the total view. But the concession that, other things being equal, there is value in extra happy people need not commit us to a simple policy of maximizing happiness. It would do so only if our way of deciding what is desirable were the kind of crude multiplication suggested by the total view. But there is no need for this. It is open to us to say that *one* thing we value is total happiness as obtained by computing numbers at different levels of happiness (though this rather abstract conception itself puts strain on our assumptions of rough measurability) without simply adopting the total view. For we may decide that we value people's lives having various qualities (which would put them high on the scale of 'worth-while life') and that the absence of these qualities cannot be compensated for by any numbers of extra worth-while lives without them. There is some analogy with common attitudes to what is valued within a single life. I enjoy eating fish and chips, but no number of extra hours eating fish and chips will compensate me for being deprived of the ability to read. (This is not to say that there are things whose value cannot be compared: it is rather to say that the ability to read is of *greater* value to me than any amount of fish and chips.)

So we can think that extra people with lives worth living are in themselves a good thing, without having to allow that there is always *some* number of such people whose existence outweighs any particular impoverishment of life.

4 An Evaluation of the Utilitarian View of Killing

For a utilitarian, killing is not intrinsically wrong, but is only wrong because of its implications for happiness and misery. He will recognize only two direct objections to killing. The minor one is the fear or pain involved in being killed. The major one is the loss of the future period of happiness the person killed would otherwise have had. On this view, there are no direct objections to killing in his sleep someone whose life is certainly going to be on balance unhappy in future.

Other utilitarian objections to killing someone appeal to the side-effects already mentioned: the loss to those who knew him and to the community, the bad precedent that may be set and any anxiety caused.

Few people would dismiss the utilitarian objections as unimportant. It is hard to dispute the undesirability of prematurely ending the life of a happy person, or to quarrel with the importance the utilitarian attaches to grief and other harmful side-effects. In this context, doubts about utilitarianism are not about the validity of the reasons given against killing, but rather about whether they are the whole story.

The first doubt concerns the extent to which the utilitarian view makes people replaceable. The central utilitarian direct objection to killing, that it results in the loss of future years of happiness, seems an equally powerful objection to deliberately not conceiving a happy child.

This problem can be dramatized by sketching an imaginary future situation. Suppose pressure on the world's resources has become so great that it is necessary to place an absolute limit on population size. Contraceptive failure is always followed by abortion unless a place in the population becomes vacant. Suppose, also, that genetic engineering is highly developed, so that we have increasing control over what our children will be like. In such a world, it may be that everyone has a fairly good life, but advances in genetic engineering suggest that the next generation should have even better lives. One way of increasing the total of worth-while life in the world might be to kill off painlessly some of the present generation in order to create vacancies in the population for new, happier people. Yet, it may be said, such a policy would be so appalling that this is a *reductio ad absurdum* of any principle telling us to maximize either the amount of worth-while life or the amount of happy life.

This criticism seems to have some force, but when side-effects are taken into account its force diminishes. For the side-effects of such a policy would obviously be calamitous. The remaining population would feel grief, resentment and insecurity on an extreme scale. The policy could be set up only in a society where 'we', the rulers, decide to kill off some of 'them', the ruled. And the members of the population remaining would come to feel that their crazed utilitarian rulers regarded them like animals in a factory farm, but one which was devoted to the production of happiness rather than milk and eggs. The terrible means to such a policy, and its terrible consequences, do not show how terrible utilitarianism is, but rather show that it is not a policy a utilitarian would favour.

The second doubt about the adequacy of the utilitarian view of killing can be brought out by a modified version of the case of the man in prison, already mentioned. The point of the case as constructed before was to show that side-effects cannot account for all the wrongness of killing, so a complete absence of harmful side-effects was built into the description. Let us keep this feature, but add some extra ones. His life in prison is not a happy one, and I have every reason to think that over the years it will get worse. In my view, he will most of the time have a quality of life some way below the point at which life is worth living. I tell him this, and offer to kill him. He, irrationally as I think, says that he wants to go on living. I know that he would be too cowardly to kill himself even if eventually he came to want to die, so my offer is probably his last chance of death. I believe that in the future his backward-looking preference for having been killed will be stronger than his present preference for going on living.

In a case like this, the utilitarian may well think it right to kill the man in prison. And even the extent to which predictions of future states of people are fallible may be insufficient to tip the scale the other way. At least in principle, it is possible for a mental state utilitarian to be committed to a 'paternalist' policy of killing someone, *in what are taken to be his own interests, but against his expressed wishes.*

It is the failure to reflect all our reasons for being reluctant to adopt such a policy which seems to me the incompleteness of the utilitarian view of killing. For this reason, the next chapter discusses the possibility of an additional principle, giving weight to a person's autonomy where his own life and death are concerned. (The principle proposed will also add to the case against the 'replacement' policy, and so may reassure anyone who is reluctant to let that case rest on side-effects alone.)

Chapter 5 Autonomy and Rights

The main argument for the direct wrongness of killing that has been accepted so far is that it is wrong to shorten a worth-while life. This argument has seemed incomplete, as suggested by consideration of the question of killing someone against his wishes where his life can be predicted to be one where he would be better off dead. (The argument will not seem incomplete to those who are prepared to support such 'paternalist' killing. Nor will it seem incomplete to those who wish to rule out such acts of killing, but who are convinced that these acts can adequately be guarded against by appeals to side-effects, or to the uncertainty both of predictions about people's future states and of the evaluation of lives as worth living or not.) I believe that the incompleteness of the argument against killing stems from its disregard of a person's autonomy in taking decisions about his own life or death. On the views adopted so far, it does not matter who takes the decision about whether I should live or die, so long as the calculations are correctly carried out. My desire in the matter is of enormous importance, but only as evidence for anyone who may be deciding the matter.

Other things being equal, people ought to have as much autonomy as possible. This is a reason for holding that, if someone wants to go on living, it may still be directly wrong to kill him even where there are good grounds for thinking his life is not worth living. Giving this weight to autonomy is a rejection of one form of paternalism.

1 Paternalism

Rejection of paternalism in such cases raises a number of disputed questions. Is it always wrong to prevent, in his own interests, an adult capable of weighing alternatives from doing or having what he wants? Many people say we never have a right to interfere on paternalist grounds. They follow Mill in thinking that restrictions of liberty may sometimes be justified by appealing to the interests of other people, but that to restrict someone's freedom for his own good is not permissible.

But in some cases we may be doubtful about giving this absolute priority to autonomy. If someone wants to start taking heroin, I will think it right to stop him if I can. This results from giving less weight to his autonomy in this matter than to sparing him the appalling suffering involved in the slow death of a heroin addict. (The heroin addict also causes suffering to people who care about him, and is a drain on the community's medical resources. These are extra reasons, of a non-paternalist kind, for stopping people taking heroin. But the concession to paternalism made here is the admission that prevention would be right even in the absence of these reasons involving other people.)

Anyone who rejects paternalism entirely has no problem in explaining his view that it is directly wrong to kill someone who wants to live. But those of us who are sometimes prepared to override a person's autonomy in what we take to be his own interests do have to face problems of drawing boundaries. If it is directly wrong to kill someone against his will, is it directly wrong to keep someone alive against his will? How can it be right that I should be forced to stay alive at great cost in pain to myself, but not be right for me to take heroin if I want, at the same cost to myself?

There are three main arguments for paternalistic prevention of heroin addiction:

(i) The suffering is very great: we can be very confident that the normal person is better off than the addict.

(ii) There is very little uncertainty that the suffering will occur.

(iii) The process is not readily reversible, so the person starting on heroin greatly restricts his future freedom of choice. (This might appeal as an argument to those whose anti-paternalism stems from valuing freedom much more than utilitarian considerations.)

It would be hard to make out a case that killing someone against his will but 'in his interests' had anything like this kind of justification. Reasons (i) and (ii) might in very rare cases apply: we would have to imagine that I am a doctor with a lot of experience of patients with your terminal illness, and I know that on our plague-ridden island medical supplies are so low that, unless I kill you now, there will be no means of avoiding your agony later. Even here, the decision about how bad a life must be for the person to be better off dead has to be taken before reason (i) applies.

Consideration of reason (iii) shows a central difference between paternalistic killing and either the heroin case or paternalistic prevention of suicide. There is the finality of an act of killing. Paternalistic prevention of suicide is different. I feel justified in stopping you killing yourself because I expect you will be glad later that I did. If I am mistaken, you will have opportunities for other attempts. Similarly, there will be other opportunities to start on heroin. But, if I kill you, this is final. You will not have second thoughts, and mine will come too late.

2 When Do Questions of Autonomy Arise?

Respect for a person's autonomy and the associated restrictions on paternalism can arise only in the context of a person who has a preference at the time when the decision affecting him is to be taken. Whatever outcome you may in future come to prefer, there can be no question of anyone now overriding your autonomy if you now have no views about the decision to be taken. (Though respect for your autonomy at least requires that this is found out by asking you.) There are three presuppositions that must be made by anyone who thinks that your autonomy should be respected in a present situation:

(a) *The existence condition:* You must already exist. There is no such thing as overriding the autonomy of a potential person. It is true that we can do things that restrict the freedom of action of future generations, perhaps by allowing the erosion of civil liberties or by using up scarce resources, but such acts are objectionable because of the weight we ought to give to the interests or liberty of future people, not because we can now be said to be flouting their autonomy.

(b) *The developmental condition:* You must be at a level of development where you can have the relevant desires. Perhaps my three-year-old son will one day have the ambition to produce a unified field theory. If I do not take steps to see he has an adequate scientific education, this may prevent him even having a chance to satisfy the ambition. But this would again be a matter of restricting his future opportunities. I cannot, if I take a decision about his education now, be overriding his autonomy. This is because, although he is in existence, he is not at the stage of development where he even *could* have the desire whose satisfaction I may be ruling out.

(c) *The possession condition:* You must have the desire whose satisfaction is in question. I override your autonomy only where I take a decision on your behalf which goes against what you actually do want, not where the decision goes against what you would want if you were more knowledgeable or more intelligent. (To say this is to talk of desires in a dispositional sense: you do not have to be conscious of your desire at the moment it is overridden. Such a condition as that would license any decision I take on your behalf the moment you are asleep. And to think of desires in this dispositional sense should also allow us to respect desires that have a stable role in a person's outlook even when they are temporarily eclipsed by conditions such as hypnosis or being drugged.)

Obviously the possession condition includes the developmental condition, which in turn includes the existence condition. The point of spelling out the first two conditions is that they are important when we consider the status of potential people, and of foetuses and babies, in the light of respect for autonomy as an objection to killing.

77

3 Respect for Autonomy as an Objection to Killing Independent of Mental-State Utilitarianism

The principle that we ought to respect people's autonomy can be seen as descended from the Kantian tradition in ethics. But someone might say that such a principle could equally well be seen as an aspect of a utilitarian policy, and therefore claim that it is superfluous to add this extra principle when utilitarian considerations have already been given weight.

In considering this objection, it is necessary to mention some differences between the desires or preferences that carry weight under the autonomy principle and those that do so under the version of utilitarianism sketched out here.

The autonomy principle stands in opposition in several ways to the mental-state version of utilitarianism discussed in the previous chapter. Where your autonomy is respected, the decision is yours, even if you opt for an outcome that you will not know about. Respect for your autonomy involves giving priority to the decision you make about your future in the light of your present outlook, even if it is predictable that your future outlook will be quite different. And, as the autonomy principle gives no weight to backward-looking preferences, it gives no support either to paternalism towards the living or to any policy of considering the interests of potential people.

Although the autonomy principle differs in these ways from mental-state utilitarianism, it could be argued that a sophisticated utilitarian would normally in practice derive from his own view the same decisions that would be generated by the autonomy principle. The case for saying this would rest partly on the bad side-effects of 'paternalist killing', partly on the fallibility of predictions about people's future happiness or misery and partly on the central role that a person's own view of his life must play in any decision whether his life is worth living.

That paternalist killing would often have disastrous side-effects is obvious. (Imagine the consequences of it becoming known that, in a certain hospital, patients were sometimes killed 'in their own interests', but against their expressed wishes.) And in the case of the proposed paternalist killing of the man in prison, mentioned in the previous chapter, it is hard to see what utilitarian would feel so confident that the man's life would get worse that he would feel justified in killing him. Even in life imprisonment, people's mental states may be relatively obscure and psychological changes hard to predict. If a man wants to go on living, although this does not force me to accept that his life is worth living, I would have to be very optimistic about my own judgement to be sure that he is wrong.

These arguments obviously go some way towards showing that a mental-state utilitarian and a believer in the autonomy principle will in practice have a common policy. If they went all the way to showing that, it might then be desirable to drop one of the two principles as redundant. That such arguments do not go all the way can be seen by considering the implications of giving up either of the two principles while retaining the other one.

Suppose we decided, where someone's life is at stake, to abandon any principle telling us to preserve worth-while lives and to be guided by the autonomy principle alone. One consequence can be seen in an imaginary case. Suppose we came upon a group of people in a remote region of the world who seemed cheerful and contented, but who had no reluctance to die. Perhaps it would be that in practice they held the view, argued for in theory by philosophers such as Lucretius, that death was no more something to regret or fear than sleep. If our only objection to killing were based on the autonomy principle, there would be no objection to killing the whole community. This seems quite unacceptable.

The deficiencies of making the wrongness of killing depend only on the autonomy principle can also be seen in a case that is not at all imaginary. If someone wants to kill himself, we often think it right to prevent him, on the grounds that he does have a worth-while life and that he will later be glad of our paternalist intervention. But if the only principle applying to matters of life and death were the autonomy principle, we would often find ourselves debarred from intervening. (Often, rather than always, because the possession condition allows us to respect desires that are briefly eclipsed. But this loophole cannot be stretched far without the autonomy principle collapsing into utilitarianism.) This degree of libertarianism does have its supporters, but to me it appears unacceptable.

Those who do not like having both principles, of utility and autonomy, involved in the wrongness of killing may think that a more plausible case can be made for retaining the utilitarian principle alone. We have already seen the arguments which show that the mental-state utilitarian will normally act in the way also prescribed by the autonomy principle. But those of us who feel that our reluctance to support paternalist killing does not depend *merely* on side-effects and on the fallibility of our judgement will want to cite respect for autonomy as an independent reason. Given a situation scarcely likely to arise in practice, where we had God-like certainty about our judgement that someone's future life was not worth living and (as in the prison case) were unhampered by side-effects, many of us would still feel that the person's own expressed wish to live should be given some weight. Anyone who shares this feeling will be dissatisfied with the mental-state version of utilitarianism on its own.

4 The Preference for Autonomy

Reasons have been given for thinking that the mental-state utilitarian and the believer in respecting people's autonomy will often act in the same way. Our preference for taking our own decisions is partly based on the greater likelihood of this bringing about outcomes we find satisfactory in other ways. But this is not the whole story. For many of us would not be prepared to surrender our autonomy with respect to the major decisions of our life, even if by doing so our other satisfactions were greatly increased.

There are some aspects of life where a person may be delighted to hand over decisions to someone else more likely to bring about the best results. When buying a secondhand car, I would happily delegate the decision to someone more knowledgeable. But there are many other decisions which people would be reluctant to delegate even if there were the same prospect of greater long-term satisfaction. Some of these decisions are relatively minor but concern ways of expressing individuality. On some council estates, there are regulations about the colour people can paint their front door, the kind of animals they can have or the sort of curtains that are allowed, and these regulations are much resented. And they would probably be resented even if it were agreed that the estate would look much worse without them. Even in small things, people can mind more about expressing themselves than about the standard of the result.

And, in the main decisions of life, this is even more so. Suppose people's marriage partners and jobs were chosen by experts, and that studies showed a far higher level of satisfaction among those whose marriages and jobs were so chosen than among people who made their own arrangements. Even so, many of us would prefer not to delegate such important decisions, for if we did so we would lose the sense of living our own lives, and we prefer to forgo a great deal of happiness, or risk a fair amount of disaster, to losing control of our lives in this way. No doubt there are disasters (being hideously tortured or going mad) which we might if necessary sacrifice all autonomy to avoid, but perhaps for *some* of us there is no degree of additional pleasure for which we would surrender control of the central decisions of our lives. It is this that partly underlies the revulsion, so hard for a mental-state utilitarian to explain, which many people have at the thought of Brave New World.

It seems plausible to suggest that, since we have this desire to take our own decisions, especially at the crucial points of our lives, a broader version of utilitarianism than the mental-state version could accommodate the emphasis given here to autonomy. For a desire so important to us would unavoidably be

81

given a central role in any utilitarianism centred around people's desires and preferences rather than around experienced states of satisfaction. But any version of utilitarianism which did justice to the role of autonomy would have to allow that in some circumstances *no* additional satisfactions of other kinds could compensate for losing control over the central decisions of life.

5 Trade-Off

Two kinds of reason have so far been allowed as legitimate direct objections to killing. One is the undesirability of shortening a worth-while life and the other is the undesirability of overriding someone's autonomy. So far, no account has been given of the relative importance of these reasons or of what should be done when they come into conflict.

It would be nice to be able to propose, at the theoretical level, some clear trade-off between the two values, preferably justified by some general argument. I have not so far found a solution to this problem which seems intellectually satisfying. In particular I am dissatisfied with any general claim about autonomy always taking priority, and have already conceded support to utilitarian paternalism in cases such as that of heroin addiction. But when killing is in question (that is in the rather few and esoteric cases where killing someone against his wishes seems to be in his interests) it is hard to draw up a principle that gives clear guidance in all possible cases. It does not seem plausible to say that there is no *conceivable* amount of future misery that would justify killing someone against his will. If I had been a Jew in Nazi Germany, I would have considered very seriously killing myself and my family, if there was no other escape from the death camps. And, if someone in that position felt that his family did not understand what the future would feel like and so killed them against their wishes, I at least am not sure that this decision would be wrong. But, in happier times and places, the independent value placed on autonomy, combined with the strong utilitarian arguments for respecting it, in practice rule out paternalist killing.

So the following principle, unsatisfactorily unspecific, suggests itself:

Except in the most extreme circumstances, it is directly wrong to kill someone who wants to go on living, even if there is reason to think this desire not in his own interests.

6 Is There a Right to Life?

Sometimes, people who want to take questions of life and death out of the realm of calculation of consequences suggest that we have a right to life. What is meant is not a legal right, but a moral right. Legal rights can be conferred or withdrawn by the appropriate legislative machinery. But the moral right to live does not depend on any laws. Moral rights are normally thought of as absolutes: they may not be infringed, however great the advantages of doing so. To say that people have a right to life is to say that it is never morally justifiable to kill them, and that the wrongness of killing is independent of any claim about the undesirability of its consequences.

Some believers in the right to life may object that their doctrine has been stated too strongly here. For some people think that we have a right to life, but that this is a right that can sometimes be overridden. Not all those who campaign against abortion under the slogan 'the right to life of the unborn child' are absolute pacifists. Their belief may not be in an absolute right, but in a *prima facie* right, which could be overruled in exceptional circumstances. But a doctrine of *prima facie* rights is of doubtful value. The approach to killing defended in this book allows that in general there is a very strong presumption that killing someone is wrong. A doctrine of absolute rights goes further than this and excludes the possibility of ever justifying killing by its consequences. But the claim that we have only a *prima facie* right to life does not exclude this possibility. It is thus not clear that it significantly differs from the view argued for here.

The doctrine that we have an absolute right to live is a genuine alternative. Any belief in absolute rights at least restricts the scope of what can be justified by beneficial consequences. But a problem arises in any moral system that allows more than one absolute right. What happens if we believe both in an absolute right to life and in an absolute right to use all necessary means to defend one's own life? There may be cases where killing in self-defence is necessary. How can I exercise my own right to self-defence without infringing my assailant's right to life? This need not be a serious difficulty for the believer in absolute rights. He can allow that certain rights have priority over others, while still insisting that we may never override someone's right for any reason except the exercise or defence of another right. Some non-pacifist campaigners for the rights of the unborn child may hold this kind of view.

Traditional doctrines of rights have often seen the existence of a right as a kind of metaphysical fact to be discovered. When rights are seen either as God-given or as being 'natural', we discover them by studying God's revelation or by contemplation of the human condition. But to those of us who find such views of the discovery of moral 'truths' either false or unintelligible, some other kinds of argument will seem necessary. Can any moral reason be given for saying we have a right to life, or is it an ultimate belief, admitting no further argument?

If there are reasons that can be given for giving this special moral priority to not killing, they are likely to appeal to the kind of considerations discussed in this and the previous chapters. But if the reasons are of this kind, the doctrine of the absolute right to life is open to objections. Either it collapses into a mere rule of thumb or else it involves a rigidity that the reasons cited in its defence cannot justify.

If, on the other hand, the absolute right to life is an ultimate moral belief, not backed by any further reasons, we may feel that it is not a very tempting doctrine. For it commits us to saying that killing is never justifiable except in the exercise or defence of other overriding rights. Until we know what other rights there are, and which, if any, are overriding, we are not in a position to accept or reject the view. If any factor we think to be morally important can qualify as someone's right then the absolute right to life may turn out to be insubstantial. (Suppose someone proposed the 'right to happiness'.) But, if we say that the right to life is the only right, or the one right that always has priority over others, this 'no trade-off' view seems too strong. Suppose there were a tyrant who, although he never killed people, inflicted hideous tortures on many of them, and who could only be stopped from this by assassination? Are we to say that there is no amount of misery whose prevention would justify killing him? Those of us who cannot accept this must reject the strong version of the view that there is an absolute right to life.

If the saying 'people have a right to life' means that killing is directly wrong where the person in question wants to go on living, or has a life worth living, then it is quite acceptable. But the doctrine of the right to life sometimes goes beyond this view, either by making killing overridingly, as well as directly, wrong, or else by making its wrongness independent of people's desires or their likely future experiences. When it does it should be rejected.

Chapter 6 Ends and Means: Double Effect

There is a further clear distinction between using means for the relief of suffering which may, as a secondary result, shorten life, and actively ending life. Here the guide is the principle known as the principle of double effect. It is a principle commonly misunderstood, but one which in fact guides doctors whenever the problem of undesirable side-effects arises with any treatment . . . The use of medicaments with the intention of relieving pain is good, and if by repeated pain relief the patient's resistance is lowered and he dies earlier than he would otherwise have done, this is a side-effect which may well be acceptable . . . On the other hand, to give an overdose *with the intention that the patient should never wake up* is morally wrong. It is killing.

Jonathan Gould and others: *Your Death Warrant? The Implications of Euthanasia*, London, 1971

The objections to killing defended here rest to a large extent on consequences, though not entirely so, because the need to respect someone's autonomy is given some weight independent of good consequences. This can be seen as accommodating part of what is valued when it is said that we ought always to treat people as ends in themselves and never merely as means.

But many people disapprove of giving the consequences of acts even the restricted, though still important, role that they play in the moral beliefs advocated here. These beliefs will to them still be sufficiently close to traditional utilitarianism to provoke the criticism that, in an objectionable way, 'the end justifies the means'. Those who make this criticism will want some set of principles according to which the relations between the consequences of an act and its morality are more indirect. In discussions of the morality of killing, two such principles are often either cited or else tacitly presupposed. One says that there is a morally significant difference between acts and omissions. This will be the subject of the next chapter. The other is the doctrine of double effect.

This doctrine can be summarized crudely as saying that it is always wrong intentionally to do a bad act for the sake of good consequences that will ensue, but that it may be permissible to do a good act in the knowledge that bad consequences will ensue. The doctrine is explained in terms of the difference between intended and foreseen consequences.

G.E.M. Anscombe, who believes in the double-effect doctrine, has illustrated it with the case of killing in self-defence.[1] If you attack me, I may, if necessary, defend myself by striking you so hard that your death results. (The 'if necessary' is important here: I have a duty to use the minimum force necessary.) But, if I know you are searching for me to kill me, I am not morally permitted to arrange for you to be poisoned before you find me.

The explanation usually given of this moral difference is that, where I arrange for you to be poisoned, I must intend your death as a means to my own safety. On the other hand, when I hit you in self-defence, I intend only to prevent you from killing me. If I only knock you unconscious, this will be just as effective. If you do die, this can be a foreseen but unintended consequence of my blow, rather than itself the intended means of my defence.

Some applications to cases of abortion of the double-effect doctrine may be mentioned. The doctrine allows that a pregnant woman with cancer of the womb may have her life saved by removal of the womb, with the foreseen consequence that the foetus dies. But, if the doctor could save only the mother's life by changing the composition of the amniotic fluid and so killing the foetus while still attached to the womb, this would

1. G.E.M. Anscombe: 'War and Murder', in W. Stein (ed.): *Nuclear Weapons, A Catholic Response*, London, 1961.

not be permitted. In the second case the death of the foetus would be an intended means; in the first case it would be merely a foreseen consequence.

The double effect doctrine is often criticized on utilitarian grounds. The two abortion cases would each have the same outcome: the death of the foetus and the saving of the mother. A utilitarian is bound to see this moral doctrine as unacceptable: depending on a distinction without a difference. If the death of the mother is a worse outcome than the death of the foetus, it seems to a utilitarian immoral to act as the double effect principle tells us.

Professor Hart has cited another application of the double effect doctrine that is open to similar objection.[2] There was a case in which a man was trapped in the cabin of a blazing lorry, with no hope of being freed. He asked a bystander to shoot him in order to save him from further agony. The bystander did so, but his act would have been condemned by the double effect doctrine. For, according to this view, if it is wrong intentionally to kill an innocent man, it is still wrong to do so even as a means to saving him from pain: better not shoot him, with the foreseen consequence that he will burn to death.

There are also problems of stating the doctrine precisely. How do we draw the line in difficult cases between an intended means and a foreseen inevitable consequence? If, as a political protest, I throw a bomb into a football crowd, causing an explosion and killing several people, are their deaths intended means to my protest or inevitable consequences of it? On what principles do we decide whether the explosion alone is included in the means or whether we must count both explosion and deaths as part of the means? This cannot be decided on the grounds of the virtual inevitability of the deaths if the explosion occurs, for the double effect doctrine tells us that there can be consequences foreseen to be inevitable, yet which do not count as intended means. The matter cannot hinge on whether or not the deaths are desired, for in the forbidden abortion case

2. H.L.A. Hart: 'Intention and Punishment', *The Oxford Review*, 1967, reprinted in H.L.A. Hart: *Punishment and Responsibility*, Oxford, 1968.

the death of the foetus is no more desired than it is in the permitted case.

It may be suggested that what is crucial is the 'closeness' of the connection between cause and effect. (Jonathan Bennett has raised the question why 'closeness' should be of any moral importance, aside from its link with the extent to which the effect is either inevitable or desired.[3] A lot of explaining seems called for.) What sort of 'closeness' is in question? Is it closeness in time? If so, having someone poisoned in order to prevent them catching and killing me will turn out not to be forbidden if the poison used is *very* slow-acting. If it is some other form of closeness, how is it specified and what degree of it is required?

The next problem in formulating the doctrine is that of identifying the class of 'bad' acts that can never be justified by appeals to consequences. Some people believe that they know the contents of the list of such bad acts, which has been laid down by an authority, perhaps by God. They have no difficulty in justifying their claim to know which acts are forbidden (apart from familiar problems of saying how they know God exists, how they know what he commands, and why they should obey his commands). If the identification of the class of forbidden acts depends on this kind of appeal to authority, those of us who are unimpressed by such appeals can discard the double effect doctrine at once. But perhaps this is too hasty. Is there any way of identifying the 'bad' acts which can never be justified by good consequences, without appealing to some authority?

These acts cannot be identified by the badness of their consequences in a particular case, for the forbidden and permitted abortions can have the same effects on the interests of all concerned. Perhaps an appeal to the beneficial consequences of a rule is involved. Because it is in general better that people do not take innocent life, a rule is made saying that it must never be done. This raises the problem: why should I obey the rule in cases where to do so does not have the best overall consequences?

3. Jonathan Bennett: 'Whatever the Consequences', *Analysis*, 1965.

There is also a further problem. For there are many things that are in general undesirable, but which are not made the subject of these absolute prohibitions. Lying is in general undesirable, but it is not commonly suggested that it is absolutely wrong to lie, for instance as a means of saving someone's life. So, why killing? Even if killing is 'in itself' worse than lying, this is surely a matter of degree. It seems hard on this basis to justify an absolute prohibition. For suppose killing is a million times worse than lying. If we can lie to avoid someone's death, how can we justify refusing to kill someone where this will save a million lives?

There is a parallel problem of deciding what kinds of foreseen but unintended consequences can be justified by the double effect doctrine. For I cannot, according to the doctrine, perform an act which brings about a small intended benefit, with disproportionately disastrous foreseen consequences. I may not tell the truth about an innocent fugitive's whereabouts to an assassin, with the foreseen consequence that he is murdered. But, having allowed this concession to utilitarian calculation, where is a line to be drawn, and why?

The situation is complicated by the difficulty of deciding where to draw the line between an act and its consequences. If we are on a desert journey and I knowingly use all the drinking water for washing my shirts, my act may be described merely as one of 'washing shirts' or of 'keeping up standards even in the desert', and our being without water may be thought of as a foreseen bad consequence. But it is at least equally acceptable to include the consequence in the description of the act, which may then be described as one of 'using up the last of the water' or of 'putting our lives at risk'. This general problem of distinguishing acts from their consequences is clearly related to the problem already mentioned, of distinguishing intended means from foreseen consequences.

It is crucial for the double effect doctrine that some limit must be set to the re-description of acts in terms of their consequences, for otherwise the doctrine will forbid nothing. Killing the foetus while it is attached to the womb will be permitted under the description 'saving the mother's life'. Eric D'Arcy[4] quotes the jingle 'Imperious Caesar, dead and turned to clay, might stop a hole to keep the wind away', but protests that it would be wrong to describe killing him with that end in view as 'blocking a draught'. D'Arcy's own solution to the problem is to claim that 'certain kinds of act are of such significance that the terms which denote them may not, special contexts apart, be elided into terms which (*a*) denote their consequences, and (*b*) conceal, or even fail to reveal, the nature of the act itself'.

This is an attractive claim, for we do feel that there is something wrong with describing Caesar's murder as 'blocking a draught'. Our objection to such an oblique description is presumably because it omits features of great importance to our moral appraisal of the act. But such incompleteness is a matter of degree. Many acts have so many facets of some relevance to moral evaluation that we often have to sacrifice completeness to brevity. In describing a man's act of rushing a seriously injured person to hospital, we do not have to include in our description of his act the consequence that he broke a promise to meet someone for lunch. We value explicitness of description, and we often disapprove of people slurring over the morally unattractive aspects of actions, especially of their own actions. But the degree of explicitness we think desirable may vary in different contexts, and there may be disagreement as to how incomplete a description can be before it reaches objectionable evasiveness.

If the doctrine of double effect is to have any content, it must stipulate that acts which fall under certain descriptions may never, for purposes of moral evaluation, be described in a way which omits this feature of them. We have seen that the drawing-up of a list of absolutely forbidden acts raises difficulties. A parallel list of un-elidable act-descriptions is likely to be morally just as debatable.

The lack of intuitive plausibility of some of the applications of the double effect doctrine, together with the difficulties both of drawing the key distinctions and of defending their relevance, are good reasons for rejecting it.

4. Eric D'Arcy: *Human Acts*, Oxford, 1963, Ch. 4, part 3.

Chapter 7   Not Striving to Keep Alive

Thou shalt have one God only; who
Would be at the expense of two?
No graven images may be
Worshipped, except the currency

Thou shalt not kill, but need'st not strive
Officiously to keep alive . . .

A.H. Clough: *The Latest Decalogue*

You are eating a hearty meal, while somewhere a baby is
starving. As the charitable appeals point out, you might have
saved it. But pleading guilty to the charge does not give you
license to strangle a neighbour's infant with your bare hands, as
though to say 'What's the difference? Both babies are dead,
aren't they?'

Mary McCarthy: *Medina*

But each one of us is guilty in so far as he remained inactive.
The guilt of passivity is different. Impotence excuses; no moral
law demands a spectacular death . . . But passivity knows itself
morally guilty of every failure, every neglect to act whenever
possible, to shield the imperilled, to relieve wrong, to countervail.

Karl Jaspers: *The Question of German Guilt*

Is it worse to kill someone than not to save his life? What we
may call the 'acts and omissions doctrine' says that, in certain contexts, failure to perform an act, with certain foreseen bad consequences of that failure, is morally less bad than to perform a
different act which has the identical foreseen bad consequences.

It is worse to kill someone than to allow them to die. Philippa Foot has discussed a case which illustrates this view.[1] She says, 'most of us allow people to die of starvation in India and Africa, and there is surely something wrong with us that we do; it would be nonsense, however, to pretend that it is only in law that we make a distinction between allowing people in the underdeveloped countries to die of starvation and sending them poisoned food'.

Another case where our intuitive response to killing differs from our response to not striving to keep alive concerns old-age pensioners. Until the introduction of automatic regular increases, the Chancellor of the Exchequer in his annual budget normally either failed to increase the old-age pension or else put it up by an inadequate amount. In either case, it was predictable that a certain number of old-age pensioners would not be able to afford enough heating in winter, and so would die of cold. We think that the decision of such a Chancellor was not a good one, but we do not think it nearly as bad as if he had decided to take a machine-gun to an old people's home and to kill at once the same number of people.

Apart from this support the acts and omissions doctrine derives from our intuitive responses to such cases, it might be argued that to abandon it would place an intolerable burden on people. For, we may think that, without it, we would have morally to carry the whole world on our shoulders. It is arguable that we would have to give money to fight starvation up to the point where we needed it more than those we were helping: perhaps to the point where we would die without it. For not to do so would be to allow more people to die, and this would be like murder. And, apart from this huge reduction in our standard of living, we should also have to give up our spare time, either to raising money or else to persuading the government to give more money. For, if a few pounds saves a life, not to raise that money would again be like murder.

Finally, it could be said that for us the acts and omissions

1. Philippa Foot: The Problem of Abortion and the Doctrine of the Double Effect, *The Oxford Review*, 1967.

doctrine is a 'natural' one: that it is presupposed by the way in which we use moral language. There is in our vocabulary a distinction between duties and those good acts that go beyond the call of duty. A doctor has no duty to risk his life by going from England to a plague-infested town in an Asian country at war in order to save lives there, and we do not blame him if he does not do so. If he does go, we think of him as a hero. But, if we abandoned the acts and omissions doctrine, we might have to abandon our present distinction between acts of moral duty and supererogation.

1 The Sources of Strength of the Acts and Omissions Doctrine

It will be argued here that we ought to reject the acts and omissions doctrine. I have no formal argument to show that it is self-contradictory or in any way incoherent. I cannot show that it is a doctrine which any rational person must reject. The argument to be used is less conclusive than that. I shall present a diagnosis of why people hold the doctrine, a cluster of reasons which seem more impressive before they are separated out than after critical examination.

The acts and omissions doctrine draws its strength from the following sources:

(*a*) Confusions between different kinds of omission.

(*b*) The fact that the doctrine is itself confused with negative utilitarianism.

(*c*) Other factors only contingently associated with the act-omission distinction.

(*d*) Other moral priorities that are themselves questionable.

(*e*) A failure to separate the standpoint of the agent from the standpoint of the moral critic or judge.

2 Varieties of Omission

Sometimes when I do not do something, it would be entirely unreasonable to blame me for this. If someone I have never heard of killed himself last week in Brazil, without my knowing or doing anything about it, I cannot be blamed for it. Even if we took the view denied by the acts and omissions doctrine (that I ought to do everything in my power to further the good and frustrate the bad) I still cannot be blamed. For my ignorance of the whole episode meant I had no opportunity to intervene, and this ignorance was not itself the result of negligence: I had in advance no reason to suppose that good would come or harm be avoided if I took the trouble to find out anything about that man.

But some omissions are at the other extreme of blameworthiness. A man who will inherit a fortune when his father dies, and, with this in mind, omits to give him medicine necessary for keeping him alive, is very culpable. His culpability is such that many people would want to say that this is not a mere omission, but a positive act of withholding the medicine. Supporters of the acts and omissions doctrine who also take this view are faced with the problem of explaining where they draw the line between acts and omissions. Is consciously failing to send money to Oxfam also a positive act of withholding? Presumably supporters of the doctrine do not want to make it an empty analytic truth, by insisting that anything we consider culpable must be counted as an act rather than an omission.

Between these extremes are other kinds of omission. Some are the result of ignorance that is negligent, where the agent could and should have avoided being ignorant. Other omissions are conscious, but are the result of some such factor as laziness, rather than some discreditable motive. It seems possible that some of the force of the acts and omissions doctrine derives from tacitly thinking of omissions in terms of examples drawn from the non-culpable end of the spectrum. The doctrine certainly seems less plausible where the omission is deliberate and results from a bad motive. But such a simple lack of discrimination is clearly by no means the whole explanation of the popularity of the doctrine.

3 Acts, Omissions and Negative Utilitarianism

In some of the cases to which the doctrine is applied, it seems to derive part of its strength from the fact that often the forbidden act would harm someone, while the permitted omission is merely a failure to benefit someone. Stealing five pounds from you is a forbidden act that harms you, while failing to make you a present of five pounds is a permitted failure to benefit you. Because of such cases, those who are attracted to negative utilitarianism, which tells us not to promote happiness, but rather to eliminate misery, often also feel attracted to the acts and omissions doctrine.

Doubt has often been cast on the attractiveness of negative utilitarianism, at least without severe restriction or modification, as the basis of a morality. (The only certain way of eliminating all misery would be the painless extermination of all conscious life.) And the distinction it depends upon is not very clear: the size of a man's income is likely to be relevant to whether stealing five pounds from him is a matter of making him unhappy or merely of reducing his happiness. And the same holds for the failure to give him five pounds.

But it can be seen, in cases where the line between positive and negative utilitarianism is intuitively relatively clear, that negative utilitarianism does not support the acts and omissions doctrine. For sending money to help the starving could reasonably be held to reduce misery, as could raising the old-age pension, and yet the failure to do either of these can shelter behind the acts and omissions doctrine. Even if we were to accept both that there was a clear distinction between eliminating unhappiness and promoting happiness, and that this was of great moral importance, we would be wrong to suppose this relevant to the defence of a view that an act and an omission *with identical consequences* can vary in moral value.

96

Philippa Foot has proposed a variant on the acts and omissions doctrine which at the same time has considerable appeal and seems to bring the doctrine closer to negative utilitarianism. For her, it is the distinction between what we do and what we allow that is crucial. On the basis of this distinction, she proposes a doctrine of positive and negative duties. Positive duties are to help people, and are taken to include acts of charity, which might normally not count as 'duties' at all. Negative duties are to refrain from injuring or harming people. Negative duties are seen as more important than positive ones. Mrs Foot says, 'It is interesting that, even where the strictest duty of positive aid exists, this still does not weigh as if a negative duty were involved. It is not, for instance, permissible to commit a murder to bring one's starving children food.'

For Mrs Foot, the distinction between negative and positive duties is not reducible to the distinction between acts and omissions. She says that 'An actor who fails to turn up for a performance will generally spoil it rather than allow it to be spoiled. I mention the distinction between omission and commission only to set it aside.' Yet, despite this disclaimer, it is not clear that the two kinds of duty can be distinguished except on the basis of the act-omission distinction. For, if I do not bring my starving children food, they will die. The harm to them may be at least as great as to someone I murder. So, if it is not permissible to commit a murder to bring one's starving children food, this prohibition cannot be based on the view that the murder would do more harm. It is hard to see how the overriding negative duty can be distinguished here from the mere positive duty to the children except by using the act-omission distinction. It is not clear that there is any acceptable half-way house between straightforward negative utilitarianism and the acts and omissions doctrine.

4 Probability of Outcome

Many acts can reasonably be said to be worse than their apparently corresponding omissions, because their bad consequences are either less avoidable or else worse. The difference in our responses to some of the cases already mentioned could be largely explained in these terms.

When the Chancellor of the Exchequer failed to raise old-age pensions, there was still some possibility of saving the lives of those who would otherwise die of cold next winter. There was still the possibility that relations, friends or private charities would step in with sufficient money, fuel, food or clothes to save those at risk. But, if someone goes to an old people's home and machine-guns the inhabitants, the deaths of most of them are inevitable. In thinking of the old-age pensioners, it would have been self-deception to suppose that adequate private rescue operations were likely, for in no year was enough done privately. And we may prefer that adequate pensions should be given to everyone as of right than that old people should have to accept private charity. But, despite these points, it remains true that probable death is preferable to certain death, and so we have at least one reason here for thinking the act worse than the omission.

But this difference is insufficient to save the acts and omissions doctrine in general, since some omissions create just as strong a probability of death as their corresponding acts. If someone is being kept alive on a respirator and I switch it off, this makes death no more certain than if, when attaching the patient to the machine, I fail to switch it on. In either case there is a chance that someone passing by will see it is off and switch it on. But the probability of this is not increased by the fact that it was on before.

5 Side-Effects

There are also differences of side-effects between the massacre and the failure to raise the old-age pension. In part they stem from the fact that people resent hostile acts more than equally hostile omissions. The Chancellor of the Exchequer allowed pensioners to die, but, if he massacred some of them, this would indicate that he actually wanted them to die. The resentment felt against the man who does not care enough to do what is necessary to keep people alive is nothing to the resentment felt against the man who wants people to die.

Another factor is that a massacre is a scene of horror. The man responsible for it may find it hard to forget and is likely to have feelings of guilt. But those who do not raise the pension (and those of us who do not campaign for higher pensions) do not have sleepless nights. This claim about differential guilt, like that about differential resentment, depends on the fact that people's responses are in line with the acts and omissions doctrine. Our present tendency to feel less guilty about allowing someone to die than about killing him might be eradicated if we renounced the acts and omissions doctrine. But, to the extent to which these psychological responses are outside our control, 'irrational' differences in strength of guilt feelings might persist after such a decision. And, even if we ourselves change our attitudes, the resentment of others who have not changed theirs will remain a factor to take into account.

Other harmful side-effects are independent of resentment or guilt. A massacre undermines our sense of security. We all feel more comfortable because we know that almost everyone in the country observes an absolute taboo on killing his fellow citizens. Our sense of security is not undermined to the same extent when we hear of old people dying quietly of cold in their rooms. This may be irrational, for we will all be old one day, and our society is still arranged so that most people have the prospect of being poor when old. But, even so, many of us are irrational in this way, and, while we stay so, there remains this difference between the side-effects of the act and of the omission.

These side-effects do not always seem great enough to justify the different moral value often placed on acts and omissions. The man responsible for a massacre has caused deaths that are more certain than those caused by the failure to raise the pension. He has also terrified his victims, aroused resentment and insecurity among other people, perhaps made himself feel guilty, and set a bad example. (The bad example carries no weight in favour of the acts and omissions doctrine, for the man who does not raise old-age pensions also sets a bad example to his successors.) The side-effects other than the bad example, harmful as they are, are not *clearly* so great as to outweigh factors on the other side. For example, although being shot in a massacre must be a terrifying experience, it may be far worse to die slowly of cold. And the extra suffering involved could possibly outweigh the extra bad effects of the act of shooting.

But even if the differences of side-effects between acts and omissions are sometimes exaggerated, it must often still be true that killing has worse total consequences than letting someone die has. Yet this is no help to the acts and omissions doctrine as it stands. That doctrine cannot explicitly be argued for on the basis of side-effects, for it claims that there is a moral difference between acts and omissions with the same total consequences. If the appeal of the acts and omissions doctrine lies in these differences of side-effects, its supporters are simply confused. For the plausible claim that many acts have worse total consequences than the omissions that apparently correspond to them supports the claim only that *these* acts are more to be avoided than *these* omissions. It provides no support for the view that, morally speaking, harmful acts are intrinsically worse than equally harmful omissions.

6 Who is Wronged?

One argument sometimes used in favour of the acts and omissions doctrine is that an act, say, of killing is always an act of killing someone in particular. But many cases of letting die do not involve knowing who it is that dies. The murderer chooses his victim, or at least knows under some description whom he is killing. But when we let people die of starvation in India or let pensioners die of cold, we are not able to say in advance which people will lose their lives. And, even after they have died, there is often no clear way of saying which people my own money could have saved. If, over the years, millions die of starvation, I could not have saved them all. Even my best efforts could only have saved some of them. And any decision that these deaths rather than those ones would have been saved by my action is bound to be fairly arbitrary. The suggestion is that killing some particular person is worse than allowing some unidentified person to die.

But it is hard to see just how this is to be taken. Is the crucial factor the lack of knowledge in advance who it is will die? If so, it is hard to see why this should be thought of any moral importance. Suppose a technician in hospital maliciously sabotages a kidney machine so that the next person to use it will not have his life saved. Why should this act be more wrong if he happens to have looked at a list and seen that the next patient to use the machine will be Mr Hedley-Smythe, proprietor of a hotel in Basingstoke? The plea 'My act was not as bad as it might have been, for only later did I discover the identity of the person whose death I caused' seems to have no mitigating force at all.

The claim may not rest on whether we know in advance whose life is at stake. If this can be found out afterwards, as in the kidney machine case, it is clear that there is a particular person whose death has been caused. But there are other cases, as when many more people die of starvation than I could have saved, where even afterwards we cannot say which lives have been lost through my inaction. But, as long as it is clear that my omission added to the number of deaths, why is it a mitigating factor that I cannot tell *which* deaths were caused by me? This certainly seems totally irrelevant to the wrongness of my failure to act. If five gunmen each fire once into a crowd, each killing one person, it may be unclear which person was killed by which gunman. Whatever the legal position, the uncertainty as to who killed whom does not reduce the moral wrong of the gunmen's acts. If it turned out that their bullets had each been numbered, their acts would not then be regarded as worse. Why should the case be any different with omissions?

7 Not Playing God

A case in which there was a choice between saving the lives of two different lots of people occurred during the Second World War.[2] A German 'spy ring' in Britain consisted of a double agent on the British side and a string of fictitious people. It was on this supposed network of agents that the German government relied for information about where the V1 and V2 rockets were falling. The aiming was broadly accurate, hitting the target of London. It was proposed that the double agent should send back reports indicating that most of them had fallen well north of London, so that the rocket ranges would correct their aim a number of miles to the south. The result of this would have been to make most of the rockets fall in Kent, Surrey or Sussex, killing far fewer people than they did in London. This proposal is said to have been resisted successfully by Herbert Morrison, on the grounds that the British government was not justified in choosing to sacrifice one lot of citizens in order to save another lot.

I do not know the details of the argument actually used, but it may have been a reluctance to play a God-like role, deciding who is to live and who is to die, that made members of the government resist the proposal. Such reluctance is very understandable.

For most of us, situations where we have to choose between saving one life or another are a nightmare we are glad not to experience. Some people, especially those concerned with the allocation of scarce medical resources, do have to face such

2. Sefton Delmer: *The Counterfeit Spy*, London, 1971, Ch. 12.

decisions, and most other people prefer not to be consulted. But the feeling that we ought not to play God in such matters can stem from something more admirable than the desire to avoid a painful choice. This is a desire not to place ourselves above other people. Choosing which of two others should live and which should die, it is natural that one may feel conscious of being presumptuous. If I regard other people as my equals, what right have I to decide between their lives? It may seem less objectionable to decide randomly than to try to judge between them.

The question of whether a choice of which person of two to save ought to be made randomly will be discussed later on. But Morrison's view about the V1 and V2 targets can be criticized independently. For here the choice was not between equal numbers of people. It was between allowing the rockets to continue to fall where they killed a larger number of people, and diverting them so that they killed a different (smaller) lot of people. Mr Morrison's view seems to depend either on the belief that numbers of deaths need be of no moral importance, or else on the belief that positive intervention is more presumptuously God-like than letting things take their course.

Objections will be made in a later chapter to the view that numbers of deaths can be morally irrelevant. But there are also problems for Morrison's other possible line of argument: that acts are more God-like than omissions. For this claim depends on holding that I am less responsible for someone's death where it is the result of my deliberate non-intervention than where it is the result of my act. This is plausible only when we make the mistake of overlooking the different varieties of omission and their corresponding degrees of culpability, or when we hold the acts and omissions doctrine which is the subject of this chapter. The belief that acts are more objectionably God-like than omissions cannot be used as an argument in support of the acts and omissions doctrine which it presupposes.

8 The View of Father Zossima's Brother, and the Impossibility of Doing All Good Things

In *The Brothers Karamazov*, there is a passage where Father Zossima narrates a conversation between his younger brother and his mother.

'And let me tell you this, too, Mother: everyone of us is responsible for everyone else in every way, and I most of all.' Mother could not help smiling at that. She wept and smiled at the same time. 'How are you,' she said, 'most of all responsible for everyone? There are murderers and robbers in the world, and what terrible sin have you committed that you should accuse yourself before everyone else?' 'Mother, my dearest heart,' he said (he had begun using such caressing, such unexpected words just then), 'my dearest heart, my joy, you must realize that everyone is really responsible for everyone and everything.'

This view of Father Zossima's brother bears an obvious resemblance to what has been argued in this chapter, but seems to have nightmare implications. There is so much misery in the world that, however hard one person tries, he cannot remove more than a fraction. Does rejection of the acts and omissions doctrine commit us to being responsible for all that is left? This seems so unreasonable that people may be attracted by the acts and omissions doctrine as an alternative. It is clearly absurd that a man who devotes his whole life to a campaign against poverty should reproach himself for, say, not having done any useful research into the causes of muscular dystrophy.

This brings out one difference between acts and omissions that is of some moral importance. Actions take time, while omissions do not. There is no end to the list of a person's omissions, while the actions he has time for during his life are limited. However heroic he is, he cannot do all the good things which, ignoring pressure of time, would be in his power. Harmful omissions are unavoidable, while most harmful acts can be avoided.

In allocating our time between actions, we have to work out priorities. The moral approach advocated here does not commit us, absurdly, to remedying all the evil in the world. It does not even commit us to spending our whole time trying to save lives. What we should do is work out what things are most important and then try to see where we ourselves have a contribution to make. We should then be able to justify the pattern of our lives. This is still a very demanding morality, which hardly anyone succeeds in living up to, but it is not the totally impossible demand made by Father Zossima's brother.

If this is not emphasized, the views argued for here are rightly open to criticism on grounds of an objectionable puritanism. This puritanism would take the form of suggesting that the only acceptable pattern of life would be one of continuous activity to save lives. But there is more to life than saving lives. Many other activities enrich people's lives, and only a view that recognized no trade-off between saving lives and other values would disallow these other activities. What is argued here does not *entail* the view that an actor rehearsing for a play, a civil servant drawing up laws to regulate pollution, or parents playing with their children, ought to be trying to raise money for Oxfam instead. (But it does make us ask the disturbing question: would we kill people if it were necessary for our pursuit of these activities?)

As well as recognizing the variety of ways in which people can contribute to the world, it is also necessary to accept the desirability of people protecting things that are worth-while in their own lives as well. This is partly because Yeats was right that too long a sacrifice makes a stone of the heart. People who make too many altruistic demands on themselves may after a time lose the inclination to go on doing good works, with the result that over the course of their lives they do less good than they would have done by starting at a sustainable rate. But it is also partly because someone's own worth-while life is a good thing in itself, not merely an instrument for creating benefits for others.

The distinction between acts and omissions can legitimately

105

be used at some points in drawing up rules of thumb by which to guide one's life. Consider a man who buys his children some chocolate and wonders whether to throw away the paper in the street. He disapproves of litter, but sees that other people have dropped their wrappers. If he does not accept the acts and omissions doctrine, he might think that throwing down one more bit of rubbish would be no worse than failing to clear up someone else's bit of rubbish, so he might either throw it down or else spend some time clearing up the street. But these alternatives are clearly unsatisfactory. We sometimes want to follow a middle course between contributing to an evil or spending our time setting it right. Either to protect our own free time or because we could make a more useful contribution to society by doing something else, we are entitled to make a rule of thumb saying that, in general, we will make the easy negative contribution of not dropping rubbish ourselves, without feeling committed to picking up any rubbish we see. Father Zossima's brother might feel responsible for all the litter in the world, but the rest of us need not share his feelings of guilt.

But it remains true that rules of thumb allowing omissions have to be justified, and there may be circumstances in which even a justifiable rule should be broken. It is hard to believe that many of us would be able to justify the degree to which we protect what we like in our own lives at the cost of starvation and death to others. (There is always the disturbing question, for those of us who reject the acts and omissions doctrine, of the extent to which we would think it legitimate to kill people, either in order to bring about things that make life interesting for the rest of us, or to protect our own lives from intolerable pressures. This Dostoyevskian question, when taken seriously, is likely to force us to reconsider *both* how justifiable it is for us to spend time playing with our children rather than helping fight starvation *and* the matter of whether positive acts of killing are quite as hard to justify as we usually suppose. The concessions made to conventional morality in the last few paragraphs are far less substantial than may first appear.) It is also hard to believe that the medical policy of refraining from killing in cases where 'not striving to keep alive' is thought morally right is a justifiable rule of thumb when the importance of what is at stake is fully appreciated.

9 Laws and Conventional Moral Rules

Macaulay, commenting on *A Penal Code Prepared by the Indian Law Commissioners*, points out the absurdity of having legislation which treats *all* deliberate omissions as on a par with acts having the same foreseen consequences:

It will hardly be maintained that a man should be punished as a murderer because he omitted to relieve a beggar, even though there might be the clearest proof that the death of the beggar was the effect of this omission, and that the man who omitted to give the alms knew that the death of the beggar was likely to be the effect of the omission. It will hardly be maintained that a surgeon ought to be treated as a murderer for refusing to go from Calcutta to Meerut to perform an operation, although it should be absolutely certain that this surgeon was the only person in India who could perform it, and that if it were not performed the person who required it would die.[3]

There are obvious reasons for agreeing with Macaulay. The standard set would be so high that almost all of us could be found guilty of murder. And it would be quite unclear which omissions people should be prosecuted for: if yesterday I read a novel, am I to be prosecuted for not saving lives by working for Oxfam, or for not doing so by holding a road-safety class at the local school?

But, from the point that the law should not punish certain harmful omissions, it does not follow that they are morally acceptable. If I see a child for whom I have no special responsibility drowning in a river and deliberately do nothing when I could save him, the law does not punish me, largely because of the difficulties of drawing clear-cut and sensible

3. Quoted in Charles Fried: *Medical Experimentation, Personal Integrity and Social Policy*, 1974.

boundaries around any proposed offence. But few of us would feel entitled to conclude that my omission is immune from criticism.

Legality does not establish that something is morally justified, but legality and illegality can make a moral difference. Doctors who think it justifiable to allow someone to die rather than prolong a painful terminal illness are no doubt right to count the risk of a murder charge as a possible reason for not administering a lethal dose of a drug. It is debatable what the law should forbid here, and debatable how strong a reason illegality is against killing in such circumstance. But some weight should be given both to the general undesirability of breaking the law and to the bad consequences of being caught.

A similar point can be made about the preservation of beneficial conventional moral rules. On the whole, the rules of conventional morality are stronger in prohibiting actions than in enjoining them. Not rescuing the drowning child is less frowned on than pushing him in to start with. Even if the conventional rules are not the best ones imaginable, there may still be a case for preserving them rather than setting a precedent which may undermine them. This is an additional reason for not killing someone which may not always apply to taking positive steps to save people.

But these reasons, which have to do with the law and with conventional practices and attitudes, may not always be decisive against killing: the question is whether killing averts a great enough evil to be justified, bearing in mind both the direct objections to killing and the side-effects, including any weakening either of the law or of a desirable common attitude. And, while the conventional revulsion against killing is an additional reason against it, this line of reasoning may not work the other way. The conventional casualness about letting people die from hunger or lack of medical care is something we should be better off without.

10 Agents and Moral Critics

Some of the plausibility of the acts and omissions doctrine may depend on confusing two different moral standpoints. There is the standpoint of the person deciding how he himself ought to act, and the standpoint of someone else wondering whether the act or omission of the first person is blameworthy. (The standpoints of the agent and of the moral judge or critic.) Because it seems reasonable to adopt a more lenient attitude in making moral judgements in many cases of harmful omission than in many cases of comparably harmful action, it is easy to assume that we are entitled to see harmful omissions as less bad when we ourselves are in the position of the agent deciding what to do. But this is doubtful, as we see when we think why it may be reasonable to judge others more leniently for omissions.

The straightforward utilitarian doctrine, according to which omissions and acts with identical consequences are equally bad, should not be interpreted crudely. That is, we should be sure that an act and an apparently corresponding omission really do have the same consequences. We have seen that there are often importantly different side-effects between what at first sight seem a corresponding pair. The utilitarian does not deny that killing someone may have worse total consequences than letting someone die has. But he does claim that, in arguing which is morally worse, we should go directly to the different consequences rather than base our view on a general principle about acts and omissions.

It is clear that, even taking side-effects into account, this utilitarian morality is a very demanding one. Although there are substantial differences of side-effects, deliberately failing to send money to Oxfam, without being able to justify our alternative spending as more important, is in the same league as murder. If this is so, a lot of us are living far below the moral standards we believe in. To deny the acts and omissions doctrine is to propose a radical and very demanding morality. I should spend my time on good works right up to the point where I can justify the claim that the disadvantage to me outweighs the benefit to others.

Living up to this demanding morality is to many of us a very unattractive prospect: it is the prospect of a huge reduction in income and the loss of a lot of our spare time. The alternatives also are not very comfortable. One is to invent some rationalization to save the acts and omissions doctrine, fitting our beliefs to our conduct rather than our conduct to our beliefs. The other approach, which I adopt, is to accept the utilitarian view, but to allow a huge discrepancy between professed beliefs and actual conduct. This is not very admirable, either.

In our present world, most of us who think about the matter fall into one of the last two categories, while only a few saints live up to the utilitarian view. Because this view sets standards so much higher than those prevailing in our present world, we are reluctant to blame the ordinary person who does not live up to them. For blame is normally apportioned at least partly in accordance with the standards of the time. We do not think that those who executed men for heresy in the sixteenth century were wicked men, although we now think that what they did was wrong. The reason why we do not think they were wicked is that we make allowances for the moral standards of the day and judge them by comparison with others in that context. The same may be said of the ordinary man who in our day fails to do enough about the evils of the world. We are reluctant to say that he is wicked, because he is not worse than other men in our historical period. But this reluctance to blame others for not living up to the utilitarian morality does not justify us in ignoring it when we are in the position of the agent.

11 The Effects of Blame for Omissions

It might be suggested that to undermine the general belief in the acts and omissions doctrine would have very bad consequences. Our greater willingness to blame people for harmful acts than for equally harmful omissions may be thought to serve a useful social purpose. What would happen if people came to view not giving to Oxfam as not very different from murder? It could be argued that this would make them, not more willing to give to Oxfam, but less reluctant to murder.

It might also be said that harmful acts often manifest different character traits from equally harmful omissions, and that it is more important to blame people for those different character traits. The man who massacres the old people exhibits some hostile motive or an unrestrained violence. The Chancellor who fails to put up the pension merely exhibits lack of imagination or concern. The suggestion is that it is more important to discourage hostility or violence than to discourage unconcern or lack of imagination, and so blame in accordance with the acts and omissions doctrine has good consequences.

None of this, even if accepted, would amount to an argument that to reject the acts and omissions doctrine would be mistaken. At best it would show that widespread rejection of it would be harmful. Arguments of this kind invite the reply made in a different context by Hume: 'There is no method of reasoning more common, and yet none more blameable, than in philosophical debates to endeavour to refute any hypothesis by a pretext of its dangerous consequences to religion and morality. When any opinion leads us into absurdities, 'tis certainly false; but 'tis not certain an opinion is false, because 'tis of dangerous consequence.' Although moral beliefs are not in any straightforward way true or false, there is something both objectionable and absurd about trying to argue for a moral view by saying how harmful its widespread rejection would be.

It may be thought that this misses the point. The suggestion may not be that the acts and omissions doctrine is defensible, but that it is a beneficial irrationality that ought not to be publicly criticized. Some people would object to this advocacy of one morality for us and another to be fostered in other people on grounds of the dishonesty and apparent condescension it involves. But it is in any case not clear that it would be harmful to undermine public belief in the acts and omissions doctrine. If we came to think of not giving to Oxfam as being very similar to a positive act of killing, this might not undermine the taboo on murder. It would obviously be a long time before most of us lived up to the high standards the belief demands, but it seems just as likely that we should move a bit in that direction as that we should relax our views on murder.

And the other claim, that it is more important to discourage positive acts of hostility than to encourage people to care more about what happens to each other, is not obviously true either. It is arguable that indifference plays as large a part in causing the world's misery as positive hostility. The existence of wars, poverty and many of the other things that destroy or stunt people's lives may be as dependent on widespread unconcern as on any positively bad motives. It may well be because of tacit acceptance of the acts and omissions doctrine that we acquiesce in the worst evils in the world.

Chapter 8   Some Conclusions

Since much of the argument so far has been opposing some influential alternative approaches to the morality of killing, the positive conclusions can be stated briefly.

It has been argued that the reasons why it is wrong to kill are not the intrinsic value of life or consciousness, nor that people have a right to life. The reasons that have been given are of two kinds. Some make killing directly wrong, while others relate to the harmful side-effects on other people.

1 The Direct Wrongness of Killing

A. It is wrong to reduce the length of a worth-while life.

B. Except in the most extreme circumstances, it is wrong to kill someone who wants to go on living, even if there is reason to think this desire not in his own interests.

C. It is wrong to kill someone where the process of being killed is frightening or painful. (This is mentioned for the sake of completeness. It is less central than the other two reasons: painless killing is not *much* less bad than other kinds.)

Reason B will normally rule out involuntary euthanasia: someone's autonomy should almost always in practice be given priority over reasons for killing him that appeal to his own interests. Do similar arguments make it wrong to kill someone in order to benefit other people? This brings up the whole question of side-effects.

2 Side-Effects and the Wrongness of Killing

Most of the side-effects which often count strongly against kill-ing someone have been mentioned. It is obvious that no exhaustive list of all possible relevant side-effects can be given. The sight of someone being murdered may so upset another man that he does not compose what would have been a great piece of music. There is no end to the possible reverberations of a single act. But some objections that will often be serious can be listed.

(i) There are the effects on the family and friends of the person killed. These can include their grief at his death, lone-liness, poverty and possible other psychological damage.

(ii) The person's contribution to the community is lost. This can be an economic contribution, if he does useful work, but can also be more intangible. The community is enriched, not only by the goods and services, inventions and works of art which someone produces, but also by the contribution that his personality and his relationship with other people make to the whole social atmosphere. (I thought this did not need saying until I read some of the economics literature on the value of human life.)

(iii) The act of killing may arouse hatred and resentment. This may be especially so where there is a tradition of family vendetta, or where a community is divided into hostile camps, as in Northern Ireland.

(iv) Killing someone may undermine the sense of security that other people have. Perhaps, if the general murder rate goes up, many will feel more scared when alone or in places they think dangerous. This danger of insecurity is particularly relevant to euthanasia, for it is very important that people going into hos-pital are not made to fear the doctor as a potential killer.

(v) Killing a person may encourage others to take killing more lightly and may also undermine one's own reluctance to kill again. Most people have a revulsion, possibly 'instinctive', against killing. (This applies at least to killing humans at close range. Many mind less about animals, and dropping bombs or firing missiles and long-range guns seem to be easier to do than killing with a bayonet.) There is often an immense resistance to killing, which armies in war often have to overcome by rigid discipline, the encouragement of patriotic or ideological fervour and by attempts to make the enemy seem less than human.

Even if our revulsion against killing is a basic human instinct, it does not follow that killing is always wrong. Instincts sometimes ought to be controlled. But the existence of this revulsion may be a restraint upon our actions that is of immense value to the human race. If so, the argument that a particular act of killing will weaken this revulsion should be taken very seriously.

3 The Possibility of Beneficial Side-Effects

The direct objections to killing, although very strong, are not being presented here as ones that cannot ever be overridden. It is possible that Hitler had a life which, from his own point of view, was worth living. He probably did not want to die. Yet it is still open to someone who holds the principles outlined here to think that, all things considered, it would have been right to assassinate him. It has not been argued that side-effects must always have less weight than the direct objections to killing.

The Hitler case is both trite and extreme. But other cases where the side-effects of killing may on the whole be beneficial are more disputable and far more morally disturbing. Some senile old people and some children born with gross abnormalities may be such an emotional burden on their families that, thinking purely of side-effects, it would arguably be better if they were dead. These situations are some of the hardest to think about, but one way not to solve the problems they raise is by supposing they do not arise.

4 Saving Lives

To kill is to shorten a life, while to save a life is merely to extend it. The conscious failure to save a life is in some circumstances conventionally regarded either as killing or as morally equivalent to it, but in other circumstances the conventional view is that they are neither identical nor morally on a par. The argument here has suggested that this conventional difference of moral evaluation is defensible to the extent that it reflects differences of side-effects. But in so far as it results from thinking that an act and deliberate omission with *identical* consequences can vary in moral value, the conventional view should be rejected. This suggests that, except for differences of side-effects, the arguments against killing are equally good arguments in favour of saving lives.

Part Three: Practice

Chapter 9 Abortion: The Traditional Approach

To my mind life begins at the moment of conception, and to suggest otherwise seems to me just the sort of casuistry which an anti-Papist might describe as Jesuitical. (Incidentally, I am not myself a Roman Catholic.) Conception is the magic moment . . .

John Grigg in the *Guardian*, 29 October 1973

I do not believe a fertilized ovum is human life in the commonsense meaning of the term: I belief human life begins at birth. Or more technically, when a foetus is sufficiently developed to be capable of living if removed from the mother's womb. That human life begins at the moment of conception is a religious tenet that makes no claim whatsoever to scientific truth.

Dee Wells in the *Guardian*, 29 October 1973

Abortion is the destruction of life after conception and before birth. It is bounded by non-conception on the one hand and by infanticide on the other. The question to be discussed here is whether or when it is morally right. The question of whether or not some or all abortions ought to be illegal is not the central topic, although the moral conclusions are relevant to an answer.

Those who defend at least some abortions tend to focus on the early stages of pregnancy, saying how different an embryo is from us and stressing how tenuous is any distinction between an early abortion and contraception.

Those who think that abortion is, at least in general, morally wrong tend to focus on the late stages of pregnancy, talking of 'the unborn child' and stressing how tenuous is any distinction between abortion and infanticide.

These opponents of abortion often rest their case on the claim that it is a person, or human being, that we kill when we abort. Mrs Jill Knight, M.P., said in a House of Commons debate in 1966:

Babies are not like bad teeth to be jerked out just because they cause suffering. An unborn baby is a baby nevertheless. Would the sponsors of the Bill think it right to kill a baby they can see? Of-course they would not. Why then do they think it right to kill one they cannot see? ... I have come to believe that those who support abortion on demand do so because in all sincerity they cannot accept that an unborn baby is a human being. Yet surely it is. Its heart beats, it moves, it sleeps, it eats. Uninterfered with, it has a potential life ahead of it of seventy years or more; it may be a happy one, or a sad life; it may be a genius, or it may be just plain average; but surely as a healthy, living baby it has a right not to be killed simply because it may be inconvenient for a year or so to its mother.

Because this view of the embryo or foetus is often central to the anti-abortion case, the debate is usually conducted on both sides in terms of drawing a line (at conception, birth or some-where between) where one starts to be either a human being or a person. Some of the rival boundaries will be mentioned here, but the conclusion will be that this approach is futile.

There are two kinds of claim, not always distinguished, on which the case against abortion usually rests. One claim is that the foetus is a human being, or a potential human being. The other is that the foetus is a person, or a potential person. Let us for the moment defer consideration of the slightly more com-plicated versions of these claims, according to which it is the *potential* for being a human being or a person that is crucial, and consider the simpler claims. Is it preferable to conduct the debate in terms of the humanity or the personhood of the foetus?

1 The Claim That the Foetus is a Human Being

If the claim that the foetus is a human being is simply the claim that it is a member of our species rather than of any other, there is a way in which this is obviously true. If we concede that the foetus is already a member of a species, then that species must surely be ours. But this is question-begging, because the disputed issue is whether the foetus has reached the developmental stage that qualifies it to be counted as a member of any species at all.

There are boundary problems that arise for this sort of approach. It is not clear that there is any uncontroversial point at which a potential human being becomes an actual one. Some have argued for conception because all the genetic ingredients are present for the first time. Others have argued for some later boundary, say when certain key anatomical components of the developed human being have emerged. But it is unclear how this kind of dispute is to be settled.

But the main difficulty is that, even if we allow that the foetus is a human being, it is hard to see how, without appealing to its potential rather than to its actual properties, we can use this to justify its protected status. Supporters of the rights of animals are quick with the accusation of 'speciesism'. This view, according to which mere membership of our species, independent of any empirical properties carried with this membership, gives a privileged claim over members of other species, was rejected in Chapter 3. If we are to defend the foetus as having a life with a stronger claim on us than animal life, we must be able to point to morally relevant properties which it has but which animals lack. It is hard to see how this could be done except in terms of its potential, which takes us away to a different argument altogether. I conclude that the claim that the foetus is already a human being will not get us far.

What about the alternative claims that the foetus is a person or a potential person? Let us start by looking at the weaker claim, that it is a potential person, and from there move on to the stronger claim that it is already a person.

2 The Foetus as a Potential Person

It is obviously true that the normal foetus is at least a potential person: it is an entity which will, barring abnormal circumstances or intervention, develop into something incontestably a person. The only question is what moral claim upon us this gives it.

The problem with using the foetus's potential for developing into a person as an anti-abortion argument is that this suggests that the person it will become is what is really valued. It is hard to see how this potential argument can come to any more than saying that abortion is wrong because a person who would have existed in the future will not exist if an abortion is performed. I would not be here if my mother, when pregnant with me, had opted for abortion. But I equally would not be here if my parents had used an effective contraceptive. It is hard to see how the potential argument can succeed against abortion without also succeeding against contraception. And even those who are against both normally want to say that abortion is morally worse than contraception.

It may be argued that the foetus is a potential person who has already got started, and that this makes abortion worse than contraception. The problem with this reply is that, if we are interested in not losing the person who will emerge at the end of the process, it is not clear what reason there can be for thinking that terminating the process is worse at one stage or another. If it is cake you are interested in, it is equally a pity if the ingredients were thrown away before being mixed or afterwards. As soon as the stage of development is allowed to make a difference (apart from side-effects) the argument has moved from potentiality to actuality: from the properties of the person the foetus may become to the properties the foetus now has. And this takes us to the debate over whether the foetus is already a person.

3 When Does One Become a Person?

(a) CONCEPTION

The argument in favour of conception as the moment at which one starts being a person is that for the first time the genetic ingredients of the future adult are together in one unit. Before conception there is no single hunk of matter about whose status we can dispute. And since development after conception follows a fairly smooth curve, later boundaries are said to have an arbitrariness that conception does not.

It is sometimes objected that conception cannot be this boundary because monozygotic twins can split at any time during the first two weeks after conception. Much of this twinning seems not to be genetically determined. So, for about two weeks after conception, we cannot be sure how many people will result. But this objection is not fatal to the case for conception as the boundary. All the supporters of that view need do is word their claim carefully: they must say that conception is the point at which at least one person emerges.

Although the boundary between contraception and abortion is in principle a sharp one, in practice some acts straddle it. Contraceptive pills not only prevent fertilization, but also change the womb lining to make it reject fertilized eggs. The I.U.D. (inter-uterine device, or 'coil') is also said to act by scraping the womb lining or by bringing on a period. These 'contraceptives' may equally be thought of as very early abortion techniques.

This blurring of the boundary between contraception and abortion need not cause those who think that one is a person from conception to change their minds. They will count the use of the pill and the I.U.D. as murder, and, if they support contraception in general, will oppose these means. They will also oppose the use of the 'morning-after' pill when it is developed.

The argument against conception as the boundary at which

123

one becomes a person is that a fertilized egg is so different from anything we normally recognize as a person. It is said that such an egg is no more a person than an acorn is an oak tree, a caterpillar is a butterfly or a bowl of unbaked ingredients is a cake. I share the feeling that a fertilized egg is not a person. But there is difficulty in demonstrating this to a determined opponent. 'A cake is still a cake, even if it is an unbaked one.' This claim seems fatuous, but the person who makes it cannot be refuted empirically and need not be making any logical mistake. The contention that a fertilized egg is a person involves stretching the word 'person' beyond its usual boundaries: it is a morally motivated piece of conceptual revision. Those who propose it do so because of a prior belief about how the egg ought to be treated. And this is a moral view which cannot be dismissed on grounds of linguistic deviance.

(b) VIABILITY

A traditional boundary was the 'quickening', when the mother first felt the foetus move. We now know that this is of no significance for the development of the foetus itself. Those who want a boundary somewhere during the period of pregnancy now more often support viability: the point where a baby could survive independently.

The argument for viability is obvious: at this point we have for the first time a potentially independent creature.

One argument against making viability the point at which one becomes a person is that such a decision seems to make potential physical independence a necessary condition of being a person. But suppose some very old person could be kept alive only at the cost of some physical dependence on another person's body. With improved medical technology, we might be able to plug into other people for periods of the day to make use of organs we lacked. If an old woman were kept alive only by being dependent on her husband in this way, she would not be 'viable'. Yet we would surely continue to count her as a person. Supporters of the theory that viability is the boundary at one end of life have to explain why it is not equally relevant at the other end.

Another argument against viability is that it is a shifting boundary. In English law there is a clear date: viability starts at twenty-eight weeks. But this sharpness is quite arbitrary. Some babies born later are not viable and some born earlier do survive. Because of medical developments, the zone of probable survival is moving further back in pregnancy. There seems something absurd about a moving boundary, so that we might say 'last year this foetus would not have been a person at this stage, but since they re-equipped the intensive care unit, it is one'. This just does not seem to be the morally significant boundary people are looking for.

Finally, it seems possible that one day we will be able to fertilize eggs and produce children entirely outside the womb. If this happens, the view that the boundary at which one becomes a person is viability will collapse into the view that the boundary is at conception.

(c) BIRTH

The attractions of birth as a sharp boundary are obvious. Also it is at birth that the baby is accepted into the human community and we start to detect the first signs of its distinct personality.

But it is against drawing the boundary here that the anti-abortionists' talk of 'the unborn child' has some force. Can we be sure that, in making birth the boundary, we are not giving more weight to our own responses than to any significant change in the foetus-baby? This point is sometimes made, as in Roger Wertheimer's admirable article 'Understanding the Abortion Argument',[1] by wondering how we would react if mothers had transparent wombs, so that foetuses were visible, or if we were even able to remove a foetus and hold it. The point is reinforced by a writer for *Life* magazine: 'Many readers of *Life*

1. Roger Wertheimer: 'Understanding the Abortion Argument', *Philosophy and Public Affairs*, 1971.

who saw Lennart Nilsson's marvellous photographs of foetuses in their sacs, especially in the later stages of development, wrote in to say that they could never again think of their *babies* as disposable *things*'.

The similarity between later foetuses and premature babies is a difficulty for the view that there is a sharp line at birth. (Some unease should be felt on reading the appendix on the disposal of foetuses after abortion in the *Report of the Committee on the Working of the Abortion Act*, where one Regional Hospital Board is reported as saying that if there is any sign of life the foetus is treated as a premature baby.)

If we could see the foetus from outside, would we still be so sure about the immense difference between the foetus-baby just before and just after birth? If we would not, this suggests that enthusiasm for this boundary is more the result of the foetus being out of sight than of any real 'onset of personality' at birth. This seems like the view that starvation and death matter less in a far-away country, since we are less aware of it than if it were happening here.

4 The Inadequacy of Sharp Boundaries

When we turn to consider side-effects, 'thin end of the wedge' arguments will be found to have some force in favour of a sharp legal boundary, after which killing is not permitted. But we are not at present considering either side-effects or what the law should be. We are asking the moral question 'what sorts of killing are directly wrong?', in the context of abortion. Some common attempts to answer this question by drawing sharp boundaries have been mentioned.

These sharp boundaries are all stipulations and cannot be 'refuted'. But I have tried to make clear the extent to which they are arbitrary. Any attempt to draw a sharp line marking the onset of state of being a person is bound to be arbitrary, for two related reasons. One is that 'person' is a loose concept; the other is that the transition from fertilized egg to adult, like many biological developments, can better be represented by a fairly steady upward curve than by a series of obviously discrete stages with abrupt transitions. To ask 'When does one start to be a person?' is like asking 'when does middle age begin?' Conventional lines for social or legal purposes could always be drawn, but we would be mistaken if we took the shadows cast by these lines for boundaries in biological reality.

(Even Michael Tooley, whose discussion of abortion seems to me the most unconventional and at the same time the most convincingly argued in the literature, presents his moral boundary in terms of when one becomes a person.[2] His thinking is in the framework of the 'right to life'. He argues persuasively that bearers of rights must have at least the capacity to desire what they have a right to, and that, in the case of the right to life, this capacity presupposes something the foetus does not have: the idea of itself as a continuing subject of experiences. But it seems unhelpful to present this thesis as an answer to the question 'when is a member of the species homo sapiens a person?' For there is some arbitrariness in stipulating that 'person' is a purely moral term, roughly equivalent to 'bearer of rights'.)

The prospect for drawing a satisfactory line round 'being a person' is poor. There is no single feature whose emergence is in question. We think of people as being conscious, having the ability to form relationships with others, being capable of some degree of thought, having some kinds of emotional responses, having some sense of their own identity. But any attempt to pick out one of these features as the person's essential ingredient is implausible. And, if a whole cluster of different factors is involved, there is no special reason to think that they all emerge over the same period or at the same rate.

It seems more defensible to abandon the view that there is an abrupt transition to the status of a person and to replace it by the view that being a person is a matter of degree. A one-year-old is much more of a person than a new-born baby or a foetus just before birth, but each of these is more of a person than the

2. Michael Tooley: 'Abortion and Infanticide', *Philosophy and Public Affairs*, 1972.

embryo. This approach obviously does not eliminate either arbitrariness or disagreement. There is room for disagreement about where the process of increasing personalization starts, where it is completed and about the rate of ascent. It is important to see that these are not factual disagreements. They could survive all parties gaining much more detailed knowledge of the facts of foetal development. They are disagreements over which aspects of personality are important and over the relative importance of different degrees of development. I do not think these disagreements would be fruitful to pursue.

Although the 'ascending-slope' view of becoming a person does not eliminate all dispute, it does avoid the implausibility of the proposed sharp boundaries and also gives some rough guidance to those who hold a principle making it intrinsically wrong to kill any human person. Combining such a principle with the 'slope' view generated the conclusion that there is not much directly wrong with an early abortion, but abortions become increasingly wrong later on, and killing a month-old baby more wrong still. This kind of 'sanctity of human life' principle was discussed earlier in the book, where it was argued to be inadequate.

Chapter 10   Abortion: Women's Rights Arguments

Would the physician be expected to terminate on the mere word of a patient that she had been raped? This would be to invite much deception, and to jeopardize all control.

Church Assembly Board for Social Responsibility: *Abortion, An Ethical Discussion*, 1965

I see it as so unarguably a basic human right for a woman to decide whether she will have an abortion or not that I am convinced the right will eventually be legally recognized and our children's children will look back on the present situation with horror – you mean in those days a *stranger* could decide whether you had the baby or not?

Jill Tweedie in the *Guardian*, 1972

Those who oppose abortion tend to concentrate on the status of the foetus. Those who think that some or all abortions are morally legitimate tend to concentrate on the position of the mother. What I shall call 'Women's Rights arguments' are those claiming that the question of abortion is essentially one of a woman's right to self-defence or of her right to control her own body. This view is put clearly in the evidence of the Women's Abortion and Contraception Campaign to the Committee on the Working of the Abortion Act: 'Women must have control over their own lives. For this we must have control over our own bodies ... The abortion issue is the cornerstone in the liberation of women. The debate on whether or not a woman may have control over her own body is a debate on the place and role of women in society.'

The difficulty with this view as it stands is that it is question-begging. For it must rest on one of two assumptions: either that the foetus is not a person at all, or that the woman's rights over her body are more important than the life of the person or part-person in her womb. Neither of these assumptions can be accepted without argument. It seems likely that most supporters of this approach just assume that the foetus is neither wholly nor partly a person, but is merely something growing in the mother's body. In assuming this without argument, supporters of the Women's Rights view fail to meet the key objection of their opponents.

Some more interesting versions of the Women's Rights approach grant that the foetus may be wholly or partly a person. There is the argument that, where the mother's life is threatened, she has a right to seek an abortion in self-defence. There is the argument that the woman's body is her own property. There is also what we may call the 'priority argument': that the woman's right to control her own life ought to have priority over the interests of the foetus. All these arguments need examination.

1 The Appeal to Self-Defence

Judith Jarvis Thomson has argued that, in cases where a pregnancy threatens the mother's life, she has a right to self-defence even at the cost of the life of the foetus and that, even when her life is not threatened, she is not morally obliged to continue with the pregnancy.[1]

In the case where the mother's life is in danger, Professor Thomson invokes the right of self-defence. She does not argue that one has a right to do *anything* necessary in defence of one's life (she would rule out torturing someone to death, even if this were the only way to save one's own life), but she argues that to save my life I may, if necessary, kill someone else, even if they are 'innocent'. She distinguishes between the question of when a

1. Judith Jarvis Thomson: 'A Defense of Abortion', *Philosophy and Public Affairs*, 1971.

third party has a right to intervene and the question of what I may do in my own defence. Even if a third party thought it wrong to choose between two innocent lives, I am allowed to save my own life at the cost of someone else's.

The appeal to the right of self-defence does have force here, provided that one is prepared to allow that this right extends to the killing of innocent people. There are those who say that killing innocent people can never be justified, even if the plea of self-defence is some kind of excuse or mitigation. There are also those who allow that it may sometimes be right to kill the innocent, but who doubt the rightness of giving automatic priority to saving one's own life, even if again self-defence is a powerful mitigating factor or excuse. But if, in other contexts, self-defence is allowed to justify killing an innocent person, then this can be used to justify abortion to save the mother's life.

2 The Ownership Argument

Professor Thomson argues that a third party (perhaps a doctor) may legitimately be swayed in favour of saving the mother rather than the foetus by the consideration that the mother owns the body which shelters the foetus. This seems dubious. I can sympathize with someone who refuses to choose between two people's lives, or who chooses between them on the grounds of the likely quality of their future lives (the foetus may be grossly abnormal), or who chooses between them on the grounds of other people's welfare (the mother may have a husband and other children). But it seems curious to be swayed by legalistic considerations of ownership.

Apart from the oddity of regarding a woman's body as a piece of her property, it seems morally objectionable to attach such weight to property rights in a context where people's lives are at stake. Mary Anne Warren has said that 'mere ownership does not give me the right to kill innocent people whom I find on my property ... It is equally unclear that I have any moral right to expel an innocent person from my property when I know that doing so will result in his death.'[2] And this can plausibly be extended even to cases where not to expel him will lead to my death. If we are in the sea after a shipwreck, some with lifebelts and some without, it is not clear that I have the backing of morality if I say, 'Get out of that lifebelt and give it to me: look, it has my name on it.'

3 The Priority Argument

We have been considering the small minority of abortion cases where the mother's life itself is threatened. It may seem that this is a specially favourable case to take if one wants to justify abortion while accepting that the foetus may be a person. But Professor Thomson has an ingenious argument designed to show that abortion need not be wrong even where the mother's life is not in danger. This argument is again connected with a woman's rights over her own body, but is also connected with a distinction between help that a decent person will give and help that someone has a right to demand.

Professor Thomson discusses a case where one person has a kidney ailment, such that he can survive only if he is plugged in to the kidneys of someone else. Suppose he needs to be attached to someone with blood of a type so rare that only I am known to have it. And suppose that I wake up one morning to find that, without my knowledge, he has been attached to my kidneys. If I unplug him, he will die. If I do not, I will have to spend a lifetime in bed with him.

The argument in this case goes as follows: Clearly I am not morally obliged to remain plugged to this person, despite the fact that to unplug him is to kill him. This is because he does not have a right to the use of my body and I have no corresponding obligation to place my body at his disposal. There is no absolute prohibition on killing people, but only on killing them unjustly. This is interpreted as forbidding us to deprive

2. Mary Anne Warren: 'On the Moral and Legal Status of Abortion', *The Monist*, 1973.

people of anything both necessary for their continued existence and *to which they have a right.* This doctrine is then applied to abortion. The question is asked: does the foetus have a right to the use of the mother's body?

In answering this question, it is suggested that the foetus has such a right only if the mother has a special responsibility towards it, in a way that I have not towards the man with kidney trouble. Professor Thomson says, 'Surely we do not have any such "special responsibility" for a person unless we have assumed it, explicitly or implicitly.' She suggests that when parents have a child whose existence they have in no way tried to prevent, and whom they have not tried to have adopted, they have assumed responsibility and have an obligation not to withdraw support. But when someone has taken all reasonable contraceptive precautions, they cannot be regarded as having assumed responsibility for an unwelcome foetus. In these circumstances the foetus does not have a right to the use of the mother's body.

Professor Thomson's view is that, where someone has no rights against one, to give them help is an act of charity rather than the performance of a moral duty. Where great benefit can be given with little trouble, the act of charity may be one that any minimally decent person would perform. As the disadvantages of an act of charity rise, it becomes less reasonable to expect someone to perform it, and eventually the point is reached where only someone of exceptional moral heroism would do so. Not aborting an unwanted foetus is, on this view, an act of charity which can involve a fairly large sacrifice. The disadvantages of being pregnant for nine months may not weigh very heavily against the loss of a person's life, but the disadvantages of either having to give away the child you bear or of having to bring up a child you do not want are clearly very great.

It is claimed as a merit of this approach that it allows for different moral attitudes to different abortions.

It allows for and supports our sense that, for example, a sick and desperately frightened fourteen-year-old schoolgirl, pregnant owing to rape, may *of course* choose abortion, and that any law which rules this out is an insane law. And it also allows for and supports our sense that in other cases resort to abortion is even positively indecent. It would be indecent in the woman to request an abortion, and indecent in a doctor to perform it, if she is in her seventh month, and wants the abortion just to avoid the nuisance of postponing a trip abroad.

This original argument is a subtle attempt to justify some abortions without either invoking the need to save the mother's life or denying that the foetus may be a person. It is, however, open to objection. Its central assumption is that I have moral duties only towards people for whom I have voluntarily assumed a special responsibility. But is this really plausible? Can we maintain this sharp distinction between people to whom I have moral duties and people to whom I may or may not be charitable?

There is a conventional view that someone has positive duties (of assistance, support, life-saving, etc.) only towards people for whom he has in some way voluntarily assumed a special responsibility, but that there are some negative duties (such as to refrain from killing or injuring) towards everyone. It has already been argued that this view depends on the acts and omissions doctrine and that we ought to reject both.

There is the other possibility, that Professor Thomson's view is not this conventional one, but that she holds the more radical view that even negative duties, such as refraining from killing, hold only for those towards whom we have voluntarily accepted a special responsibility. But this also ought to be rejected. It commits us to holding that, where torturing or killing someone would be to my advantage, I will refrain from doing so if I am a decent, charitable person, but, if he is a complete stranger to whom I have assumed no special obligations, there is no *moral* objection to my going ahead. (It scarcely needs saying that this interpretation of Professor Thomson's views is unlikely to be the correct one.)

4 Abortion and Extraction

The Women's Rights arguments, even if accepted, justify abortion only because the alternative of extraction followed by rearing is at present not technically possible. That is, the Women's Rights arguments at most support the claim that a woman is not obliged to carry and give birth to a child she does not want. If it were possible safely to extract the foetus from the womb and to rear it artificially, this would be compatible with respecting the claim about a woman's rights over her own body. To have a right not to carry and bear a child, as Professor Thomson recognizes, is not to have a right to demand its death as well as its removal.

There are various factors relevant to the desirability or otherwise of rearing children outside the womb ('test-tube babies'). We may soon have to make moral decisions about completely artificial reproduction, with no womb involved at any stage, about the rearing of fertilized eggs removed from natural wombs. One relevant consideration is obviously the likely quality of life of a child produced in this way. It will not have a natural mother and so will either be adopted or reared in an institution. Adoptions vary, and so do institutions. If theories about the importance of early parental bonds are correct, it is arguable that children brought up in institutions have a less good chance of a worth-while life than other children. Another possible disadvantage is that the substitute womb may lack some feature of the natural womb that is important for development. Then there are considerations affecting people other than the child. There is the question of whether we want a larger or a smaller population. There is the fact that, if there is a shortage of children for adoption, artificially reared children may bring great happiness to childless couples. On the other hand, if the child was originally extracted from the womb of its natural mother, its continued existence may be a source of great distress to her.

But those who both hold a principle of the sanctity of human life, and hold that the fertilized egg, embryo or foetus is already a human being, are committed to artificial rearing whenever possible, once extraction has taken place. For such people, the considerations mentioned may be taken into account in deciding whether or not to fertilize eggs in order to rear them artificially, but, once fertilization has taken place, the issue is settled by invoking the sanctity of life. And, to anyone who holds that kind of view, the Women's Rights arguments can at most justify extraction rather than abortion.

Earlier in this book principles concerning the sanctity of life were rejected in favour of an approach based on respecting people's autonomy and on the nature of their lives. It is time to see the implications of this for abortion.

Chapter 11 Abortion Reconsidered

There is a common assumption that, in terms of direct wrong (that is, irrespective of side-effects on other people), killing a new-born baby is worse than abortion, which in turn is worse than the use of contraception. This sliding scale is accepted by many people with very different views about how wrong any one of these acts is. It is accepted by many who think contraception wrong, and by many who think contraception entirely legitimate. It is accepted by many opponents and supporters of legalized abortion on demand.

I shall argue that we should reject this sliding scale when considering whether these acts are *directly* wrong, except in so far as different knowledge is avoidable at different stages. But something like this sliding scale will re-appear when side-effects are taken into account.

So far two general approaches to abortion have been discussed. One of them involves arguing for (or assuming) some boundary marking the point at which one becomes a person. This rests on some prior assumption that killing persons is intrinsically wrong: a principle of the sanctity of human life or of the rights of persons. The other approach, the 'priority' version of the Women's Rights argument, failed to establish the woman's right to an abortion while a sanctity of life principle was retained. But suppose we think that sanctity of life principles should be abandoned, and replaced by a set of principles concerning people's autonomy and the quality of their lives?

1 Abandoning the Sanctity of Life

It has been argued earlier that there is nothing intrinsically good in a person merely being alive and that the idea of a 'right to life' should be rejected. The alternative view proposed is that the objections to killing (apart from side-effects and any pain involved) are two: it is wrong to reduce the amount of worthwhile life, and it is wrong to override someone's autonomy when he wants to go on living.

How does this alternative view apply to abortion? The reasons given for the direct wrongness of killing put abortion virtually on a level both with killing a new-born child and with deliberate failure to conceive a child. This is quite out of line with the conventional sliding scale of direct wrong.

Consider the objection to killing that it is wrong to reduce the amount of worth-while life. Unless one is a supporter of the acts and omissions doctrine, it is clear that deliberate failure to conceive someone who would have a worth-while life is in this respect on a par with killing a foetus who would have a worth-while life. In either case the result is one less such person than there might have been. And the same goes for killing a new-born baby. The only relevant differences here can be ones of knowledge of how the potential person will turn out. We normally know more about this potential after birth than we do before birth, and we normally know very little about it before conception. When the greater knowledge we have at the later stages supports the view that the person will be normal, this tends to make infanticide worse than abortion, and abortion worse than non-conception. But where what was an apparently normal foetus turns out to be an abnormal baby, infanticide becomes less (directly) wrong than abortion would have been. And, where a woman has German measles early in her pregnancy, or where amniocentesis detects genetic abnormalities in the foetus, abortion becomes less (directly) wrong than deliberate non-conception.

The claim that killing is directly wrong because it overrides someone's autonomy does not apply to non-conception, abortion or to the killing of a new-born baby. However much one may regard a new-born baby as a person, it would be absurd to suppose that it has any desire not to die, or even the concepts of being alive or dead on which such a desire depends. There are of course great difficulties in saying at what stage such concepts and desires do start to appear, or even what are the criteria by which we decide whether or not they have appeared. But, although the acquisition of a concept may sometimes be a flickering, gradual affair, and although the phase at which the concepts of life and death develop may be disputed, it cannot plausibly be said that very young babies have a desire to go on living rather than to die. If we accept that they do not have this desire, the second main argument for the direct wrongness of killing provides no reason against either infanticide or abortion. So far as this factor goes, they are both on a par with not conceiving a child.

The third and least of the direct objections to killing is the pain involved. Non-conception and, presumably, very early abortions do not involve painful death. In so far as later abortions and early infanticide do involve any pain, they are to that extent worse. For simplicity, let us assume that painless abortion and infanticide are possible, bearing in mind that in any actual case where pain *is* involved we must take this into account.

So, on the approach argued for earlier in this book, non-conception, abortion and the killing of a baby are all on the same level of direct wrong in cases where there is the same expectation of a normal child. Since unfertilized eggs, foetuses and new-born babies are all without even the capacity for any desire for life, they all fall outside the scope of the principle of autonomy. The only argument for the direct wrongness of failure to conceive, or of these killings, is the 'impersonal' one concerned with not reducing the amount of worth-while life. But, since this is an impersonal principle, there is in its terms nothing wrong with eliminating one potential worth-while life, provided that another is substituted. (Arguments against abortion that appeal only to the *potential* of the foetus cannot discriminate between abortion and the use of contraceptives.)

In other words, foetuses and babies are, in terms of these principles, replaceable. If a woman knows that to conceive now would result in a handicapped child, while to conceive in three months would probably result in a normal child, many of us would support her decision to wait. There is nothing special about fertilizing *this* egg, but it is important that the outcome should be a person with a worth-while life. On the principles I have argued for, we ought (until we consider side-effects) to take the same view about the foetus and the baby. If the mother will have other children instead, it is not directly wrong to prevent *this* foetus or *this* baby surviving. If this foetus or baby has a poor chance of having a worth-while life, it will be directly wrong *not* to replace it by a baby with a better chance. But in many cases these direct considerations will be outweighed by the harmful side-effects of such an act.

2 How Wrong is Deliberate Non-Conception?

The impersonal principle that we ought to maximize the amount of worth-while life commits us to the view that, other things being equal, we ought to conceive as many children as possible who have a good chance of having worth-while lives. But other things are not equal.

There are the familiar problems of over-population. It seems likely than an increase in the population often makes the lives of those already living less worth-while than they would otherwise be. There may be less food to go round, and greater pressure may be placed on the world's resources of energy and raw materials. People may suffer from a sense of overcrowding. All these factors have to be set against the worth-while lives of the additional members of the population. I do not know how one should decide what the optimum population would be, either for the world or for a particular country. There are difficult questions about the weight to give to extra people with worth-while lives as against any reduction in the general quality of life that may result from a larger population. There are also complex factual questions about the possibility of producing more food, of finding new sources of energy and of dealing with shortages of raw materials. But, however hard it is to decide on an ideal population size, it is reasonable to suggest that sometimes a population can be too large, and that this will then count as a reason against conceiving even someone whose life will probably be well worth living.

There are also special problems of unwanted children and their parents. People will not mind the thought that they ought to have a child where this is what they want anyway. But if they do not want a child, what is the situation then?

Sometimes an unplanned and originally unwanted baby becomes a loved and wanted child. Then no special problems exist. But in other cases the parents continue to feel that it would have been better if the child had not been born. These are the hard-core cases of unwanted children. Such situations are especially likely to arise where the family is already large and the mother already overworked and exhausted, or where the marriage is broken, or where there is poverty, overcrowding or bad health (mental or physical). An unwanted child is likely to place a great extra strain on both parents, and especially on the mother. Any other children in the family are also likely to suffer from this additional member, either through shortage of money or space or through the psychological pressures on their parents.

An unwanted child is also less likely to have a thoroughly worth-while life than a wanted child. (A great deal of my argument here rests on this factual assertion, which I do not support with any evidence.) It is also likely that the most anti-social adults are often those who have not been loved enough as children.

For all these reasons, affecting the child, the family and society at large, it is very undesirable that children who are (and will remain) unwanted should be conceived. Other things being equal, there should be as many people with worth-while lives as possible. But where the happiness of a potential unwanted child is so problematic and the diminution of the happiness of others so relatively unproblematic, it seems reasonable to suggest that *there should be as few unwanted children as possible.* The only exception to this would be in the extreme case where a population was so dangerously small that desperate measures were necessary to avoid extinction. This is a case which for practical purposes we can at present ignore. We can take it that, when we consider all relevant factors, including side-effects, it is morally justifiable deliberately to prevent conception of a child one does not want.

3 Side-Effects of Abortion

If the side-effects of abortion were the same as those of deliberate failure to conceive a child, the question of its morality would be answered already. There should be as few unwanted children as possible, so non-conception and abortion would be equally justifiable. But there are large and relevant differences.

There are the effects of abortion on the mother. An abortion, especially a late one, can cause emotional distress. Physical and chemical changes during pregnancy, making the mother psychologically adjusted to accept a baby, can lead to great grief after a late abortion. There is also the danger to the mother's fertility and even life. The risk to a mother's life with an early abortion is negligible, but a late abortion is a major operation. Even if these risks are not considered sufficient to cause anxiety, the emotional upheaval often involved is in itself a powerful objection to treating abortion as merely an alternative method of birth control.

There are also the effects, particularly of a late abortion, on the surgeons who perform it and the nurses involved. Some surgeons and nurses object to abortion on principle, but even those who do not are often revolted or distressed by the actual performance of it. And some surgeons understandably feel that the saving of human life is a more satisfying daily activity than

142

its destruction. This provides another reason for saying that late abortion at least is not morally equivalent to birth control.

Then there are the more oblique effects of abortion on society at large. There is the possibility, hard to assess, that increasing numbers of abortions may gradually undermine the general reluctance to kill, with disastrous social consequences. There is the danger, though surely a remote one, that maternal affection for children might be damaged by an easy acceptance of abortion. And, finally, abortions use up the time and equipment of doctors and hospitals: scarce resources that could be used to help others.

All these actual or possible side-effects of abortion are sufficient to show that it would be wrong to regard abortion as an equally acceptable alternative to contraception. But abortion at an early stage is very different from late abortion. Early abortion involves little danger to the mother and probably much less distress than late abortion. The early operation, using the suction method, need not be particularly upsetting to surgeons and need not be such a burden on medical resources. And, since many fewer people regard the very early embryo as a person, there is less threat to common attitudes towards killing or towards children.

Some of the harmful side-effects of abortion will be eliminated when an 'abortion pill' is developed. Once such a pill is safe, without its own harmful effects, a woman will be able to perform her own abortion without anyone else even knowing she has been pregnant.

And some of the distress caused to doctors and nurses could even now be reduced by changing moral and social attitudes. If abortion is widely thought of as a minor kind of murder, this adds to the unpleasantness of it. But we could regard doctors and nurses who perform or help with abortions as especially heroic, doing something intrinsically distasteful which yet prevents much unhappiness. If this attitude became more widespread, there might be some lessening of the reluctance to perform abortions.

143

4 The Morality of Freely Available Abortion

I have argued that, in terms of direct wrong, abortion is on a level with deliberate failure to conceive a child. And I have argued that, even given a commitment to maximizing the number of worth-while lives in the world, there should be as few unwanted children as possible. For this reason, it is legitimate to prevent the conception of a child you believe you will not want.

Abortion differs morally from deliberate non-conception only in its side-effects. Because it has worse side-effects, it would be wrong to adopt it in preference to contraception. And, since the side-effects are worse when the abortion is later, it would be wrong for either a mother or a doctor, deliberately and without a strong reason, to postpone an abortion until late.

But these harmful side-effects of abortion do not seem to me to outweigh the objections to bringing unwanted children into the world. For this reason, I think it is always right for a qualified person capable of performing an abortion to do so when requested by the mother. Those who are more optimistic about the happiness of unwanted children and of their families may disagree. But, taking this view, I regard a law which forbids even some cases of abortion as being objectionable on moral grounds. This does not mean (the misleading suggestion in the popular phrase 'abortion on demand') that doctors with conscientious objections should have to perform abortions.

One argument against these conclusions, which deserves to be taken seriously, is that put by a couple who wrote a letter to the *New Statesman* in 1972:

We have two adopted children, both attractive, intelligent and likeable (most of the time). If abortion on demand had been easily available the chances are that the natural mothers would have taken advantage of the facilities and we would never have known our children. At a time when adoption societies are closing through lack of babies to place with clamouring prospective adopters, it must be disheartening for childless couples who have the love and the means to provide a good life for the 'unwanted' child to read of foetuses being slaughtered and thrown out with the slops from hundreds of operating theatres.

The possibility of providing children for those who want them but cannot have them naturally or by A.I.D. is not something simply to dismiss. The feelings of deprivation must often be very great. But I doubt whether their elimination justifies forcing women to bear children they do not themselves want and then to give them away. This seems likely to cause more misery than it prevents.

It is sometimes said that few of those who support freely available abortion can really think abortion morally acceptable in all possible cases. Do not even the most liberal feel some disapproval of the mother who has a late abortion because her pregnancy will prevent a holiday abroad? The suggestion is that most of us do not regard the foetus as merely replaceable.

But this suggestion need not be accepted. For it is quite possible to be shocked by the mother's act while still considering the foetus replaceable. The side-effects of a late abortion have already been mentioned, and they alone justify criticism. But the central ground for disapproval is tied up with the relationship between a mother and her child. We feel that people who are unenthusiastic about having children are less likely to be good mothers, and a woman who cares more about a holiday abroad than about killing her potential child should not have got pregnant or should have had an abortion at once. For all these reasons we can criticize the mother's choice without giving up the view that all unwanted foetuses should be aborted.

5 When It Is Wrong Not to Have an Abortion

One reason for rejecting the claim that the question of abortion is merely a matter of the woman's rights over her own body is that on a utilitarian view it is sometimes wrong to refuse to have

145

an abortion. If tests have established that the foetus is abnormal in a way that will drastically impair the quality of its life, it will normally be wrong of the mother to reject abortion.

Most of us would accept that it would be wrong deliberately to conceive a handicapped child rather than a normal one, if the choice were available. On the moral system defended here, this can be extended to abortion. If aborting the abnormal foetus can be followed by having another, normal one, it will be wrong not to do this. The side-effects of abortion will not in general be bad enough to outweigh the loss involved in bringing into the world someone whose life is much less worth-while than that of a normal person who could be conceived instead.

Some qualifications must at once be made here. There will be cases where the side-effects of abortion will be exceptionally bad, pershaps where the mother has had previous abortions and is not in a state to take another. And foetuses can be abnormal to various degrees. To be born with a finger missing may not make much difference to the quality of one's life. On the other hand, some abnormalities are so gross as to make life not worth living at all. There will obviously be different views of how serious an abnormality must be in order to justify abortions causing different degrees of distress. I have no general formula to offer. But it is worth saying that on the whole people recover from abortions after a while, but a handicap normally lasts a lifetime.

Another reservation should be mentioned. In arguing that a woman sometimes has a moral duty to have an abortion, I am not arguing that she should be compelled to perform this duty. Many women will want an abortion if they know the foetus is severely abnormal. Those who do not will sometimes be open to moral persuasion. Where they are not, it seems best to leave them alone. The horrors of some system of compelling women to accept abortion, against their will and perhaps against their moral principles, seem to outweigh the likely advantages of such a policy.

The claim that sometimes one ought to have an abortion has been argued so far in terms of the desirability of aborting an abnormal foetus in order to replace it by a normal one. But there are cases where the possibility of replacement may not exist. Perhaps any child of a particular mother will be abnormal to the same degree. Or perhaps she is at the very end of the child-bearing age, or she no longer has a husband.

In cases of this sort, unusually strong reasons are necessary for it to be wrong not to abort. Where the foetus is so abnormal that it cannot have a life worth living it still ought to be aborted. But milder handicaps may make a life less worth-while without destroying its worth altogether. A blind person has a less favourable start in life than a normal person, but it would be absurd to say that his life is likely not to be worth living. And the same goes for many other severe handicaps, especially when the handicapped person has the support of other people.

6 Handicap and Worth-While Life

I have admitted that I can offer no general formula stating what a worth-while life is or indicating the point at which a life is not worth living. Obviously people disagree a lot here. There is also a widespread and natural reluctance to consider these questions too closely in the context of handicap and disability. We do not want to hurt handicapped people or those close to them by the suggestion that it would have been better if they had not been born. For the same reason, we are even reluctant to say that people with disabilities have on the whole less worth-while lives than normal people. There is also the belief in treating all people as our equals, which commits us to a lack of condescension towards the physically or mentally weak.

But our view of conception and abortion in certain cases should be bound up with our view of the extent to which the potential person will have a worth-while life. If we are sure that his life will not be worth living, we ought not to conceive him, or, failing that, an abortion should be obtained. It is sometimes morally wrong to evade the question of whether someone's life is likely to be worth living.

And, when we think of handicaps such that life is still very clearly worth living, there is some self-deception in not admitting that a handicapped person is likely to have a less worthwhile life than a normal person. Of course this is only a matter of probability: no doubt many individual handicapped people have more satisfying lives than many individual normal people. And it is also true that the quality of such a person's life depends a lot on the attitudes and responses of those close to them and of the wider society. But, despite all this, it remains true that severely handicapped persons stand a less good chance than a normal person in the same situation of an equally worthwhile life. The fact that we recognize this is shown by the choices we would make, if we were able, when conceiving: virtually everyone would think it wrong deliberately to conceive a handicapped child rather than a normal one.

And we can say that a severely handicapped person is likely to have a less good life than a normal person, while treating him as our equal. If someone with a handicap is conceived instead of a normal person, things turn out less well than they might have done. It would have been better if the normal person had been conceived. But things of this sort can be said about almost any of us. If my own conception was an alternative to the conception of someone just like me except more intelligent, or more athletic or more musical, it would have been better if that person had been conceived. Most of us are ourselves pleased to have been conceived and glad that some other person was not conceived instead. But being glad to have been conceived is quite compatible with the recognition that, from an impartial point of view, it would have been even better if some more gifted or happier person had been conceived instead.

It is true that a severely handicapped person, unlike a normal one, is particularly badly off, with a potential below average. But he is not helped by the pretence that this is not so. Nor does the admission that it is so prevent us from giving his interests equal weight with our own, or make the relationship between us one of inequality. And, if it is better that a normal person should be born rather than a handicapped person, our recognition of this will be important for our beliefs about abortion.

7 A Consequence of Some 'Sanctity of Life' Views

Any belief that a foetus is not in moral terms replaceable, and hence that abortion is directly wrong in a way that contraception is not, is in danger of generating socially disastrous consequences. The alternative view outlined here positively encourages abortion of all seriously abnormal foetuses. The view that the foetus has a right to life discourages such abortions, with the result that the proportion of people who are genetically defective is higher than it might be. And, unless we believe in the acts and omissions doctrine, the argument against killing an abnormal foetus also enjoins us wherever possible to save a foetus from spontaneous abortion. Presumably medical technology will one day enable us to save many embryos and foetuses at present spontaneously aborted. A high proportion of these are likely to be grossly abnormal. Acceptance of views about the sanctity of the life of the foetus (unless combined with the acts and omissions doctrine) would in such circumstances commit us to a policy of drastically increasing the proportion of the population who are seriously abnormal.

Chapter 12 Infanticide

What is abortion if not a form of euthanasia? Why can one kill perfectly good babies and yet if they are actually born (but turn out wrongly) insist they live, even to the extent of operations, incubators and oxygen tents; then place them in hellish institutions for the rest of their lives? Or confine their mother to a living hell? What kind of morality is this?

Letter to the *Guardian*, from a parent of a child with spina bifida, December 1971

1 The Problem

The sister at the hospital, she knew, and she didn't believe much and thought they ought to leave him alone. I mean, he would have died if they'd left him alone, you see. We all know that years ago there wouldn't have been a chance and we all said they ought to have left him alone and let him have gone. But there you are. Doctors say they have to save a life, and they did. There's nothing you can do about it.

I think one thing – it's against my upbringing, it's against my religion, it's against everything I want ever to believe and that's one thing I think – I think that with all the aids and with all the help that's given to them, I think myself that they should put them to sleep. It would be more merciful for the child and for the parents to be told the child was dead and never thought of – forgot. Because – it would ruin no bond, really – you know – up to twelve months. Sure, what if you're heartbroken for a while, it's going to wear away, you know? Whereas the ache of this never wears away. That never wears away. Whether I send him away or keep him at home, it's going to be a heartbreak

150

either way, isn't it, you know? I won't feel very happy about it, whereas if he'd been taken as a baby I'd have forgotten now.

Mothers, quoted in Sheila Hewett: *The Family and the Handicapped Child*, London, 1970

Still, it stands very close to the elbow to ask how many normal children would equal one seriously abnormal child in assessing the real threat to the life and health of a mother and of her family.

Paul Ramsey: *Reference Points in Deciding About Abortion* in J. Noonan (ed.): *The Morality of Abortion*, Cambridge Mass., 1970

Two weeks ago, magistrates at Hull Juvenile Court put a 13-month-old boy into the care of the local authority in order that Hull Corporation could give consent to an operation designed to relieve a rapid deterioration in the baby's health resulting from spina bifida. The parents, a young couple, had refused such consent, and the father attended the court hearing in a final attempt to prevent the operation taking place.

Donald Gould, *New Statesman*, 1972

The newspapers reported recently the prosecution of an elderly woman who shot her severely mentally and physically handicapped adult child because she was frightened she might die before him. A few months ago we read about handicapped children who live subhuman existences in hospital year after year because there is nobody to give them the attention they need. Earlier this year the mother of a crippled boy attempted suicide when he was returned to her care after being in hospital.

Article in the *Guardian*, 5 December, 1971

There is a tendency to use only the most cursory efforts at resuscitation (or none at all) at the birth of an anencephalic infant ... We tend to feel it is kinder to the mother who may subsequently produce a healthy child to have to tell her she had a still birth than to have to burden her with a malformed infant who can never realize the hopes and dreams parents have for their children. The picture changes, of course, if the child breathes spontaneously. Our morality will not permit us (and should not permit us) to destroy the child. This is violative of the expectation of the public of the function of the physician, an image which we share.

Professor Sidney Shindell, *Yale Journal of Biology and Medicine*, 1965

COHEN: ... Supposing you have a child born physically apparently well, but virtually an ament. I am sure you would say that child must remain alive; so you would differentiate, as it were, between the omission of means of saving life, and the commission of means of destroying life. Am I right in that?

MILLER: Yes. In other words, I don't think there's any point in operating on a congenital heart defect in a Mongolian idiot, on the other hand there is no excuse for going around slaughtering healthy Mongols.

COHEN: I think this really comes down, doesn't it, to A.H. Clough's observation, 'Thou shalt not kill, but need'st not strive officiously to keep alive.' I think most doctors would follow that doctrine, don't you?

MILLER: Yes.

From *Keeping People Alive* in A. Clow (ed.): *Morals and Medicine*, London, 1970

Active treatment is the easy way out. Most of us don't have the moral courage to think of other approaches.

A surgeon, quoted in Gerald Leach: *The Biocrats*, London, 1972

Sir, Few parents of spina bifida children are able to adopt the clear-cut views of some of your correspondents. We are more likely to be living in a perpetual cloud of conflicting feelings.

When my two-year-old son was born the team of doctors in

charge thought his outlook was good and so operated immediately (they told me that if they did not operate he might not die but survive in a worse state). A year later we knew he would not only never walk but never even sit unsupported. Meanwhile he receives from physiotherapists, doctors, social workers and all his family an immense amount of loving care. I think we all carry a double wish: that he will grow and prove intelligent and able to cope with life; and at the same time that he might die painlessly should life prove intolerable.

The emotional pendulum swings one way when we read of families who cope, of children who seem happy; and when we realize how much support and encouragement our society offers. It swings the other way when we read of the horrors of life for institutionalized adolescents, and realize how many people would like the problem swept away drastically. One day I think I am a moral coward for not being prepared to solve it by drastic means myself; the next I reproach myself for insufficient courage and optimism in thinking of the future.

There is certainly a good case for leaving spina bifida children unoperated at birth (though I wonder how many doctors would leave their own children); but I suspect that some of those who advance it are trying to tidy up the world in a way that can never be done. What about mongol children, spastics, children injured in accidents? In hospital waiting rooms I have been *envied* by other mothers for my bright, strong-armed little boy.

Could the medical profession not produce some generally agreed guiding advice for future parents, suggest, in fact, a national policy? At the moment the fate of a spina bifida baby seems to depend to some extent on chance factors (which hospital you are in perhaps); considering the numbers born and the severity of the handicap, this may well add to the confusion and bitterness felt by some parents.

A letter to *The Times*, August 1972

Mr and Mrs Jones foresaw a time when they could no longer carry on, so they planned ahead for the inevitable breakdown.

They agreed to kill their son and take their own lives when the strain of caring for him became too great. In the event it was Dorothy who ended the struggle for Graham and herself. Perhaps she felt that her husband could yet find some peace and happiness before he, too, had to die. But when a policeman called at the home he found John Jones kneeling beside his dead wife's body in deep distress, saying, over and over again, how he wished she had waited for him so that they could have gone together.

Donald Gould *New Statesman*, 1975

2 Some Traditional Answers

Most of us prefer not to think too closely about the type of problem raised in the previous section, with the result that the national policy asked for by the mother who wrote to *The Times* is not in sight. And the problem will become more pressing. Future medical advances, combined with a determination to save the lives of all foetuses, could lead to a greatly increased proportion of severely handicapped people in the population. As a result of current medical knowledge, sometimes combined with a determination to keep babies alive wherever possible, we are already moving in that direction. We are able to save premature babies at increasingly early stages of pregnancy, and as a result we save a higher proportion of people with severe defects. Operations on abnormal babies, and protection against what would otherwise be fatal illnesses, have the same result. Many more mentally subnormal babies survive; many more also survive with such handicaps as spina bifida.

Only those with the crudest and most complacent outlook could feel that no problem exists. They easily accept either a blanket policy of infanticide or the misery caused by a policy of saving lives wherever possible. But for those who agree that there is a problem, it is often hard to know how to start thinking about it. There are the different traditional views about killing, and people often fall back on one or other of them with

154

relief, since when taking decisions of this kind almost any framework of thought seems better than none. Let us look first at the implications of the traditional views that are often invoked in the context of these problems.

Those who believe in the sanctity of life hold that to kill a baby is intrinsically wrong and that this is so even if the life ahead of it is one of unrelieved misery. Although the doctrine of the sanctity of life does not rule out the possibility that side-effects in exceptional circumstances may justify killing someone, most of those who hold it would not allow killing in order to spare other members of a family from suffering. Many who believe that life is sacred are not absolute pacifists, but they would often argue that to kill in war is justified because other lives are being defended. This is the 'no trade-off' position: killing may be justified if it prevents other deaths, but cannot be justified in defence of the *quality* of other lives or by the miserable life of the person killed.

The strictest version of the view that life is sacred, which generates absolute pacifism, allows no justification for killing. The no trade-off version rules out all infanticide except in the very rare cases where someone else's life is at stake. (If such things could be predicted, the attempted suicide of the mother of the crippled boy, or the actual suicide of Mrs Dorothy Jones, might be considered relevant here. The no trade-off view has never been developed in sufficient detail to give an answer.)

The belief that life is sacred is normally combined with the doctrine of double effect, the acts and omissions doctrine or some similar view, to temper the obligation to take all steps needed to save as many lives as possible. But it is worth noting that, without these other doctrines, it would commit us to taking all possible positive steps to save the life of any baby, however terrible its state. If the life of a feeble-minded child in permanent pain *could* be saved, we should go to every effort or expense to do so, up to the point where the effort or money would have to be diverted from other life-saving activities.

Those who think that life is sacred often avoid this consequence by appealing to the acts and omissions doctrine. They think, with Professor Shindell, Lord Cohen and Dr Miller, and probably most other doctors, that it is wrong to take positive steps to kill a baby, but that it may sometimes be right to allow a baby to die. This belief in passive infanticide is a clear view, although its supporters, like those of active infanticide, have the difficult problem of drawing boundaries: how serious a condition qualifies for passive infanticide?

An alternative modification of the doctrine of the sanctity of life is to combine it with the principle of double effect. Infanticide is then ruled out as an intended act, but in certain cases a course of action with the death of the baby as a foreseen consequence is acceptable. Yet another modification appeals to the distinction between ordinary and extraordinary means of life-saving. On this view we are obliged to use all ordinary means to save a baby's life, but are not obliged to go to exceptional lengths.

In this book, it has been argued that we should give up the doctrine of the sanctity of life, give up the acts and omissions doctrine and also give up the doctrine of double effect. The arguments will not be repeated here. The distinction between ordinary and extraordinary means will be discussed later in the context of euthanasia, where I shall suggest that it also is unsatisfactory.

The view advocated here as an alternative to these traditional views is that questions about killing should be decided by considering the autonomy of the person whose life is at stake, the extent to which his life is worth living and the effects of any decision on other people. Let us now look at the bearing of these considerations on infanticide.

3 Autonomy

Killing someone overrides his autonomy where it goes against his own preference for staying alive. This objection to killing provides no argument against infanticide, for new-born babies have no conception of death and so cannot have any preference for life over death.

This may seem an absurdly sweeping dismissal. It may be said that babies, although unable to think about death, behave in ways that increase their chances of survival. They have the sucking reflex and cry when in pain. Is this not some indication of a preference for life?

The answer to this is simply 'no'. It is an objection rooted in biological and philosophical confusion. The existence of a pattern of behaviour that increases the chance of survival can be explained in familiar Darwinian terms, but such an explanation need make no mention of any specific desire to survive. The behaviour pattern, such as infant crying, is there because in the past those with this behaviour managed to survive better than those without it. It is redundant to suggest that the baby who cries when in danger does this because he understands the causal link between the danger and his possible death.

It is clear that babies do not have the concept of death. Anyone who doubts this should spend some time with a baby trying to see what degree of understanding of the world he has. Another way of dispelling illusions here is to talk to two-year-olds and three-year-olds and see how much they grasp the idea of death.

It may be said that it is scholastic to make having a desire depend on having a concept. The suggestion is that babies may have the desire to go on living although they do not have the concepts of life and death. I suspect this derives what plausibility it has from a naïve assumption that having a concept is the same as being able to use a word. It would certainly be objectionable to suppose that people have only those desires that they can formulate adequately in words. People, whether children or adults, often know exactly what they want without being able to give proper verbal expression to this. (A simple example is provided by the poverty of most people's colour vocabulary: I may go to buy paint, with a clear mental image of the colour I want, without having any idea of its name.) So, of course, it would be wrong to suppose that babies, or animals, have no desire to avoid death *simply because they cannot say so*. That would be an argument both scholastic and fallacious.

Desires do not presuppose words, but they do presuppose concepts. A baby can want to be fed, or be changed, or to go to his mother, although he does not speak. Innumerable signs of recognition and pleasure show us that he has these concepts. But a baby cannot want to escape from death any more than he can want to escape the fate of being a chartered accountant when grown up. He has no idea of either.

This shows that killing a baby cannot be objected to on the grounds of overriding a straightforward desire to live. But, at this point, someone wanting to invoke the autonomy objection might quote Spinoza: 'No one can desire to be blessed, to act well, or live well, who at the same time does not desire to be, to act and to live, that is, actually to exist.'[1] The satisfaction of most desires, including those of babies, presupposes the continued existence of the person who has them. If a baby wants to see his mother, his desire will not be satisfied if he is no longer alive when she reaches him.

It is not clear to what extent it makes sense to talk of a baby desiring whatever is necessary for the realization of his desire to see his mother. But, even if we grant that this does make sense, it still does not make the autonomy argument a very powerful objection to killing babies. For, in killing a baby, someone is overriding the baby's autonomy to no greater extent than he would be if he prevented the mother from coming home that day. So far as the autonomy argument goes, the objection to infanticide is *at most* no stronger than the objection to frustrating a baby's current set of desires, say by leaving him to cry unattended for a longish period.

The autonomy argument is either entirely or largely inapplicable as an objection to infanticide.

4 Worth-While Life

The other main direct objection to killing is that it is wrong to destroy a worth-while life. But this is an 'impersonal' objection,

1. *Ethics*, Part IV, Prop. 21.

having to do with potential. In terms of this objection, new-born babies, like foetuses, are replaceable. It is wrong to kill a baby who has a good chance of having a worth-while life, but *in terms of this objection* it would not be wrong to kill him if the alternative to his existence was the existence of someone else with an equally good chance of a life at least as worth-while.

To illustrate this point with the easiest sort of case, let us consider a pair of Siamese twins joined in such a way that they cannot both survive. Where there is no difference between their chances of a worth-while life, and where an operation will kill one but allow the other to survive, what should be done? The value placed on worth-while life (unless modified by the acts and omissions doctrine) will enjoin that the operation be performed, but it will be a matter of indifference which baby is killed and which is helped to survive.

The impersonal nature of this objection to killing is relatively easy to accept in the case of the Siamese twins, because the two lives are at stake at the same time. But the time at which a worth-while life is lived is irrelevant to its value. It follows that babies are, in terms of this objection, replaceable in a stronger sense. If a mother is resolved to have exactly one child and no more, the death of her first baby may cause her to have another. If the second baby has just as good a life as the first one would have done, then, in terms of the worth-while life objection, the death of the first baby has not mattered at all. And, if the first baby would have had a less good life, its death was in this respect a good thing.

The 'replacement view' already influences many people with regard to foetuses. Pregnant women who have German measles sometimes opt to abort the foetus who may have been damaged and conceive another one instead. If for the moment we ignore the complex side-effects and simply consider the two main direct objections to killing, we find that they generate the extension of the replacement view to babies. (Those who resist this should consider premature babies. Why should it make a difference whether or not a creature at the same stage of development is inside or outside the womb?) A defective baby is

159

better replaced by a later, normal one, as a more worth-while life is the result. And the autonomy principle, which in the case of adults gives existing people preference over potential people, does not apply to babies. (When we turn to side-effects, we shall see the limitations of applying the replacement view to babies.)

The objection to killing someone whose life is worth-while can in principle be deflected by considerations of replacement. But many of the problems it raises are in situations where replacement is not relevant. These are the problems of deciding whether someone's life is worth living at all. The questions can be seen in cases of babies born with spina bifida.

Of babies born with spina bifida, the great majority of those who receive no treatment die in the first year. The results of full medical treatment can be seen by looking at what happened in Sheffield, when it was the policy there to give maximum treatment to all spina bifida babies. A survey by Dr John Lorber shows that, even with this treatment, 59 per cent of those born between 1959 and 1963 were dead by 1971.[2] Dr Lorber gives a detailed description of the condition of the 41 per cent who survived, which he then summarizes as follows:

At the most 7 per cent of those admitted have less than grossly crippling disabilities and may be considered to have a quality of life not inconsistent with self-respect, earning capacity, happiness and even marriage. The next 20 per cent are also of normal intelligence and some may be able to earn their living in sheltered employment, but their lives are full of illness and operations. They are severely handicapped and are unlikely to live a full life span. They are at risk of sudden death from shunt complications or are likely to die of renal failure at an early age. The next 14 per cent are even more severely handicapped because they are retarded. They are unlikely to earn their living and their opportunities in life will be severely restricted.

Some comparison can be made with babies born with spina bifida in 1967 and 1968, again treated in Sheffield. The two year

2. J. Lorber: 'Results of Treatment of Myelomeningocele', *Developmental Medicine and Child Neurology*, 1971, and J. Lorber: 'Spina Bifida Cystica', *Archives of Disease in Childhood*, 1972.

survival rate rose from 50 to 64 per cent in this second group. But in this group the proportion of babies treated who survived as members of the most severely handicapped category rose from 14 to 23 per cent. Dr Lorber says, 'Passage of time can only alter this balance by the likely higher mortality among those most severely affected.'

The question which most of us prefer to evade is whether it is a good or a bad thing when one of these 'most severely affected' children dies. Because we are discussing the point about worthwhile life, let us for the moment artificially exclude effects on other people, such as parents or brothers and sisters. Is this kind of life, seen from the child's own point of view, one which is worth living?

How can we think about this question? It is obvious that, when it concerns a particular group of children with a special set of handicaps, no answer is worth listening to unless given by someone with knowledge and experience of that medical condition and of the social context of the lives in question. For this reason, I am going to give no answer to the question about the spina bifida children, but only suggest a way of thinking about it.

In a previous chapter, it was argued that a person's own view about whether he wants to go on living, while not a conclusive test, is normally evidence of overriding importance. The problem with babies is that they cannot have a view. So we have to find a test to substitute for asking them what they prefer. The best substitute will be for us to ask whether we ourselves would find such a life preferable to death.

This substitute question is in various ways unsatisfactory. It is clear that people will often disagree in their answers in a particular case. Also, such a thought experiment reveals the limitations of our imagination. It is so hard even to see things from the point of view of other people who are normal that judgements of what it would be like to be, say, a feeble-minded person have a high proportion of guesswork. (There is a large literature on the adequacy or otherwise of answering moral questions by trying to imagine yourself in someone else's place, stimulated by the illuminating work of R.M. Hare. I have nothing original to contribute to it. There are serious difficulties in this approach, but when dealing with questions like the present one, no less problematic alternative has been proposed.)

The method of trying to assess the quality of someone's life by trying to imagine oneself in his place may generate answers that differ from those suggested by our immediate responses. Many of us feel horror or revulsion when confronted with some gross abnormalities. Although this response in other people may itself impair the quality of a person's life (and should for that reason be resisted as much as possible) it is not a reliable guide to how the person himself feels.

Perhaps there are people who, in performing the proposed thought experiment, would think that for them any kind of life would be preferable to death. (Aristotle would be one of them, if he were prepared to stand by this uncharacteristic *non sequitur:* 'Now death is the most terrible of all things; for it is the end, and nothing is thought to be any longer good or bad for the dead.'[3]) The rest of us can either feel doubts about their imagination or else admire their resilience. But those of us who think that we would opt for death rather than some kinds of lives have a good reason for holding that some lives are not worth living. In these cases, depending on the degree of impairment, the quality of the life either simply ceases to be an objection to killing or else becomes a positive argument in favour of it.

5 The Relative Weakness of the Direct Objections to Infanticide

The appeal to autonomy is virtually useless as an argument against infanticide. The argument that it is wrong to destroy a worth-while life holds in most cases, although not always, and in some extreme cases the predictable quality of someone's life works as an argument the other way. But even where the worth-

3. *Nicomachean Ethics*, 1115[a].

while life argument does hold, it is no stronger against infanticide than against not conceiving a child. In either case, there is one less person with a worth-while life. And, considering this reason in isolation, babies are replaceable. Just as it may be right to defer conception if later you stand a better chance of having a normal child, so, in terms of this consideration, it can be right to kill a defective baby and then have a normal one you would not otherwise have.

The limited force of these objections to infanticide will be disturbing to many people. And it is also disturbing that the autonomy argument, which makes the difference between adults and babies, has such blurred boundaries of application. It is so unclear when it is sensible to say that a child has the desire not to die. The vision of a nightmare society looms up in which the casual 'replacement' of babies starts to spread up the age groups, causing an open-ended threat to the lives of children. The worst fears of those who oppose abortion on grounds of the thin end of the wedge, or the slippery slope, would be realized. But this nightmare prospect derives its plausibility from neglect of side-effects. With the direct objections to infanticide relatively weak, how does the picture alter when side-effects are taken into consideration?

6 Side-Effects: Those Closely Affected

The main people affected by an act of infanticide, apart from the baby, are the parents and other family, and, if it is in hospital, the doctors and nurses involved. But the cumulative effect of a general policy of infanticide in certain kinds of case can involve society as a whole.

The parents, especially the mother, are likely to be greatly distressed by the killing of their baby. It seems much worse than an abortion, a miscarriage or a still-birth. But, where the abnormality is sufficiently serious, this may be less terrible for the parents than having to live with their child and bring him up. It is an unpalatable truth that appeals to side-effects can sometimes be among the strongest arguments *for* infanticide. And this can be further increased by taking into consideration the interests of any other children in the family, either those already in existence or those who will be born later.

For any doctors and nurses involved, infanticide must often be extremely unpleasant. Those who have chosen work which has among its main aims the saving of lives can hardly be expected to find killing babies any more tolerable a task than the rest of us would find it. Those of us who are not involved are not in a position to lecture those who are about their duty here, but should give proper weight to the feelings involved. However, in weighing up this factor, we should not forget that the misery of the surviving baby and his family may last a lifetime.

The side-effects on those most closely involved in a single act of infanticide may be rather mixed. While the side-effects of killing a wanted, normal baby are so entirely awful that they alone would constitute an overwhelming objection, even in the absence of direct considerations, other cases are far less clear. Where the handicap is sufficiently serious, the killing of a baby may benefit the family to an extent that is sufficient to outweigh the unpleasantness of the killing (or the slower process of 'not striving to keep alive').

7 Side-Effects and Society: The Wedge Problem

It seems that, in a fair number of cases of extreme abnormality, both direct considerations and the side-effects on those most closely involved will combine to support the case for infanticide. But the position is complicated when the social effects of a general policy of infanticide in such cases are considered.

Let us first look at some possibly beneficial side-effects. There are couples who know that they run an unusually high risk of having abnormal children and who, because of this, do not have the children they want. If they could rely on infanticide if things went wrong, they might then go ahead and have children. Their own lives would be fuller, and the worth-while lives of their children count for something.

One problem connected with spina bifida would also be eased. To operate on a baby with spina bifida increases the chance of survival, but the quality of future life can be uncertain. Some parents would opt for the operation if a greatly improved state were certain, but, because of the chances of survival in a poor state, prefer to leave their child unoperated. If an operation with disastrous results could be followed by death, this would make it easier for parents to choose the operation. This might lead to the saving of some children who would have worth-while lives, but who now die.

But there are social dangers, as well as benefits, in an infanticide policy in some kinds of case. The thin end of the wedge argument seems to have more force here than it does with abortion. For birth is a clear boundary, while the age boundary round permissible infanticide is not a natural and clear-cut one. This is especially so when the main direct difference between infanticide and later killing is the autonomy argument, with its boundary partly dependent on such things as the hazy region where children start to grasp the idea of death. One main difference of side-effects is that the relationships other people (even the mother) have with a new-born baby are much more slender than they later become. This difference also hardly generates a sharp boundary.

Problem cases seem likely to create pressures to extend the scope of infanticide once it is made legitimate at all. If it is allowed at birth for children with some grave abnormality, what will we say about an equally serious abnormality that is only detectable at three months? And another that is only detectable at six months? And another that is detectable at birth and only slightly less serious? And another slightly less serious than that one? Those of us who think that, in some individual cases, infanticide is right because of the interests of the child, or of those closest to him, have to take seriously the argument that any advantages to those involved may be outweighed by the disadvantages of inserting the thin end of this wedge.

The wedge argument has two different versions which are not sufficiently often distinguished. There is a logical version and an empirical version.

The logical version makes no predictions about the actual consequences of allowing the thin end of a wedge to be inserted, but says that it is impossible to *justify* accepting the thin end while rejecting the rest of it. A cut-off point anywhere between the two ends is bound to be arbitrary and so hopeless to justify. But this claim that cut-off points with an element of arbitrariness cannot be justified seems mistaken. Father John Ford, in his article 'The Morality of Obliteration Bombing',[4] rightly says, 'I think it is a fairly common fallacy in legal and moral argumentation to conclude that all is lost because there is a field of uncertainty to which our carefully formulated moral principles cannot be applied with precision.'

Why is this a fallacy? Consider the case of speed limits. A supporter of the logical version of the wedge argument might argue that we should either ban cars altogether or else allow driving at any speed anywhere. For how can a speed limit of thirty miles an hour possibly be defended as better than one of twenty-nine or thirty-one miles an hour? The point that, in terms of safety, there may be no discriminable difference between two speed limits that vary by one mile an hour is an obviously feeble one. Suppose that the smallest discriminable difference of safety is between speed limits differing by five miles an hour. A limit of thirty is safer than one of thirty-five. This shows that it is not permissible to continue to add sub-threshold amounts and to claim that they make no difference. The *maximum* claim that can be made is that it does not matter within four miles an hour where the limit is: it can vary, say, between twenty-eight and thirty-two. This then allows us to argue that blurred limits are less effective than precise ones, and so opt for any one speed between twenty-eight and thirty-two. The logical wedge argument fails.

4. John C. Ford, s.j.: 'The Morality of Obliteration Bombing', *Theological Studies*, 1944, reprinted in Richard A. Wasserstrom (ed.): *War and Morality*, Belmont, 1970.

The empirical version of the wedge argument claims that, once you allow the thin end to be inserted, the result will *in fact* be that more and more of the wedge follows. But this needs to be backed by more evidence than is usually provided. Not all such boundaries are constantly being pushed along, even where there is some pressure on them: many people start to drink without ending up as alcoholics. What is needed is a good reason for thinking that, in any particular case, more of the wedge will be inserted than is desirable.

In the case of infanticide, there are some pressures that might bear on any boundary. Sympathy for a child's suffering, horror at his deformity, parental reluctance to take on a heavy burden, and the preference for drastic but rapid solutions over long, messy ones are all strong pressures. But, on the other hand, the revulsion of parents, doctors and nurses against an act of killing, and our collective social awareness of the dangers of creeping extensions of killing, are strong pressures the other way. I do not think that the case for the empirical version of the wedge argument is sufficiently convincing to outweigh the considerations that favour infanticide in certain cases. This depends on my (fallible) assessment of the relative strengths of these different pressures. Those who make a different assessment can still support a policy of no infanticide, even if they accept the general framework of principles suggested in this book.

Those of us who do not find the empirical version of the wedge argument sufficiently strong to rule out all infanticide still have the 'speed-limit' problem of deciding where to draw a boundary. For it is relevant to estimating the strength of the wedge argument whether there is to be a boundary that is clear and sharp or one that depends on vague factors such as psychiatric assessment of family circumstances. To move from tolerating abortion to tolerating infanticide is to remove the sharp boundary of birth. If this change in moral outlook is to be reflected in our legal and social arrangements, it is of importance that the new boundary is made very sharp. For, if it is not, the wedge argument has greatly increased force against the whole proposal.

8 Towards a Social Policy

It has been argued here that the moral issues involved in a decision about the life or death of a seriously abnormal baby are complicated. The predicted quality of life has to be considered, along with a mass of side-effects both on those closely involved and on the wider society. Not only is the issue a complicated one, but each component factor involves difficult questions of judgement about which people can reasonably disagree.

But this murkiness of the issue itself provides two reasons why those of us who think that infanticide is sometimes right should press for the working-out of a social policy with great explicitness and detail. One reason has been given: the wedge problem. The other reason is that a particular set of parents or a particular doctor needs help in taking decisions. Everyone is fallible here, but it seems more sensible to trust any consensus that emerges among those with knowledge and experience (parents of severely affected children and doctors specializing in the field) than a particular person's immediate view at a time of crisis.

I have nothing to contribute to the emergence of this policy, beyond the attempt in this book to undermine some of the general views (the sanctity of life, the acts and omissions doctrine) that at present obstruct it. The policy must be worked out by those in a better position to do so. It may be that there should be an absolute time limit for all cases. (Dr Francis Crick once proposed a two-day period for detecting abnormalities, after which infanticide would not be permissible.) Or it may be that the limit should vary for some abnormalities less immediately detectable. It may be that infanticide should be permissible in all cases of one abnormality, but that with another abnormality other tests should be crucial. Dr Lorber's work on the different outcomes to be expected in spina bifida cases with different degrees of seriousness at birth is the sort of information that is relevant here. What is needed for a coherent policy is more work of this kind and more attempts to reach agreement on its implications.

168

To advocate such a policy is not to suggest that babies should be killed against the wishes of their parents or that doctors who do not agree with infanticide should be forced to act against their conscience. It is rather to advocate that society should set clear limits to what will be treated as permissible. At present, a fair number of severely abnormal children die because individual doctors or parents support a policy of 'not striving to keep alive'. But, as the mother who wrote to *The Times* said, the haphazard results of this can lead to confusion and bitterness. There is no moral case for matters of life and death depending to such a degree on chance factors.

Chapter 13   Suicide and Gambling with Life

I'm sure most of us, confronted with the sight of a man walking towards the edge of a precipice, would rugger tackle him first and seek to dissuade him second. But how about the man who is patently drinking himself to death? How about the man who, faced with the statistics, still elects to smoke? Should we also legislate to tie them down, lock them away because of these life-threatening habits? And if we did, how long before we were passing further laws against those who lead too sedentary a life – for the same reason?

Ian Martin: 'Slow Motion Suicide', *New Society*, October 1974

It was once common to think of a person who killed himself with strong moral disapproval. In England, suicide was illegal right up to 1961. The arguments for the traditional moral condemnation varied. Sometimes the appeal was simply to the sanctity of life, sometimes it was to the view that the right of life and death belongs, not to the person himself, but to God, or even the king or the state. Of these arguments, the only one to be touched on here is the assertion that a man must not usurp God's right to decide the time of his death. This one is interesting only because of the elegance of its decisive refutation by David Hume:

Were the disposal of human life so much reserved as the peculiar province of the Almighty that it were an encroachment on his right, for men to dispose of their own lives; it would be equally criminal to act for the preservation of life as for its destruction. If I turn aside a stone which is falling upon my head, I disturb the course of nature, and I invade the peculiar province of the Almighty by lengthening out my life beyond the period which by the general laws of matter and motion he had assigned it.[1]

The view that suicide is morally wrong has been held so strongly that some have treated it as one of the purest cases of an obviously wrong kind of act. Wittgenstein said,

If suicide is allowed then everything is allowed. If anything is not allowed then suicide is not allowed. This throws a light on the nature of ethics, for suicide is, so to speak, the elementary sin. And when one investigates it it is like investigating mercury vapour in order to comprehend the nature of vapours. Or is even suicide in itself neither good nor evil?[2]

But in the sixty years since these remarks were made, it has come to seem less obvious that suicide is wrong at all, even to people who are far from holding that everything is allowed.

The reaction against responding to suicide with horror and condemnation has made widespread the view that the question is not in any way a moral one. Suicide is sometimes thought of as an irrational symptom of mental disturbance and so as a 'medical' problem. On a different view, it is a matter for each person's free choice: other people should have nothing to say about it, and the question for someone contemplating it is simply one of whether his future life will be worth living. Against these views, it will be argued here that consideration of a possible act of suicide raises moral questions, for the person himself and for other people, of the same complexity as other acts of killing. (It does not, of course, follow from this that it would in some cases be a good thing to revert to traditional attitudes of disapproval towards those who have attempted suicide.) It will also be argued here that the moral case which justifies some acts of intervention to prevent a suicide has implications for social policy on a wider range of issues than is at first apparent.

1. David Hume: 'Of Suicide', in his *Essays*.
2. Ludwig Wittgenstein: *Notebooks*, 1914–16, concluding paragraphs.

1 The Variety of Suicidal and Near-Suicidal Acts

There are many different kinds of suicidal act. The act of someone whose life is fundamentally a happy one but who tries to kill himself in a state of severe but temporary depression differs from the act of someone who, after prolonged deliberation, decides to kill himself rather than face any more of his incurable illness. And the case is different again when people kill themselves for reasons that we, even if not Durkheim, can call 'altruistic', perhaps because they do not want to be a burden to others, or as a protest against some political or social evil, or as a gesture in support of some cause. Here distinguishable but related acts vary from voluntary acceptance of a martyr's death at the hands of others, to slow suicide by hunger strike, and public and dramatic suicide (such as that of Jan Palach in Czechoslovakia or some of the Buddhist suicides in Vietnam).

Apart from these, there is a whole range of acts on the border of suicide. Some of the most interesting work on the explanation of suicide is that of Professor Stengel and others suggesting that many apparent attempts at suicide may not have been intended to succeed.[3] Comparison of those 'attempts' which end in death and those which do not shows some significant differences. More men than women make attempts ending in death, while more women than men make 'attempts' which they survive. The peak age for fatal attempts is between fifty-five and sixty-four, while the peak age for non-fatal ones is between twenty-four and forty-four. Such discrepancies make it plausible to suggest that not all 'attempts' are the result of an equally firm decision to die. Some may be a cry for help without any real intention to die. Others may be made in a state of mind where a gamble is taken with some risk of death and some chance of survival followed by help.

As well as the dramatic case of a suicide 'attempt', there are other instances where people gamble with their lives. People in

3. Erwin Stengel: *Suicide and Attempted Suicide*, Harmondsworth, 1964.

172

wars volunteer for high-risk missions, sometimes out of altruism or duty, but sometimes because they do not value their lives much, or even half want to die. The same may be true of some who take on dangerous jobs, such as soldier or war correspondent, or some of those who like dangerous sports. Then there are those who drink or smoke heavily, or who eat too much and exercise too little, all in the knowledge of the earlier death that will probably result.

In the cases mentioned, we would not count a course of action as even near-suicidal unless the risk of death was welcomed, or at least accepted with indifference. A member of a bomb-disposal squad may very much want to live, and do his work out of public spirit: it would be quite inappropriate to call him suicidal. And the same is true of heavy smokers who want a long life but who cannot escape their addiction.

But in all cases where people opt for the risk or certainty of their own death, whether or not with suicidal intent, it is possible to raise two moral questions. Ought they to risk their lives? Should other people intervene to prevent them? One reason for thinking that to raise the question of the morality of an act of suicide is inappropriate is the belief that an act of suicide must be done in such a state of disturbance that moral considerations stand no chance of influencing the decision. But thinking about the variety of suicidal and near-suicidal acts should cast doubt on this belief.

2 Questions for the Person Thinking of Suicide

Where someone contemplating suicide is sufficiently in control of himself to deliberate about his course of action, two factors are relevant to the decision. What would his own future life be like, and would it be worth living? What effect would his decision (either way) have on other people?

The difficulties in answering the question about one's own future life are obvious. If life is at present sufficiently bad to make a person think suicide may be in his own interest, he will need to have some idea of how likely or unlikely is any improvement in his state. This is often hard to predict (except in cases where the blight on his life is an absolutely incurable illness). Most of us are bad at giving enough weight to the chances of our lives changing for better or worse. And people sometimes contemplate suicide without exploring the possibility of less radical steps to deal with their problems. Someone who would normally not even consider such upheavals as leaving his family, changing his job, emigrating, or seeking psychiatric help, should not absolutely rule out any of them once he enters the region where killing himself is not ruled out either. And, since many of us are bad at predicting our own futures, it is worth talking to other people who may see the thing differently, whether friends or the Samaritans.

The other difficulty is deciding what sort of life is worth living. One test has to do with the amount of life for which you would rather be unconscious. Most of us prefer to be anaesthetized for a painful operation. If most of my life were to be on that level, I might opt for permanent anaesthesia, or death. But complications arise. It may be that we prefer to be anaesthetized for an operation only because we have plenty of other times to experience life without pain. It may be worth putting up with a greater degree of pain where the alternative is no life at all. And, even if we can decide about when we would rather be unconscious, the question whether a life is worth living cannot be decided simply by totting up periods of time to see if more than half our waking life is below zero in this way. Some brief periods of happiness may be of such intensity as to justify much longer periods of misery. (Equally, some brief periods of agony or despair may outweigh longer periods of mild cheerfulness.)

Our estimates of the quality of our lives are especially vulnerable to temporary changes of mood, so that the only reasonable way to reach a serious evaluation is to consider the question over a fairly long stretch of time. Even this has limitations, because of the difficulty of giving the right weight to estimates made at different times and in different moods, but anything less is hopelessly inadequate.

The other question to be answered is about the effects on other people of a decision for or against the suicide. No doubt there are some people whose lives are so desperately bad that their own interests should come before any loss to other people. But sometimes an act of suicide can shatter the lives of others (perhaps parents) to a degree the person might never have suspected. Suicide cannot be seen to be the right thing to do without the most careful thought about the effects on all those emotionally involved. There is also the question of the loss of any general contribution the person might make to society.

To kill oneself can sometimes be the right thing to do, but much less often than may at first sight appear. (Evidence of a reasonably respectable kind could come from studies of the later lives of those whose 'attempts' fail and of the lives of families after one member kills himself.) To suggest that some acts of suicide may be morally wrong is not to advocate that those who make failed 'attempts' ought to be responded to with condemnation or reproach: it is obvious that the last thing that is helpful is any pressure of this kind.

It is interesting that the case against suicide is also a case against gambling with one's life. There are familiar stories of the wives of racing-car drivers pleading with their husbands to retire. This kind of thing is not just a marginal feature of dangerous jobs or sports, but something which ought to be considered very seriously before starting on them.

3 Intervention: The Problems

The moral question for the person contemplating suicide is simply whether his being dead would be a better state of affairs for himself and others or a worse one. ('Simply' does not imply that this question is easy.) But for other people contemplating intervention to prevent a suicide, the matter is more complicated. They have to ask the same question about whether the death would on the whole be a good or a bad thing. But, if they decide it would be a bad thing, they also must ask the further

175

question, whether it would be right for them to intervene. This will seem not to be a separate question only to someone who thinks that we are always entitled to interfere in other people's lives where they would otherwise do something wrong.

The question of intervention can take various forms. Are we entitled to use our powers of persuasion in an attempt to stop someone killing himself? If our persuasion fails, or we have no opportunity to use it, may we then use coercion? If we can use some coercion, how far may we go? (This problem is clearly illustrated by the use of forcible feeding on people killing themselves by hunger strike.) If someone arrives in hospital after a suicide attempt, should doctors make efforts to revive him?

These questions are related to others not involving suicide: to what extent ought there to be persuasion, social pressure or legislation of a paternalist kind, to try to stop people risking their lives? These questions arise about matters such as seat belts in cars, drugs, smoking, obesity, dangerous sports or safety standards in houses.

4 Intervention: A Policy

Apart from consideration of side-effects, the guiding principles to be applied are two. It is desirable where possible to save a worth-while life. It is desirable where possible to respect a person's autonomy. The prevention of suicide is obviously a place where these two principles will sometimes conflict, and I have no general formula for deciding priorities. The policy to be suggested here is that there should be an attempt to save the maximum number of worth-while lives compatible with using paternalist restrictions of autonomy only temporarily in the case of sane adults. Some people may accept the same general principles, but strike a different balance between them where they conflict.

Where we think someone bent on suicide has a life worth living, it is always legitimate to reason with him and to try to persuade him to stand back and think again. There is no case against reasoning, as it in no way encroaches on the person's autonomy. There is a strong case in its favour, as where it succeeds it will prevent the loss of a worth-while life. (If the person's life turns out not to be worth-while, he can always change his mind again.) And if persuasion fails, the outcome is no worse than it would otherwise have been.

Where someone has decided that his life is not worth living and is not deflected from his decision for suicide by persuasion, it is legitimate to restrain him by force from his first attempt, or even several attempts. (I do not attempt to draw any precise boundary here.) This legitimacy depends on our belief that his life will be worth living: those of us who do not believe in the sanctity of life will not agree to overriding someone's autonomy in order to make him endure a life not worth living. And we ought to limit severely the number of times we use force to frustrate a person's decision to kill himself, because a persistent policy of forcible prevention is a total denial of his autonomy in the matter. If we prevent him once or a few times this gives him a chance to reconsider, and the decision later is still his own. Even those who do not set any independent value on autonomy may feel in the case of a rational person that his persistent suicide attempts cast doubt on their own judgement that his life is worth living.

The endorsement of limited coercion given here does not extend to the forcible feeding of those on hunger strike. Someone set on a slow death of this kind has plenty of time to reconsider the decision, and so the justification of temporary intervention does not apply. In addition, much stronger justification would be needed for imposing the pain and humiliation that normally accompany forcible feeding than for the relatively harmless methods of frustrating a normal suicide attempt.

The question of forcible prevention is easier to answer in the case of a rational person calmly deciding that his life is not worth living than it is in the case of someone prone to bouts of suicidal depression. In the case of the rational person we intervene to give him a chance to think again, but should ultimately respect his decision. But should we equally respect the decision for suicide taken in a temporary but recurring mood of despair?

There is no difficulty in justifying intervention in the case of someone in a suicidal mood for the only time in his life. He is given time to think again, and he never again decides to kill himself. His life has been saved at minimal cost to his autonomy. But what are we to say of someone whose emotional life is a constant series of ups and downs, who alternates between very much wanting to go on living and moods of suicidal depression? If we treat him on a par with the person who calmly and rationally contemplates suicide, we will, after frustrating a few attempts, allow him to go ahead. But the rightness of this seems much more doubtful where moods of temporary depression are involved.

This is partly because a sustained and reflective preference for suicide seems much better evidence that a person's life is not worth living than are frequent changes of mind about it. And it is also because overriding a decision that is the product of a passing mood is less disrespectful of autonomy than overriding a preference that plays a stable role in a person's outlook. Where someone fluctuates between optimism and pessimism about his life, there may be no neutral vantage point from which he can take a 'rational' decision. In such a case, he does not fully possess the desire either to live or to die, in the dispositional sense of 'possess' that is relevant to the autonomy principle. It is hard to see in such a case that we can decide about intervention on any basis other than our views about the likely quality of his future life, together with any side effects we think relevant. (If we are unable to judge whether his future life is likely on balance to be worth living, we may allow the scale to be tipped by the effects of his suicide on his family.)

Some decisions about intervention have to be taken largely in ignorance of the state of mind and reasons behind the person's decision to kill himself. A mere passer-by may be in a position to intervene, or, more often, a doctor in a hospital may be in a position to revive someone after an attempt. In all such cases, the intervention is justified. This is for the same reason that intervention is justified in any first attempt. There is the chance of saving a worth-while life at the cost of only a temporary interference with autonomy: there is a very strong chance that someone calmly determined to kill himself will have other opportunities.

5 Paternalism and Gambling with Life

To what extent is intervention justified when someone places his own life at risk? When ought we to try to persuade people not to run risks or even compel them by law not to do so? These questions again do not have simple answers. We need to take into account the benefits that may result from running the risks, the degree of risk involved and the drawbacks of the different kinds of intervention. Whether or not persuasion should be used may also vary in individual cases according to the likely side-effects of a death. If someone volunteers for a highly useful but dangerous job, such as bomb-disposal, it may not be right to try to argue him out of this. But the position changes if he has a large family and there are plenty of bachelor volunteers. (The arguments for intervention are not all paternalist ones.)

As the benefits from a risky course of action decrease and the risk increases, so the case for trying to persuade someone to change his mind increases. And there comes a point where the risks are so disproportionate to the benefits that, if persuasion is unsuccessful, there is justification for stronger pressure, and perhaps legislation. So much injury and loss of life results from the failure to wear seat belts in cars that it is right for the law to make wearing them compulsory. Those who resist this proposed legislation use arguments appealing to people's freedom from paternalist interference and say that persuasion is better than compulsion. So it is, but freedom from such a trivial piece of compulsion is purchased at too great a cost in lives and happiness.

We rightly value having a large area of our lives free from fussy state interference. And for the state to intervene to prevent us taking any risk to life, however small, would involve an officious paternalism which nearly everyone would find not worth-while. But when the risks increase, the objections should diminish. Against this, we have to set the benefits for which the risks are run. Having to spend a moment putting on a seat belt is an extremely trivial disadvantage to weigh against avoiding a high risk. But having to give up an activity like mountaineering might be a large sacrifice for those who like it, and so a much larger degree of risk would be necessary to justify banning it.

I do not know where the boundaries of legislation should be. A great deal of investigation and argument is needed. But it is at least fairly clear that our intuitive responses to this question probably need to be revised. Social traditions grow up in which some things are thought of as outside the scope of legislation simply because they have never been legally controlled. We are used to paternalist laws making motorcyclists wear crash helmets, but the idea of laws forbidding people to smoke cigarettes shocks us as an infringement of traditional liberties. Yet our location of smoking within the realm of individual free decisions is a tradition that grew up before we knew the facts about its effects. A rational social policy would be concerned with striking a balance between minimizing risks and minimizing the kinds of restrictions that frustrate people in things that really matter to them. It is not at all clear that our traditional frontiers of legislation achieve this.

The argument here is that reasons for preventing suicides are also reasons for social policies of risk reduction, if necessary by legislation. To some it may appear odd that I have argued in favour of legislation to prevent people taking certain risks with their lives, but have not argued for the re-introduction of legislation against suicide. The reason for this is that suicide is a special case. Legislation seems, hardly surprisingly, to be of little use in reducing the suicide rate, and its main effect was to impose an additional ordeal on those who survived their suicide attempts. There is also the thought that some suicide decisions are quite rational, being taken by people with a very clear assessment of their future lives, so that interference is unjustified.

And the appeal to autonomy has much more force where the person's decision is of such importance to him than it has when it concerns a person's decision not to bother to put on his seat belt. There is nothing to be said for a substantial erosion of autonomy that is also ineffective. There is a lot to be said for saving many people who want to live, but who, for trivial advantages, thoughtlessly gamble with their lives.

Chapter 14 Voluntary Euthanasia

A certain West German doctor, who elects to remain anonymous, during the last war, at fearful risk to himself, provided Jewish acquaintances about to be deported to torture and extermination with tablets so they could kill themselves. (He also for a while harboured a Jew and thereby saved him.) To be sure, to furnish the means of suicide is not quite the same as to kill; but suppose he had directly injected a paralysed Jew, who was unable to handle the tablets, òr a small child? It would not detract from the nobility of his conduct.

Professor D. Daube: 'Sanctity of Life', in *Symposium on the Cost of Life, Proceedings of the Royal Society of Medicine,* 1967

All those who work with dying people are anxious that what is known already should be developed and extended and that terminal care everywhere should become so good that no one need ever ask for voluntary euthanasia.

Dr Cicely Saunders: 'The Care of the Dying Patient and his Family', in *The Problem of Euthanasia, Documentation in Medical Ethics,* 1972

The word 'euthanasia' will be used here to mean killing some-one where, on account of his distressing physical or mental state, this is thought to be in his own interests. It is to include killing someone about to enter such a state as well as someone already there. Voluntary euthanasia is done at the request of the person himself. When, if ever, is voluntary euthanasia right? (This question is not one about its legality, but about its morality. Its illegality is obviously relevant to the rightness or otherwise of doing it. But it is possible to raise the moral question independently, perhaps as part of a discussion of whether the law should be changed.)

When unassisted suicide is possible, there is no need to ask for help. A person's unnecessary request for help would be evidence that his suicide 'attempt' was not genuine, but an appeal for support. But when unaided suicide is impossible, various degrees of help may be asked for. The person may ask for the means of suicide to be made available: he may be too ill to go out and buy poison, or he may be in hospital and unable to leave. He may ask for the act of killing to be performed by someone else: he may be unable to inject himself, or unable to pick up a pill and place it in his mouth. To give the first kind of help is to assist a suicide. To give the second is an act of voluntary euthanasia.

The case for legal discouragement of helping people to commit suicide is a strong one. It is more often desirable to encourage the person considering suicide to have second thoughts than it is to help him kill himself. And it is desirable to do whatever possible to discourage a kind of self-interested oblique murder, committed by encouraging a suicide. But, despite the case for a general social policy of discouragement, it may in a particular instance be right to provide the help needed for suicide.

Various conditions must be met before it is right for me to help your suicide. I must be convinced that your decision is a serious one: it must be properly thought out, not merely the result of a temporary emotional state. I must also think your decision a reasonable one. (If I think your life will be worth living, the case for preserving a worth-while life starts to pull in the opposite direction from the case for respecting your autonomy.) These considerations are parallel to those relating to the morality of frustrating someone's suicide attempt. It is also necessary to think about the circumstances that make assistance necessary for suicide. If these circumstances are only temporary, this counts against giving assistance, as failure to help is not a permanent frustration of autonomy: unaided suicide will be possible later. But, if unaided suicide will never be possible, or will not be possible for a long time, the situation is different. To refuse to provide help is a very serious denial of the person's autonomy over the matter of his own life and death, and is only to be justified by powerful arguments appealing either to the future quality of his life or to side-effects. (If it is right to stand aside and let someone kill himself, it is hard to see why it is wrong to provide necessary assistance. There may be differences of side-effects, perhaps to do with feelings of guilt, with establishing a precedent or with the consequences of an illegal act. But, where these side-effects are not strong enough to justify the difference of moral evaluation, it must depend on some view such as the acts and omissions doctrine.)

If it is sometimes right to assist a suicide, say by bringing pills to someone's bedside for him to take, is it ever right to perform an act of voluntary euthanasia? The difference between voluntary euthanasia and assisted suicide is that the final act is performed by someone else. Someone who is sceptical about the importance of this may say that, so far as the person providing help is concerned, the only difference is that euthanasia involves one more physical movement: the two kinds of act are otherwise the same in intention and outcome. I want to suggest that the sceptic is here guilty of over-simplification, but that the underlying attitude is right.

If assisted suicide is possible, it is always to be preferred to voluntary euthanasia. If we know that a person himself knowingly took a lethal pill, there is by comparison with euthanasia little ambiguity about the nature of his decision. Whether his act was well thought out or one resulting from temporary depression, there is strong reason to think that at that moment he was acting on his own decision to die. (Any residual doubt can only be about whether the 'attempt' was meant to succeed.) But where the person does not perform the final act himself, there is always more room for doubt about the extent to which he desired death. It seems possible that someone might ask for pills and at the last minute not take them, but feel inhibited about expressing a last-minute change of mind to the person about to carry out his request to give him a lethal injection.

Although the sceptic wrongly ignores this difference, we should support his basic attitude. For, unless we hold a view such as the acts and omissions doctrine, it is hard to see why it matters *in principle* who actually puts the pill in the man's mouth. If we were in a position to have no serious doubt about the person's considered and strong preference for death, the fact that I put the pill in his mouth rather than left it at his bedside would be in itself of no moral importance. As the sceptic points out, both intention and outcome are the same.

If this view is correct, voluntary euthanasia is justified in those cases where we know that the person would commit suicide if he could, and where we believe that the conditions that would make it right to allow or assist a suicide are satisfied. This general principle may be modified in application by the consideration of side-effects. In practice it also raises difficulties concerning the genuineness of a request for euthanasia, and in cases where genuine requests are followed by changes of mind.

1 Problems of the Euthanasia Request

If someone in hospital is in a bad state and says he wants to die, there are real problems in interpreting his remark. It may be an expression of a carefully considered decision or it may be a cry of temporary despair. It may not even be meant seriously at the time. There is such a range of possible degrees of commitment to such a statement, that further exploration is obviously needed before taking it as expressing a clear decision. But after a thorough discussion, repeated on several occasions, it should be possible to form a better impression of the person's actual preference. There is the further problem of finding out the extent to which the request is well based: it would be less worth taking seriously if it depended on an exaggerated view of the pain involved in a particular illness. But this again could be cleared up by a sufficiently thorough discussion.

There are also problems posed by existence of unstable preferences. As with suicide, someone may be undecided about

185

having euthanasia, and there may be no neutral vantage point from which he can see his 'real' preference. In such a case it seems right not to carry out a request for euthanasia. To refuse it is less to deny autonomy than to flout a preference of a more persisting kind. The existence of periods of preferring to be alive makes debatable the view that, on balance, his life is not worth living.

2 Side-Effects

Some of the arguments against euthanasia appeal to side-effects. A practice of euthanasia might make patients afraid when they went into hospital. Or it is argued that the mass murders of the Nazi period had their small beginnings in the Nazi euthanasia programme. These objections, whatever their force against non-voluntary euthanasia, do not carry much weight against voluntary euthanasia. When a voluntary euthanasia programme is properly understood (and publicity could be used to make it so) patients will not fear going to hospital, for they will know that euthanasia would be carried out only at their request. And the Nazi objection is also weak. It was not from *voluntary* euthanasia that the extermination policy grew. And it is hard to see why such results should follow from a voluntary euthanasia policy motivated by the desire to relieve suffering and by respect for a person's autonomy.

Other objections based on side-effects do have more relevance to voluntary euthanasia. One is the suggestion that, if voluntary euthanasia were known to be an option, people might put pressure on their burdensome relations to volunteer. It is hard to evaluate this objection. It seems to me rather implausible, but perhaps I am being too optimistic. In advance of trying a voluntary euthanasia policy, we do not know how people would behave. (Is there any evidence of such pressures in a country where voluntary enthanasia is not illegal?)

A related objection is that, even without pressure being

brought by relations, people who felt they were a burden might think that, although they had lives worth living, they ought to volunteer for euthanasia. This gains some support from the fact that there have been cases of suicide by people whose motive was a reluctance to be a burden on others. Part of the difficulty of evaluating this objection is that it is hard to predict how widespread such feelings would be. Another difficulty is the more fundamental uncertainty about whether it is right in such a case to override the person's autonomy. Where he is wrong in thinking he is a burden, he should not be given euthanasia, but should be persuaded of the truth. (It seems possible that, with so much talk of old people almost as though they were members of another species, many old people who are loved and wanted members of a family do have unnecessary fears that they are a nuisance to the others.) But there are sometimes cases where a person who is old or ill does put a great strain on a family, and where he sees this and would rather die than have the situation continue, it is not obvious that a paternalist refusal to carry out his wishes is justified.

Another possible bad side-effect of voluntary euthanasia concerns the treatment of dying patients. Is there a danger that allowing such a policy would hamper the development of the kind of terminal care which would make euthanasia unnecessary? The policy of total rejection of euthanasia may have the advantage of strengthening people's commitment to developing more humane and imaginative forms of terminal care. Certainly some of the most sensitive and impressive work here, such as that of Cicely Saunders and others, has been done in the context of a principled refusal to comply with euthanasia requests. But it is not clear that voluntary euthanasia would seem an alternative rather than a supplement to better terminal care. A hospital with a voluntary euthanasia policy could still have a staff that did all they could to make euthanasia requests unnecessary. The view that voluntary euthanasia would be accepted as an easy alternative to improved care under-rates the deep revulsion against killing which most people have, and which often seems especially strong among those in professions like nursing. (Perhaps this is again too optimistic. Is there any clear evidence relevant to this?)

3 Suggestion

The general view of the morality of killing adopted in this book makes it reasonable to regard voluntary euthanasia as acceptable in principle in those cases where helping someone commit suicide would also be justifiable. But this acceptance in principle of voluntary euthanasia is subject to there not being overridingly bad side-effects, as well as to there being some reliable way of identifying which requests signify a stable and thought-out preference for death.

In my view thorough discussion should enable us to sort out the serious requests from the others, and the arguments from side-effects are not sufficiently strong to constitute an overriding objection. But the side-effects are difficult to predict and evaluate, and someone holding the same general principles might legitimately take a more pessimistic view. Social policy in these matters is usually not empirical enough. Why rely on guesses and intuitions, whether my optimistic ones or someone else's pessimistic ones, rather than try a social experiment? We could first look at practice in other countries and then modify the law for a trial period here. We would then be in a much better position to assess the side-effects. (Some people may say that if there are bad side-effects we would pay a price even for a trial period of a voluntary enthanasia policy. But this has to be set against the price we already pay in suffering and loss of autonomy by maintaining the status quo.)

Any such trial period should be of a policy in which the question has first to be raised by the person whose life is in question. Any alternative would make it far more doubtful that death was genuinely the person's own considered preference, and would also make some of the possible bad side-effects far more likely.

There is an aspect of any voluntary euthanasia policy that

188

should be mentioned. This is the issue of whether or not there should be a very formal system for validating requests for euthanasia. On the one hand, it is held that witnessed signatures on forms of consent provide safeguards. On the other hand, it is said that bureaucratic procedures would interfere with relationships between doctors and patients and would make the whole procedure harder for both. It seems to me worth trusting doctors not to take life unjustifiably, and so to prefer a code of medical ethics to any formal procedure. But, if we think voluntary euthanasia can be right, there is a serious case for devising some system under which, when performed by some kinds of hospital doctor, it would not be illegal. Some people defend the view that, while doctors ought sometimes to perform acts of voluntary euthanasia, these acts ought to remain illegal, so that the intervention of cumbersome legal procedures is avoided. This policy exposes doctors quite unfairly to the risk of a murder charge and probably contributes to excessively conservative decisions.

Chapter 15　Euthanasia without Request

A man who killed the woman he loved because she was dying from cancer was sent to a mental hospital for an indefinite period . . . The judge told Searby: '. . . She was enduring terrible physical misery but she had a right to live. Her misery could well have been discounted by your love. I will not accept that you killed her out of affection. Love doesn't kill life, it supports and sustains it.'

Daily Telegraph, 25 March 1972, quoted in Ian Robinson: *The Survival of English*, 1973

This is a difficult decision, for example, in the chronic respiratory cripple. It may sometimes be possible to rescue such a patient from an acute exacerbation of chronic disablement, but the discomfort and stress of intensive procedures are such that at a certain stage it must certainly be kinder to spare the patient an ordeal that can but leave him at the best more severely incapacitated.

Professor Henry Miller: *Economic and Ethical Considerations*, in *Symposium on the Cost of Life, Proceedings of the Royal Society of Medicine*, 1967

We are now always able to control pain in terminal cancer in the patients sent to us and only very rarely indeed do we have to make them continually asleep in so doing . . . I certainly agree . . . that there is much suffering among the dying in this country, but, without going into the reasons why I personally think that euthanasia as advocated is wrong, I would like to emphasize again that it should be unnecessary and is an admission of defeat.

Dr Cicely Saunders: *The Lancet*, 2 September 1961

No medical or theological argument could convince me that it is right for a human being to lie in bed incontinent, blind, deaf, for one whole year.

Mrs Jean Drewery: *The Listener*, 13 February 1975

These are extremely difficult problems which will stop troubling us only when we can ensure that everyone, even when fatally ill, has a life that is unambiguously worth living. They are problems that will trouble us for some time to come.

1 Repudiation of Involuntary Euthanasia

It is necessary to distinguish between involuntary and non-voluntary euthanasia. Involuntary euthanasia is killing someone, supposedly in his own interests, in disregard of his own views. It may be to kill him against his expressed preference for staying alive. Or it may be to kill him without taking the trouble to find out his views. What is crucial is that he is in a position to express views, but that any views he has are overridden.

Non-voluntary euthanasia is killing someone, supposedly in his own interests, but where he is either not in a position to have, or not in a position to express, any views on the matter. It is non-voluntary euthanasia that is a live issue for doctors and is the one which is to be discussed here.

Involuntary euthanasia can under all normal circumstances be ruled out. It falls foul of the autonomy objection and it is likely to have appalling side-effects. The only conceivable case for it is a judgement that someone's future life will be utterly hellish (sufficiently so to justify overriding his autonomy *and* outweighing the bad side-effect). But the person's own view on the matter is normally strong evidence to correct any such judgement made by someone else. The only sorts of case I can think of are those involving a future so awful that the person cannot grasp what it will be like. (Perhaps someone going to a Nazi concentration camp, or a mental defective about to be

191

tortured to death.) But even in the concentration camp case it is not obvious that involuntary euthanasia is justified: the most that can be said is that it is not obvious it can be ruled out. For practical purposes, ignoring these nightmare cases, all there is to be said about involuntary euthanasia is that it should be clearly repudiated.

2 Non-Voluntary Euthanasia

Non-voluntary euthanasia is an issue for doctors, because there are people whom we think may have lives worse than death, but who are not in a position to express any decision of their own on this. Babies born with terrible abnormalities are an example which we have already discussed. Other are people, usually adults, who would normally be able to decide such things for themselves, but whose disorder either prevents this or at least prevents them expressing any decision. They may be so senile that they cannot understand the question, or totally paralysed, or, like the person mentioned by Mrs Drewery, blind and deaf, and so out of communication with us.

There are two central problems here: When, if ever, is it justifiable to conclude that someone's life is not worth living? And, if we do think someone's life is not worth living, what should our policy be? There is a range of alternatives between the two extremes of killing and of making maximum efforts to save life.

3 Lives Not Worth Living

As suggested in Chapter 12, there is no adequate test for deciding the point at which someone's life is not worth living. Any general formula seems either too indeterminate or too contentious, or both. What is crucial is how much the person himself gets out of life, and, where he is not in a position to express a view on this himself, the least unsatisfactory test is to ask what one would choose for oneself: would I choose death rather than have that sort of life?

This, while still contentious, is less so than a formula mentioning particular degrees of pain or kinds of handicap. It is unsatisfactorily indeterminate, because the thought experiment required will not lead to everyone giving the same answer, and in some cases life of a certain kind may be so difficult to imagine that many of us will not feel confident about any answer. Part of the problem is factual uncertainty. (Just how painful is such and such a kind of cancer? How much does a certain analgesic remove pain and how much does it merely damp down the expression of pain?) Part of the problem is more theoretical: when I put myself in someone else's place, how much of *me* should I put there? I would rather live without hands than die, but a friend whose main activities are painting and music lived through the blitz concerned much more about her hands being blown off than about being killed. If I had to put myself in her place, I would have to eliminate those of my preferences that are known to differ from hers, as well as any that seem highly personal to me. There seem real difficulties about knowing where to draw the boundary between those preferences I take with me in the thought experiment and those I leave behind.

These difficulties are serious, and the proposed test will not always lead to agreement. But, as suggested in Chapter 12, there seems no less unsatisfactory test. And there will sometimes be some independent evidence. If most other informed people doing the thought experiment disagree with my answer, this will be a reason for thinking that I have been biased by preferences peculiar to me. General unanimity, on the other hand, will strengthen confidence in such a judgement: if nearly everyone has a certain preference, this gives us a reason for thinking that the person in question would have it. Other evidence may come from the actual choices of people able to make them in similar situations. If people with a certain severe handicap have a very high suicide rate this is some evidence one way. If they do not, this is some evidence the other way. The same is true of the

193

suicide rates of doctors (who may be supposed to be well informed) when they know they have some illness.

But such evidence is at best inconclusive, and the choices of those able to make them will usually bear only obliquely on someone in a state where he either cannot reach or cannot express a decision. Obviously there is a strong case for extreme caution in judging that someone would, if able to choose, prefer to be dead, as there is a risk of being wrong. But it should be remembered that the opposite view may also be wrong, and just as disastrously so. Some of us would rather run a risk of being dead than the same degree of risk of being for years unable to communicate with anyone.

It is mainly with people in their terminal illness that this is a live issue. If Dr Saunders is right, the problem could be virtually eliminated, at least in the case of terminal cancer patients, by using the appropriate methods of controlling pain. But, where pain is not so successfully controlled, the fact that it *could* be is not much comfort to the patient, and it may still be that his life is so painful that death would be preferable. And, in cases of people totally unable to communicate or be communicated with, whether because of paralysis or the failure of various senses, the important thing is not physical pain, but loneliness, claustrophobia and boredom to the point of madness.

4 The Alternatives

Where someone is not able to express his own view about being alive or dead, it may sometimes happen that we think that his life is not worth living. (Any confidence in this will certainly not be justified unless we have both considered any available information with any bearing on the question and discussed it with other people.) But, where we hold this opinion with reasonable confidence, we have the question of what course of action to take or support. The first question must be whether there is anything which can be done to make his life worth living: in the case of a fatal illness, this is the question prompted by the remark of Dr Saunders that euthanasia 'should be unnecessary and is an admission of defeat'. But if his life cannot be improved to the point where we alter our view that it is not worth living, there are various alternatives. The main ones are:

(i) Taking all possible steps to preserve life.

(ii) Taking all 'ordinary' steps to preserve life, but not using extraordinary' means.

(iii) Not killing, but taking no steps to preserve life.

(iv) An act which, while not intended to kill, has death as a foreseen consequence.

(v) A deliberate act of killing.

I shall assume here that we can reject the strongest life-saving policy, which would require us to use not merely all 'ordinary' means, but all possible means for saving someone's life where we judge that it is not worth living. This strongest policy is one which is not widely thought obligatory even in cases where the person's life is worth living: other claims on doctors' time and lack of money are normally thought to set limits to the steps that can be required of people to save lives. No doubt we have not yet thought clearly enough on the question how much money we should as a society be prepared to spend on saving lives, but, without adopting the no trade-off view, we cannot reject financial limitations altogether. And acceptance of any such constraints in the case of people whose lives are worth living makes rejection of them in the cases under discussion totally perverse. For this reason, most of those who think that in such cases we ought still to try to preserve life make use of the distinction between ordinary and extraordinary means.

5 Ordinary and Extraordinary Means

The distinction drawn between ordinary and extraordinary means of saving life is not based on the line between what is and is not medically orthodox, but on a cluster of features clearly supposed to be relevant to the question: do the likely results justify the drawbacks of the methods?

In discussions of this distinction, aspects of the means relevant to whether or not they are extraordinary are said to be the degree to which they are expensive, unusual, difficult, painful or dangerous. And the extent to which the outcome is satisfactory is also thought relevant to assessing the 'ordinariness' of the means: it is sometimes suggested that, where the means have many of the drawbacks listed, they are not ordinary if their outcome is to leave the patient severely disabled or a heavy burden on his family.

The trouble with this distinction (whatever its virtues as a rough-and-ready rule for doctors) is that it tries to do too much at once. The decision about the 'ordinariness' of the means involves assessing how worth-while the life saved will be, assessing the side-effects on the family and the cost in effort and money, and then in the light of all this making an overall assessment of the desirability of the life-saving project. So a stand has to be taken on a number of the largest questions about relative priorities before an answer can be given about ordinariness. It is clear both that there is much room for disagreement about answers here and that to present this cluster of questions as though they were a single one, and almost a technical one concerning 'means' at that, is highly misleading.

The confusion of thought involved in this way of presenting the questions can be seen by looking at those of the factors usually cited that really are to do with the means. We are supposed to assess the extent to which the means are expensive, unusual, difficult, painful or dangerous. The obvious question is what 'unusual' is doing in this list. It seems either redundant or undesirable. For, if the unusual treatment is expensive, difficult, painful or dangerous, we can object to it already on those grounds. But where an effective treatment is cheap, easy, painless and risk-free, only someone whose conventionality verges on dementia will object to it because of its being unusual.

Those who ask whether the outcome will be a high enough chance of a life good enough to justify the pain, or the cost in time, effort or money involved in some life-saving procedure, are asking the unavoidable and central question. What

196

is important is to face this as involving decisions about priorities, and not to slur it over in a way which implies that the answer depends on how often the techniques are used.

6 Not Prolonging Dying

When someone has an illness from which he has no hope of recovering and which is bound to kill him soon, it is often suggested that medical intervention which goes beyond easing his pain or distress is not saving life but 'prolonging the act of dying'. It is because the period of lingering on in such a state is thought not worth having that this description carries an implied or explicit criticism. For, in other circumstances, we think it worth postponing death, even if only for a few days or weeks.

Where we think someone's life is not worth living and he is beyond expressing a view, it is hard to see what case there can be (apart from possible side-effects) for taking *any* steps to postpone his death. This is what is half conceded in the small print of the literature on ordinary and extraordinary means, when the kind of life that will be saved is allowed to be relevant.

The increased power of medical techniques means that it is often possible to keep fatally ill patients alive much longer, and sometimes indefinitely, in states which few can really think are preferable to death. This changed technical situation has, in the view of many doctors, transformed the moral question about euthanasia. It is said that, instead of being the 'yes' or 'no' question it used to be ('Is it right to kill someone to spare him this degree of misery?'), the problem has become one of degree: when is it right to withdraw the medical intervention which is holding back death?

The view that the moral questions have been utterly changed is exaggerated. For the central issues are the same: does this person have a life that is worth living? Does this kind of life justify the effort that is going into preserving it, and the effects on other people that its preservation is having? But the technical changes have made one aspect more acute. Because prolonging

197

life in terminal illness is something we can do more often and for longer, a policy of doing so where possible will have a much greater impact on the community now than it would have done once. The diversion of funds and of doctors' energies into this would, if taken to its extreme, have calamitous effects elsewhere. And for this reason the pressure to reach a decision whether a life is worth preserving is much more obvious.

7 An Assessment of the Alternatives

Let us look again at the main alternative policies available in a situation of this kind where we think that the person will not have a life worth living.

If for the moment we ignore possible side-effects, it is clear that there is no case for taking any positive steps to prolong life. The autonomy issue does not arise, since we do not know of any preference the person himself has, and where the life is not worth living the other direct argument for life-preservation collapses. So, unless there are strong arguments based on side-effects, we can rule out taking all possible steps to preserve life and equally rule out taking any steps at all, 'ordinary' or otherwise.

We then have to choose between the other three policies. There is the 'neutral' policy: not performing any act that will either postpone or hasten death. There is the 'double effect' policy of performing an act with some other object, such as the relief of pain, which will also predictably speed up death. There is finally the possibility of an intentional act of killing.

The neutral policy will obviously appeal to supporters of the acts and omissions doctrine. But there are circumstances in which even those of us who reject that doctrine will be justified in pursuing the neutral policy. This will be right in cases where death will come rapidly in any case, so that any positive intervention would make very little difference, or where it is of no importance how soon death comes. Where someone's life is not worth living because of great distress, the rapidity of death will be important, but from his own point of view the time of death will not matter in cases where the patient is in a coma. Even in the case of unconscious patients, the distress a lingering death causes to their family will normally be a reason for thinking an accelerated death desirable. It may be unpleasant for doctors and nurses to take part in a positive act which will speed up death, and this is a factor pulling the other way. But, apart from this, the case for the neutral policy seems powerful only where death is not necessary as an escape from distress and where there is no serious burden imposed on friends and family by a slower death.

In cases where there are reasons sufficient to justify departing from the neutral policy and speeding up death, how should we decide between the 'double effect' policy and intentional killing? Put like this, the question is odd. For we cannot aim at death via the double effect policy, as the whole point of the use of double effect in these contexts is that the death is foreseen but not aimed at. The aim is the relief of pain, and death is the foreseen but unintended by-product of the medical means used. Reasons were given in Chapter 6 for rejecting the double effect doctrine. But it may be that, just as the neutral policy can sometimes be defended without invoking the acts and omissions doctrine, so a 'double effect' policy can sometimes be justifiable without appealing to the doctrine of double effect. This 'double effect' policy would be one of bringing about death by a means which also had some other desirable effect: perhaps stepping up the dose of some drug knowing that this will both knock out pain and speed up death. To do this need not involve the intellectually dubious rigmarole of those who really hold the double effect doctrine: saying that one of these consequences is intended while the other is not. And, where it is possible to follow this policy, it has the advantage of perhaps being less distressing to the person who has to carry it out. For even someone thoroughly clear-headed about these matters may feel an emotional revulsion against an 'undiluted' act of killing, which would be reduced if the act also relieved pain. The 'double effect' policy also has a blurring quality which makes prose-

199

cution less likely than in the case of an act with the un-ambiguous aim of speeding death.

These are good reasons for normally preferring an act with such a double effect to an undiluted act of killing. But what of cases where this choice is not available? A non-medical instance was that of the man inescapably trapped in a burning lorry who asked to be shot rather than endure being burnt to death. (Even the most sophistical stretching and squeezing of concepts could scarcely make it plausible that such a shooting had death as merely a foreseen and unintended consequence. Or, if concepts are as malleable as this, the doctrine of double effect rules out nothing.) A medical case would be either where the question of pain relief did not arise, or where it was possible to relieve pain without death, but where the person's life would be at such a low level of consciousness as to be not worth living.

In such cases, there are obvious arguments for an intentional and undiluted act of killing. The alternative may impose too much suffering on the person whose life is in question (the lorry driver being burnt to death) or on other people involved (such as the family of a patient kept in a semi-comatose state in hospital for years). Many people have such revulsion against an act of killing that we should not rush in to rebuke those who cannot bring themselves to kill in such cases. And this reluctance to kill is one defence against slipping into a far more bloody kind of world, a defence we should hesitate to weaken. But, when this has been said, it should also be said that in these rare cases the undiluted act of killing may not be a wrong act, but an act of a decent and generous person. To shoot the lorry driver is an appalling thing for a passer-by to have to do, arousing deep revulsion and possibly involving a risk of prosecution. We should respect rather than condemn someone who manages to do it.

8 Side-Effects: Franz Stangl

Once there are grounds for thinking someone would be better off dead, the argument seems to glide disturbingly smoothly towards the conclusion that undiluted killing is right where weaker policies fail to bring about the same result. I do not wish to retreat from this view, but one widespread anxiety must be mentioned.

Since the Second World War, no one can write with the degree of sympathy shown here for speeding up death without being haunted by the Nazi experience. We know that the extermination camps had their beginnings in the euthanasia programme, and that Franz Stangl, the commandant of Treblinka, and many of those under him, came from running that programme.[1]

The Nazi euthanasia programme was not carried out by people with the outlook advocated here, and Franz Stangl was not the kind of person you might easily find working for the National Health Service. In the context of the attitudes that prevail among doctors in England now, fears that a policy of switching off the respirator more often and sooner might start a slide towards extermination camps are bound to seem a bit farfetched. But we cannot totally dismiss the anxieties. There were doctors who disgraced their profession in the Nazi camps, and people who could be induced to behave as they did must exist anywhere. The question is: given the case which exists in some circumstances for deliberately terminating life where the person is not in a position to request it, can we act on this without contributing towards attitudes of indifference or worse towards killing in less justifiable situations? Pessimism here seems hard to reconcile with any knowledge of the deeply ingrained attitudes of most doctors and nurses. There is a widespread reluctance to kill, and much awareness of the difficulty of knowing that someone's life is not worth living. Any profession contains

1. Cf. Gitta Sereny: *Into That Darkness: From Mercy Killing to Mass Murder*, London, 1974.

some people who are callous, unscrupulous or too willing to obey evil orders of the established authorities. The lesson of the German experience is a political one: not to allow power to pass to a government under which that kind of doctor will be at home. We need not draw the over-simple moral that, because of what the Nazis did, doctors should be encouraged to leave the respirator on beyond the point where life is worth-while.

Chapter 16 Numbers

I implied that 18,000 successful detections of early tuberculosis might be worth the risk of 20 more deaths from leukaemia, just as it is worth slaughtering 100 cattle to save the rest from foot and mouth disease. This kind of calculation may seem almost indecent in peacetime, although in wartime we should be shocked if campaigns were planned without reckoning the deaths it would cost to win a battle.

Lord Adrian: *Priorities in Medical Responsibility, Proceedings of the Royal Society of Medicine*, 1963

Deterrence theorists sometimes seem to suggest that the 'utility' of human life is linear. One wonders if the difference between 28,654,833 deaths and 28,654,832 deaths is really as morally significant as the difference between one death and none, or if saving a few lives in a war which has taken millions is a very great contribution.

Phillip Green: *Deadly Logic*, Ohio, 1966

What is the moral context in which we should see those killed by violence? There exists a view that one violent death has the same moral value as a thousand or a million deaths. Presumably 'moral value', in this view, is kept in jars of concentrated essence on the shelves of philosophers, or in the divine pantry. The killer cannot add to his sin by committing more than one murder. However, every *victim* of murder would claim, if he could, that his death had a separate moral value.

Gil Elliot: *The Twentieth Century Book of the Dead*, London, 1972

Two famous nineteenth-century court cases illustrate moral problems where some lives can only be saved by sacrificing others. In the case of *U.S.* v. *Holmes* (1842), the defendant was a member of a ship's crew in an overcrowded lifeboat, who obeyed the orders of the mate and helped to throw overboard sixteen male passengers. The judge, directing the jury to convict him on the charge of manslaughter, said that the first people to be sacrificed should have been chosen by lot.

In the other case, *R.* v. *Dudley* (1884), it was found that shipwrecked sailors who killed a cabin boy for food were guilty of murder, despite the likelihood that, without this act of cannibalism, all would have died, with the already weakened cabin boy probably dying first.

Even if moral views influence such decisions, the findings of the courts concern legality rather than ethics. But obvious moral questions are raised. Is it ever right to kill someone in order to save other lives? Does it make a difference if the person is killed outright, as in the Dudley case, or is merely thrown overboard to an overwhelmingly probable death? Does morality demand that the lives of passengers be given priority over those of sailors, or that women and children have priority over men? Does it make a moral difference if the victims are chosen by lot? Is it relevant that the victim would die anyway, or would die first?

These rather repellent cases dramatize problems which have to be taken seriously in less extreme situations. Although few of us will ever have to decide for or against throwing someone out of a lifeboat, decisions are often taken in our name as to who shall live and who shall die. There are choices to be made about the allocation of scarce medical resources: some drugs are in short supply; we lack facilities to give intensive care to all whose lives might be saved; there are shortages of transplant donors. There are sometimes choices for doctors between the life of the woman in labour and her baby. There are questions of the morality of medical experiments that risk the lives of patients in the hope of developing techniques that may save more lives in future. How should we decide which classes of people to conscript into the army during a war? We have to decide whether to spend more money on road safety or more on the National Health Service. Even a decision as to which streets in a town should take most of the traffic involves placing some lives at greater risk than others.

The two court cases pose the problems peculiarly starkly because they involve the killing or throwing overboard of identifiable people in order to improve the chances of survival of other identifiable people. Some of the other choices mentioned seem less stark for several reasons. They are in general cases of deciding whom to allow to die, rather than whom to kill. Some of them are choices between unknown people. And some of them are choices which involve allocating different probabilities of death rather than certain death. It is psychologically easier for a town planner to decide against installing some traffic lights, knowing that someone may get killed as a result, than it would be for the same man in a lifeboat to throw a person back into the sea. But these differences should not obscure the fact that which particular people will die depends upon the medical or social choices made. This is clear when scarce medical resources are being allocated and the other choices mentioned are in this respect the same. Are there any general principles to guide these choices?

1 Choices in Ignorance

Normally, life and death choices between people are made with some knowledge about the people concerned. When a drug in short supply is being allocated, at least the medical histories of the potential recipients are known. When planners are deciding which streets should have heavy traffic, they are at least in a position to know which streets have schools or old people's homes. But if we imagine a case of idealized simplicity, where the choice is between the lives of two people about whom we know nothing át all, it is obvious that the choice must be random. And the same is true where we have to choose to save one life out of a larger sample than two. So long as we really know nothing about the people, not even names, sexes or ages, we cannot but choose randomly.

The problems start when we turn back to real situations where we have some knowledge. One question takes priority over others. Are we ever justified in departing from the nearest approximation to random choice? There is a widespread and understandable view that it is objectionable for someone to make God-like choices between different people's lives on the basis of what he knows about them. On this view we ought to allocate scarce life-saving resources randomly, or else have a minimum intervention policy such as allocating them on a 'first come, first served' basis. Random allocation is not the same as a minimum intervention policy, as positive steps can be taken to ensure greater randomness than would result from letting 'nature' take its course. Minimum intervention might favour those who live near a major teaching hospital, while random allocation on a national basis would not. Having noted this difference, I shall not pursue it, but will in an over-simplified way treat these policies as being approximately the same. I shall argue that sometimes we ought to depart from such policies. The type of case to be considered in this chapter is where the argument is easiest: where a departure from randomness leads to greater numbers of lives saved.

2 The Maximizing Policy

Other things being equal, we ought to intervene in a non-random way if the result will be a smaller loss of life. This commits us to what is already the normal policy of doctors and others allocating scarce life-saving equipment: to take some account of the probability of a treatment's success with different people. Suppose there is a drug in short supply that stands a good chance of curing a fatal disease in carefully selected patients, but only a rather poor chance with the average sufferer from the disease. To give it on a 'first come, first served' basis is virtually certain to save fewer lives than to give it to patients selected on the basis of probable responsiveness. It is not being suggested that numbers of lives saved should be the only factor to be considered, but that it would be wrong to think that numbers need be of no importance.

This involves rejecting both an extreme and a moderate belief in the irrelevance of numbers. The extreme belief is that it is wrong to decide against the life of one person in order to save another even if non-intervention will result in the death of both. This extreme belief may have been combined with the acts and omissions doctrine in what was, at least at one time, part of the official Catholic view of abortion. A Decree of the Holy Office of 5 May 1902 condemned the abortion of a foetus growing outside the uterus, for example in the Fallopian tube. Failure to abort would result in both mother and foetus dying.

The more moderate belief in the irrelevance of numbers is that, while it is important that someone should be saved, we need not think it morally preferable to save a larger number rather than a smaller number of people. This view has been stated clearly by G.E.M. Anscombe.[1] She cites a case where a lot of people are stranded on a rock, and a single person is stranded on another rock. If, for some reason, there is only time to go to one of these rocks on a rescue mission, ought I to go to the one with more people?

G.E.M. Anscombe says that, while the larger numbers may weigh with me as a good reason for going to that rock, there is nothing wrong with choosing to rescue the single person instead. Her argument for this is to say that the others have no cause for complaint. 'They are not injured unless help that was owing to them was withheld. There was the boat that could have helped them; but it was not left idle; no, it went to save the other one. What is the accusation that each of them can make? What wrong can he claim has been done him? None whatever: unless the preference signalizes some ignoble contempt.' Professor Anscombe goes on to say that a man 'doesn't act badly if he uses his resources to save X, or X, Y and Z, *for no bad reason*,

1. G.E.M. Anscombe: 'Who is Wronged?', *The Oxford Review*, 1967.

and is not affected by the consideration that he could save a larger number of people. For, once more: who can say he is wronged? And if no one is wronged, how does the rescuer commit any wrong?'

This doctrine, that numbers of lives saved need not be of any moral importance, has some odd consequences. Sometimes when an aircraft is about to crash, the pilot aims to hit the least densely populated piece of ground he can reach. But, according to the Anscombe view, there is nothing wrong with a quite different policy. So long as *someone* will be killed whichever building he hits, there is nothing wrong with a pilot choosing to crash into a crowded hospital in order to save the life of the solitary caretaker in the warehouse next to it. The only escape from this consequence seems to be to say that aiming for the warehouse leads to a higher chance of no one being killed. But in the many cases where some loss of life is for practical purposes certain, this escape is not open.

And the mention of such a possible escape brings out one of the moral assumptions underlying the moderate belief in the irrelevance of numbers. Professor Anscombe thinks we should always save one life rather than no lives, but that it is acceptable to save one life rather than two. This presupposes either that the rightness of saving a life has nothing to do with its desirable outcome, or the unstated belief that the time at which someone's life is in jeopardy is relevant to the moral importance of saving it. One of these curious assumptions is a necessary feature of the position, as we can see from consideration of some more people stranded on rocks.

Suppose there are two rocks, and on Monday the lifeboatman hears that A and B are stranded, one on each rock. He has only time to go to one rock before both are submerged by the tide. Neither rock is harder to reach than the other. He knows nothing about the identity of either A or B. Here we might all agree that it is morally indifferent which rock he goes to. Now suppose that on the next day, Tuesday, a third person, C, is stranded on one of the two rocks. We may all agree that it is of some moral importance that the lifeboatman should go and rescue him. But, according to the Anscombe view, if C had instead been stranded with either A or B on Monday, the prospect of saving him as well as one of the others need not have been considered of any moral importance at all. This moderate view of the irrelevance of numbers seems linked to the unacceptable view that saving lives consecutively is more worth-while than saving lives simultaneously. (The alternative assumption is that the rightness of saving a life has nothing to do with any value placed on the life which is saved.)

The policy being defended here, that, other things being equal, we ought always to prefer to save a larger to a smaller number of people, can be called the maximizing policy. Obviously the acceptability to different people of a maximizing policy in life-saving operations will depend a lot on the interpretation of 'other things being equal'. One difference of interpretation is so central that it is worth making explicit at once. Many people would be prepared to accept what might be called a weak maximizing policy. According to this, it is right to save the larger number of stranded people or to be guided by numbers of lives expected to be saved when originally allocating scarce medical resources. But it is not right to throw out someone already in a lifeboat to make room for someone with a better chance of survival, nor is it right to remove someone with poor prospects from intensive care in order to treat someone with better prospects, even if such acts would result in more lives saved. The strong maximizing policy, on the other hand, allows positive interventions of the kind the weak policy rules out.

Those who accept the acts and omissions doctrine are likely, if they accept a maximizing policy at all, to hold a weak one on principle. Those of us who reject the acts and omissions doctrine will decide between the two versions in any particular case by trying to weigh up the balance of advantages. In the case of medical shortages, it will be necessary to estimate how many extra lives would be saved by a strong rather than a weak policy, but to balance this against the likely bad side-effects of adopting the strong one. Among these would be the awfulness for a patient who thought his life was saved being disappointed, the appalling task for a doctor of breaking the news to the patient and later removing his treatment, and the insecurity felt by patients having treatment when they heard about the strong policy.

Those who find non-random acts of choice between people's lives totally unacceptable will reject a maximizing policy. But, even for those of us who accept a maximizing policy, there is some room for debate about what, if any, are the other aims, as well as minimizing loss of life, which should influence us in these decisions.

3 Certain Death for a Known Person and 'Statistical' Death

Guido Calabresi has drawn attention to the discrepancy between what society will sometimes spend on saving the life of a known person in peril and what it will spend to reduce the future level of fatal accidents.[2] He takes the case of a trapped coal-miner, and contrasts the effort and expense that are poured out to rescue him with the failure to abolish dangerous level crossings, which would save more lives for the amount spent.

Calabresi considers the possible charge of irrationality which could be made against this bias in favour of the known person at risk, but suggests that the bias can be defended. He argues:

We are committed to 'humanism', to the dignity of the individual, and to human life. Much of the fabric of our society depends on our belief in this commitment, as do most of our traditional and 'cherished' liberties. Accident law indicates that our commitment to human life is not, in fact, so great as we say it is; that our commitment to life-destroying material progress and comfort is greater. But this fact merely accentuates our need to make a bow in the direction of our commitment to the sanctity of human life (wherever we can do so at a reasonable total cost). It also accentuates our

2. Guido Calabresi: ' Reflections on Medical Experimentation in Humans ', in Paul A. Freund (ed.): *Experimentation on Human Subjects*, London, 1972.

need to reject any societal decisions that too blatantly contradict this commitment. Like 'free will', it may be less important that this commitment be total than that we believe it to be there. Perhaps it is for these reasons that we save the man trapped in the coalmine. After all, the event is dramatic; the cost, though great, is unusual; and the effect in reaffirming our belief in the sanctity of life is enormous. The effect of such an act in maintaining the many societal values that depend on the dignity of the individual is worth the cost.

The difficulty with this defence is that it suggests that the best way of 'reaffirming our belief in the sanctity of life' is by adopting a policy which saves fewer lives than we could save for the same trouble and expense. There seems something unserious about a commitment best demonstrated in such a paradoxical way. Calabresi's approach involves people responding to image and publicity rather than reality. There must be either a division between the ruled and the manipulative rulers or else an act of collective self-deception by society as a whole. The avoidance of a sufficiently great catastrophe might perhaps justify either of these states of affairs. But what are the reasons for thinking that our belief in 'the dignity of the individual' depends on this intellectual sleight of hand? The suggestion seems to be that social and moral collapse would follow the declared government adoption of a maximizing policy, with known and unknown persons having equal weight. But where is the evidence for this?

It is only a contingent fact that preference for known over unknown lives is usually associated with giving priority to present over future peril. There could be a case where a mixture of known and unknown people are at risk at the same time. If two trawlers in a fishing fleet both send an S.O.S. message over the radio, but only one message includes the names of captain and crew, it seems implausible that the ship with the named crew should have moral priority in the rescue operation.

In understanding the bias in favour of the trapped miner over 'statistical' lives, we need to disentangle various different elements. Time bias often comes in, because the 'statistical' lives will usually be saved in the future. There is our lack of

211

emotional response to the fate of people about whom nothing is known: our knowledge of the trapped miner can vary from mere knowledge of his name to fairly detailed descriptions of what sort of person he is with corresponding increases in emotional response. Also there are the desperately anxious members of his family, perhaps seen on television, and we have a very strong desire that their nightmare should end happily. We find it much harder to envisage the reaction of the families as yet unknown to us when the 'statistical' lives are lost. But all these variations in emotional response reflect our limitations rather than any differences that can readily be defended as morally important. Suppose we rescue the coal-miner, but the next year he becomes one of the 'statistical' lives claimed by the dangerous level crossings we chose not to abolish? The loss to him and his family is no less serious because the rest of us are no longer involved. (To say that our difference of response is a limitation is not to say that the dehumanizing alternative, where we would not care about the miner and his family, would be better. The limitation in our nature is not that we do care about the near and known, but that we cannot care about the distant and unknown people at risk.) We perhaps cannot very much alter the limitations of our sympathies, but we need not use these limitations as an argument for saying that a policy of relatively downgrading 'statistical' lives is morally right.

There is a different kind of consideration that may operate in support of saving known lives. This relates to a preference many of us have where our own life is at stake. Anatol Rapoport recounts a case of air crews on high-risk missions in the Second World War. At a certain place, a pilot's chances of surviving his thirty bombing missions were only one in four. It was calculated that one-way missions, by reducing the fuel load, could increase the load of bombs, so that only half the pilots need fly. Selection would be by lot, with half the pilots escaping altogether and half going to certain death. On this system, fatalities would be halved, but it was not adopted. Obviously there could be various reasons for not adopting the system, including the possibility that those who drew lots for certain death would not carry out the order. But there is also an extreme horror which most of us have at the thought of being in a position where we can see certain death ahead. The condemned cell is a lot of the awfulness of capital punishment. Many of us would be extremely reluctant to opt for the one-way mission system, despite the halving of the risk of death. Even those of us who would, reluctantly, opt for the system of one-way missions would be prepared to accept *some* additional risk of death in preference to risking a condemned-cell situation, with a waiting period during which certain death could be anticipated. And, if we have this trade-off in our preferences where our own lives are at risk, it seems right to give weight to the similar attitudes of others when we are thinking about social policy.

But this line of thought does not go far to justify the discrepancy between our efforts to save known lives and our efforts to save 'statistical' lives. It suggests that we ought to give some additional weight to avoiding slow death rather than sudden and unexpected death. If people are usually killed instantly on the dangerous level crossings, avoiding a level-crossing death is (a bit) less important than rescuing the trapped miner. But often the contrast between known and 'statistical' lives involves no discrepancy of this sort. The choice may be between rescuing a trapped miner now and spending the money on an improved warning system in the mine, so that fewer miners will be trapped in future. Then the condemned-cell aspect counts on both sides and is no longer an argument against a maximizing policy.

4 Medical Experiments

In order to test the effects of a possible new method of treatment on people with an illness, it is necessary to give it to some and withhold it from others. General physiological or pharmacological theories, together with the results of animal trials, will often give a fairly good idea of the benefits and risks to be expected. But, in advance of human trials, such knowledge is inconclusive. The moral problems raised by this are obvious. In the first human trials with a new drug, the doctor administering it is imposing some degree of risk on those given it, and, what is less often discussed, is depriving the control group of a possible cure. Advances which benefit succeeding generations of patients depend on some risks being taken. It may seem that the ethics of medical experiments are a simple case of the conflict between known and 'statistical' lives. This is an element of the problem, but only one.

In one way all medical treatment should be experimental, in that the doctor should monitor its effects and be alert to the possibility that a particular case may reveal that some modification is required to the accepted view of the value of a treatment. But the moral problems arise only where embarking on or withholding a course of treatment can plausibly be thought to involve some increased risk of harm to the patient. This can be either the giving of a treatment as yet untried in humans or withholding a venerable form of treatment in an attempt to establish what its effects really are.

In the case of a new treatment, trying it should obviously be ruled out where there is not sufficient evidence (from animal studies, etc.) to suggest that it is unlikely to have seriously harmful bad effects, and that it is at least reasonably likely to be an effective treatment. (The imprecision of these phrases is deliberate.) It should also be uncontroversial that a trial can be ruled out when it is too poorly designed to provide results clear enough to be useful. But when these minimal requirements have been satisfied, the difficult problems arise.

Suppose some new drug seems likely to be valuable in treating a serious illness, but there is reason to believe it will require modification to eliminate harmful side-effects. And suppose there is no way of being certain what, if any, the harmful side-effects will be until clinical trials have taken place. What principles should guide us here? Is the crucial thing that the doctor should only carry out an experiment which he would be prepared to have carried out on himself if he were in the patient's situation? Is it ever right to apply a medical technique to a patient purely for the sake of research, without there being any serious possibility of direct benefit to him?

The problems raised by these questions are enormous, and they cannot be adequately discussed here. I am merely concerned to show that some familiar safeguards are not obliterated by a qualified adoption of a maximizing policy. These safeguards are that doctors should observe at least the following restrictions:

(a) *Informed consent:* The patient should be fully informed about the likely risks and benefits, and should decide, without any pressure being brought to bear, whether or not he consents to the procedure. Patients not in a position to give informed consent (children, or people who are senile or of subnormal intelligence) should be used as subjects for an experiment only if there is no possibility of asking for participants from among those in a position to give consent (for instance a drug which may cure senility, or a disorder confined to children). Those not capable of giving consent should not be used as subjects simply because all those asked for consent have refused it. Groups of people under various kinds of duress, such as prison inmates, should never be used, because of the requirement that the consent is given free from any kind of pressure.

(b) *The doctor's own judgement:* The doctor should not ask the patient to submit to any medical procedure which he would not himself be prepared to submit to in similar circumstances.

The point of the second requirement, involving the doctor's own judgement, is to remedy some of the deficiencies of the informed-consent requirement. Patients will often, even after careful explanation, have only a hazy grasp of the facts, and most of us find it hard to make vivid to ourselves different probabilities of risk or benefit. The likelihood that patients will sometimes consent without clear-headed understanding and deliberation makes further safeguards necessary, and the one about the doctor's own judgement, although itself a fallible test, is an obvious requirement. (What would we think if we gave our consent to some treatment and then in the course of it

215

discovered that the doctor would not dream of consenting to it himself in the same circumstances?)

These safeguards, which may need supplementing by others, might at first sight seem inconsistent with any kind of maximizing policy or with the attempt to eliminate the habitual downgrading of 'statistical' lives relative to known people at risk. But it is possible, starting from the assumption that the interests of everyone who has or will have a certain illness should be thought of equal importance, to defend rough and ready rules which are biased towards the interests of the person who is at present the patient. No doubt some of the projects ruled out by observing these safeguards would have contributed to medical progress, and so, in ruling them out, we are denying some people future escape from illness and even death. But the risk to the known person is often clearer than the future benefit, and there is also the possibility that a cure may be discovered by some technique not available to us yet, and so make our proposed experiment superfluous. There is such temptation to unfounded optimism in scientific research, and such temptation to exaggerate the importance of one's own line of investigation, that rules emphasizing the consent and interests of the present patient are needed to counteract these tendencies. Also, the effect on patients' attitudes towards hospitals and doctors needs to be taken into account, and a known code of practice of this kind gives ground for confidence unobtainable by other means.

The aim is to have the maximum curing of illness and saving of life, both now and in the future. But this is a matter where allowing the enthusiastic researcher unrestricted appeal to that aim in defending medical experiments would be likely to be self-defeating. For that reason, among others, the safeguards are necessary.

Chapter 17   Choices Between People

In Glasgow there was still a small neurosurgical unit with four
consultant neurosurgeons for 3.8 million people. They did not
like exercising the 'arrogance' of saying who would or would
not have the superlative treatment which it was obviously
possible to give to a few, but they must not delude themselves
into thinking that if they did not exercise the choice then no one
did. The decision to say 'no' could be passed 'down the line' but,
nevertheless, it was being exercised in the hospital by some
doctor. He did not necessarily think that these doctors were
arrogant in saying the cost of life was too great for the present
resources to bear. All would like to give the best sort of
treatment to all in need, but the amount of cases which were
being referred to neurosurgeons ...

Reported remarks of Mr Robert Tym, in discussion of *Severe
Head Injuries, Symposium on the Cost of Life, Proceedings of
the Royal Society of Medicine*, 1967

In one of the oldest haemodialysis laboratories in this country,
there are many potential beneficiaries of the machine who have
to be rejected. As I understand the procedure followed in that
laboratory, an anonymous committee of lay people who live in
the area make the decisions with physicians used primarily as
consultants. They take into consideration many things about
the patient such as his general health, his morality, his social
and family responsibilities, the part he plays in community life
and its economy, and many others.

Dr James Z. Appel: *Ethical and Legal Questions Posed by
Recent Advances in Medicine, Journal of the American Medical Association*, 1968

It is much easier to allow a board or an office or a profession to make decisions than it is to establish principles whose rational application will in fact yield just results. Moreover, the public acceptability of a life–death decision may depend on traditional deference to the discretion of the decision maker. The absence of a consensus on the principles to be applied may undermine acceptability once the principles of decision have been made explicit. Yet if the protection of the individual against arbitrariness and the rule of law rather than men is the mark of a civilized society, then the 'black box' that yields decisions unpredictably and uncomprehensively is tolerable only until society becomes sophisticated enough to generate rules to replace it.

from a note on *Scarce Medical Resources, Columbia Law Review*, 1969

1 Interventionism

An interventionist policy involves giving some people preference over others when their lives are at stake. There are various drawbacks to such a policy.

One is the desirability of a society without different grades of people. Those of us who dislike any kind of class system, and want a community where people think of themselves as equals, are likely to have doubts about any decision implying that one person's life is more worth saving than another, at least in all cases where we are sure that those concerned have lives worth living. And, even if we think that some people have more worth-while lives than others, we may recognize the strong utilitarian case against setting up inequalities of treatment based on our fallible judgements of this. The whole social climate is affected when some groups of people are not confident that their interests will be given the same weight as those of others. And with something so fundamental as the saving of life this effect may be especially strong. It was said at one time that in some hospitals people over sixty-five had on their identification labels the letters 'NTBR', indicating that in the event of breathing failure they were 'not to be resuscitated'. It needs little imagination to guess the effect on someone's morale of discovering what the letters on his label meant.

Another disadvantage of interventionism is the unpleasantness of making non-random choices between people's lives. Even deciding by lot must be fairly unpleasant, but it must be much more distressing to decide by making judgements about the value of the lives of different people. This could be made even worse if a patient or his desperate relations put emotional pressure on a doctor having to allocate scarce life-saving treatment. (Though this extra pressure could be eliminated by laying down rigid rules governing the choice, or by giving the decision to an anonymous committee.)

Another possible disadvantage is that it *may* be worse to die as the result of a reasoned decision that saving someone else is more important than it would be to die as the result of a random process. But some people might find the result easier to accept if it seemed justifiable. It is hard to know whether to give any weight to this factor.

Social policy is often discussed in ways that reflect the attractiveness of views that do not require us to weigh up very many considerations. In discussions of interventionism versus random choices between people, two kinds of over-simplification are attractive. There is a simplifying moral radicalism that completely overrides the drawbacks of interventionism, giving them no weight at all. There is also a simplifying moral conservatism that places what amounts to an infinite weight on the drawbacks and unconditionally rules out the possibility of interventionism ever being justified. The position adopted here differs from both of these: it is that the drawbacks of interventionism have to be weighed against the drawbacks of random choice. But the position stated at this level of generality has little content. It is necessary to discuss some of the possible criteria that could guide an interventionist policy in order to see what, if anything, is lost by keeping to random choices. Factors sometimes thought relevant include age, dependants, contribution to society, the quality of the person's own life and the person's 'moral' status.

2 Lives or Life-Years: The Relevance of Age

It is widely held that expectation of life is relevant to a choice between saving one life or another. In the lifeboat situation, many of us would prefer to rescue a normal person rather than someone who was in the late stages of a terminal illness. A young person would often be rescued in preference to someone in his nineties. In states with capital punishment, someone who was ill and in the condemned cell would probably not be given priority in the queue for scarce medical resources. Those of us who think that these preferences are right show that we are interested not merely in numbers of lives saved, but also in the period for which life is extended. If I rescue someone from drowning, but he is run over and killed an hour later, the brevity of the interval does not alter the fact that I saved his life. Those interested merely in numbers of lives saved, but not at all in time-span, think that there is as much value in postponing a death for ten minutes as in postponing it for ten years. This seems absurd.

If we think that expected length of life is relevant, should we adopt a simple time-span criterion? This would be to say that, other things being equal, we are not interested in numbers of lives saved, but rather in numbers of life-years saved. This has been advocated by Dr Donald Gould:

In the name of justice, as well as efficiency, we have got to adopt new methods of medical accounting. One such assesses the relative importance of threats to health in terms of the loss of life-years they cause. Calculations are based upon the assumption that all who survive their first perilous year ought then to live on to the age of 70 (any extra years are a bonus). In Denmark, for example, there are 50,000 deaths a year, but only 20,000 among citizens in the 1–70 bracket. These are the ones that count. The annual number of life-years lost in this group totals 264,000. Of these, 80,000 are lost because of accidents and suicides, 40,000 because of coronary heart disease, and 20,000 are due to lung disease. On the basis of these figures, a large proportion of the 'health' budget ought to be spent on preventing accidents and suicides and a lesser but still substantial amount on attempting to prevent and cure heart and lung disease. Much less would be spent on cancer, which is predominantly a disease of the latter half of life, and which therefore contributes relatively little to the total sum of life-years lost. Little would go towards providing kidney machines, and even less towards treating haemophiliacs. No money at all would be available for trying to prolong the life of a sick old man of 82.[1]

On this view, we would be committed to a general preference for saving younger people rather than older ones. In assessing such a policy, it is hard to separate differences of age from differences in the kind of life it is possible to live, and from side-effects. People of forty usually have a fuller life and more dependants than people of eighty; children are so important to their parents.

It has been argued in earlier chapters that the direct objections to killing relate both to the value of a worth-while life and to respect for people's autonomy. These factors are also relevant to decisions about saving lives. If we think it wrong to shorten a worth-while life, this implies the placing of some value on time span. But if we think it important that, as far as possible, people's desires to go on living should not be overridden, this implies the placing of some value on numbers of people saved. (And rules out Dr Gould's policy of spending *nothing at all* on saving a sick old man of eighty-two.)

If we choose to save one person for a predicted span of sixty years, rather than saving five people each for a predicted span of ten years, we have gained ten extra life-years at the cost of overriding the desires of four extra people. The two direct reasons for saving lives pull different ways here. Both factors ought to be given some weight, but I am unable to think of any

1. Donald Gould: 'Some Lives Cost Too Dear', *New Statesman*, November 1975.

general principle governing the trade-off between them. (Side-effects will often count in favour of saving the larger number of people, but that is another matter.)

3 Side-Effects

If there are two people whose lives are in question and we have to choose to save only one, the number of people dependent on them should be regarded as very important. If other things are equal, but one has no family and the other is the mother of several young children, the case against deciding between them randomly is a strong one. Since other things are equal, the choice would be random if dependants were left out of account. Refusal to depart from random choice when knowledge about their dependants is available is to place no value on avoiding the additional misery caused to the children if the mother is not the one saved. (Or it is to place some value on this, but so little that it does not outweigh the general drawbacks of interventionism.)

In a case like this, it seems perverse to allow the drawbacks of interventionism to outweigh the great loss to the children, particularly since one of the main drawbacks seems less serious here. A large part of the case against interventionism is the undesirability of creating a two-tier community, saying that we value some people more than others. This seems obviously objectionable if our preference is based on the belief that one of the people is nicer, more intelligent or morally superior to the other person. But the objection loses a lot of its force when the preference is justified by citing the interests of dependants rather than the merits of the person selected.

If we give some weight to the interests of dependants, should we take into account more generalized side-effects, such as the relative importance of the contributions to society made by different people? There are good grounds for rejecting this as a general policy. It is a truism that we have no agreed standard by which to measure people's relative contribution to society. How does a mother compare with a doctor or a research scientist or a coal-miner? Any list of jobs ranked in order of social value seems, at least at present, to be arbitrary and debatable. It also seems to introduce the offensive division of people into grades that we have seen to be one of the most serious disadvantages of interventionism.

But, while rejecting discrimination based on supposed social worth as a general policy, it would be wrong to rule out the possibility of exceptions in extreme cases. It seems doctrinaire to say that, if Winston Churchill in 1940 had been in the lifeboat situation, it would have been wrong to give him priority. (Or consider a case where we can prevent only one of two aircraft from crashing, and one contains most of the country's leading surgeons.) It does not seem fruitful to try here to draw a precise boundary round the exceptions. The arguments given suggest only that they should be very few.

4 Quality of Life

Should we be influenced in our choices between people by our estimates of the relative quality of their lives? In one hospital a man given intensive care turned out to be a tramp and a meths drinker, and some people wondered if it would have been better to have provided the care for someone else. But even here it is hard to be sure how much the implied judgement of the quality of the man's life was influenced by mere social distance. I know very little about meths drinkers, and those who know more may have good reason for thinking their lives to be unhappy. But, if the doubts were partly based on the fact that the man was a tramp, we ought to be very suspicious of them.

The less we sort people into different grades the better, especially given the fallibility of our judgements about the quality of people's lives. But again it seems doctrinaire to rule out the possibility of ever allowing weight to the sort of life the saved person can expect. If we accept that some people have lives so terrible as to be not worth living, it seems hard to deny the existence of a neighbouring grey area where a life may be worth

223

living but is less worth living than normal. It would clearly be absurd to give priority in life-saving to someone whose life is not worth living. Yet it is hard, without making an artificially sharp cut-off point, to accept this while refusing to be influenced in selection by the fact that someone is in a state only a little less bad.

The policy supported here is one of putting aside considerations of the quality of a person's life, except in cases where we enter the region where questions could be raised about whether his life is worth living. This policy again lacks precision. I doubt whether it is fruitful to look for greater precision while talking in these generalities. Only by a familiarity with detailed cases, which I lack, is anyone likely to work out more precise guidelines.

5 Moral Status

The most disturbing part of the quotation from Dr Appel at the start of this chapter was his report that a patient's morality might be taken into account when he was being considered as a candidate for scarce medical resources. An echo of this is to be found in the remarks on abortion, by Professor T.N.A. Jeffcoate, of the Department of Obstetrics and Gynaecology, University of Liverpool:[2]

If this is to be done with maximum safety, it has to be arranged at the earliest possible moment, so feckless girls and women with unwanted pregnancies have to be admitted as a matter of urgency, taking precedence over women anxiously waiting to have their prolapse, or other disability, cured. Is it right that the promiscuous girl, who has not troubled to practise contraception, should have priority over the decent married woman, who has been waiting perhaps twelve months for admission for investigation of sterility?

Is the unease about this just an irrational prejudice? There are some good reasons for thinking it is not.

2. In A. Clow (ed.): *Morals and Medicine*.

In the first place, deciding not to choose a person for treatment because of a judgement about his moral worth looks disconcertingly like a kind of reluctant but retributive capital punishment. There are obvious differences, but the similarity is that a life or death decision is made to depend on a person's desert. As well as familiar arguments against deciding such matters on the basis of desert (not *all* of which need be accepted) there are additional objections in this medical context which do not apply in cases of capital punishment. The question is not one of someone's desert being weighed up by considering whether or not he broke a law in the absence of recognized excusing conditions. Desert is assessed on the much more nebulous basis of a judgement of moral character. It seems highly unlikely that doctors will have enough information to make a judgement on someone's whole life, and even if they had a great deal of information a judgement of moral worth would still be a very difficult matter. With friends I have known closely for most of my life, I would find a demand that I should estimate their relative moral worth often not merely absurd, but hopelessly difficult. There is also the capriciousness of the choice: doctors are likely to vary in the moral standards they apply. There are none of the safeguards against unfairness that the law builds in where it is legal guilt that is in question. And it seems doubtful whether the application of moral criteria by doctors could fail to arouse justifiable resentment and bitterness.

We should reject moral evaluation of patients as a general basis of choice. But, perhaps even here, we should not be doctrinaire. Suppose there is one place in the intensive care unit, and two people in need of it are brought into the hospital. One is a seriously wounded bank robber and the other is a man who was equally seriously wounded when he heroically went to the aid of a policeman under fire from the bank robber. It seems intuitively preposterous that, with all other considerations equally balanced, we should toss a coin to decide between the two. But this feeling can be justified, both by the difference of desert between the men and by a general utilitarian argument based on the desirability that the risks of helping policemen should as far as possible be reduced relative to the risks of armed robbery. And, if we allow the difference of desert in this case, where the risk to life so directly results from the acts being judged, this is by no means the same as allowing general character evaluations by doctors treating natural disorders.

6 Theory and Practice

The theme of this discussion has been the complexity of these decisions between people's lives. (This is not the banal point that such decisions are difficult or distressing.) In the light of the reasons given earlier in this book for avoiding deaths (the undesirability of a worth-while life being shortened, respect for autonomy, and side-effects) various simplifications have been rejected. One is the refusal to allow interventionism at all, which has been rejected because our reasons for avoiding deaths are reasons also for preferring larger numbers of lives saved, and for giving some weight to such factors as age, dependants and quality of life. Another simplification rejected is that of a policy of thorough-going interventionism, giving automatic priority to people well qualified on these grounds. This has been rejected because of the drawbacks of interventionism, which should be taken account of by anyone who accepts that some weight should be given to undesirable side-effects.

The views expressed earlier about why killing is wrong commit anyone who accepts them to weighing up many conflicting considerations when making these choices between different lives. I have tried to lay down some guidelines in this chapter and the previous one. But it should be said that someone who shared the same theoretical position might give very different weightings to the various factors from those given here. But the possibility of these practical differences does not rob the theoretical moral position of content. The situation is like that in a different field of social policy whose principles have received more philosophical attention, that of punishment. From the fact that two utilitarians may disagree in their as-

226

sessment of the advantages and disadvantages of a penal policy, it does not follow that the theoretical issues between utilitarians and retributivists have no practical importance. To say that I would rather my local hospital was one where these decisions were taken on the lines suggested here, rather than those advocated by either Appel or Calabresi, is to say something which could be disagreed with by decent and rational people. But it is not to say something devoid of content.

Chapter 18 Execution and Assassination

The Penal Law is a Categorical Imperative; and woe to him
who creeps through the serpent-windings of Utilitarianism
to discover some advantage that may discharge him from the
Justice of Punishment, or even from the due measure of it . . .
For if Justice and Righteousness perish, human life would
no longer have any value in the world . . . Whoever has
committed murder must *die*.

Immanuel Kant: *The Philosophy of Law*

It is curious, but till that moment I had never realized what it
means to destroy a healthy, conscious man. When I saw the
prisoner step aside to avoid the puddle I saw the mystery, the
unspeakable wrongness, of cutting a life short when it is in full
tide. This man was not dying, he was alive just as we are alive.
All the organs of his body were working – bowels digesting
food, skin renewing itself, nails growing, tissues forming – all
toiling away in solemn foolery. His nails would still be growing
when he stood on the drop, when he was falling through the air
with a tenth of a second to live. His eyes saw the yellow gravel
and the grey walls, and his brain still remembered, foresaw,
reasoned, even about puddles. He and we were a party of men
walking together, seeing, hearing, feeling, understanding the
same world; and in two minutes, with a sudden snap, one of us
would be gone – one mind less, one world less.

George Orwell: 'A Hanging', *Adelphi*, 1931

The debate about capital punishment for murder is, emotionally at least, dominated by two absolutist views. On the
retributive view, the murderer must be given the punishment he
deserves, which is death. On the other view, analogous to

pacifism about war, there is in principle no possibility of justifying capital punishment: in execution there is only 'the unspeakable wrongness of cutting a life short when it is in full tide'. Supporters of these two approaches agree only in rejecting the serpent-windings of utilitarianism.

Let us look first at the retributive view. According to retributivism in its purest form, the aim of punishment is quite independent of any beneficial social consequences it may have. To quote Kant again:

Even if a Civil Society resolved to dissolve itself with the consent of all its members – as might be supposed in the case of a people inhabiting an island resolving to separate and scatter themselves throughout the whole world – the last Murderer lying in the prison ought to be executed before the resolution was carried out. This ought to be done in order that everyone may realize the desert of his deeds, and that blood-guiltiness may not remain upon the people; for otherwise they might all be regarded as participators in the murder as a public violation of justice.

This view of punishment, according to which it has a value independent of its contribution to reducing the crime rate, is open to the objection that acting on it leads to what many consider to be pointless suffering. To impose suffering or deprivation on someone, or to take his life, is something that those of us who are not retributivists think needs very strong justification in terms of benefits, either to the person concerned or to other people. The retributivist has to say either that the claims of justice can make it right to harm someone where no one benefits, or else to cite the curiously metaphysical 'benefits' of justice being done, such as Kant's concern that we should have 'blood-guiltiness' removed. I have no way of refuting these positions, as they seem to involve no clear intellectual mistake. I do not expect to win the agreement of those who hold them, and I am simply presupposing the other view, that there is already enough misery in the world, and that adding to it requires a justification in terms of non-metaphysical benefits to people.

229

This is not to rule out retributive moral principles perhaps playing a limiting role in a general theory of punishment. There is a lot to be said for the retributive restrictions that *only* those who deserve punishment should receive it and that they should never get more punishment than they deserve. (The case for this, which at least partly rests on utilitarian considerations, has been powerfully argued by H.L.A. Hart.)[1] But the approach to be adopted here rules out using retributive considerations to justify any punishment not already justifiable in terms of social benefits. In particular it rules out the argument that capital punishment can be justified, whether or not it reduces the crime rate, because the criminal deserves it.

This approach also has the effect of casting doubt on another way of defending capital punishment, which was forthrightly expressed by Lord Denning: 'The ultimate justification of any punishment is not that it is a deterrent, but that it is the emphatic denunciation by the community of a crime: and from this point of view, there are some murders which, in the present state of public opinion, demand the most emphatic denunciation of all, namely the death penalty.'[2] The question here is whether the point of the denunciation is to reduce the murder rate, in which case this turns out after all to be a utilitarian justification, or whether denunciation is an end in itself. If it is an end in itself, it starts to look like the retributive view in disguise, and should be rejected for the same reasons.

If we reject retribution for its own sake as a justification for capital punishment, we are left with two alternative general approaches to the question. One is an absolute rejection in principle of any possibility of capital punishment being justified, in the spirit of Orwell's remarks. The other is the rather more messy approach, broadly utilitarian in character, of weighing up likely social costs and benefits.

1. H.L.A. Hart: 'Prolegomenon to the Principles of Punishment', *Proceedings of the Aristotelian Society*, 1959–60.
2. Quoted in the *Report of the Royal Commission on Capital Punishment*, 1953.

1 The Absolutist Rejection of Capital Punishment

To some people, it is impossible to justify the act of killing a fellow human being. They are absolute pacifists about war and are likely to think of capital punishment as 'judicial murder'. They will sympathize with Beccaria's question: 'Is it not absurd that the laws which detest and punish homicide, in order to prevent murder, publicly commit murder themselves?'

The test of whether an opponent of capital punishment adopts this absolutist position is whether he would still oppose it if it could be shown to save many more lives than it cost: if, say, every execution deterred a dozen potential murderers. The absolutist, unlike the utilitarian opponent of the death penalty, would be unmoved by any such evidence. This question brings out the links between the absolutist position and the acts and omissions doctrine. For those of us who reject the acts and omissions doctrine, the deaths we fail to prevent have to be given weight, as well as the deaths we cause by execution. So those of us who do not accept the acts and omissions doctrine cannot be absolutist opponents of capital punishment.

There is a variant on the absolutist position which at first sight seems not to presuppose the acts and omissions doctrine. On this view, while saving a potential murder victim is in itself as important as not killing a murderer, there is something so cruel about the kind of death involved in capital punishment that this rules out the possibility of its being justified. Those of us who reject the acts and omissions doctrine have to allow that sometimes there can be side-effects associated with an act of killing, but not with failure to save a life, which can be sufficiently bad to make a substantial moral difference between the two. When this view is taken of the cruelty of the death penalty, it is not usually the actual method of execution which is objected to, though this can seem important, as in the case where international pressure on General Franco led him to substitute shooting for the garrotte. What seems peculiarly cruel

231

and horrible about capital punishment is that the condemned man has the period of waiting, knowing how and when he is to be killed. Many of us would rather die suddenly than linger for weeks or months knowing we were fatally ill, and the condemned man's position is several degrees worse than that of the person given a few months to live by doctors. He has the additional horror of knowing exactly when he will die, and of knowing that his death will be in a ritualized killing by other people, symbolizing his ultimate rejection by the members of his community. The whole of his life may seem to have a different and horrible meaning when he sees it leading up to this end.

For reasons of this kind, capital punishment can plausibly be claimed to fall under the United States constitution's ban on 'cruel and unusual punishments', so long as the word 'unusual' is not interpreted too strictly. The same reasons make the death penalty a plausible candidate for falling under a rather similar ethical ban, which has been expressed by H.L.A. Hart: 'There are many different ways in which we think it morally incumbent on us to *qualify* or *limit* the pursuit of the utilitarian goal by methods of punishment. Some punishments are ruled out as too barbarous to use *whatever their social utility*'[3] (final italics mine). Because of the extreme cruelty of capital punishment, many of us would, if forced to make a choice between two horrors, prefer to be suddenly murdered rather than be sentenced to death and executed. This is what makes it seem reasonable to say that the absolutist rejection of the death penalty need not rest on the acts and omissions doctrine.

But this appearance is illusory. The special awfulness of capital punishment may make an execution even more undesirable than a murder (though many would disagree on the grounds that this is outweighed by the desirability that the guilty rather than the innocent should die). Even if we accept that an execution is worse than an average murder, it does not follow from this that capital punishment is too barbarous to use *whatever its social utility*. For supposing a single execution deterred

3. H.L.A. Hart: 'Murder and the Principles of Punishment', *Northwestern Law Review*, 1958.

many murders? Or suppose that some of the murders deterred would themselves have been as cruel as an execution? When we think of the suffering imposed in a famous kidnapping case, where the mother received her son's ear through the post, we may feel uncertain even that capital punishment is more cruel than some 'lesser' crimes than murder. The view that some kinds of suffering are too great to impose, whatever their social utility, rules out the possibility of justifying them, however much more suffering they would prevent. And this does presuppose the acts and omissions doctrine, and so excludes some of us even from this version of absolutism.

2 A Utilitarian Approach

It is often supposed that the utilitarian alternative to absolutism is simply one of adopting an unqualified maximizing policy. On such a view, the death penalty would be justified if, and only if, it was reasonable to think the number of lives saved exceeded the number of executions. (The question of what to do where the numbers exactly balance presupposes a fineness of measurement that is unattainable in these matters.) On any utilitarian view, numbers of lives saved must be a very important consideration. But there are various special features that justify the substantial qualification of a maximizing policy.

The special horror of the period of waiting for execution may not justify the absolutist rejection of the death penalty, but it is a powerful reason for thinking that an execution may normally cause more misery than a murder, and so for thinking that, if capital punishment is to be justified, it must do better than break even when lives saved through deterrence are compared with lives taken by the executioner.

This view is reinforced when we think of some of the other side-effects of the death penalty. It must be appalling to be told that your husband, wife or child has been murdered, but this is surely less bad than the experience of waiting a month or two for your husband, wife or child to be executed. And those who think that the suffering of the murderer himself matters less than that of an innocent victim will perhaps not be prepared to extend this view to the suffering of the murderer's parents, wife and children.

There is also the possibility of mistakenly executing an innocent man, something which it is very probable happened in the case of Timothy Evans. The German Federal Ministry of Justice is quoted in the Council of Europe's report on *The Death Penalty in European Countries* as saying that in the hundred years to 1953, there were twenty-seven death sentences 'now established or presumed' to be miscarriages of justice. This point is often used as an argument against capital punishment, but what is often not noticed is that its force must depend on the special horrors of execution as compared with other forms of death, including being murdered. For the victim of murder is innocent too, and he also has no form of redress. It is only the (surely correct) assumption that an innocent man faces something much worse in execution than in murder that gives this argument its claim to prominence in this debate. For, otherwise, the rare cases of innocent men being executed would be completely overshadowed by the numbers of innocent men being murdered. (Unless, of course, the acts and omissions doctrine is again at work here, for execution is something that we, as a community, *do*, while a higher murder rate is something we at most *allow*.)

The death penalty also has harmful effects on people other than the condemned man and his family. For most normal people, to be professionally involved with executions, whether as judge, prison warder or chaplain, or executioner, must be highly disturbing. Arthur Koestler quotes the case of the executioner Ellis, who attempted suicide a few weeks after he executed a sick woman ' whose insides fell out before she vanished through the trap'.[4] (Though the chances must be very small of the experience of Mr Pierrepoint, who describes in his autobiography how he had to execute a friend with whom he often sang duets in a pub.[5]) And there are wider effects on

4. Arthur Koestler: *Reflections on Hanging*, London, 1956.
5. Albert Pierrepoint: *Executioner: Pierrepoint*, London, 1974.

society at large. When there is capital punishment, we are all involved in the horrible business of a long-premeditated killing, and most of us will to some degree share in the emotional response George Orwell had so strongly when he had to be present. It cannot be good for children at school to know that there is an execution at the prison down the road. And there is another bad effect, drily stated in the *Report of the Royal Commission on Capital Punishment*: 'No doubt the ambition that prompts an average of five applications a week for the post of hangman, and the craving that draws a crowd to the prison where a notorious murderer is being executed, reveal psychological qualities that no state would wish to foster in its citizens.'

Capital punishment is also likely to operate erratically. Some murderers are likely to go free because the death penalty makes juries less likely to convict. (Charles Dickens, in a newspaper article quoted in the 1868 Commons debate, gave the example of a forgery case, where a jury found a £10 note to be worth 39 shillings, in order to save the forger's life.) There are also great problems in operating a reprieve system without arbitrariness, say, in deciding whether being pregnant or having a young baby should qualify a woman for a reprieve.

Finally, there is the drawback that the retention or re-introduction of capital punishment contributes to a tradition of cruel and horrible punishment which we might hope would wither away. Nowadays we never think of disembowelling people or chopping off their hands as a punishment. Even if these punishments would be specially effective in deterring some very serious crimes, they are not regarded as a real possibility. To many of us, it seems that the utilitarian benefits from this situation outweigh the loss of any deterrent power they might have if re-introduced for some repulsive crime like kidnapping. And the longer we leave capital punishment in abeyance, the more its use will seem as out of the question as the no more cruel punishment of mutilation. (At this point, I come near to Hart's view that some punishments are too barbarous to use whatever their social utility. The difference is that I think that arguments for and against a punishment should be based on social utility,

235

but that a widespread view that some things are unthinkable is itself of great social utility.)

For these reasons, a properly thought-out utilitarianism does not enjoin an unqualified policy of seeking the minimum loss of life, as the no trade-off view does. Capital punishment has its own special cruelties and horrors, which change the whole position. In order to be justified, it must be shown, with good evidence, that it has a deterrent effect not obtainable by less awful means, and one which is quite substantial rather than marginal.

3 Deterrence and Murder

The arguments over whether capital punishment deters murder more effectively than less drastic methods are of two kinds: statistical and intuitive. The statistical arguments are based on various kinds of comparisons of murder rates. Rates are compared before and after abolition in a country, and, where possible, further comparisons are made with rates after reintroduction of capital punishment. Rates are compared in neighbouring countries, or neighbouring states of the U.S.A., with and without the death penalty. I am not a statistician and have no special competence to discuss the issue, but will merely purvey the received opinion of those who have looked into the matter. Those who have studied the figures are agreed that there is no striking correlation between the absence of capital punishment and any alteration in the curve of the murder rate. Having agreed on this point, they then fall into two schools. On one view, we can conclude that capital punishment is not a greater deterrent to murder than the prison sentences that are substituted for it. On the other, more cautious, view, we can only conclude that we do not know that capital punishment is a deterrent. I shall not attempt to choose between these interpretations. For, given that capital punishment is justified only where there is good evidence that it is a substantial deterrent, either interpretation fails to support the case for it.

If the statistical evidence were conclusive that capital punishment did not deter more than milder punishments, this would leave no room for any further discussion. But, since the statistical evidence may be inconclusive, many people feel there is room left for intuitive arguments. Some of these deserve examination. The intuitive case was forcefully stated in 1864 by Sir James Fitzjames Stephen:[6]

No other punishment deters men so effectually from committing crimes as the punishment of death. This is one of those propositions which it is difficult to prove, simply because they are in themselves more obvious than any proof can make them. It is possible to display ingenuity in arguing against it, but that is all. The whole experience of mankind is in the other direction. The threat of instant death is the one to which resort has always been made when there was an absolute necessity for producing some result ... No one goes to certain inevitable death except by compulsion. Put the matter the other way. Was there ever yet a criminal who, when sentenced to death and brought out to die, would refuse the offer of a commutation of his sentence for the severest secondary punishment? Surely not. Why is this? It can only be because. 'All that a man has will he give for his life.' In any secondary punishment, however terrible, there is hope; but death is death; its terrors cannot be described more forcibly.

These claims turn out when scrutinized to be much more speculative and doubtful than they at first sight appear.

The first doubt arises when Stephen talks of 'certain inevitable death'. The Royal Commission, in their *Report*, after quoting the passage from Stephen above, quote figures to show that, in the fifty years from 1900 to 1949, there was in England and Wales one execution for every twelve murders known to the police. In Scotland in the same period there was less than one execution for every twenty-five murders known to the police. Supporters of Stephen's view could supplement their case by advocating more death sentences and fewer reprieves, or by optimistic speculations about better police detection or

6. James Fitzjames Stephen: Capital Punishments, *Fraser's Magazine*, 1864.

greater willingness of juries to convict. But the reality of capital punishment as it was in these countries, unmodified by such recommendations and speculations, was not one where the potential murderer faced certain, inevitable death. This may incline us to modify Stephen's estimate of its deterrent effect, unless we buttress his view with the further speculation that a fair number of potential murderers falsely believed that what they would face was certain, inevitable death.

The second doubt concerns Stephen's talk of 'the threat of instant death'. The reality again does not quite fit this. By the time the police conclude their investigation, the case is brought to trial, and verdict and sentence are followed by appeal, petition for reprieve and then execution, many months have probably elapsed, and when this time factor is added to the low probability of the murderers being executed, the picture looks very different. For we often have a time bias, being less affected by threats of future catastrophes than by threats of instant ones. The certainty of immediate death is one thing; it is another thing merely to increase one's chances of death in the future. Unless this were so, no one would smoke or take on such high-risk jobs as diving in the North Sea.

There is another doubt when Stephen very plausibly says that virtually all criminals would prefer life imprisonment to execution. The difficulty is over whether this entitles us to conclude that it is therefore a more effective deterrent. For there is the possibility that, compared with the long term of imprisonment that is the alternative, capital punishment is what may appropriately be called an 'overkill'. It may be that, for those who will be deterred by threat of punishment, a long prison sentence is sufficient deterrent. I am not suggesting that this is so, but simply that it is an open question whether a worse alternative here generates any additional deterrent effect. The answer is *not* intuitively obvious.

Stephen's case rests on the speculative psychological assumptions that capital punishment is not an overkill compared with a prison sentence; and that its additional deterrent effect is not obliterated by time bias, nor by the low probability of execution, nor by a combination of these factors. Or else it must be assumed that, where the additional deterrent effect would be obliterated by the low probability of death, either on its own or in combination with time bias, the potential murderer thinks the probability is higher than it is. Some of these assumptions may be true, but, when they are brought out into the open, it is by no means obvious that the required combination of them can be relied upon.

Supporters of the death penalty also sometimes use what David A. Conway, in his valuable discussion of this issue, calls 'the best-bet argument'.[7] On this view, since there is no certainty whether or not capital punishment reduces the number of murders, either decision about it involves gambling with lives. It is suggested that it is better to gamble with the lives of murderers than with the lives of their innocent potential victims. This presupposes the attitude, rejected here, that a murder is a greater evil than the execution of a murderer. But, since this attitude probably has overwhelmingly widespread support, it is worth noting that, even if it is accepted, the best-bet argument is unconvincing. This is because, as Conway has pointed out, it overlooks the fact that we are not choosing between the chance of a murderer dying and the chance of a victim dying. In leaving the death penalty, we are opting for the certainty of the murderer dying which we hope will give us a chance of a potential victim being saved. This would look like a good bet only if we thought an execution substantially preferable to a murder and either the statistical evidence or the intuitive arguments made the effectiveness of the death penalty as a deterrent look reasonably likely.

Since the statistical studies do not give any clear indication that capital punishment makes any difference to the number of murders committed, the only chance of its supporters discharging the heavy burden of justification would be if the intuitive arguments were extremely powerful. We might then feel justified in supposing that other factors distorted the murder

7. David A. Conway: 'Capital Punishment and Deterrence', *Philosophy and Public Affairs*, 1974.

rate, masking the substantial deterrent effect of capital punishment. The intuitive arguments, presented as the merest platitudes, turn out to be speculative and unobvious. I conclude that the case for capital punishment as a substantial deterrent fails.

4 Deterrence and Political Crimes by Opposition Groups

It is sometimes suggested that the death penalty may be an effective deterrent in the case of a special class of 'political' crimes. The 'ordinary' murder (killing one's wife in a moment of rage, shooting a policeman in panic after a robbery, killing someone in a brawl) may not be particularly sensitive to different degrees of punishment. But some killings for political purposes have a degree of preparation and thought which may allow the severity of the penalty to affect the calculation. Two different kinds of killing come to mind here. There are killings as part of a political campaign, ranging from assassination through terrorist activities up to full-scale guerrilla war. And then there are policies carried out by repressive governments, varying from 'liquidation' of individual opponents with or without 'trial' to policies of wholesale extermination, sometimes, but not always, in wartime.

Let us look first at killings by groups opposed to governments. Would the various sectarian terrorist groups in Ireland stop their killings if those involved were executed? Would independence movements in countries like Algeria or Kenya have confined themselves to non-violent means if more executions had taken place? Could the Nazis have deterred the French resistance by more executions? Could the Americans have deterred guerrilla war in Vietnam by more executions?

To ask these questions is to realize both the variety of different political situations in which the question of deterrent killing arises, and also to be reminded, if it is necessary, that moral right is not always on the side of the authorities trying to do the deterring. But let us, for the sake of argument, assume a decent government is trying to deal with terrorists or guerrillas whose cause has nothing to be said for it. People have always gone to war knowing they risk their lives, and those prepared to fight in a guerrilla war seem scarcely likely to change their mind because of the marginal extra risk of capital punishment if they are arrested. If the case is to be made, it must apply to lower levels of violence than full-scale guerrilla war.

Given the death penalty's drawbacks, is there any reason to think it would be sufficiently effective in deterring a campaign of terrorist violence to be justified? The evidence is again inconclusive. In many countries there have been terrorist campaigns where the authorities have responded with executions without stopping the campaign. It is always open to someone to say that the level of terrorist activity might have been even higher but for the executions, but it is hard to see why this should be likely. Those who do the shooting or the planting of bombs are not usually the leaders and can be easily replaced by others willing to risk their lives. Danger to life does not deter people from fighting in wars, and a terrorist gunman may be just as committed to his cause as a soldier. And executions create martyrs, which helps the terrorist cause. They may even raise the level of violence by leading to reprisals.

But it may be that a sufficiently ruthless policy of executions would be effective enough to overcome these drawbacks. It has been claimed that the policy of the Irish government in 1922–3 is an instance of this. David R. Bates describes it as follows:[8]

In the turbulent period following the establishment of the Irish Free State, military courts with power to inflict the death penalty were set up to enable the Irregulars (opposing the Treaty) to be crushed. These powers were first used on 17 November 1922, when four young men were arrested in Dublin and, on being found to be armed, were executed. Shortly afterwards the Englishman, Erskine Childers, captured while carrying a revolver, was also executed. On 7 December two Deputies were shot (one fatally) by the Irregulars. The Minister for Defence, with the agreement of the Cabinet, selected four Irregular leaders who had been in prison since the fall of

8. Professor David R. Bates, Letter to *The Times*, 14 October 1975.

the Four Courts on 29 June. They were wakened, told to prepare themselves, and were executed by firing squad at dawn. During a six-month period, almost twice as many Irregular prisoners were executed as had been executed by the British from 1916 to 1921. At the end of April 1923, the Irregulars sought a ceasefire to discuss terms. The Free State Government refused. In May 1924, the Irregulars conceded military defeat.

This is an impressive case, and it may be that this degree of ruthlessness by the government involved fewer deaths than would have taken place during a prolonged terrorist campaign. But against this must be set some doubts. What would have happened if the terrorists had been as ruthless in reprisal as the government, perhaps announcing that for every man executed there would be two murders? Is it clear that after a period of such counter-retaliation it would have been the Irregulars rather than the government who climbed down? Does not any net saving of lives by the government's ruthless policy depend on the terrorists refraining from counter-retaliation, and can this be relied on in other cases? And is there not something dangerous in the precedent set when a government has prisoners executed without their having been convicted and sentenced for a capital offence? And, in this case, is it even clear that the defeat of the Irregulars ended once and for all the violence associated with the issues they were campaigning about? I raise these questions, not to claim that the government policy was clearly wrong, but to show how even a case like this is ambiguous in the weight it lends to the argument for using the death penalty against terrorism.

I do not think that the chance of a net saving of lives will in general outweigh the combination of the general drawbacks of capital punishment combined with the danger of its merely leading to a higher level of violence in a terrorist situation. But this is a matter of judgement rather than proof, and I admit that it *may* be that the opposite view had better results than mine would have had in 1922.

5 Deterrence and Political Crimes by the Authorities

The other category of political crimes which sometimes seems so special as to justify the death penalty is atrocities committed by governments or their agents. The executions of leading Nazis after the Nuremberg trials and the execution of Eichmann after his trial in Jerusalem come to mind. The justification usually advanced for these executions is retributive, and it is hard to imagine any more deserving candidates for the death penalty. But, for those of us who do not consider retribution an acceptable aim of punishment, the question must be whether executing them made their kind of activity less likely to happen again in the future. For, if not, we have no answer to the question asked by Victor Gollancz at the time of the Eichmann trial: why should we think we improve the world by turning six million deaths into six million and one?

The chances of people who design or carry out governmental policies of murder being tried and sentenced must often be very small. Sometimes this happens as the result of revolution or defeat in war, but those in power stand a fairly good chance of being killed under these circumstances anyway, and the additional hazard of capital punishment may not have much deterrent effect. As with 'ordinary' murderers, the hope of not being caught reduces the punishment's terrors. Some of those who murdered for Hitler were executed; their opposite numbers under Stalin paid no penalty. The torturers who worked for the Greek colonels were brought to trial, but those now at work in Chile, Brazil and South Africa have every expectation of not being punished.

When considering isolated cases of governmental murder (perhaps the assassination of a troublesome foreign leader by a country's intelligence agency, or the single killing of a political opponent) there seems no reason to think capital punishment more of a deterrent than it is of 'ordinary' non-political murder. If anything, it is likely to be less of a deterrent because

243

of the reduced chance of a murder charge ever being brought. So there seems no case for treating these crimes as other than ordinary murders. But when considering large-scale atrocities, on the scale of those of Hitler or Stalin, or even on the scale of Lyndon Johnson in Vietnam or General Gowon in Nigeria, a version of the best-bet argument comes into play. There are two possible advantages to the death penalty here. One is simply that of totally eliminating the chance of the same mass murderer occupying a position of leadership again. Suppose Hitler had been captured at the end of the Second World War and the question of executing him had arisen. If he had not been executed, it is overwhelmingly probable that he would have spent the rest of his life in Spandau prison, writing his memoirs and giving increasingly senile lectures on world history to visiting journalists. But there would always be the very slight risk of an escape and return to power in the style of Napoleon. This slight risk is removed by execution. The other advantage of the death penalty is the chance, which we have seen to be probably very slight, of deterring repetition of such policies by other leaders.

The best-bet argument in these cases can be used by someone who accepts that the dangers of a defeated leader returning to power are very small and that the chances of execution deterring future leaders from similar policies are also very small. The argument is simply that, where the prevention of such enormous atrocities is in question, even an extremely small probability of prevention is valuable. Consider a case where numbers and probabilities are parallel, but where act and omission are reversed. Suppose someone in hospital can have his life saved only by the making of some organism which has previously been banned. The reason for the ban is that there is a danger, but only a very faint one, of the organism getting out of control. If it does this, the death rate will run into millions. Let us suppose that our intuitive estimate of the unquantifiable risk here is the same as our intuitive estimate of the unquantifiable reduction of risk caused by executing the murdering leader. Those who would rather let the hospital patient die than breach the ban on the dangerous organism must either rely on the acts

244

and omissions doctrine, or else rely on some difference of side-effects, if they are not prepared to support executing the murdering politician or official.

Part of the difficulty in interpreting comparisons of this sort arises from the fact that we are dealing with probabilities that cannot be measured. And, even if they could be measured, most of us are unclear what sacrifices are worth making for the reduction of some risk that is already very small. But if we make the highly artificial assumption that the alterations in probability of risk are the same in the medical case as in the execution case, the dilemma remains. Let us suppose that the risk is one that we would not take in the medical case to save a single life. Those of us who do not accept the acts and omissions doctrine must then either find some difference of side-effects or else support the execution.

Side-effects do go some way towards separating the two cases. For, to breach the ban on producing the organism, even if it does no harm itself, contributes by example to a less strict observance of that ban (and possibly others) in cases where the risk may be much greater. While, in the case of the Nazi leaders, such bad side-effects as exist follow from execution rather than from saving their lives. These side-effects include the contribution made to a climate of opinion where the death penalty seems more acceptable in other contexts, and the precedent which may encourage politicians to have their overthrown rivals, at home or abroad, executed. This last effect could be mitigated by more effort than was made at Nuremberg to remove the impression of the defeated being tried by the victors. It would be possible to set up a court of a genuinely international kind, independent of governmental pressure, to which prosecutions for a large-scale murder could be brought. But the general effect on the public consciousness of having capital punishment as a serious possibility would remain. I am uncertain how to weigh this against the small chance of helping to avert a great evil. For this reason my own views on this question are undecided.

6 Assassination and Terrorism

In executing people in order to reduce killings elsewhere, we are gambling with lives, just as we are when we run the risk of other killings by deciding against execution. The policy advocated here is one of maximizing the numbers of lives saved, subject to some additional weight being given to the cruelty of the death penalty and to its bad side-effects. The question is a bit like that of medical experiments on patients which may save future lives. The side-effects are sometimes so bad that a very heavy burden of proof lies on those who propose them, yet this is not to say that such a policy cannot in principle ever be justified. But the question perhaps even more closely resembles that of whether assassination could be an acceptable policy.

Those who support assassination do so most plausibly when they point to the deaths many political leaders cause, with the implication that the changes following the death of a single statesman may save many lives. Edward Hyams has said that 'it is a curious instance of the perversity of mankind ... that we think of the mass slaughterer Harry Truman, with his H-bomb, as a great war leader; of the man who shoots a single president as a villain'.[9] And others who support acts of killing for political purposes sometimes show by their choice of terminology the links they wish to claim between their acts and other kinds of killing more widely accepted as legitimate: members of Catholic or Protestant groups in Ireland who kill people often talk in terms either of acts of war or of executions.

Many of us respond to the assassination of a leader with special feelings of horror. These feelings are special, not merely by comparison with our response to hearing of a fatal road accident, but special even by comparison with our response to other deliberate acts of killing. Perhaps this is partly the result of leaders being 'known' to us, especially now that we often see them on television. Perhaps it is also because of a kind of magi-

9. Edward Hyams: *Killing No Murder, A Study of Assassination as a Political Means*, London, 1969.

cal belief that a leader is in some way sacred. Many world leaders are responsible for huge numbers of deaths, and yet there are relatively few assassination attempts in a time when many people are prepared to kill for political ends. It may be that this is to be explained partly by this possession by leaders of both sanctity and familiarity. Another factor, simple fear of reciprocation, may be relevant to explaining why leaders so rarely have each other assassinated, even in wartime.

Those of us who do not think of leaders as in any way sacred may think that assassination could in principle sometimes be justified. But, as with other killings, there is a large burden of justification. George Orwell has criticized any casual acceptance of this kind of killing in his rebuke to W.H. Auden for the line in *Spain*: 'The conscious acceptance of guilt in the necessary murder.' Orwell says:

> Notice the phrase 'necessary murder'. It could only be written by a person to whom murder is at most a *word*. Personally I would not speak so lightly of murder. It so happens that I have seen the bodies of numbers of murdered men – I don't mean killed in battle, I mean murdered. Therefore I have some conception of what murder means – the terror, the hatred, the howling relatives, the post mortems, the blood, the smells. To me murder is something to be avoided.[10]

And the scenes after a murder are only a small part of the case against it. But, as with execution, assassination cannot be dismissed without taking into account the possibility of benefits, including the saving of many lives. The fact that we do not know the people whose lives may be saved by assassinating some dictator or bellicose politician does not make them less important.

Only those who support the acts and omissions doctrine are entitled to say that political killing cannot in principle ever be justified, even if it saves many lives. But this does not mean that the rest of us have to pursue a simple maximizing policy: supporting any assassination that could be shown to save at least two lives. (This view would suggest that the murder of a feeble

10. George Orwell: *Inside the Whale*, London, 1940.

Minister of Health or an incompetent factory inspector would be justified if they could not be removed by less drastic means.) As with executions, the bad side-effects of assassinations are sufficient to set severe limits to any simple maximizing policy.

Political killings have side-effects often greater than intended, most spectacularly when the assassination at Sarajevo acted as the trigger for the First World War. No doubt the chances of that kind of 'side-effect' are very small. But political killings, whether the dramatic assassination of a leader or the less publicly traumatic killings of a terrorist campaign whose targets are customers of shops and pubs, virtually always have terrible and cumulative side-effects. People are made to feel less secure. This may be irrational, given the insignificant chances of being a victim of terrorism compared to other dangers such as road accidents. But, whether or not it is irrational, people do feel far more insecure when murderers are at large than they do when crossing the road. And, where a small group are obvious targets, such as members of governments, the protective arrangements made necessary can create an atmosphere of separation from people that is undesirable. Much more seriously, a political killing sets a precedent which can soon build up a tradition of attempts to change society by violence rather than persuasion. It is hard to be sure here about cause and effect, but it seems at least possible that the assassination of John Kennedy set an example which made more likely such acts as the assassinations of Robert Kennedy and Martin Luther King, and the attempted assassinations of George Wallace and Gerald Ford. And whenever one group wages a terrorist campaign this makes other groups with other political aims more likely to regard terrorism as a live option. Since any society has its dissenters, the danger is of political killing becoming established like an ineradicable infectious disease. It seems worth putting up with some fairly appalling leaders, or allowing some good causes to fail, in order to avoid that. It is easy here to focus in a short-sighted way on the immediate consequences of a proposed act, ignoring its contribution to a downward spiral of violence.

The presumption against assassination and terrorism becomes

immense when, to the harmful side-effects, is added the fallibility of these methods in bringing about their political goals. Trotsky suggests that, outside civil war, they are never effective:[11] 'Are the given means really capable of leading to the goal? In relation to individual terror, both theory and experience bear witness that such is not the case. To the terrorist we say: It is impossible to replace the masses; only in the mass movement can you find expedient expression for your heroism.' I am not as confident as Trotsky that assassination or terror campaigns by minority groups cannot be politically effective, but at least usually their success is highly doubtful. There may be rare cases where history could have been changed by an assassination: perhaps an assassination of Hitler in 1933 would have averted a great evil; perhaps the assassination of Churchill in 1940 would have brought one about. But policies are rarely created by, or dependent upon, a single man. It is hard to believe that the assassination of Lyndon Johnson would have ended the Vietnamese war, or that South Africa would be transformed by a successful attempt on the life of a Prime Minister. On the other hand, the death of Stalin did lead to a more relaxed policy and no doubt to the saving of many lives. The record is ambiguous. And this means that assassination has at best only a fair prospect of success, which makes it highly unlikely to be justifiable, even against fairly terrible policies. It is only in very extreme cases, where the evil to be averted is on the scale of war or large-scale massacre, that a version of the best-bet argument gives a serious possibility of justification.

7 Gambling with the Lives of Others

The debates over the death penalty and over political killing have a similar structure. In each debate there are those who, presupposing the acts and omissions doctrine, rule out in principle the possibility of such killings being justified in any circumstances. At the other end of the spectrum are those who

11. Leon Trotsky: *Their Morals and Ours*, 4th edition, New York, 1969.

justify the killings without feeling the need to cite beneficial consequences: retributivists over the death penalty and political killers motivated by a fanaticism unmodifiable by evidence about probable outcomes.

One of the middle positions in these debates is that advocated here. Where the consequences, either of the death penalty or of the assassination of some politician whose career has been costly in lives, are so uncertain, we are gambling with lives whether we kill or not. Those who support the executioner or the assassin on grounds of probable life-saving are gambling the certain death of a murderer or a politician against the chance of averting a number of other deaths. Those of us who, in virtually all circumstances, are opposed to the activities of the executioner or the assassin are gambling with the unknown 'statistical' lives of potential murder victims, or of those who may die in war or concentration camps. Unless we accept the acts and omissions doctrine, we must accept that either gamble requires careful calculation. But the special evils of execution and of its side-effects create a strong presumption against the death penalty, which normally only the probability of substantial net savings in lives will outweigh. And there is an even stronger presumption against the use of assassination or terrorist killing for political means, which seem likely to have long-term side-effects of an altogether different magnitude.

Chapter 19   War

The question of the rights and wrongs of a particular war is generally considered from a juridical or quasi-juridical standpoint: so and so broke such and such a treaty, crossed such and such a frontier, committed such and such technically unfriendly acts, and therefore by the rules it is permissible to kill as many of his nation as modern armaments render possible. There is a certain unreality, a certain lack of imaginative grasp about this way of viewing matters. It has the advantage, always dearly prized by lazy men, of substituting a formula, at once ambiguous and easily applied, for the vital realization of the consequences of acts.

Bertrand Russell: The Ethics of War, *International Journal of Ethics*, 1915

It is widely held that killing in war is quite different. It is not, and we need to think about the implications of this.

It is striking how casually most people accept the reasons offered by governments for acts of war. Even many of those who resist abortion, infanticide or euthanasia, on the grounds of a belief in the sanctity of life, sometimes acquiesce with only cursory thought when their governments embark on large-scale destruction of life in war. We compartmentalize our thinking, finding it hard to think about both the large scale and the small scale in proper perspective. The circumstances seem so exceptional that we feel the general taboo on killing is unaffected by its suspension in the context of war.

This compartmentalization has two opposed effects. On the one hand, we regard killing in war as less serious than other deliberate killing. A man who kills as a soldier in war is not regarded in the same way as a civil murderer, even by pacifists or by those who think he fought on the wrong side. On the other hand, partly because they are the result of deliberate killing, deaths in war still cause more horror and revulsion than deaths which no one intended. We think of the First World War as one of the greatest evils of our century. We scarcely remember the influenza epidemic that followed it, although the influenza claimed more lives than the war. The reasons for these differences of attitude are complex. Here I am not trying to explain the differences, but simply drawing attention to them. The first theme of this chapter is that, apart from important special side-effects, killing in war is morally on a par with other killing. Declarations of war, military uniforms and solemn utterances by national leaders in no way reduce the burden of justification for an act of killing.

The second theme is that our thinking about the morality of war is distorted because the questions are usually presented in too simple a form. The central moral question is usually taken to be about the rightness or wrongness of absolute pacifism. It is too easily assumed that the good arguments that make absolute pacifism implausible end the matter. But the rejection of an absolute ban on killing is only a starting point in a serious discussion of whether a particular act of killing, or participation in a particular war, is justifiable.

War is not a unitary phenomenon, and different considerations may affect the morality of taking part in different kinds of war. There are nuclear wars and conventional wars, world wars and local wars, colonial wars and revolutionary wars, guerrilla wars, civil wars, religious wars, tribal wars and others. And, even if we concentrate on the 'simple' case of a conventional war between two countries, there are various moral issues that should be separated. There is the question whether the government is justified in committing the country to war. There is the question for an individual, once the war has started, whether or not he should participate (and the related question of what provisions the country should make for conscientious objection). Then there are questions about the morality of various general policies or individual acts carried

252

out while fighting a war: questions about the use of nuclear weapons, chemical and biological warfare, saturation bombing, or torture by the military authorities, and questions about certain acts of cruelty or killing carried out by individual members of the forces.

Some people say it is pointless to discuss the morality of war, since, even if it is always immoral, it can never be eliminated, for reasons having to do with human nature or the nature of society. The reply to them is that the biological and anthropological evidence is inconclusive. It is not yet clear that men have an ineradicable predisposition to war, nor that the aspects of our psychology which now contribute to war could not find other outlets. We have hardly begun to experiment with the different forms of society and education which might change our situation. Of course it *may* be that war is ineradicable, but the bare possibility of this is not an argument for abandoning our present discussion.

Let us look first at some general positions adopted about the morality of war, and later turn back to some of the questions distinguished above.

1 The Views of Patriots and Other Believers

Among those who are prepared to discuss the morality of war, those who often seem most convinced of the rightness of a particular war are patriots and people who hold beliefs closely analogous to patriotism. The beliefs relevant to war which are associated with patriotism vary in strength. At the strong extreme (absolute patriotism) is 'my country right or wrong': the view that one's country is entitled to use whatever means necessary to further its interests, and that the citizen ought to participate in any war justified in these terms. At the mild end of the spectrum there is the belief that one ought to fight for one's country, subject to some condition such as that the war be a just one or, perhaps more stringently, a defensive one. Beliefs at any point along this spectrum can be combined with any degree of crudity or sophistication either about what one's country's interests are or about the criteria for a war being just.

Analogous to patriotic attitudes to war are the attitudes of those who can be called 'Believers'. A Believer is like a patriot except that the cause he believes in is not simply that of a country. He is prepared to fight for socialism or communism, democracy or the free world, colonial liberation or white civilization, and he is often inclined to believe that his ism is embodied in the present or future practice of one side or other in a war. (In the period of the cold war, a Believer was the opposite of the kind of person with whom Camus identified himself in 1946, when he spoke of 'so many of us in Europe who are not of any party – or ill at ease in the party we have chosen – who doubt socialism has been realized in Russia or liberalism in America, who grant to each side the right to affirm its truth but refuse it the right to impose it by murder, individual or collective'.)[1]

As with patriotism, Belief can vary in degree. And no doubt most of us are to some degree Believers at least some of the time: never to be so would be never to prefer one cause to another. At the strong end of the spectrum is the man who has no uncertainties about his values, no doubt that they are already, or are about to be, embodied in the practice of his chosen group, and thinks it obvious that they are worth the price of war. There are various factors which tend to push people towards the other end of the spectrum, where support is lent rather than given. One is the awareness of how parochial our perception of the world so often is and how liable our values are to modification through further experience and thought. Another is the recognition that there is something crude and arbitrary about the various political loyalties between which we are supposed to choose. This kind of scepticism is familiar in connection with the old parties to the cold war. How many people are there left who feel identified with something called the 'socialist camp' or something else called the 'free world'? But it applies with almost equal force to the more

1. Albert Camus: *Neither Victims nor Executioners*, Chicago, 1972.

specific sets of political doctrines we are offered. Consider the isms available now for a Western European. We can choose between fascism, conservatism, liberalism, anarchism, socialism, various kinds of nationalism, or communism. There seems no special reason why any of these ideological package deals should give the right relative weight to happiness, justice, freedom and whatever other basic values a person has. The more critically people think about their own values, and the more clearly they see political movements for the shifting coalitions that they are, the more likely they are to be conditional or qualified Believers rather than absolute ones.

There is no way of 'refuting' the many versions of patriotism and Belief that do not *depend* on inconsistencies or factual mistakes. But those whose patriotism or Belief is absolute can often be turned into holders of a more qualified version by the pressure of certain questions. Are there reasons for supporting this country or that ideology? How do we assess the strength of those reasons relative to the importance of avoiding the suffering and loss of life of war? Or is the avoidance of war to be given no weight at all? Fairly soon in a discussion of this sort, most people who are worth arguing with will turn out not to hold absolute views, but will have started towards Russell's 'vital realization of the consequences of acts'.

2 Absolute Pacifism

The varieties of pacifism are almost as great as of patriotism. Some versions of pacifism forbid only killing, while others forbid the use of 'force' or 'violence'. There are differences about what counts as force or violence. Some versions allow degrees of force otherwise prohibited to be used in self-defence or the defence of others, but no recognizable version of pacifism allows killing even as a defensive act. In order to avoid disputes about the point at which interference with someone else's aggressive act itself starts to count as violence, let us consider versions stated in terms of the wrongness of killing. The arguments which apply to the relatively clear-cut form of pacifism can be adapted with few modifications to fit the broader and less precise version.

Absolute pacifism says that it is never right to kill another person, however evil the consequences (including loss of life) of not doing so. This doctrine itself can have its basis in various different kinds of belief. It may be based on some religious command, or on some secular version of the doctrine of the sanctity of life. Or the objections to killing may be based on respect for people's autonomy or rights. As we shall see, principles about the sanctity of life, or respect for autonomy or rights, support absolute pacifism only when they are combined with other principles not often made explicit.

Part of the attractiveness of absolute pacifism is that to adopt it eliminates a discrepancy that exists in many people's moral outlook between their attitudes to killing within and outside war. For many people would absolutely rule out the possibility of an isolated act of killing a particular person being justified, however bad the consequences of not doing so. This line of thought is clearly expressed in Tolstoy's *Letter to a Non-Commissioned Officer*:

> You are surprised that soldiers are taught that it is right to kill people in certain cases and in war, while in the books admitted to be holy by those who so teach, there is nothing like such a permission, but, on the contrary, not only is all murder forbidden but all insulting of others is forbidden also, and we are told not to do to others what we do not wish done to us. And you ask, is not this a fraud? And why do these people shoot at their brothers? Because it has been instilled into them that the oath they were obliged to take on entering the service is binding, and that, though it is generally wrong to murder people, it is right to do so at the command of their superiors.

It is sometimes suggested that, despite its intuitive appeal, absolute pacifism can be briskly dismissed on the ground that it is self-contradictory. This has been clearly put by Narveson.[2] (He presents the argument in terms of violence, but the logic

2. Jan Narveson: 'Pacifism: A Philosophical Analysis', *Ethics*, 1965.

would be the same if expressed in terms of killing.) He says that, if we claim that violence is morally wrong, we are saying that 'those to whom it is done have a right *not* to have it done to them'. And he argues that for people to have such a right includes having the 'right to anything else that might be necessary (other things being equal) to prevent the deprivation from occurring'. And one thing that might be necessary is force or violence. Narveson's suggestion is that absolute pacifism is inconsistent because, in saying that violence or killing is wrong, we are committed to the view that we have a right to use violence or killing if necessary to protect our own right not to be the victim.

If saying that a kind of action is wrong committed us to the view that those harmed by it had this kind of unrestricted right to use all means necessary to prevent its occurrence, then absolute pacifism would indeed be self-contradictory. But it is not clear that moral disapproval does carry with it any strong commitment of this kind. I think it is wrong to spread malicious gossip about people. But I do not see that it follows from this that I have the right to kill someone if I cannot find any other way of stopping his slanders against me. To think something is wrong does not entail that potential victims of that kind of act have a no-holds-barred right of self-defence, and so the pacifist position is not shown by Narveson's argument to be inconsistent.

But there are other considerations which make absolute pacifism seem implausible. These are its two alternative theoretical presuppositions, which are not often made explicit. First, the absolute pacifist may be committed to the 'no trade-off' view about the value of human life. He holds that it is wrong to take life even if the alternative is to bring about other kinds of harm, *no matter how serious*. One explanation of this would be his adherence to the no trade-off view. But this view has the consequence, which many attracted to pacifism may find embarrassing, that society ought to give the saving of life overriding priority over other claims on its resources. The consequences of this for the *quality* of life in such a society scarcely need emphasis. The absolute pacifist may of course deny that he holds the no trade-off view. He may say that we do not have to give saving life such priority: it is *not taking life* that has this special moral status. But here he avoids commitment to the no trade-off view only by accepting the acts and omissions doctrine. Those of us who are not prepared to accept either of these presuppositions are debarred from being absolute pacifists.

3 Contingent Pacifism

The view which John Rawls[3] has called 'contingent pacifism' does not hold that there is an absolute prohibition on killing in war, such that it is inconceivable that such killing could be justified. The contingent pacifist appeals to the 'vital realization of the consequences of acts', and says that, while there is in principle the possibility of a war being justified, this is in practice a possibility so remote that we can disregard it. The contingent pacifist engages in the same calculations as the person who holds some qualified version of patriotism or Belief, but comes up with different conclusions, either through factual disagreement or through giving different relative weight to different outcomes.

A powerful defence of one form of contingent pacifism is in Richard Wasserstrom's illuminating article 'On the Morality of War'.[4] He focuses on the difficulty of justifying the killing of an innocent person in peacetime, and argues that an equally heavy burden of justification applies to the killing of the innocent in war. He points out that current military techniques have made a large-scale killing of the innocent an inescapable feature of modern war, and concludes: 'the argument from the death of the innocent does, I believe, make it clear both where the burden is and how unlikely it is today to suppose that it can be honestly discharged'.

3. John Rawls: *A Theory of Justice*, Harvard, 1971, section 58.
4. Richard A. Wasserstrom: 'On the Morality of War: A Preliminary Enquiry', *Stanford Law Review*, 1969.

There has been considerable dispute as to the possibility of drawing a clear boundary in modern war between the innocent and the guilty. And it is also open to doubt whether the distinction has the moral importance in war that it is sometimes credited with. Discussion of the issue can here be deferred for a few pages, as contingent pacifism need not rest on this particular distinction. The evils of war, the suffering, the killing of innocents and others, are obvious. A contingent pacifist can point to all these evils and use Wasserstrom's argument. There is an immense burden of justification, and it is by no means obviously wrong to say that with modern war it is unlikely ever to be honestly discharged. The parallel is with the ordinary policy many of us have with regard to individual acts of killing. It is *conceivable* that a situation will arise such that it will be right for me to carry out a premeditated murder of someone I come across in my private life. But in reality the chances of this are so remote that my policy is indistinguishable from that of an absolute pacifist. The justification would need to be so great that the question is not a live issue.

There is a further argument in favour of contingent pacifism which appeals to longer-term considerations than the horrors of a particular war. This argument appeals to the effects of breaching or of helping to establish a precedent. Since war is such a major evil, the argument goes, the establishing and maintaining of a tradition of repudiating it as a means of policy will have far more beneficial overall consequences than the most desirable outcome of any war. Every time we go to war, even in such a relatively clear-cut case as to defeat Hitler, we make a contribution to a tradition in which war is legitimate. But every time we refuse to continue politics by the 'other means' of war, we contribute to the establishment of the alternative tradition, which may be the most important thing in the world.

In this argument, there is an analogy with the historical abandonment of particularly brutal forms of punishment. When a form of punishment has recently been abolished (as with capital punishment in England) there is often still pressure for its reintroduction. But when a cruel punishment (such as mutilation) has not been used for a very long time it seems so terrible that

259

its reintroduction is never seriously discussed. The benefits of a more humane penal policy outweigh the loss of any short-term gain there might be in using one of these cruel punishments to stamp out some especially horrible kind of crime. It seems very plausible that a situation in which war was no longer regarded as a live option would be so beneficial that it is worth forgoing short-term advantages to help establish it.

These considerations – both Wasserstrom's reminder that wartime killing needs as much justification as other acts of killing that most of us would scarcely contemplate, and consideration of the long-term effects of decisions about war – make a powerful case for contingent pacifism. But this form of pacifism rests on the claim that total renunciation of war by a nation will have better consequences than a decision in any circumstances to wage war. And there are other considerations which to some extent tell against the general claim.

In the first place, we should feel some hesitation about accepting that the awfulness of war is always worse than that of the wrong side winning. This is obviously often so, but in a case like that of the war against Hitler, the contingent pacifist view is, to put it mildly, open to debate. Anyone who reflects both on the horrors of the Second World War and on what the Nazis managed to do in what would otherwise have been only their *first* twelve years should be able to see how decent and rational people can take different views here.

The case of the Second World War raises a general doubt about the consequences of a pacifist policy: the pursuit of a pacifist policy by some countries gives unlimited power over them to those non-pacifist countries who care to use it. Either actual invasion or else use of the threat of invasion as blackmail will give great power to those prepared to use them in an otherwise pacifist world. And the non-pacifist governments using these means are unlikely to be those who would put power to best use.

There is also a doubt about the strength in any particular case of the point about contributing to a climate where war is no longer an acceptable means to political ends. For *both* parties to a dispute must renounce war as a solution in order to generate the most satisfactory outcome. Then indeed there is another contribution to the non-violent tradition. But where one side is prepared to resort to war, the long-term impact of a pacifist policy on the other side is more ambiguous. It may be that people will remember the fine example of the country that preferred its cause to be lost rather than go to war. But the episode may equally be remembered as another depressing example of success going to those prepared to use force.

I conclude that, while there is a very strong presumption against a war being justifiable (just as there is in the case of individual acts of murder), particular cases have to be considered on their merits. Despite its rejection by various kinds of pacifists and Believers, this conclusion has a platitudinous quality and needs to be supplemented by rather more detailed considerations. Let us turn back to some of the different questions distinguished earlier.

4 Government Decisions for and against Nuclear War

Decisions for and against war by governments (or, in the case of civil war or revolution, by other groups of leaders) are obviously more momentous than any decision taken by an individual about whether or not to support a war. Governments are not always known for their interest in ethics, but this need not discourage us from forming our own views. We even have some duty to do so if we live in a country where governmental policies are at all sensitive to public opinion. The variety of kinds of war poses an obvious problem in formulating adequate general principles, but let us distinguish between nuclear and conventional war and start by considering the extreme case: full-scale nuclear war.

When is full-scale nuclear war justified? For anyone having the sort of outlook defended in this book, where great weight is given both to numbers of lives saved and to the extent to which people's lives are worth-while, it would require a most bizarre interpretation of the alternatives to think that such a nuclear war could be justified. We all know the rough order of magnitude of deaths. We remember President Kennedy's phrase that 'the survivors will envy the dead'. We all have a fair idea, both of how much of what we value would be left, and of the genetic horrors that would still be in store. We know that even the worst regime is likely to be changed in less time than it would take to undo those effects that can be undone of a major nuclear war. Finally, we all know that a sufficiently widespread or prolonged nuclear war could be the end of the human race. So far as full-scale nuclear war goes, the case for contingent pacifism is overwhelming.

We have seen that the Hitler case raises a serious problem for a general contingent pacifism, as the Second World War may have been a lesser evil than the survival and growth of the Nazi regime. But, when we think soberly about the worst hypothetical choice in the world, it is hard not to conclude that a Nazi society, including the extermination camps, would be less terrible than a major nuclear war. Those of us who share this view are pacifists with respect to full-scale nuclear war. The form of pacifism defended here is contingent. The suggestion is not that there could be no imaginable world in which major nuclear war would be justified, but rather that, in the world as it is, there is no serious possibility of its justification. If you construct an imaginary case in which the *only* way to stop the leaders of a country releasing a virus that will kill everyone on earth is to wage nuclear war, I will agree that in those circumstances nuclear war would be justifiable. But when we return to the world as it is, contingent pacifism as regards major nuclear war reasserts itself.

It is often pointed out that nuclear wars vary in scale. To take a pacifist view of full-scale nuclear war does not in itself entail renunciation of any use of nuclear weapons. It may be said that, while, a major nuclear war between super-powers should be avoided at all costs, a local nuclear war between small countries would be much less serious, as would a war between major powers waged with only tactical nuclear weapons.

The approach adopted here, where any kind of acceptable pacifism is at best contingent, commits us to examining cases on their merits. And perhaps major nuclear war is the only case where we can propose a general rule of pacifism without there being any serious possibility at all of justifiable breaches of the rule. If we allow the possibility of justifying the Second World War, we cannot rule out the possibility that some minor use of nuclear weapons could be justified in equally dire circumstances. But we should remember how very heavy the burden of justification is for large-scale killing, and how rarely it is likely to be discharged.

There is a special argument against the small-scale use of nuclear weapons, in addition to those against conventional war, which appeals to the long-term consequences. There is widespread recognition of the appallingness of nuclear warfare, and even the use of the smallest nuclear weapon in a good cause would send a wave of revulsion round the world. The killing of larger numbers of people in conventional war would not arouse disgust and horror to anything like the same degree. (Figures are disputed, but it is likely that more lives were lost in the bombing of Dresden than at Hiroshima.) This predictable reaction to the use of nuclear weapons is one of our defences against their use. Since Hiroshima and Nagasaki, a tradition has grown up of not using nuclear weapons, which may make a statesman a bit more reluctant to incur the odium of using them. The use of nuclear weapons again, however small in scale, will greatly weaken this defence against their future use, perhaps on a larger scale and with less justification. (This argument applies with most force to the first breach of the nuclear taboo, but, if that breach does occur, a weaker but still important argument will be relevant: it will still matter not to contribute to the tradition of using nuclear weapons.)

This special anti-nuclear argument appeals to the 'thin end of the wedge'. The taboo on using nuclear weapons is more fragile than is desirable, and is admittedly only one of the factors restraining governments from full-scale nuclear war. But when we are considering such an overwhelming evil, we should give correspondingly greater importance to preserving even minor aspects of our defensive system against it. (The enormity of the evil is one reason why the wedge argument is so much more powerful here than in its more common use in connection with abortion or infanticide. Another reason is that the grounds for scepticism about the empirical version of the wedge argument in those contexts rested on the attitudes of parents and doctors involved in the decisions. We cannot have the same confidence in the decisions likely to be taken by governments either at war or contemplating war.)

The other special argument against the use of small-scale nuclear weapons appeals to more immediate consequences. This is that there will often be a danger of war escalating from a small nuclear conflict into a large one. The boundary between Dresden and Hiroshima may not be *in itself* of very great moral significance, but this line between conventional and nuclear war is highly visible, and so there is less danger of gently drifting across it than there is of gently drifting up the scale from small to large nuclear conflict.[5]

If it is hard to justify any war, it is especially hard to justify large-scale wars. The extra arguments against even the small-scale use of nuclear weapons seem to me to make the chances of justifying any form of nuclear war, however limited, vanishingly small. But such a view depends on a combination of general principles and factual assessment. Someone could share the moral outlook defended here, but differ in his estimate of the chances of it ever being right to use nuclear weapons, as the result of a radically different view of likely outcomes.

5 Nuclear Threats and Deterrence

It may be thought that, if the chances of a government being justified in using nuclear weapons are so remote, the possession of nuclear weapons and threats to use them are unjustifiable. But this does not immediately follow, and some separate consideration of nuclear threats is necessary. There are many

5. cf. Thomas C. Schelling: *The Strategy of Conflict*, Harvard, 1960, Ch. 1.

different uses to which a nuclear threat can be put. There are aggressive uses of the nuclear threat, as when it is used in an attempt to make another country cede some territory or change some aspect of its foreign or domestic policy. There are defensive uses of the nuclear threat, when it is used to deter the enemies of a country from attacking it. Nuclear retaliation can be the threatened response to *any* attack, or only to nuclear attack. Rather different considerations apply in these different cases. Here I shall consider only the defensive use of the nuclear threat and only the case where the threat is made to deter nuclear attack. I take this case partly because in practice it is the most important, partly because it is the use most likely to be justifiable, and partly because it illustrates an interesting discrepancy between the morality of using nuclear weapons and the morality of threatening their use.

Consider Russia and America, each capable of massive nuclear retaliation in the event of a nuclear attack by the other. Suppose one did launch a nuclear attack on the other. On the views argued for in this book, it would be clearly wrong actually to use nuclear retaliation upon the population of the aggressor country. It is too late to avoid the catastrophic damage to the victim country, and so retaliation would merely double the size of the catastrophe to no useful purpose. If we believe in a maximizing policy, we must accept this, as we must if our moral views tell us not to inflict pointless suffering or not to embark on pointless killing.

On this view, where there is a balance of terror, where each side is only restrained from attack by fear of retaliation, there is a clear rank ordering of possible outcomes. The best outcome is for neither side to suffer nuclear devastation, the next best is for only one side to do so and the worst outcome is for both sides to be devastated. This rank ordering might seem to be that of any sane man, but D.H. Hodgson has produced an interesting argument purporting to show that it is a self-defeating outlook.[6] He says that someone holding it as leader of a nation in a balance-

6. D.H. Hodgson: *Consequences of Utilitarianism*, Oxford, 1967, Ch. 4, part 1.

of-terror situation is debarred from securing what he himself considers to be the best outcome: neither side being devastated. This is because he is debarred from actually retaliating when attacked, and when the other side realizes this there will be nothing to restrain them from attack.

It is worth noting that this argument applies only to a pure balance-of-terror situation. Where, as we may hope is the case in most real conflicts, other restraining factors operate as well as fear of retaliation, knowledge that the leaders of one side hold the sane man's rank ordering will not automatically lead to an attack by the other side. (Although it will, of course, still remove one major restraint.) A more important limitation of the argument is that it only shows that in certain circumstances the sane man's rank ordering will have disastrous consequences *if the other side gets to know of it.* The Hodgson argument does not show that to possess the rank ordering is self-defeating, but it does show that, in a balance-of-terror situation, it may be necessary to conceal the rank ordering by making insincere threats of retaliation. If we accept that actual retaliation would not be justified, our discussion of the ethics of nuclear deterrence comes down to a discussion of whether or not insincere threats of nuclear retaliation can be justified.

What is the case against the use of these insincere threats? The first problem is that it is hard to see how a government could make insincere threats of retaliation seem genuine to another government without equally deceiving its own population. Governments are too often willing to deceive the people of a country, and it is a very serious drawback to a policy that it requires constant deception of a population on such a major issue by a government. It is, apart from anything else, a serious departure from the idea of democratic government if the basic principles of policy cannot be openly stated and discussed.

A further problem is that the deception and propaganda can work too well. Insincere threats can be made to look sincere only by governments saying that actual retaliation would be justified. And, if they say this convincingly enough, some people, perhaps including the politicians of the next generation, will be convinced. As people replace each other in government, especially where public opinion has been persuaded to look on actual retaliation as a legitimate option, the insincerity may disappear and a genuine threat emerge.

There are also the serious, though familiar, objections that a nuclear arms race is very expensive and carries with it some danger of accidental war. The pure form of accidental war involves some technical error either in the systems used to detect attack or in the system controlling the nuclear weapons themselves. But there is also something like accidental war, when politicians on one side misjudge how far they can go in some confrontation without bringing on nuclear retaliation. We are all lucky to have escaped this kind of 'accident' in the Cuban missiles crisis of 1962. To some extent the dangers of this kind of miscalculation can be reduced by 'hot-line' devices, and by clear conventions about permissible acts by parties to a nuclear stalemate. But it is hard to see how this sort of danger could be totally eliminated.

In the long term, the most important objection to the use of nuclear deterrence may be the effects on the attitudes of people whose governments tell them that the waging of retaliatory nuclear war would be legitimate. If a population develops the degree of hostility to the other side that may be necessary for sustained support of such a policy, this will work against the development of trust and the other attitudes necessary if the two sides are ever to escape from the balance-of-terror situation.

All these considerations make a powerful case against the use of nuclear deterrence, but in some circumstances they could be outweighed by arguments in favour of the insincere threat of nuclear retaliation. These are circumstances where such a threat seems the only plausible way of deterring another country either from making a nuclear attack or from using its own nuclear weapons to an intolerable degree as a means of black-mail. But, although nuclear deterrence *can* be justified, the drawbacks of the policy are such that it should only be a last

267

resort, and it is (as with war in general) too readily assumed that to show that it can be justified is enough to show that in a particular case it *is* justified.

6 Government Decisions for and against Conventional War: Aggression and Defence

Private acts of killing, most of us think, are extremely hard to justify. Wars are killing on a large scale and are that much harder to justify. The greater the war looks like being, the greater the evil it must avert to be justified. (And it must be clear that the evil cannot be averted by less drastic means.) And, as well as the difficulty of justifying so much killing and misery, there is the long-term case against resorting to war, resting on the danger of strengthening the tradition of resorting to war. And, in some cases, there is the danger that a conventional war may escalate into a nuclear one, so that the special arguments against nuclear war tell also against resorting in the first place to the conventional war.

But, with all these arguments against war, it is possible that war is sometimes the lesser evil, and perhaps the Second World War was one of those times. Such a decision can only be reached by calculating gains and losses, which, even with hindsight, cannot be done with any precision. And the decision at the time in such a case is immensely difficult: who in 1939 could predict how long the war would last? On the one hand, who could predict that the war would include the use of nuclear weapons? On the other hand, who in 1939 could predict the *full* results of Nazism? (When in 1945 Richard Dimbleby sent the first report from Dachau, the Governors of the BBC could not believe it and refused to broadcast it until there was confirmation by newspaper correspondents.) We cannot be at all confident of being right about the consequences of a decision in a situation such as that in 1938, when the decision was against war, or in 1939, when the decision was for war. But the fact that we cannot be sure of the consequences does not absolve us from the duty to base our decision upon the best judgement of them that we can make.

One popular alternative to the evaluation of probable consequences is to rely on the distinction between aggressive and defensive war. Many people take the view that it is always wrong for a government to start a war, but always legitimate for a government to meet external aggression with force. But even this plausible-looking view is open to criticism. G.E.M. Anscombe has spoken sharply of it: 'The present-day conception of "aggression", like so many strongly influential conceptions, is a bad one. Why *must* it be wrong to strike the first blow in a struggle? The only question is, who is in the right.'[7] There seems no reason in principle why it should always be wrong to start a war. If other governments had foreseen what the Nazis would do, they would probably have been right to invade Germany to remove Hitler in the early 1930s, or to wipe out all the leading Nazis by a bombing raid on one of the Nazi rallies at Nuremberg. Either of these courses of action would have avoided the far worse calamities that actually took place. Equally, it is not clearly right to wage a defensive war in all circumstances. If there is no prospect of winning, as in Czechoslovakia in 1968, a defensive war is only pointless bloodshed. And, even if there is prospect of winning, the cost may be too great.

But, while the distinction between aggression and defence does not automatically mark off justifiable from unjustifiable wars, it is still of some importance. This is partly because those who are prepared to start wars are likely to be worse governments than average, and the best outcome is usually that they should not win. But, more fundamentally, the distinction is important because of the role it can play in building up a tradition of settling disputes peacefully rather than by war. One way in which this tradition can be fostered is by declarations, treaties and agreements. We all know that these cannot be entirely relied on, but nevertheless they probably do make a con-

7. G.E.M. Anscombe: 'War and Murder', in W. Stein (ed.): *Nuclear Weapons, A Catholic Response*, London, 1963.

tribution to a climate of opinion in which war is less likely. But few, if any, governments or peoples are at present likely to enter into any agreement by which they renounce the use of war even as a means of self-defence. Since governments and peoples are more ready to give up the aggressive use of war in exchange for similar renunciations by other countries, it is worth having such agreements rather than no agreements.

Although the question of who starts a war is morally less central than is sometimes thought, the matter of establishing traditions gives it considerable oblique importance. The tradition of renouncing war even as a means of defence has not got off the ground. But the tradition of renouncing aggressive war is much more powerful, and so any act of aggression does more harm by doing damage to what is at present a more valuable mental barrier against war.

7 Individual Decisions about Participation in War

When a war starts, people living in the countries involved have to decide to what extent they are justified in participating in it. In practice, many people do not ask such a question, and some of those who do are intimidated, either by public opinion or by governmental pressure, from pursuing the question too far. But prison sentences and patriotic indignation do not make moral questions go away. Taking part in large-scale killing should not be decided upon with so much less thought than one could give to the decision about a private act of killing. How should this question about participation be answered?

For absolute patriots and absolute pacifists, the question presents no problem. For those of us without such certainties the matter is more complicated. In part, it involves thinking about all the questions already discussed in the context of governmental decision for and against war. But when a person has reached his own decision about whether a particular side is justified in fighting a war, this does not end the matter. For, once the war has already started, there is a changed situation which must be taken into account. Obviously the major part of the question will normally be about the rightness or wrongness of the war. And usually it will be right to participate in a justifiable war and wrong to participate in an unjustifiable war. But there are exceptions to these general rules.

The reasons for refusing to participate in a justified war are of little general interest. If my absence will drive my schizophrenic brother to suicide, or I am on the verge of making a great advance in cancer research, these matters may be of more importance than one man's contribution to the war effort, and I may be justified in refusing or evading participation in the war effort. (Lytton Strachey is supposed to have replied to a woman who taxed him with not being in uniform: 'Madam, I am the civilization for which they are fighting.') Such special cases need not detain us here.

The reasons which may make it right to participate in an unjustifiable war are of more general relevance. Consider the position of someone who during the Second World War took the view that the Hitler regime was a very great evil, but that the world war was an even greater one. On this view, the war should never have been started. It would not follow from this that he should not participate. For his non-participation will do nothing to bring the war to an end, but will merely make a very small contribution to weakening the forces against Hitler. Once the war is on, his preferred outcome is Hitler's defeat rather than Hitler's victory, and he may think the difference between these outcomes important enough to justify his own participation. There need be no inconsistency here, as his first preference, no war at all, is now unavailable.

There are some considerations that count against participation in an unjustifiable war. One is the desirability of standing out against social pressures and war hysteria. This will make it easier for other people to do the same, and may even lead to a substantial movement against the war, as did early opposition in the United States to the war in Vietnam. It will also strengthen the tradition of citizens making independent

271

judgements, which itself may operate as some check on governments embarking on further unjustifiable wars in the future.

A further reason for hesitation, even before participation in a justifiable war, is the open-ended nature of a commitment to military service. Wars once started can change their character, either politically or technologically, but the commitment to participate is hard to revoke. This danger has to be balanced against the desirability of contributing towards the best outcome as seen at the moment.

It is a feature of the approach advocated here that people who, on these sorts of grounds, refuse to participate in some war will normally not be granted exemption as conscientious objectors. Most countries that make provision at all for conscientious objection lay down criteria that require absolute pacifism rather than selective objection to individual wars considered on their demerits. It is also often required that the pacifism is based on some religious belief. There is no good reason why these restrictive criteria should not be liberalized. The present narrow criteria could scarcely be defended except by the following three arguments, each of which is inadequate. The first argument is that only absolute pacifism or religious-based pacifism count as genuine moral grounds for objecting to war. This view is not worth discussing. The second argument is that broadening the criteria for conscientious objection would let so many people through the net as seriously to impair the war effort. But if a really substantial section of the population think a war unjustified, this is in itself a powerful reason for doubting whether a government should have embarked on it. Having regulations which make it harder for governments to take to war a country seriously divided on the issue seems likely to be a benefit rather than a loss. The third argument is that broadening the criteria would give greater scope for frauds escaping the army by feigned conscientious objection. This argument fails: there is no reason to think that sophisticated moral beliefs are easier to feign than crude ones.

Those of us who believe in more rational public discussion of moral issues, or simply in civil liberties, should support liberal rather than restrictive criteria for conscientious objection in times of compulsory military service.

8 War Crimes and the Rules of War

Once a war is on, and let us for the sake of argument suppose it to be a justifiable one, are there any moral restrictions on the numbers or kinds of deaths that may be brought about in pursuit of victory? I have already suggested that there are good reasons for not crossing the boundary between conventional and nuclear war. There is a tradition of other restrictions that has influencèd modern declarations and treaties concerning the conduct of war. According to the tradition, killing must be necessary for a military objective and must not be disproportionate to the goal achieved. Also, according to the tradition, there must be no intentional killing of non-combatants ('the innocent'), whether civilians or prisoners. And certain methods of waging war, including various kinds of weapons, are absolutely forbidden. Those who support this tradition do so usually for one of two reasons. They sometimes hold certain absolute moral principles, such as the wrongness of the intentional killing of the innocent, which must not be flouted even in a context of war. Or else they say that the evils of war can to some extent be reduced by the parties to a war accepting these rules.

Critics of the traditional approach point to the apparent arbitrariness of some of the rules. Why is it morally acceptable to kill someone conscripted into the army, but not acceptable intentionally to kill the civilians who work in the war ministry? Why is gas outlawed but not napalm? The critics also suggest that having a special category of 'war crimes' helps to make other aspects of war seem more legitimate and so contributes to an undesirable degree of acceptance of war as a means of policy. Let us look at these defences and criticisms of the rules of war.

Take first the prohibition of the intentional killing of the innocent, interpreted in this context as the intentional killing of non-combatants. If *moral* guilt and innocence are in question, many politically active civilians may bear more guilt for a war than many conscripted soldiers. And, if the concepts of guilt and innocence are simply revised to coincide with the distinction between combatants and non-combatants, there is still a grey area which includes workers in munitions factories and those who supply the army with food. Father John Ford and others have defended the possibility of drawing the distinction against criticisms of this kind, but even if the distinction can be drawn there is the question of why it should be thought morally important. The death of a soldier is not a more trivial matter for him or his family than the death of a civilian.

An absolutist defence of the prohibition of killing non-combatants has been given by Thomas Nagel.[8] His argument consists partly in a criticism of the utilitarian approach to the matter, and partly in an attempt to unearth the fundamental consideration underlying the morality of absolute prohibitions. His criticism of the utilitarian view focuses on the consequences of its adoption. He says:

> Someone unfamiliar with the events of this century might imagine that utilitarian arguments, or arguments of national interest, would suffice to deter measures of this sort. But it has become evident that such considerations are insufficient to prevent the adoption and employment of enormous anti-population weapons once their use is considered a serious moral possibility. The same is true of the piecemeal wiping out of rural civilian populations in airborne anti-guerrilla warfare. Once the door is opened to calculations of utility and national interest, the usual speculations about the future of freedom, peace, and economic prosperity can be brought to bear to ease the consciences of those responsible for a certain number of charred babies.

When Nagel turns to his positive explanation of absolute prohibitions, he notes that the prohibitions in war are restrictions either on the people who may be attacked or on the means of attack. He suggests that these can be combined under the prin-

8. Thomas Nagel: 'War and Massacre', *Philosophy and Public Affairs*, 1972.

ciple that 'hostile treatment of any person must be justified in terms of something *about that person* which makes the treatment appropriate' and says that 'hostility is a personal relation, and it must be suited to its target.' He expands on this idea of the relation one ought to have to other people: 'I believe it is roughly this: whatever one does to another person intentionally must be aimed at him as a subject, with the intention that he receive it as a subject. It should manifest an attitude towards *him* rather than just to the situation, and he should be able to recognize it and identify himself as its object.' He also says that a restriction is absolute if there cannot be a justification for violating it, and suggests that in this context a justification for what one does to another person must be such that it can be offered to *him*.

Nagel's criticism of utilitarianism does not amount to a convincing claim that the utilitarian approach is in principle mistaken, but at most makes a case for arrangements which deny to armies or governments unrestricted use of utilitarian arguments. The reason that Nagel's criticism does not tell against utilitarianism in principle is that it appeals to the supposed bad consequences of taking these decisions by straightforward utilitarian calculation. These bad consequences, if they exist, could be taken into account by a consistent utilitarian. He might then decide that the best way of maximizing utility would be by adopting an oblique strategy, such as encouraging governments and armies to treat certain restrictions as if they were absolute prohibitions. Traffic regulations are not absolute moral principles, but serve the end of reducing accidents. The overall aim of accident reduction is not discredited by the fact that it may best be achieved, not by encouraging drivers to work out their own strategy towards this aim, but rather by encouraging them to obey conventional regulations. It should also be said that genuine utilitarian calculation is not discredited by the fact that the American war in Vietnam was sometimes defended by the use of incompetent calculations, based on dubious factual predictions and a doubtfully utilitarian scale of values.

Nagel's positive discussion of the basis of absolute pro-

275

hibitions in war is of obvious interest and appeal. He does not present it as in any way a fully worked-out account, but as a first approximation worth further exploration. For this reason, objections to it may prove unfounded when it is worked out in detail. But, as it stands, it should not be accepted. The principle in its present form is so vague that it is not clear either what it allows or what it rules out. It seems to lay down two requirements, one about my attitude to the person I attack, the other about his acceptance of my attitude as justifiable. Take my attitude first. Must I feel personal hostility towards the soldier I kill in war? If I feel sorry for him as a possibly reluctant conscript, does this alter the morality of killing him? Suppose I feel hostility towards civilian supporters of the war but not to soldiers forced to fight it? Does this make killing civilians right and killing soldiers wrong? It may be that answers to these questions are supposed to be provided by the second requirement, about the possibility of justifying my attitude to the person I attack. But what does this requirement come to? Why can I not offer to a civilian the justification that his death is a necessary means to the avoidance of a great evil, the victory of his side in the war? If the answer is that he would not accept this, then suppose the fighting soldier does not accept it either? Perhaps the claim is not that the soldier *will* accept it, but that he *would* accept it, if ... But, if what? Unless the theory is developed to answer some of the questions, we must look for something else.

R.B. Brandt has suggested that people both impartial and rational would choose rules of war that would maximize expectable utility.[9] (Any difference between that approach and the perhaps more complicated objections to killing outlined in this book is scarcely likely to be significant in the context of war, where the calculations are bound to be very coarse-textured.) On the utilitarian view, there is obviously everything to be said for those humanitarian restrictions that are no hindrance to military effectiveness, and it is clear that mutual agreement to

9. R.B. Brandt: 'Utilitarianism and the Rules of War', *Philosophy and Public Affairs*, 1972.

observe these restrictions is in the interests of all parties to a war. The difficult problem arises over the question of restrictions that do impair effectiveness. Brandt proposes the rule:

a military action (e.g. a bombing raid) is permissible only if the utility (broadly conceived, so that the maintenance of treaty obligations of international law could count as a utility) of victory to all concerned, multiplied by the increase in its probability if the action is executed, on the evidence (when the evidence is reasonably solid, considering the stakes), is greater than the possible disutility of the action to both sides multiplied by its probability.

He admits that this rule is vague and requires considerable exercise of judgement in actual situations. He also admits that both sides in a war will normally assign positive overall utility to their own victory. But he claims, with justification, that his rule is very different from a blanket permission of any act that may contribute to victory.

Brandt's proposed rule seems to me persuasive as an underlying approach to the question of war crimes, but inadequate as a rule to be agreed on by an international convention. It is persuasive as a general approach because it allows us to assign proper weight both to the aims of a justified war and to the desirability of limiting the horrors both of a present war and of future ones. Absolute bans on acts necessary to victory may involve giving too little weight to the avoidance of these evils which justify the war. On the other hand, the Brandt approach prevents us from forgetting that a good end justifies some means but not others. The acceptance of a restriction of this kind is a natural corollary of the view that wars can at best be justified on balance. As the horror of a war increases, it may pass the point where it is the lesser of the two evils.

The reason why Brandt's rule is likely to be inadequate as an instruction to appear in army manuals is that it leaves too much to the judgement of the soldier or strategist. If it is compared with some of the present rules, its lack of detail is striking. The United States army rules forbid any attack on civilians 'for the sole purpose of terrorizing the civilian population'. Brandt says that utilitarian considerations cannot justify a rule as stringent as this, and says, 'I fear we have to say that at this point the Army's theory has gone somewhat too far.' (It is not every day that an army is rebuked by a philosopher for *this*.) It is true that the army's prohibition of such attacks does not allow for those *very* rare circumstances in which the utilitarian approach might allow them. But it seems likely that a better outcome in utilitarian terms will be obtained by clear-cut rules, that give approximately the same results as utilitarian calculation, than by leaving so much of the calculation itself up to those waging war.

It is of course true that in some respects the present agreements about conduct in war depart radically from those that could be justified on the utilitarian approach. This is strikingly so in the case of weapons that are allowed and forbidden. But even where this is so, there is still a strong case for conforming to their prohibitions. As George I. Mavrodes has argued, what is right often depends on what conventions are already in existence.[10] The rule in England about driving on the left is no better than a rule telling us to drive on the right would have been. It would probably be better if our rule conformed to that in most other countries, so that people travelling between different countries did not have to change. But since the rule is there, accidents are reduced by obeying it. Even where the rules of war are imperfect, it is important to bolster the tradition that they are obeyed rather than to undermine it, as the system as a whole is better than having no system of restraints. (This does not rule out pressing for the system to be reformed by international agreement.)

Some people would disagree with the claim that the present rules of war are better than no rules. They might argue that all war is barbarism and that having rules forbidding some acts has the disastrous result of making the rest of war seem more legitimate than it is, and so the rules of war hinder progress towards its total abolition. If it can be shown that rules of war do make

10. George I. Mavrodes: 'Conventions and the Morality of War', *Philosophy and Public Affairs*, 1975.

war itself seem more acceptable as a policy, this is a very powerful case against such rules. I doubt whether they do have *any* significant effect of this kind, and so I continue to support their existence. But it is not clear how to settle this question, and it may be that evidence will one day show that the rules do have this effect, so undermining the position adopted here.

It should be said that there is the possibility, on very rare occasions, of a breach of the rules of war being justified. This is not inconsistent with the view that there ought to be rules of war or even with the view that the existing rules of war are the right ones. (I can consistently think that the authorities have chosen the right speed limit in a town, but still think I am right to break it when rushing someone to hospital.) The sort of rare case where breaking the rules of war will be justified is where doing so is essential to an enterprise that is likely to make a substantial contribution to the chances of victory, and where defeat would involve enormous evils. Consider the morality of bombing a hospital where Hitler is lying ill. Bombing a hospital is a terrible thing in itself, and will contribute towards undermining the very desirable general rule granting hospitals immunity from attack in war. But against this has to be set the contribution the death of Hitler might make to a quicker end to the war or a Nazi defeat, both of which will also save lives. I do not put forward any view about this case, but only suggest that we cannot totally rule out the possibility of such a war crime being justified. This does not undermine the case for doing what we can to encourage obedience to the rules of war as the norm.

9 Revolution and Wars of National Liberation

So far this discussion has mainly been in terms of the morality of wars between independent nations. But it is worth considering the view that revolutions and related phenomena have a special moral status. Several different cases need to be distinguished. There are times when a government is changed by a coup which can be relatively or even totally bloodless. There are wars of independence or of national liberation, where foreign rule is fought against and which may last for many years, as in Algeria or Angola. And there are revolutions within countries which already have national independence, such as the French and Russian revolutions. The bloodless coup scarcely raises issues that need be considered here. But revolutions that do involve killing, and wars of national liberation, are sufficiently like other wars to raise the question of whether or not the same standards of justification apply to them.

There are two views according to which revolutions can be set apart morally from other wars. The first is an extreme Hobbesian view, defended in our time by G.E.M. Anscombe, which says that revolution is a form of war which is never justified. The second view, that of Lenin, says that revolution is the only kind of justifiable war.

G.E.M. Anscombe says, 'The right to attack with a view to killing is something that belongs only to rulers and those whom they command to do it. I have argued that it does belong to rulers precisely because of that threat of violent coercion exercised by those in authority which is essential to the existence of human societies.'[11] This argument is unconvincing as a defence of an absolute ban on violent revolution. It may be true that force or threats are necessary for holding society together (though some thinkers take a more optimistic view), but it does not follow from this that the *existing* authorities should always be conceded a monopoly of force. It may be that some societies are so bad that force should be used to transfer power to other people.

Lenin expressed his view in a denunciation of the pacifist response to the First World War:[12]

If the present war rouses among the reactionary Christian Socialists, among the whimpering petty bourgeoisie, *only* horror and fright, only aversion to all use of arms, to bloodshed, death, etc., then we must say: capitalist society is always an *endless horror*. And

11. G.E.M. Anscombe, op. cit.
12. V.I. Lenin: *The War Programme of the Proletarian Revolution*, 1916.

if this most reactionary of all wars is now preparing a *horrible end* for that society, we have no reason to drop into despair. At a time when, as everyone can see, the bourgeoisie itself is paving the way for the only legitimate and revolutionary war, namely, civil war against the imperialist bourgeoisie, the 'demand' for disarmament, or more correctly, the dream of disarmament, is, objectively, nothing but an expression of despair.

In saying that the *only* legitimate war is that against the bourgeoisie, Lenin, obviously no absolute pacifist, is adopting an attitude of contingent pacifism towards all other wars. What marks off the proletarian revolution from other wars must be the greater evil it avoids, the greater benefit it brings, or the less killing and suffering it involves. Since there is no reason to think the proletarian revolution especially bloodless, its special justification must be in terms of the evils of the old society and the benefits of the new one. This does not involve claiming that the tests of whether revolution is justified differ from the tests proposed here for wars in general. For Lenin, the tests are the same, but only the proletarian revolution passes them. But this is a claim that needs a lot more detailed argument than is usually given in revolutionary literature. It is not enough (especially when confronting people thinking of the horrors of the First World War) simply to say that 'capitalist society is always an *endless horror*'. We can accept that capitalist society has its own evils, and we need not forget that lives are lost, as well as blighted, by poverty and bad conditions. But the argument is still incomplete. A more detailed description than is usually given of the society expected to result is needed, together with some indication of the degree of confidence we can have in these predictions. And, especially, some idea is needed of how much killing and misery is likely to take place in order to bring about the revolution.

As with wars between countries, these calculations are impossible to carry out with precision and are virtually certain to involve mistakes. But this does not absolve those who advocate or oppose revolution from taking their decision in the light of the best estimates they can make. As with other wars, people advocate revolution with a casualness about detailed argument that they would never show in other contexts where lives were at stake.

Some writers set these acts of killing apart from others by a mystique of revolutionary violence, to which they ascribe special benefits. Jean-Paul Sartre, in his preface to Frantz Fanon's book *The Wretched of the Earth*,[13] says,

I think we understood this truth at one time, but we have forgotten it – that no gentleness can efface the marks of violence; only violence itself can destroy them. The native cures himself of colonial neurosis by thrusting out the settler through force of arms. When his rage boils over, he rediscovers his lost innocence and he comes to know himself in that he himself creates his self.

Sartre also says,

The rebel's weapon is the proof of his humanity. For in the first days of the revolt you must kill: to shoot down a European is to kill two birds with one stone, to destroy an oppressor and the man he oppresses at the same time: there remain a dead man and a free man; the survivor, for the first time, feels a *national* soil under his foot. At this moment the Nation does not shrink from him; wherever he goes, wherever he may be, she is; she follows and is never lost to view, for she is one with his liberty.

Even those who believe in these supposed psychological benefits to the killer will be hard put to think that they get us far in defending the killing, unless they make the tacit assumption that the interests of the person killed count for little or nothing. But, just as killing in war is morally less different from other killing that people suppose, so killing in revolution is as hard to justify as in any other war. The death of a person does not matter less to him or his family because he is a colonial settler or a member of the middle classes.

The case for a revolution can be argued adequately only by detailed analysis of likely gains and losses. The fact that this is difficult does not mean that there is never any possibility of

13. Translated by Constance Farrington, London, 1965.

doing it to an adequate extent. For, while there is a heavy burden of justification on those who propose violent revolution, there is sometimes also a heavy burden of justification on those who propose acquiescing in the status quo. For, unless we accept the acts and omissions doctrine, we must weigh against those we might kill in a revolution those we allow to die by accepting the status quo. These include not only those killed by a repressive regime, but also those who die because of a government's inactivity.

The case against a revolution depends partly on disagreeing with the revolutionary's estimate, either of present evils or of future benefits, or else of the costs in lives and misery of the revolutionary period itself. It is also possible to oppose a revolution on the ground that, while a successful revolution might be desirable, the chances of bloodshed being followed by failure are too high. There are also special evils associated with revolution, to some extent related to the features regarded as beneficial by Sartre. Nadezhda Mandelstam, discussing the period of the Russian revolution and its aftermath says,

Why is it so easy to turn young people into killers? Why do they look on human life with such criminal frivolity? This is particularly true in those fateful periods when blood flows and murder becomes an ordinary everyday thing. We were set on by our fellow men like dogs, and the whole pack of us licked the hunter's hand, squealing incomprehensibly. The head-hunting mentality spread like a plague. I even had a slight bout of it myself.[14]

There is also a long-term argument against revolution, similar to one used against other kinds of war. Revolutions strengthen the tradition of resorting to violence and killing in order to change society. Even if, in a particular situation considered on its own merits, revolution is justified, this long-term effect is something that still may outweigh the immediate considerations.

14. Nadezhda Mandelstam: *Hope Against Hope*, translated by Max Hayward, London, 1971, Ch. 25.

The conclusion, that a justification for revolution (like war) is possible but extremely difficult to provide, has a platitudinous air. But it is a platitude often ignored by the followers of Lenin and those of Hobbes.

10 Concluding Note

In this chapter I have argued against absolute pacifism, against the view that it is always wrong to fight in an unjustified war, and even against regarding the prohibitions on various kinds of war crimes as being absolutely binding. To say all this is to lean over backwards to recognize the possibility of complex moral justifications for acts which would normally outrage the sensibilities of most decent people. The trouble with allowing the *possibility* of such acts being justified is that this view can be corrupted by enthusiastic 'realists' into a defence of whatever war or atrocity is thought to serve their national or ideological interests. So I should like to say here that it is hard to believe that more than an insignificant number of all the wars in history have been justified. The act of refusal to participate, which seems so minute in its immediate effects, often contributes to a tradition of dissent and criticism that makes future wars less likely. And decisions against committing war crimes, which may seem like pointless gestures, also contribute in the long term to traditions that limit the barbarism of war. Our thinking about the morality of war is easily distorted by the time bias which exaggerates the importance of the immediate relative to the long term. It takes a conscious effort to begin to escape from this.

But the most fundamental distortion of our thinking here is the compartmentalization of our minds, which goes so deep that we are usually quite unaware of it. Sometimes the compartmentalization breaks down, as with the regimental doctor in Vietnam treating an enemy soldier, who remembered the Hippocratic Oath when his commanding officer said, 'Just keep him alive for a few minutes so we can question him. After that he can die. It doesn't matter to me.'[15] It is obvious that we will not abolish war simply by altering states of mind. It is necessary to find better political arrangements and to find some way of reducing the dangers created by the existence of separate nation states. But political changes are not totally separate from changes in our thinking: the causal influence goes both ways. One change must be to stop regarding killing in war as almost by magic immune from moral criticism. This will help us to retain our scepticism when governments and Believers present the impassioned and rubbishy arguments normally used in support of war.

15. Gordon S. Livingston: 'Letter from a Vietnam Veteran', in Richard A. Falk, Gabriel Kolko and Robert Jay Lifton: *Crimes of War*, New York, 1971.

Chapter 20   Moral Distance

Of philosophical opinions I embrace for preference those that are most substantial, that is to say most human, and most natural to us.

Montaigne: *On Experience*

Who will direct our anger against that which is truly terrible, and not that which is merely near?

Alexander Solzhenitsyn: *'One Word of Truth...'* London, 1972

To many people, the views advocated in this book will seem to have an excessive rationalism. In matters of killing and saving lives, the right thing to do has been identified with what creates (in a broad interpretation of this phrase) the best total outcome. This jars with a whole range of 'natural' intuitive feelings. Our revulsion against killing is enormously greater than our reluctance to let people die. Killing in war does not elicit the same response as a spectacular murder case. We care more about a dramatic rescue operation to save a single miner than about safety measures that will save many lives. Those who support abortion are often appalled at the thought of infanticide. It has been argued here that the right thing to do will sometimes go against these intuitive feelings.

It may be objected that, while this might be a morality for a God or a Martian, it is not a morality for human beings. Various criticisms can be implied here. The suggestion may be that such a rationalist morality is not one that we are capable of living by. Or it may be said that, since morality must be rooted in our intuitive responses, this rationalist morality fails because it does not have enough intuitive appeal. Or it may be that, even if we could do so, to guide our conduct by it would destroy the human quality of relationships.

Part of the defence of the kind of rationalism in question is to look at the most general features of the 'natural' morality contrasted with it. Here and there in the discussion of these issues, echoes of taboo and magic can perhaps be heard, as when people say that life is sacred or that conception is the 'magic moment' when life begins. Sometimes there is a belief in the transforming power of words, as when people who agree on all the facts of foetal development try to settle the question of abortion by arguing about whether the word 'person' applies to the foetus. And, when thinking about the doctrine of double effect, or the acts and omissions doctrine, I wonder whether it is far-fetched to see something like a belief in ritual, in the concern with the shape of the causal pathway by which an outcome is reached, or the concern with whether it is reached by act or omission. But more important, and less speculative, is the phenomenon of moral distancing.

1 Moral Distance

In his famous experiments on obedience, Stanley Milgram found that certain kinds of distancing influenced people's willingness to obey orders to inflict pain.[1] The subjects of the experiment thought (wrongly) that when they obeyed an order, they were inflicting a severe electric shock on someone. Where the 'victim' could be dimly seen through a silvered glass, those obeying the orders often looked away. One of them said, 'I didn't want to see the consequences of what I had done.' To test the influence of distancing, the situation was varied. At one extreme the victim was in another room and could not even be heard. At the other extreme, the person obeying the order had to force the 'victim's' hand on to a shock plate. When the shocks were supposedly given to an unheard person in another room

1. Stanley Milgram: *Obedience to Authority, an Experimental View*, London, 1974.

twice as many subjects obeyed as when they would have to force the victim's hand. Even if other factors also contributed to this discrepancy, it seems plausible that psychological distancing played an important part.

This distancing is familiar in other contexts. We care more if the child down the road gets drowned than if thousands die in a flood in another country. And it is especially evident in war. Mary McCarthy, writing of the My Lai massacre,[2] says,

Though it would have changed nothing for the victims, most of us would prefer to think that those women and babies and old men had died in a raid rather than been singled out, one by one, for slaughter. Logic here is unpersuasive: the deliberate killing of unresisting people *is* more repugnant than the same result effected by mechanical means deployed at a distance and without clear perception of who or what is below.

She also says,

If one and the same person can condemn Calley and still 'live with' the B-52 raids in Laos and Cambodia, which he *knows* must be killing an unknown number of peasants on a daily basis, this only means that he is not totally callous. He knows, if he stops to think, but mercifully he is not obliged to think twenty-four hours a day. There are knowledge and inescapable knowledge. Somewhere in between lies the toleration threshold, differing, obviously, in different people. In the air war, the magnitude of the effect produced by the mere everyday pressing of a button or releasing a catch surpasses the imagination of those concerned, which was not the case with Lt Calley emptying and reloading his rifle or with the men who watched.

These remarks bring out both how it is easier to kill at a distance and how we take a more charitable view of others who kill at a distance than of those who do so at close range. There is the feeling that because killing at a distance is easier, one would not have to be such a monster to do it.

Psychological distancing can depend on distance in time as well as space. A proportion of those who start smoking this year will be killed by cigarettes in the future, but neither cigarettes

2. Mary McCarthy: *Medina*, London, 1973.

nor advertisements for them are banned. Yet if there were a food that killed the same proportion of its consumers by immediate poisoning, it is hard to believe that people or governments would care so little. Time bias is combined with other factors in the widespread downgrading of the value of saving 'statistical' lives.

Our responses also vary with people's external appearance. Babies with repulsive physical deformities are less likely to arouse protective responses than babies who look normal but who are feeble-minded. Perhaps an extreme case of this is part of what accounts for the barrier between abortion and infanticide: we respond to the baby's appearance, while the foetus cannot be seen at all. Photographs of foetuses are used a lot in campaigns against abortion. The physical repulsiveness that sometimes comes with extreme old age may, for a similar reason, be a double curse. Unpleasant in itself, it may also dull the responses of others. If the very old looked as attractive as children, would some geriatric wards be left as they are?

Our responses also vary with the extent to which we ourselves are already emotionally involved with those affected. This is obvious in the case of our greater concern for our family and friends than for strangers. But there are less obvious instances. The Home Office regulations governing scientific experiments on animals give far greater protection to species whose members are often objects of human affection, such as dogs, cats and horses, than they do to monkeys.

We are also often victims of a kind of size illusion generated by contexts where large numbers of people are involved. When considering the problem of world poverty, we sometimes think that there is no point in sending money to relief agencies. 'The most I could do would be to save a handful of people from starvation, and this is a mere drop in the ocean, for millions of lives are at stake.' Huge problems produce a kind of paralysis of the imagination, so that we do not bring sharply into focus exactly what we can do. For in other contexts, such as in a burning building, we would take very seriously the possibility of saving a handful of lives.

2 Defence Mechanisms

Both the importance given to words and the phenomena of moral distancing can be plausibly explained as defence mechanisms that serve a valuable purpose. There is a psychological need for clear categories, and for cut-and-dried decision procedures. Also certain jobs, sometimes of great social value, might be psychologically too demanding if those doing them did not to some extent work with a deadened imagination or with simple categories limiting their sense of responsibility. More generally, it is arguable that we all need the protection of such defence mechanisms: that anyone with a steady imaginative grasp of the extent of the avoidable evil in the world would suffer some kind of psychological collapse.

It has been suggested by Mary Douglas, in her anthropological writings, that many cases of 'moral' revulsion are founded on our emotional hostility to things that blur the sharp boundaries between the categories in terms of which we normally see the world.[3] A view of this kind is highly suggestive, yet of great elusiveness when the question of testing its truth is raised. But whether or not a preference for sharp boundaries is valuable in the explanation of natural moralities, it is clearly true that sharp category distinctions are found helpful by people taking certain moral decisions. This is illustrated by the eagerness with which people embrace some all-or-none view when asked whether or not the foetus is a person. Or again, there is the use of the word 'murder'. To many people, the assassination in time of peace of a repulsive dictator would be murder, and so wrong, while the killing of many of his subjects in time of war would not be murder, and so could even be one's duty. These simple categories spare people much hard intellectual work in thinking about consequences, and, more importantly, spare people much moral agonizing.

It is especially important for people doing some jobs to have clear-cut rules. Many doctors, taking what I believe to be often

3. e.g. Mary Douglas: *Purity and Danger*, London, 1966.

good decisions against further efforts to prolong a life, are able to preserve peace of mind because of the psychological distance put between their decision and murder by the acts and omissions doctrine. And the doctrine of double effect operates in the same way for the administering of death-inducing doses of morphine.

Having an imagination at least partly anaesthetized can make life easier for a decision-maker, but often with disastrous consequences. Politicians, humane in private life, going to war for inadequate reasons are perhaps the most obvious instance. A striking illustration of the effect on decision-taking of a numbed imagination concerns the forcible deportation to Russia, in accordance with the Yalta Agreement, of large numbers of Soviet citizens in the West.[4] They were forcibly herded on to trains by troops, and many committed suicide. On arrival they faced either labour camps or death. The Foreign Office official who defended this policy against army protests no doubt found his task easier because of his own psychological distance from the victims. But when, from among all those to be deported, a single woman managed to see this official and clung to his knees crying, she was spared. We can bring ourselves to sign documents consigning large numbers of people to their deaths more easily than we can refuse to save the person in front of us.

A case like this may make us think these defence mechanisms entirely harmful. If the decision-makers had thought of all the victims of the deportation policy as vividly as the official had to think of the woman, they would have been unable to stomach the policy and a better decision would have been reached.

Other cases seem to show the defence mechanisms in a more favourable light. Sometimes, it may be right to refuse to give in to political blackmail, and yet it may take a rather numbed imagination to do so. Suppose some terrorists say they will massacre captive children unless their demands are met. Our capitulation now may put many future people at risk from the increasingly confident terrorists, and so it may be right to stand firm. And the people taking the decision may only be able to

4. cf. Nicholas Bethell: *The Last Secret*, London, 1974.

refuse the demands if they avoid thinking too much about the plight of the children now at risk. But such a case only shows that, where one defence mechanism is already operating, the operation of another may counteract the bias and so lead to the right decision. For it is only in the context of our inability to think sufficiently vividly about the plight of future victims as yet unknown that we have to reach the right decision by means of damping down our responses to those now at risk.

This suggests an idealized picture of the moral sensibilities appropriate to rationalist morality. Let us look at the psychology of rationalist man, so that we may understand ourselves better by contrast.

3 Rationalist Man

Rationalist man would lack *any* of the distorting effects of the defence mechanisms. He would respond emotionally to all the foreseeable reverberations across time and space of his acts and omissions, just as much as to consequences immediately experienced. His responses would not be altered by the shape of the causal pathway leading to the outcome, nor by the decision to apply a word to phenomena in other respects already understood.

Rationalist man would have to differ from us in other important ways if he were to have much happiness. Suppose I decide to spend some money on a concert ticket rather than give it to a famine relief agency. The result may be that ten fewer sick Indian children are included in a medical programme than would have been if I had sent the money. The defence mechanisms normally have a great influence here. If, in order to buy the concert ticket, I had to take medicine from the children and sell it, I would no longer enjoy the concert. Most of us would be unable to act in this way. If rationalist man retained our present revulsion against such behaviour, he would feel just the same about merely buying the ticket with money that could have gone to Oxfam. Even if his conscience would not be quite as tender as that of Father Zossima's brother, it would be very different from ours. He would either have to live a life spectacularly self-sacrificing by our standards or else have many of his pleasures overshadowed by guilt. Perhaps his more intense responses to things we can feel distant from would increase rationalist man's capacity for altruism. But, if his capacity remained as limited as ours, he might become suicidally depressed. If so, part of the case for the defence mechanisms is that they protect people from an intolerable burden of guilt and despair.

(It is hard to tell how much we could rid ourselves of the defence mechanisms. If we could at least to some extent eliminate them, the argument for retaining them would stress the burden of guilt they avoid. Against this would have to be set the drawbacks of the status quo, where so much death and misery results from decisions taken by people whose defence mechanisms are in excellent working order.)

4 Difficulty and Intuitive Basis

One criticism says that rationalist morality, going against many of our intuitive responses, is impossibly difficult to live by. Another, related, criticism is that rationalist morality will not be even aspired to by people, since it is so lacking in intuitive appeal.

There are many psychological barriers which common-sense morality depends on. Most of the common-sense views criticized in this book share a single feature. They forbid what is intuitively repugnant or difficult and allow what is not, regardless of the total effects on others. These views fit our psychological barriers so well that the suspicion arises that they are not based on concern for others at all, but on our own need to feel comfortable about the behaviour to which we are naturally inclined.

Hume is surely right in his scepticism about the extent of our concern for others:

293

In general, it may be affirmed, that there is no such passion in human minds as the love of mankind, merely as such, independent of personal qualities, of services or of relation to ourself. It is true, there is no human, and indeed no sensible creature, whose happiness or misery does not, in some measure, affect us, when brought near to us, and represented in lively colours: but this proceeds merely from sympathy, and is no proof of such a universal affection to mankind.[5]

It is possible to speculate that these limitations of emotional involvement were relatively unimportant in the environment of primitive man. Concern restricted to a few people, and to what happens near by in space and time, is adequate for people whose actions have effects limited in the same way. But now we can kill or save lives at a distance and greatly influence the lives of future generations. And we are able to ask whether we are justified in downgrading the interests of people outside the range of our emotional responses. At this point, for many of us, the dilemma arises. We cannot see any justification for downgrading people because they live far away or in the future, and yet we cannot escape the limitations of our psychology. Our beliefs start to diverge from the emotional responses natural to us.

It is tempting to eliminate this tension by saying that it is our beliefs which must give. On such a view, rationalist philosophy, which so often involves standing back and allowing criticism and theory to come between our feelings and our decisions, would be replaced by a celebration of the spontaneous and the intuitive. One danger of this is that we will take ourselves (adult humans not yet old) as the centre of the moral universe, and such 'morality' as we have will be limited by our inability to imagine ourselves in other positions. When our 'morality' is biased in this way, it is open to the charge of being mere rationalization of self-interest.

Those of us who, for this and other reasons, are not prepared to accept that intuitive responses and natural attitudes are sac-

5. David Hume: *A Treatise of Human Nature*, Book 3, Part 2, Section 1.

rosanct have the problem of seeing how far these responses can, where desirable, be modified or else acted against.

It is hard to tell how far it is in our power to modify some of our deepest intuitive responses. There seems to be no general consensus among historians and anthropologists on the question of whether there is a constant central moral framework underlying the surface differences between societies. And neither the presence nor the absence of such a framework would settle conclusively the question how far a deliberate change of outlook is possible. Critical discussion can at least enable us to withhold our intellectual assent from some of our emotional attitudes, and this may help to weaken the grip they have on us.

We know that we can sometimes act against strong intuitive responses, though the extent of this is again unclear. People carrying out abortions, or soldiers in war, can overcome their revulsion against killing. Various social pressures are obviously at work. But also important are the beliefs, linked in their turn with countervailing intuitive responses, by which they justify these acts of killing. In what circumstances, and how far, our thought out beliefs can override feelings of revulsion or the limitations of our imagination are empirical questions. They have not had the attention which, in view of their importance for our future, they deserve.

5 Moral Conservatism

The view that we cannot significantly modify or act against our deeply ingrained pre-reflective attitudes may be put forward with relief or regret. Reasons for relief (and corresponding regret if we turn out after all to have scope for substantial change) can be based on two different kinds of moral conservatism.

Pure moral conservatism is opposed to changes in moral outlook because it simply endorses current beliefs or attitudes. If we already have the right morality, any change must be for the worse. I have nothing further to say here about this view. It will appeal to all those who think that common-sense morality forms an entirely consistent system which has only acceptable logical consequences.

Utilitarian moral conservatism takes a different form. Here the appeal is to the possibility that casting doubt on deeply ingrained moral attitudes might have an appalling outcome. There are cases where the collapse of traditional moral attitudes have had terrible consequences. The Ik, an African tribe deprived of their hunting grounds, seem, in the description given by Colin Turnbull, to be very close to being a group of people without any concern for each other at all.[6] And we know how much of the range of human responses the Nazis were able to abandon.

There is obviously no easy way of being sure how likely desirable changes in moral outlook are to bring undesirable ones with them. But there are some assumptions underlying the utilitarian moral conservative's position which should be brought out into the open. There is an assumption of a high degree of interdependence in our present attitudes: the view that we cannot relax the prohibition on infanticide without weakening our psychological defences against the extermination camps. There is the assumption that the reasons we have for the policies we choose are relatively unimportant to the reverberations of those policies in other parts of our system of attitudes. This is the view that switching off the respirator will make the doctor who does it more casual about the value of life in other contexts, no matter how carefully the decision was reached and regardless of the reasons. There is the assumption that current attitudes form a static system, or, less implausibly, that there is a natural or desirable rate of moral change which would be exceeded by whatever particular change of outlook the moral conservative is engaged in resisting.

None of these assumptions can be dismissed out of hand, but equally none of them should be put forward as obviously true without need of further discussion. Many people have killed in

6. Colin Turnbull: *The Mountain People*, London, 1973.

war without their attitudes to other kinds of killing showing any apparent ill effects, which casts some doubt on the supposed high degree of psychological interdependence of different parts of our outlook. It may be objected that this is one of the pieces of the compartmentalization that might be broken down by rationalist morality. This is true, but is it obvious that the results of this would be more murders rather than fewer wars? We know rather little about these aspects of our psychology, which is no doubt a good reason for taking a gradual approach to moral change. (It is scarcely likely that changes of attitude resulting from discussion and criticism, rather than from uglier techniques, will be anything other than gradual.)

The effects of changes of belief and attitude are uncertain. To say that this is a case for letting change be gradual is not to concede that our present attitudes are all in order, nor to concede that it is too dangerous to tamper with them at all. Are we entitled to accept so readily the kind of world they have helped to bring about? Our defence mechanisms no doubt spare us from great psychological discomfort, and contribute a lot to the freedom from pressure on which so much of our happiness may depend. There is an obvious case for preserving them. But the question remains: at what cost in misery and loss of life are we entitled to do so?

Bibliography

Chapter 2   The Scope and Limits of Moral Argument

R. B. Brandt: *Ethical Theory*, Englewood Cliffs, 1959, Chs. 1 and 2.

Alan Gewirth: 'Positive Ethics and Normative Science', *Philosophical Review*, 1960.

R. M. Hare: *Freedom and Reason*, Oxford, 1963, Chs. 6 and 11.

Philippa Foot: 'Moral Arguments', *Mind*, 1958.

B. A. O. Williams and R. F. Atkinson: 'Consistency in Ethics', *Proceedings of the Aristotelian Society*, Supp. Volume, 1965.

Alexander Solzhenitsyn: *'One Word of Truth . . .'*, London, 1972.

Alasdair MacIntyre: 'How Virtues Become Vices', *Encounter*, 1975.

Chapter 3   The Sanctity of Life

(a) THE BOUNDARY BETWEEN LIFE AND DEATH

Glanville Williams: *The Sanctity of Life and the Criminal Law*, London, 1958, Ch. 1.

Ad Hoc Committe of the Harvard Medical School to Examine the Definition of Brain Death: 'A Definition of Irreversible Coma', *Journal of the American Medical Association*, 1968.

Task Force on Death and Dying of the Institute of Society, Ethics and the Life Sciences: 'Refinements in Criteria for the Determination of Death, An Appraisal', *Journal of the American Medical Association*, 1972.

P. D. G. Skegg: 'Irreversibly Comatose Individuals: "Alive" or "Dead" ', *Cambridge Law Journal*, 1974.

Lawrence C. Becker: 'Human Being: The Boundaries of the Concept', *Philosophy and Public Affairs*, 1975.

BIBLIOGRAPHY

(b) DEATH AND LENGTH OF LIFE

Lucretius: *The Nature of the Universe*, translated by R. E. Latham, Harmondsworth, 1951.

Marcus Aurelius: *Meditations*, translated by Maxwell Staniforth, Harmondsworth, 1964.

Augustine: *The City of God*, Book 13.

B. Pascal: *Pensées*, section on Diversion.

A. Schopenhauer: *The World as Will and Representation*, translated by E. J. F. Payne, New York, 1969, Book 4, section 54, and supplements to the Fourth Book, Ch. 41.

Leo Tolstoy: *The Death of Ivan Ilich.*

Ludwig Wittgenstein: *Tractatus Logico-Philosophicus*, translated by D. F. Pears and B. F. McGuinness, London, 1971. Propositions 6.431–6.4312.

P. L. Landsberg: *The Experience of Death*, London, 1953.

William H. Poteat: ' "I Will Die": An Analysis', *Philosophical Quarterly*, 1959.

Paul Edwards: 'My Death', in *The Encyclopaedia of Philosophy*, New York, 1967.

Arnold Toynbee: 'The Relation between Life and Death, Living and Dying', in Arnold Toynbee and others: *Man's Concern with Death*, London, 1968.

Thomas Nagel: 'Death', in James Rachels (ed.): *Moral Problems*, New York, 1971.

Mary Mothersill: 'Death', in James Rachels (ed.): *Moral Problems*, New York, 1971.

James Van Ezra: 'On Death as a Limit', *Analysis*, 1971.

Bernard Williams: 'The Makropulos Case', in *Problems of the Self*, Cambridge 1973.

Michael A. Slote: 'Existentialism and the Fear of Dying', *American Philosophical Quarterly*, 1975.

(c) THE PROHIBITION OF KILLING

Thomas Aquinas: *Summa Theologica*, Secunda Secundae, section 64.

Karl Barth: *Church Dogmatics: The Doctrine of Creation*, Part 4.

Albert Schweitzer: *The Teaching of Reverence for Life,* London, 1966.

Bruno Bettelheim: *The Informed Heart,* London, 1961, Ch. 6.

Richard Robinson: *An Atheist's Values,* Oxford, 1964, Ch. 2, Section 2.

Edward Shils: 'The Sanctity of Life', in D. H. Labby (ed.): *Life or Death: Ethics and Options,* London, 1968.

Abraham Kaplan: 'Social Ethics and the Sanctity of Life', in D. H. Labby (ed.): *Life or Death: Ethics and Options* London, 1968.

T. Goodrich: 'The Morality of Killing', *Philosophy,* 1969.

Daniel Callahan: *Abortion: Law, Choice and Morality,* New York, 1970, Ch. 9.

R. E. Ewin: 'What is Wrong with Killing People?', *Philosophical Quarterly,* 1972.

Marvin Kohl: *The Morality of Killing,* London, 1974, Chs. 1 and 2.

Eike-Henner W. Kluge: *The Practice of Death,* New Haven, 1975, Ch. 6.

Chapter 4   Actual and Potential People

(a) GENERAL WORKS ON UTILITARIANISM

John Stuart Mill: *Utilitarianism,* 4th edition, London, 1871.

Henry Sidgwick: *The Methods of Ethics,* 7th edition, London, 1907, Book 4.

G. E. M. Anscombe: 'Modern Moral Philosophy', *Philosophy,* 1958.

R. M. Hare: *Freedom and Reason,* Oxford, 1963, Ch. 7.

Anthony Quinton: *Utilitarian Ethics,* London, 1973.

J. J. C. Smart and Bernard Williams: *Utilitarianism, For and Against,* Cambridge, 1973.

(b) UTILITARIANISM, POPULATION SIZE AND KILLING

Henry Sidgwick: *The Methods of Ethics,* 7th edition, London, 1907, Book 4, Ch. 1.

F. Dostoyevsky: *Crime and Punishment.*

BIBLIOGRAPHY

G. Tedeschi: 'On Tort Liability for "Wrongful Life" ', *Israel Law Review*, 1966.

Jan Narveson: 'Utilitarianism and New Generations', *Mind*, 1967.

Jan Narveson: *Morality and Utility*, Baltimore, 1967, pp. 46–50.

Hermann Vetter: 'Utilitarianism and New Generations', *Mind*, 1971.

Richard G. Henson: 'Utilitarianism and the Wrongness of Killing', *Philosophical Review*, 1971.

John Rawls: *A Theory of Justice*, Harvard, 1971, sections 27–30.

R. Steven Talmage: 'Utilitarianism and the Morality of Killing', *Philosophy*, 1972.

Stuart Hampshire: *Morality and Pessimism*, Cambridge, 1972.

Leonard C. Lewin: *Triage*, London, 1972.

Jan Narveson: 'Moral Problems of Population', *The Monist*, 1973.

Eike-Henner W. Kluge: *The Practice of Death*, New Haven, 1975, Ch. 6.

Derek Parfit: 'Overpopulation', *Philosophy and Public Affairs*, forthcoming.

Chapter 5   Autonomy and Rights

John Stuart Mill: *On Liberty*, 3rd edition, London, 1864.

H. L. A. Hart: 'Are There Any Natural Rights?', *Philosophical Review*, 1955.

Norman St John-Stevas: *The Right to Life*, London, 1963.

Gerald Dworkin: 'Paternalism', in Richard A. Wasserstrom (ed.): *Morality and the Law*, Belmont, 1971.

Joel Feinberg: 'Legal Paternalism', *Canadian Journal of Philosophy*, 1971.

Michael Tooley: 'Abortion and Infanticide', *Philosophy and Public Affairs*, 1972, revised version in Joel Feinberg (ed.): *The Problem of Abortion*, Belmont, 1973.

John Finnis: 'The Rights and Wrongs of Abortion: A Reply

to Judith Thomson', *Philosophy and Public Affairs*, 1973.

Joel Feinberg: 'The Rights of Animals and Unborn Generations', in William T. Blackstone (ed.): *Philosophy and Environmental Crisis*, Georgia, 1974.

H. J. McCloskey: 'The Right to Life', *Mind*, 1975.

Chapter 6   Ends and Means: Double Effect

G. E. M. Anscombe: *Mr Truman's Degree*, Oxford, 1958, reprinted in *The Human World*, 1973.

G. E. M. Anscombe: 'Modern Moral Philosophy', *Philosophy*, 1958.

Glanville Williams: *The Sanctity of Life and the Criminal Law,* London, 1958, Ch. 6.

G. E. M. Anscombe: 'War and Murder', in Walter Stein (ed.): *Nuclear Weapons, A Catholic Response*, London, 1961.

Eric D'Arcy: *Human Acts*, Oxford, 1963, Ch. 1, part 1; Ch. 3; Ch. 4, part 3.

Jonathan Bennett: 'Whatever the Consequences', *Analysis*, 1966.

H. L. A. Hart: 'Intention and Punishment', *The Oxford Review*, 1967, reprinted in H. L. A. Hart: *Punishment and Responsibility*, Oxford, 1968.

Anthony Kenny: 'Intention and Purpose in Law', in R. S. Summers (ed.): *Essays in Legal Philosophy*, Oxford, 1968.

Philippa Foot: 'The Problem of Abortion and the Doctrine of the Double Effect', *The Oxford Review*, 1967, reprinted in James Rachels (ed.): *Moral Problems*, New York, 1971.

G. G. Grisez: 'Toward a Consistent Natural Law Ethics of Killing', *American Journal of Jurisprudence*, 1970.

L. Geddes: 'On the Intrinsic Wrongness of Killing Innocent People', *Analysis*, 1973.

R. A. Duff: 'Intentionally Killing the Innocent', *Analysis*, 1973.

John Finnis: 'The Rights and Wrongs of Abortion: A Reply to Judith Thomson', *Philosophy and Public Affairs*, 1973.

Judith Jarvis Thomson: 'Rights and Deaths', *Philosophy and Public Affairs*, 1973.

James G. Hanink: 'Some Light on Double Effect', *Analysis* 1975.

R. G. Frey: 'Some Aspects to the Doctrine of Double Effect', *Canadian Journal of Philosophy*, 1975.

Chapter 7   Not Striving to Keep Alive

Graham Hughes: 'Criminal Omissions', *Yale Law Journal*, 1958.

J. O. Urmson: 'Saints and Heroes', in A. I. Melden: *Essays in Moral Philosophy*, Washington, 1958.

Joel Feinberg: 'Supererogation and Rules', *Ethics*, 1961, reprinted in Joel Feinberg: *Doing and Deserving*, Princeton, 1970.

Eric D'Arcy: *Human Acts*, Oxford, 1963, Ch. 1.

Jonathan Bennett: 'Whatever the Consequences', *Analysis*, 1966.

P. J. FitzGerald: 'Acting and Refraining', *Analysis*, 1967.

Philippa Foot: 'The Problem of Abortion and the Doctrine of the Double Effect', *The Oxford Review*, 1967.

Daniel Dinello: 'On Killing and Letting Die', *Analysis*, 1971.

John Casey: 'Actions and Consequences', in John Casey (ed.): *Morality and Conduct*, London, 1971.

Myles Brand: 'The Language of Not Doing', *American Philosophical Quarterly*, 1971.

Peter Singer: 'Famine, Affluence and Morality', *Philosophy and Public Affairs*, 1972.

Michael Tooley: 'Abortion and Infanticide', *Philosophy and Public Affairs*, 1972.

J. M. Freeman: 'Is There a Right to Die – Quickly?' *Journal of Paediatrics*, 1972.

Michael Walzer: 'Political Action: The Problem of Dirty Hands', *Philosophy and Public Affairs*, 1973.

Bernard Williams: 'A Critique of Utilitarianism' (Sections 3, 4 and 5), in J. J. C. Smart and Bernard Williams: *Utilitarianism, For and Against*, Cambridge, 1973.

John Harris: 'The Marxist Conception of Violence', *Philosophy and Public Affairs*, 1974.

John Harris: 'Williams on Negative Responsibility', *Philosophical Quarterly*, 1974.

Charles Fried: *Medical Experimentation: Personal Integrity and Social Policy*, Oxford, 1974, Ch. 3.

John Harris: 'The Survival Lottery', *Philosophy*, 1975.

Gerard Hughes: 'Killing and Letting Die', *The Month*, 1975.

Richard L. Trammell: 'Saving Life and Taking Life', *Journal of Philosophy*, 1975.

James Rachels: 'Active and Passive Euthanasia', *New England Journal of Medicine*, January 1975.

Chapters 9, 10 and 11   Abortion

(a) GENERAL

Glanville Williams: *The Sanctity of Life and the Criminal Law*, London, 1958, Chs. 5 and 6.

Church Assembly Board for Social Responsibility: *Abortion, An Ethical Discussion*, London, 1965.

H. Forrseman and Inga Thuwe: '120 Children Born after Application for Therapeutic Abortion Refused', *Acta Psychiatrica Scandinavica*, 1966.

G. Tedeschi: 'On Tort Liability for "Wrongful Life" ', *Israel Law Review*, 1966.

Joshua Lederberg: 'A Geneticist Looks at Contraception and Abortion, Colloquium on Ethical Dilemmas from Medical Advances', *Annals of Internal Medicine*, 1967.

Paul Ramsey: 'The Morality of Abortion', in D. H. Labby (ed.): *Life or Death: Ethics and Options*, London, 1968.

John T. Noonan: 'Deciding Who is Human', *Natural Law Forum*, 1968.

John T. Noonan (ed.): 'The Morality of Abortion', *Legal and Historical Perspectives*, Cambridge, Mass., 1970.

Daniel Callahan: *Abortion: Law, Choice and Morality*, New York, 1970, especially Chs. 10 and 11.

G. G. Grisez: *Abortion: The Myths, Realities and Arguments*, New York, 1970.

T. N. A. Jeffcoate and Philippa Foot: 'Abortion', in A. Clow (ed.): *Morals and Medicine*, London, 1970.

BIBLIOGRAPHY

B. A. Brody: 'Abortion and the Law', *Journal of Philosophy*, 1971.

Roger Wertheimer: 'Understanding the Abortion Argument', *Philosophy and Public Affairs*, 1971.

R. J. Gerber: 'Abortion: Parameters for Decision', *Ethics*, 1972.

D. Gerber: 'Abortion: The Uptake Argument', *Ethics*, 1972.

R. B. Brandt: 'The Morality of Abortion', *The Monist*, 1972.

Gerald Leach: *The Biocrats*, London, 1972, Ch. 1.

Michael Tooley: 'Abortion and Infanticide', *Philosophy and Public Affairs*, 1972, revised version in Feinberg, 1973 (below).

R. Howell and others: 'Correspondence', *Philosophy and Public Affairs*, 1973.

Stanley Benn: 'Abortion, Infanticide and Respect for Persons', in Feinberg, 1973 (below).

Joel Feinberg (ed.): *The Problem of Abortion*, Belmont, 1973.

B. Sarvis and H. Rodman: *The Abortion Controversy*, New York, 1973, Ch. 2.

B. A. Brody: 'Abortion and the Sanctity of Human Life', *American Philosophical Quarterly*, 1973.

Joseph Margolis: 'Abortion', *Ethics*, 1973.

Report of the Committee on the Working of the Abortion Act, London, 1974, especially sections E, F, G, H and L.

Marvin Kohl: *The Morality of Killing*, London, 1974, Chs. 3 and 4.

Joel Rudinow: 'On "The Slippery Slope" ', *Analysis*, 1974.

Anne Lindsay: 'On the Slippery Slope Again', *Analysis*, 1974.

H. Tristram Engelhardt: 'The Ontology of Abortion', *Ethics*, 1974.

L. W. Sumner: 'Toward a Credible View of Abortion', *Canadian Journal of Philosophy*, 1974.

R. M. Hare: 'Abortion and the Golden Rule', *Philosophy and Public Affairs*, 1975.

Lawrence C. Becker: 'Human Being: The Boundaries of the Concept', *Philosophy and Public Affairs*, 1975.

(b) WOMEN'S RIGHTS ARGUMENTS

Judith Jarvis Thomson: 'A Defense of Abortion', *Philosophy and Public Affairs*, 1971.

B. A. Brody: 'Thomson on Abortion', *Philosophy and Public Affairs*, 1972.

John Finnis: 'The Rights and Wrongs of Abortion: A Reply to Judith Thomson', *Philosophy and Public Affairs*, 1973.

Judith Jarvis Thomson: 'Rights and Deaths', *Philosophy and Public Affairs*, 1973.

Mary Anne Warren: 'On the Moral and Legal Status of Abortion', *The Monist*, 1973.

Report of the Committee on the Working of the Abortion Act, London, 1974, Vol. I, paras 160–73 and 186–273.

Marvin Kohl: *The Morality of Killing*, London, 1974, Ch. 5.

Lorenne M. G. Clark: 'Reply to Professor Sumner', *Canadian Journal of Philosophy*, 1974.

Raymond M. Herbenick: 'Remarks on Abortion, Abandonment and Adoption Opportunities', *Philosophy and Public Affairs*, 1975.

Chapter 12   Infanticide

(a) GENERAL

Glanville Williams: *The Sanctity of Life and the Criminal Law*, London, 1958, Ch. 1.

Nigel Walker: *Crime and Insanity in England*, Vol. I, Edinburgh, 1968, Ch. 7.

R. B. Zachary: 'Ethical and Social Aspects of Treatment of Spina Bifida', *Lancet*, 1968, and ensuing letters.

J. M. Freeman: 'Is There a Right to Die – Quickly?' *Journal of Paediatrics*, 1972, and ensuing letters.

Gerald Leach: *The Biocrats*, London, 1972, Ch. 7.

Michael Tooley: 'Abortion and Infanticide', *Philosophy and Public Affairs*, 1972, revised version in Feinberg, 1973 (below).

R. Howell and others: Correspondence, *Philosophy and Public Affairs*, 1973.

BIBLIOGRAPHY

Stanley Benn: 'Abortion, Infanticide and Respect for Persons', in Joel Feinberg (ed.): *The Problem of Abortion*, Belmont, 1973.

Eliot Slater and others: 'Severely Malformed Children', *British Medical Journal*, May 1973.

R. S. Illingworth: 'Some Ethical Problems in Paediatrics', in J. Apley (ed.): *Modern Trends in Paediatrics*, 4, London, 1974.

Eike-Henner W. Kluge: *The Practice of Death*, New Haven, 1975, Ch. 4.

(b) THE CHILD'S DESIRE TO LIVE

P. Schilder and D. Wechsler: 'The Attitudes of Children Towards Death', *Journal of Abnormal and Social Psychology*, 1934.

M. Nagy: 'The Child's Theories Concerning Death', *Journal of Genetic Psychology*, 1948.

J. M. Natterson and A. G. Knudson, Jr: 'Concerning Fear of Death in Fatally Ill Children and their Mothers', *Psychosomatic Medicine*, 1960.

Marjorie E. Mitchell: *The Child's Attitude to Death*, London, 1966.

Sylvia Anthony: *The Discovery of Death in Childhood and After*, Harmondsworth, 1971.

Robert Kastenbaum and Ruth Aisenberg: *The Psychology of Death*, New York, 1972, Ch. 2.

(c) QUALITY OF LIFE

R. M. Hare: *Freedom and Reason*, Oxford, 1963, Ch. 7, especially section 5.

C. C. W. Taylor: Critical Notice of *Freedom and Reason, Mind*, 1965.

G. D. Stark: 'Neonatal Assessment of the Child with a Myelomeningocele', *Archives of Disease in Childhood*, 1971.

J. Lorber: 'Results of Treatment of Myelomeningocele, An Analysis of 524 Unselected Cases, with special reference to possible selection for treatment', *Developmental Medicine and Child Neurology*, 1971.

J. Lorber: 'Spina Bifida Cystica. Results of treatment of 270 consecutive cases with criteria for selection for the future', *Archives of Disease in Childhood*, 1972.

G. D. Stark and Margaret Drummond: 'Results of Selective Early Operation in Myelomeningocele', *Archives of Disease in Childhood*, 1973.

D. B. Shurtleff and others: 'Myelodysplasia: Decision for Death or Disability', *New England Journal of Medicine*, 1974.

(d) SIDE-EFFECTS

Gillian Tindall: *The Youngest,* London, 1967.

Peter Nichols: *A Day in the Death of Joe Egg,* London, 1967.

John Stallworthy: 'The Almond Tree', in *Root and Branch*, London, 1969.

Sheila Hewett, with John and Elizabeth Newson: *The Family and the Handicapped Child, A Study of Cerebral Palsied Children in their Homes*, London, 1970.

B. M. Freeston: 'An Enquiry into the Effect of a Spina Bifida Child upon Family Life', *Developmental Medicine and Child Neurology*, 1971.

J. H. Walker, M. Thomas and I. T. Russell: 'Spina Bifida and the Parents', *Developmental Medicine and Child Neurology*, 1971.

Charles Hannam: *Parents and Mentally Handicapped Children*, Harmondsworth, 1975.

Hannah Mussett: *The Untrodden Ways*, London, 1975.

(e) THE WEDGE ARGUMENT

John C. Ford, S.J.: 'The Morality of Obliteration Bombing', *Theological Studies*, 1944, reprinted in Richard A. Wasserstrom (ed.): *War and Morality*, Belmont, 1970.

Max Black: *Margins of Precision*, Ithaca, 1970, Ch. 1.

R. J. Gerber: 'Abortion: Parameters for Decision', *Ethics*, 1972.

D. Gerber: 'Abortion: The Uptake Argument', *Ethics*, 1972.

Joel Rudinow: 'On "The Slippery Slope" ', *Analysis*, 1974.

Anne Lindsay: 'On The Slippery Slope Again', *Analysis*, 1974.

Joel Rudinow: 'Further in the Modest Defence', *Analysis*, 1975.

Chapter 13   Suicide and Gambling with Life

Augustine: *The City of God*, Book I, Chs. 17–27.

Voltaire: *Of Suicide*.

David Hume: *Of Suicide*.

Immanuel Kant: 'Suicide', in *Lectures on Ethics*.

A. Schopenhauer: 'On Suicide', in *Essays and Aphorisms*, selected and translated by R.J. Hollingdale, Harmondsworth, 1970.

Émile Durkheim: *Suicide*, 1897, London, 1952.

Ludwig Wittgenstein: *Notebooks, 1914–16*, concluding paragraphs.

Sidney Hook: 'The Ethics of Suicide', *International Journal of Ethics*, 1927.

Albert Camus: *The Myth of Sisyphus*, 1942, New York, 1955.

Glanville Williams: *The Sanctity of Life and the Criminal Law*, London, 1958, Ch. 7.

Norman St John-Stevas: *Life, Death and the Law*, London, 1961, Ch. 6.

John Cohen: *Behaviour in Uncertainty and its Social Implications*, London, 1964, Chs. 5 and 6.

Richard Robinson: *An Atheist's Values*, Oxford, 1964, Ch. 2, section 2.

Erwin Stengel: *Suicide and Attempted Suicide*, Harmondsworth, 1964.

R. F. Holland: 'Suicide', in G. N. A. Vessey (ed.): *Royal Institute of Philosophy Lectures 2: Talk of God*, London, 1969.

A. Alvarez, *The Savage God, A Study of Suicide*, London, 1971.

Gerald Dworkin: 'Paternalism', in Richard A. Wasserstrom (ed.): *Morality and the Law*, Belmont, 1971.

Joel Feinberg: 'Legal Paternalism', *Canadian Journal of Philosophy*, 1971.

David Daube: 'The Linguistics of Suicide', *Philosophy and Public Affairs*, 1972.

Ian Martin: 'Slow Motion Suicide', *New Society*, October 1974.

Jenny Barraclough: 'The Bomb Disposal Men', *The Listener*, October 1974.

Richard B. Brandt: 'The Morality and Rationality of Suicide', in Seymour Perlin (ed.): *A Handbook for the Study of Suicide*, New York, 1975.

Eike-Henner W. Kluge: *The Practice of Death*, New Haven, 1975, Ch. 2.

Ivan Morris: *The Nobility of Failure*, London, 1975.

Chapters 14 and 15   Euthanasia

J. Michael and H. Wechsler: 'A Rationale of the Law of Homicide', *Columbia Law Review*, 1937.

Pius XII: *Allocution* on Ordinary and Extraordinary Means, 24 November 1957.

Glanville Williams: *The Sanctity of Life and the Criminal Law*, London, 1958, Ch. 8.

Norman St John-Stevas: *Life, Death and the Law*, London, 1961, Ch. 7.

Cicely Saunders: letter in the *Lancet*, 2 September 1961.

Church Assembly Board for Social Responsibility: *Decisions about Life and Death*, London, 1965.

C. Blomquist: 'Moral and Medical Distinction between "Ordinary" and "Extraordinary" Means', in *Decisions about Life and Death* (above).

Simone de Beauvoir: *A Very Easy Death*, 1964, English edition, London, 1966.

W. St C. Symmers, Sen.: 'Not Allowed to Die', *British Medical Journal*, 17 February 1968.

John Hinton: *Dying*, Harmondsworth, 1967.

George P. Fletcher: 'Prolonging Life', *Washington Law Review*, 1967.

Cicely Saunders: 'The Moment of Truth: Care of the Dying Person', in Leonard Pearson (ed.): *Death and Dying – Current Issues in the Treatment of the Dying Person*, Cleveland, 1969.

A. B. Downing (ed.): *Euthanasia and the Right to Death, The*

Case for Voluntary Euthanasia, London, 1969, especially papers by Flew, Kamisar and Williams.

Elisabeth Kübler-Ross: *On Death and Dying*, London, 1970.

Henry Miller and Anthony Bloom: 'Keeping People Alive', in A. Clow (ed.): *Morals and Medicine*, London, 1970.

Paul Ramsey: *The Patient as Person, Explorations in Medical Ethics*, New Haven, 1970, Ch. 3.

E. F. Shotter (ed.): *Matters of Life and Death*, London, 1970.

Symposium on Euthanasia, *Proceedings of the Royal Society of Medicine*, 1970.

Jonathan Gould: *Your Death Warrant? The Implications of Euthanasia*, London, 1971.

British Medical Association: *The Problem of Euthanasia*, London, 1971.

The Voluntary Euthanasia Society: *Doctors and Euthanasia*, London, 1971.

G. R. Dunstan and others: *The Problem of Euthanasia*, Documentation in Medical Ethics, 1972.

Alastair P. Campbell: *Moral Dilemmas in Medicine*, Edinburgh, 1972, pp. 169–86.

Hugh Trowell: *The Unfinished Debate on Euthanasia*, London, 1973.

Marvin Kohl: *The Morality of Killing*, London, 1974, Part III.

P. D. G. Skegg: 'A Justification for Medical Procedures Performed Without Consent', *Law Quarterly Review*, 1974.

Gitta Sereny: *Into That Darkness: From Mercy Killing to Mass Murder*, London, 1974.

Eike-Henner W. Kluge: *The Practice of Death*, New Haven, 1975, Ch. 3.

Church Information Office: *On Dying Well, An Anglican Contribution to the Debate on Euthanasia*, London, 1975.

James Rachels: 'Active and Passive Euthanasia', *New England Journal of Medicine*, January 1975.

'Euthanasia: A Good End?', *The Listener*, 13 February 1975.

Lawrence C. Becker: 'Human Being: The Boundaries of the Concept', *Philosophy and Public Affairs*, 1975.

Donald Gould: 'Some Lives Cost Too Dear', *New Statesman*, 21 November 1975.

Chapter 16   Numbers

(a) GENERAL

R v. *Dudley and Stephens*, 1884, 14 QBD.

Decree of the Holy Office, 5 May 1902.

Lon L. Fuller: 'The Case of the Speluncean Explorers', *Harvard Law Review*, 1949.

Glanville Williams: *The Criminal Law: The General Part*, London, 1961, Ch. 17.

Lord Adrian: 'Priorities in Medical Responsibility', *Proceedings of the Royal Society of Medicine*, 1963.

Anatol Rapoport: *Strategy and Conscience*, New York, 1964, Ch. 10.

Phillip Green: *Deadly Logic*, Ohio, 1966.

G. E. M. Anscombe: 'Who is Wronged?', *The Oxford Review*, 1967.

W. J. Warwick: 'Organ Transplantation: A Modest Proposal', *Medical Opinion and Review*, 1968.

'Note on Scarce Medical Resources', *Columbia Law Review*, 1969.

Charles Fried: *An Anatomy of Values, Problems of Personal and Social Choice*, Cambridge, Mass., 1970, Chs. 11 and 12.

Gerald Leach: *The Biocrats*, London, 1970, Ch. 11.

Gil Elliot: *The Twentieth Century Book of the Dead*, London, 1972.

John Harris: 'The Survival Lottery', *Philosophy*, 1975.

Onora Nell: 'Lifeboat Earth', *Philosophy and Public Affairs*, 1975.

Donald Gould: 'Some Lives Cost Too Dear', *New Statesman*, 21 November 1975.

(b) SAVING LIVES AS A SOCIAL PRIORITY

G. Stickle: 'What Priority Human Life?', *American Journal of Public Health*, 1965.

Guido Calabresi: 'The Decision for Accidents: An Approach to Non-Fault Allocation of Costs', *Harvard Law Review*, 1965.

Symposium on The Cost of Life, *Proceedings of the Royal Society of Medicine*, 1967.

BIBLIOGRAPHY

'Note on Scarce Medical Resources', *Columbia Law Review*, 1969.

Thomas C. Schelling: 'The Life You Save May Be Your Own', in S. B. Chase (ed.): *Problems in Public Expenditure Analysis*, Brookings Institute, 1969.

Charles Fried: *An Anatomy of Values, Problems of Personal and Social Choice*, Cambridge, Mass., 1970, Chs. 11 and 12.

Gerald Leach: *The Biocrats*, London, 1970, Ch. 11.

Guido Calabresi: *The Cost of Accidents: An Economic and Legal Analysis*, 1970.

E. J. Mishan: 'Evaluation of Life and Limb: A Theoretical Approach', *Journal of Political Economy*, 1971.

T. C. Sinclair: *A Cost Effectiveness Approach to Industrial Safety*, London, 1972.

Craig Sinclair, Pauline Marstrand and Pamela Newick: *Innovation and Human Risk, The Evaluation of Human Life and Safety in Relation to Technical Change*, London, 1972.

E. G. Knox: 'Negligible Risks to Health', *Community Health*, 1975.

(c) MEDICAL EXPERIMENTS

Claude Bernard: *Introduction to the Study of Experimental Medicine*, 1856, translated by H. C. Greene, London, 1962.

United States v. Karl Brandt, Trials of War Criminals Before the Nuremberg Military Tribunals, Vols. 1 and 2: The Medical Case, Washington, 1948 – extracts in Katz (below).

Henry K. Beecher: *Clinical Investigation – Medical, Ethical and Moral Aspects*, Boston, 1963.

World Medical Assembly: *Declaration of Helsinki*, 1964.

'New Dimensions in Legal and Ethical Concepts for Human Research, *Annals of the New York Academy of Science*, 1970.

Henry K. Beecher: *Research and the Individual, Human Studies*, Boston, 1970.

Paul Ramsey: *The Patient as Person, Explorations in Medical Ethics*, New Haven, 1970.

Lord Platt: 'Human Guinea-Pigs', in A. Clow (ed.): *Morals and Medicine*, London, 1970.

A. L. Cochrane: *Effectiveness and Efficiency*, London, 1972.

Jay Katz (ed.): *Experimentation with Human Beings*, New York, 1972.

Guido Calabresi: 'Reflections on Medical Experimentation in Humans', in Freund (below).

Paul A. Freund (ed.): *Experimentation on Human Subjects*, London, 1972.

Charles Fried: *Medical Experimentation: Personal Integrity and Social Policy*, London, 1974.

Brian P. Bliss and Alan G. Johnson: *Aims and Motives in Clinical Medicine, A Practical Approach to Medical Ethics*, London, 1975, Chs. 7, 8, 9 and 10.

Chapter 17   Choices Between People

Bernard Williams: 'The Idea of Equality', 1962, reprinted in *Problems of the Self*, Cambridge, 1973.

L. Shatin: 'Medical Care and the Social Worth of a Man', *American Journal of Orthopsychiatry*, 1966.

Symposium on the Cost of Life, *Proceedings of the Royal Society of Medicine*, 1967.

J. D. N. Nabarro, F. M. Parsons, R. Shackman and M. A. Wilson: 'Selection of Patients for Haemodialysis', *British Medical Journal*, March 1967.

D. Sanders and J. Dukeminier: 'Medical Advance and Legal Lag: Haemodialysis and Kidney Transplantation', in Symposium: Reflections on the New Biology, *U.C.L.A. Law Review*, 1968.

James Z. Appel: 'Ethical and Legal Questions Posed by Recent Advances in Medicine', *Journal of the American Medical Association*, 1968.

'Note on Scarce Medical Resources', *Columbia Law Review*, 1969.

N. Rescher: 'The Allocation of Exotic Lifesaving Therapy', *Ethics*, 1969.

315

BIBLIOGRAPHY

Paul Ramsey: *The Patient as Person, Explorations in Medical Ethics*, New Haven, 1970, Ch. 7.

Charles Fried: *An Anatomy of Values, Problems of Personal and Social Choice*, Cambridge, Mass., 1970, Chs. 11 and 12.

B. A. Brody: 'Abortion and the Sanctity of Human Life', *American Philosophical Quarterly*, 1973.

Onora Nell: 'Lifeboat Earth', *Philosophy and Public Affairs*, 1975.

Chapter 18   Execution and Assassination

(a) CAPITAL PUNISHMENT

Cesare Beccaria: *An Essay on Crimes and Punishments,* 1769.

James FitzJames Stephen: 'Capital Punishments', *Fraser's Magazine*, 1864.

The Hon. Mr Gilpin: Speech Against Capital Punishment, *Hansard*, April 1868, reprinted in Ezorsky (below).

John Stuart Mill: Speech in Favour of Capital Punishment, *Hansard*, April 1868, reprinted in Ezorsky (below).

Leo Tolstoy: *War and Peace*, 1869, Book 12, Ch. 11.

George Orwell: 'A Hanging', *Adelphi,* 1931, reprinted in *Decline of the English Murder and other essays*, Harmondsworth, 1965.

J. Michael and H. Wechsler: 'A Rationale of the Law of Homicide', *Columbia Law Review*, 1937.

Royal Commission on Capital Punishment, 1949–1953, Report, London, 1953.

Arthur Koestler: *Reflections on Hanging*, London, 1956.

Albert Camus, 'Reflections on the Guillotine', 1957, in *Resistance Rebellion and Death*, New York, 1961.

W. B. Gallie: 'The Lords Debate on Hanging, July 1956: Interpretation and Comment', *Philosophy*, 1957.

H. L. A. Hart: 'Murder and the Principles of Punishment', *Northwestern Law Review*, 1958, reprinted in *Punishment and Responsibility*, Oxford, 1968.

H. L. A. Hart: 'Prolegomenon to the Principles of Punishment', *Proceedings of the Aristotelian Society*, 1959–60, reprinted in *Punishment and Responsibility*, Oxford, 1968.

Arthur Koestler and C. H. Rolph: *Hanged by the Neck*, Harmondsworth, 1961 (adaptation of Koestler's book above).

Ludovic Kennedy: *10 Rillington Place*, London, 1961.

Christopher Hibbert: *The Roots of Evil*, London, 1963, Part 7, Ch. 1.

Hannah Arendt: *Eichmann in Jerusalem, A Study in the Banality of Evil*, London, 1963.

H. A. Bedau: 'A Social Philosopher Looks at the Death Penalty', *American Journal of Psychiatry*, 1967.

E. Van den Haag: 'On Deterrence and the Death Penalty', *Ethics*, 1968.

Herbert Morris: 'Persons and Punishment', *The Monist*, 1968.

Gertrude Ezorksy (ed.): *Philosophical Perspectives on Punishment*, Albany, 1972.

Steven Goldberg: 'On Capital Punishment', *Ethics*, 1974.

David A. Conway: 'Capital Punishment and Deterrence, Some Considerations in Dialogue Form', *Philosophy and Public Affairs*, 1974.

Albert Pierrepoint: *Executioner: Pierrepoint*, London, 1974.

David R. Bates: Letter to *The Times*, 14 October 1975.

(b) ASSASSINATION AND TERRORISM

Leon Trotsky: *Their Morals and Ours*, 1938, 4th edition, New York, 1969, section on *Dialectic Interdependence of Ends and Means*.

Albert Camus: *Les Justes*.

Conor Cruise O'Brien: *Murderous Angels*, London, 1969.

Edward Hyams: *Killing No Murder, A Study of Assassination as a Political Means*, London, 1969.

Robert Paul Wolff: 'On Violence', *Journal of Philosophy*, 1969.

Hannah Arendt: *On Violence*, London, 1970.

Richard Wollheim: 'On Democracy and Violence', *The Listener*, 17 February 1972.

Joseph Margolis: 'On the Ethical Defense of Violence and Destruction', in Virginia Held, Kai Nielsen and Charles Parsons (eds): *Philosophy and Political Action*, New York, 1972.

BIBLIOGRAPHY

E. J. Hobsbawm: 'The Rules of Violence', in *Revolutionaries, Contemporary Essays*, London, 1973.

John Harris: 'The Marxist Conception of Violence', *Philosophy and Public Affairs*, 1974.

Anthony Arblaster: 'What is Violence?', in Ralph Milliband and John Saville (eds.): *The Socialist Register*, 1975.

Ted Honderich: *Three Essays on Political Violence*, Oxford, 1976.

Chapter 19 War

(a) COLLECTIONS

John C. Bennett: *Nuclear Weapons and the Conflict of Conscience*, New York, 1962.

Walter Stein: *Nuclear Weapons, A Catholic Response*, London, 1963.

Peter Mayer: *The Pacifist Conscience*, London, 1966.

Leon Bramson and George W. Goethals: *War: Studies from Sociology, Psychology, Anthropology*, revised edition, New York, 1968.

Richard A. Wasserstrom: *War and Morality*, Belmont, 1970.

Michael Walzer: *Obligations: Essays on Disobedience, War and Citizenship*, Cambridge, Mass., 1971.

Richard A. Falk, Gabriel Kolko and Robert Jay Lifton: *Crimes of War*, New York, 1971.

Virginia Held, Kai Nielsen and Charles Parsons: *Philosophy and Political Action*, New York, 1972.

Peter A. French: *Individual and Collective Responsibility, Massacre at My Lai*, Cambridge, Mass., 1972.

Virginia Held, Sidney Morgenbesser and Thomas Nagel: *Philosophy, Morality and International Affairs*, New York, 1974.

Marshall Cohen, Thomas Nagel and Thomas Scanlon: *War and Moral Responsibility*, Princeton, 1974.

(b) GENERAL

Carl von Clausewitz: *On War*, 1832.

Leo Tolstoy: *Christianity and Patriotism*, 1894.

Leo Tolstoy: *Letter to a Non-Commissioned Officer*, 1902.

William James: *The Moral Equivalent of War*, 1910.

Bertrand Russell: 'The Ethics of War', *International Journal of Ethics*, 1915.

Sigmund Freud: *Thoughts for the Times on War and Death*, 1915, *Complete Works*, Vol. 14, London, 1957.

Albert Einstein and Sigmund Freud: *Why War?*, 1933, reprinted in Mayer (above).

Morris Ginsberg: 'The Causes of War', *Sociological Review*, 1939.

Bronislaw Malinowski: 'An Anthropological Analysis of War', *American Journal of Sociology*, 1941.

George Orwell: 'Notes on Nationalism', *Polemic*, 1945, reprinted in *Decline of the English Murder and Other Essays*, Harmondsworth, 1965.

Albert Camus: *Neither Victims Nor Executioners*, 1946, English-language edition, Chicago, 1972.

Arnes Naess: 'A Systematization of Ghandian Ethics of Conflict Resolution', *Conflict Resolution*, 1958.

Major-General J. F. C. Fuller: *The Conduct of War, 1789–1961*, London, 1961.

Paul Ramsey: *War and the Christian Conscience*, Durham, N.C., 1961.

G. E. M. Anscombe: 'War and Murder', in Stein (above).

Jan Narveson: 'Pacifism: A Philosophical Analysis', *Ethics*, 1965.

Alastair Buchan: *War in Modern Society, An Introduction*, London, 1966.

M. J. Whitman: 'Pacifism: A Philosophical Analysis – A Reply', *Ethics*, 1966.

Raymond Aron: *Peace and War, A Theory of International Relations*, New York, 1966.

Jan Narveson: 'Pacifism: A Philosophical Analysis – A Rejoinder', *Ethics*, 1966.

Michael Walzer: 'Moral Judgement in Time of War', *Dissent*, 1967.

BIBLIOGRAPHY

Arnold Toynbee: 'Death in War', in Arnold Toynbee and others: *Man's Concern with Death*, London, 1968.

Paul Ramsey: *The Just War*, New York, 1968.

Donald A. Wells: 'How Much Can "The Just War" Justify?', *Journal of Philosophy*, 1969.

Richard Wasserstrom: 'The Morality of War: A Preliminary Enquiry', *Stanford Law Review*, 1969, reprinted in Wasserstrom (above).

Michael Walzer: 'World War II, Why Was This War Different?', *Philosophy and Public Affairs*, 1971.

R. M. Hare: 'Peace', in *Applications of Moral Philosophy*, London, 1972.

Barrington Moore, Jr: *Reflections on the Causes of Human Misery*, London, 1972, Ch. 2.

Gil Elliot: *Twentieth Century Book of the Dead*, London, 1972.

Tom Regan: 'A Defense of Pacifism', *Canadian Journal of Philosophy*, 1972.

Michael Walzer: 'The Problem of Dirty Hands', *Philosophy and Public Affairs*, 1973.

Jeffrie G. Murphy: 'The Killing of the Innocent', *The Monist*, 1973.

James Turner Johnson: 'Toward Reconstructing the Jus ad Bellum'. *The Monist*, 1973.

Iredell Jenkins: 'The Conditions of Peace', *The Monist*, 1973.

Robert L. Holmes: 'On Pacifism', *The Monist*, 1973.

Joseph Margolis: 'War and Ideology', in Held, Morgenbesser and Nagel (above).

Robert Jay Lifton: *Home from the War, Vietnam Veterans: Neither Victims nor Executioners*, London, 1974.

(c) NUCLEAR WAR AND DETERRENCE

John C. Ford, s.j.: 'The Morality of Obliteration Bombing', *Theological Studies*, 1944, reprinted in Wasserstrom (above).

Bertrand Russell: *Common Sense and Nuclear Warfare*, London, 1959.

Thomas C. Schelling: *The Strategy of Conflict*, Harvard, 1960.

Herman Kahn: *On Thermonuclear War*, Princeton, 1960.

Anatol Rapoport: *Fights, Games and Debates*, Ann Arbor, 1960, parts I and II.

Thomas C. Schelling and Morton Halperin: *Strategy and Arms Control*, New York, 1961.

Hedley Bull: *The Control of the Arms Race*, London, 1961 (revised edition, 1965).

Bertrand Russell: *Has Man a Future?*, London, 1961.

Karl Jaspers: *The Future of Mankind*, Chicago, 1961.

Gunter Lewy: 'Superior Orders, Nuclear Warfare and the Dictates of Conscience: The Dilemma of Military Obedience in the Atomic Age', *American Political Science Review*, 1961.

John Strachey: *On the Prevention of War*, London, 1962.

John C. Bennett (ed.): *Nuclear Weapons and the Conflict of Conscience*, New York, 1962.

Walter Stein (ed.): *Nuclear Weapons, A Catholic Response*, London, 1963.

J. L. Allen: 'The Relation of Strategy and Morality', *Ethics* 1963.

Theodore Roszack: 'A Just War: Analysis of Two Types of Deterrence', *Ethics*, 1963.

Anatol Rapoport: *Strategy and Conscience*, New York, 1964.

Robert M. Palter: 'The Ethics of Extermination', *Ethics,* 1964.

Robert Levine: 'Open Letter from a Military Intellectual to a Sophisticated Liberal Leader', *Bulletin of the Atomic Scientists*, 1964.

Thomas C. Schelling: *Arms and Influence*, New Haven, 1966.

Phillip Green: *Deadly Logic*, Ohio, 1966.

D.H. Hodgson: *Consequences of Utilitarianism, A Study in Normative Ethics and Legal Theory*, 1967, Ch. 4, part 1.

Arthur Lee Burns: *Ethics and Deterrence. A Nuclear Balance Without Hostage Cities?*, *Adelphi Papers*, Institute of Strategic Studies, London, 1970.

Douglas Lackey: 'Ethics and Nuclear Deterrence', in James Rachels (ed.): *Moral Problems*, 2nd edition, New York, 1975.

(d) CONSCIENTIOUS OBJECTION

Carl Cohen: 'Conscientious Objection', *Ethics*, 1968.

BIBLIOGRAPHY

Michael Walzer: *Obligations: Essays on Disobedience, War and Citizenship*, Cambridge, Mass., 1971.

John Rawls: *A Theory of Justice*, Harvard, 1971, section 58.

Hugo Adam Bedau: 'Military Service and Moral Obligation', *Inquiry*, 1971, revised version in Held, Nielsen and Parsons (above).

David Malament: 'Selective Conscientious Objection and the *Gillette* Decision', *Philosophy and Public Affairs*, 1972.

Alan Gewirth: 'Reasons and Conscience: The Claims of the Selective Conscientious Objector', in Held, Morgenbesser and Nagel (above).

Donald A. Peppers: 'War Crimes and Induction: A Case for Selective Conscientious Objection', *Philosophy and Public Affairs*, 1974.

(e) WAR CRIMES AND RULES OF WAR

John C. Ford, s.j.: 'The Morality of Obliteration Bombing', *Theological Studies*, 1944, reprinted in Wasserstrom (above).

G. E. M. Anscombe: *Mr Truman's Degree*, Oxford, 1958, reprinted in *The Human World*, 1973.

Gunter Lewy: 'Superior Orders, Nuclear Warfare and the Dictates of Conscience', *American Political Science Review*, 1961.

D. Irving: *The Destruction of Dresden*, London, 1963.

R. J. Krickers: 'On the Morality of Chemical/Biological Warfare', *Journal of Conflict Resolution*, 1965.

Paul Ramsey: *The Just War*, New York, 1968.

Gordon S. Livingston: Letter from a Vietnam Veteran, *Saturday Review*, 1969, reprinted in Falk, Kolko and Lifton (below).

Richard Wasserstrom: 'The Relevance of Nuremberg', *Philosophy and Public Affairs*, 1971.

Richard A. Falk, Gabriel Kolko and Robert Jay Lifton: *Crimes of War*, New York, 1971.

Sydney D. Bailey: *Prohibitions and Restraints in War*, Oxford, 1972.

Peter A. French (ed.): *Individual and Collective Responsibility, Massacre at My Lai*, Cambridge, Mass., 1972.

Ronald J. Frankenberg: 'Taking the Blame and Passing the

Buck', in Max Gluckman (ed.): *The Allocation of Responsibility*, Manchester, 1972.

Thomas Nagel: 'War and Massacre', *Philosophy and Public Affairs*, 1972.

R. B. Brandt: 'Utilitarianism and the Rules of War', *Philosophy and Public Affairs*, 1972.

R. M. Hare: 'Rules of War and Moral Reasoning', *Philosophy and Public Affairs*, 1972.

Sandford Levinson: 'Responsibility for Crimes of War', *Philosophy and Public Affairs*, 1973.

Michael Walzer: 'The Problem of Dirty Hands', *Philosophy and Public Affairs*, 1973.

Mary McCarthy: *Medina*, London, 1973.

Marshall Cohen, Thomas Nagel and Thomas Scanlon (eds.): *War and Moral Responsibility*, Princeton, 1974.

Hugo Adam Bedau: 'Genocide in Vietnam?', in Held, Morgenbesser and Nagel (above).

George I. Mavrodes: 'Conventions and the Morality of War', *Philosophy and Public Affairs*, 1975.

Robert K. Fullinwider: 'War and Innocence', *Philosophy and Public Affairs*, 1975.

(f) REVOLUTION

V. I. Lenin: *Socialism and War*, 1915.

V. I. Lenin: *The War Programme of the Proletarian Revolution*, 1916.

V. I. Lenin: *Bourgeois Pacifism and Socialist Pacifism*, 1917.

Leon Trotsky: *Their Morals and Ours*, 1938, 4th edition, New York, 1969.

Frantz Fanon: *The Wretched of the Earth*, 1961, with preface by Jean-Paul Sartre, translated by Constance Farrington, London, 1965.

Karl Popper: 'Utopia and Violence', in *Conjectures and Refutations*, London, 1963.

G. E. M. Anscombe: 'War and Murder', in Stein (above).

Hannah Arendt: *On Revolution*, revised edition, London, 1965.

Herbert Marcuse: 'Ethics and Revolution', in Richard T. De George (ed.): *Ethics and Society*, Kansas, 1966.

Kai Nielsen: 'On the Choice between Reform and Revolution', *Inquiry*, 1971, revised version in Held, Nielsen and Parsons (above).

Nadezhda Mandelstam: *Hope Against Hope*, translated by Max Hayward, London, 1971, Ch. 25.

Peter Caws: 'Reform and Revolution', in Held, Nielsen and Parsons (above).

John Harris: 'The Marxist Conception of Violence', *Philosophy and Public Affairs*, 1974.

Robert L. Heilbroner: *An Inquiry into the Human Prospect*, New York, 1974, Ch. 2.

Chapter 20   Moral Distance

Stanley Milgram: *Obedience to Authority, An Experimental View*, London, 1974.

Mary McCarthy: *Medina*, London, 1973.

Mary Douglas: *Purity and Danger, An Analysis of Concepts of Pollution and Taboo*, London, 1966.

Mary Douglas: *Natural Symbols, Explorations in Cosmology*, London, 1970.

Nicholas Bethell: *The Last Secret*, London, 1974.

David Hume: *A Treatise of Human Nature*, London, 1739, Book III, Part II, Section 1.

Colin Turnbull: *The Mountain People*, London, 1973.

Konrad Lorenz: *On Aggression*, London, 1966, Ch. 7.

P. F. Strawson: 'Freedom and Resentment', in *Freedom and Resentment and Other Essays*, London, 1974.

Index

Discover more about our forthcoming books through Penguin's FREE newspaper...

Penguin
Quarterly

It's packed with:

- exciting features
- author interviews
- previews & reviews
- books from your favourite films & TV series
- exclusive competitions & much, much more...

Write off for your free copy today to:
Dept JC
Penguin Books Ltd
FREEPOST
West Drayton
Middlesex
UB7 0BR
NO STAMP REQUIRED

READ MORE IN PENGUIN

In every corner of the world, on every subject under the sun, Penguin represents quality and variety – the very best in publishing today.

For complete information about books available from Penguin – including Puffins, Penguin Classics and Arkana – and how to order them, write to us at the appropriate address below. Please note that for copyright reasons the selection of books varies from country to country.

In the United Kingdom: Please write to *Dept. JC, Penguin Books Ltd, FREEPOST, West Drayton, Middlesex UB7 OBR*

If you have any difficulty in obtaining a title, please send your order with the correct money, plus ten per cent for postage and packaging, to *PO Box No. 11, West Drayton, Middlesex UB7 OBR*

In the United States: Please write to *Penguin USA Inc., 375 Hudson Street, New York, NY 10014*

In Canada: Please write to *Penguin Books Canada Ltd, 10 Alcorn Avenue, Suite 300, Toronto, Ontario M4V 3B2*

In Australia: Please write to *Penguin Books Australia Ltd, 487 Maroondah Highway, Ringwood, Victoria 3134*

In New Zealand: Please write to *Penguin Books (NZ) Ltd,182–190 Wairau Road, Private Bag, Takapuna, Auckland 9*

In India: Please write to *Penguin Books India Pvt Ltd, 706 Eros Apartments, 56 Nehru Place, New Delhi 110 019*

In the Netherlands: Please write to *Penguin Books Netherlands B.V., Keizersgracht 231 NL–1016 DV Amsterdam*

In Germany: Please write to *Penguin Books Deutschland GmbH, Friedrichstrasse 10–12, W–6000 Frankfurt/Main 1*

In Spain: Please write to *Penguin Books S. A., C. San Bernardo 117–6° E–28015 Madrid*

In Italy: Please write to *Penguin Italia s.r.l., Via Felice Casati 20, I–20124 Milano*

In France: Please write to *Penguin France S. A., 17 rue Lejeune, F–31000 Toulouse*

In Japan: Please write to *Penguin Books Japan, Ishikiribashi Building, 2–5–4, Suido, Bunkyo-ku, Tokyo 112*

In Greece: Please write to *Penguin Hellas Ltd, Dimocritou 3, GR–106 71 Athens*

In South Africa: Please write to *Longman Penguin Southern Africa (Pty) Ltd, Private Bag X08, Bertsham 2013*

READ MORE IN PENGUIN

PSYCHOLOGY

Introduction to Jung's Psychology   Frieda Fordham

'She has delivered a fair and simple account of the main aspects of my psychological work. I am indebted to her for this admirable piece of work' – C. G. Jung in the *Foreword*

Child Care and the Growth of Love   John Bowlby

His classic 'summary of evidence of the effects upon children of lack of personal attention ... it presents to administrators, social workers, teachers and doctors a reminder of the significance of the family' – *The Times*

Recollections and Reflections   Bruno Bettelheim

'A powerful thread runs through Bettelheim's message: his profound belief in the dignity of man, and the importance of seeing and judging other people from their own point of view' – William Harston in the *Independent*. 'These memoirs of a wise old child, candid, evocative, heart-warming, suggest there is hope yet for humanity' – Ray Porter in the *Evening Standard*

Sanity, Madness and the Family   R. D. Laing and A. Esterson

Schizophrenia: fact or fiction? Certainly not fact, according to the authors of this controversial book. Suggesting that some forms of madness may be largely social creations, *Sanity, Madness and the Family* demands to be taken very seriously indeed.

I Am Right You Are Wrong   Edward de Bono

In this book Dr Edward de Bono puts forward a direct challenge to what he calls the rock logic of Western thinking. Drawing on our understanding of the brain as a self-organizing information system, Dr de Bono shows that perception is the key to more constructive thinking and the serious creativity of design.

READ MORE IN PENGUIN

PSYCHOLOGY

Psychoanalysis and Feminism Juliet Mitchell

'Juliet Mitchell has risked accusations of apostasy from her fellow feminists. Her book not only challenges orthodox feminism, however; it defies the conventions of social thought in the English-speaking countries ... a brave and important book' – *New York Review of Books*

The Divided Self R. D. Laing

'A study that makes all other works I have read on schizophrenia seem fragmentary ... The author brings, through his vision and perception, that particular touch of genius which causes one to say "Yes, I have always known that, why have I never thought of it before?"' – *Journal of Analytical Psychology*

Po: Beyond Yes and No Edward de Bono

No is the basic tool of the logic system. *Yes* is the basic tool of the belief system. Edward de Bono offers *Po* as a device for changing our ways of thinking: a method for approaching problems in a new and more creative way.

The Informed Heart Bruno Bettelheim

Bettelheim draws on his experience in concentration camps to illuminate the dangers inherent in all mass societies in this profound and moving masterpiece.

The Care of the Self Michel Foucault
The History of Sexuality Vol 3

Foucault examines the transformation of sexual discourse from the Hellenistic to the Roman world in an inquiry which 'bristles with provocative insights into the tangled liaison of sex and self' – *The Times Higher Education Supplement*

Mothering Psychoanalysis Janet Sayers

'An important book ... records the immense contribution to psychoanalysis made by its founding mothers' – Julia Neuberger in the *Sunday Times*

READ MORE IN PENGUIN

POLITICS AND SOCIAL SCIENCES

National Identity   Anthony D. Smith

In this stimulating new book, Anthony D. Smith asks why the first modern
nation states developed in the West. He considers how ethnic origins,
religion, language and shared symbols can provide a sense of nation and
illuminates his argument with a wealth of detailed examples.

The Feminine Mystique   Betty Friedan

'A brilliantly researched, passionately argued book – a time-bomb flung
into the Mom-and-Apple-Pie image ... Out of the debris of that shattered
ideal, the Women's Liberation Movement was born' – Ann Leslie

Peacemaking Among Primates   Frans de Waal

'A vitally fresh analysis of the biology of aggression which deserves the
serious attention of all those concerned with the nature of conflict, whether
in humans or non-human animals ... De Waal delivers forcibly and clearly
his interpretation of the significance of his findings ... Lucidly written'
– *The Times Higher Educational Supplement*

Political Ideas   David Thomson (ed.)

From Machiavelli to Marx – a stimulating and informative introduction to
the last 500 years of European political thinkers and political thought.

The Raw and the Cooked   Claude Lévi-Strauss

Deliberately, brilliantly and inimitably challenging, Lévi-Strauss's sem-
inal work of structural anthropology cuts wide and deep into the mind of
mankind, as he finds in the myths of the South American Indians a
comprehensible psychological pattern.

The Social Construction of Reality
Peter Berger and Thomas Luckmann

The Social Construction of Reality is concerned with the sociology of
'everything that passes for knowledge in society', and particularly with
that 'common-sense knowledge' that constitutes the reality of everyday
life for the ordinary member of society.

READ MORE IN PENGUIN

POLITICS AND SOCIAL SCIENCES

Conservatism Ted Honderich

'It offers a powerful critique of the major beliefs of modern conservatism, and shows how much a rigorous philosopher can contribute to understanding the fashionable but deeply ruinous absurdities of his times' – *New Statesman & Society*

Karl Marx: Selected Writings in Sociology and Social Philosophy Bottomore and Rubel (eds.)

'It makes available, in coherent form and lucid English, some of Marx's most important ideas. As an introduction to Marx's thought, it has very few rivals indeed' – *British Journal of Sociology*

Post-War Britain A Political History Alan Sked and Chris Cook

Major political figures from Attlee to Thatcher, the aims and achievements of governments and the changing fortunes of Britain in the period since 1945 are thoroughly scrutinized in this stimulating history.

Inside the Third World Paul Harrison

This comprehensive book brings home a wealth of facts and analysis on the often tragic realities of life for the poor people and communities of Asia, Africa and Latin America.

Medicine, Patients and the Law Margaret Brazier

'An absorbing book which, in addition to being accessible to the general reader, should prove illuminating for practitioners – both medical and legal – and an ideal accompaniment to student courses on law and medicine' – *New Law Journal*

Bread and Circuses Paul Veyne

'Warming oneself at the fire of M. Veyne's intelligence is such a joy that any irritation at one's prejudice and ignorance being revealed and exposed vanishes with his winning ways ... *Bread and Circuses* is M. Veyne's way of explaining the philosophy of the Roman Empire, which was the most successful form of government known to mankind' – *Literary Review*

BY THE SAME AUTHOR

I: The Philosophy and Psychology of Personal Identity

Am I *the same person* now as when I was a child? Is there some underlying unity that holds together every shred of an individual's life? And can we, to large extent, *create* our own personality and character?

In this challenging book the author of *Causing Death and Saving Lives* tackles the vexed questions of the personal identity. Cases of split brains and multiple personalities suggest that our consciousness can perhaps be divided, fragmented or even shared; philosophers have upset many of our commonsense assumptions, yet few people doubt that they are the same unique person throughout their life. And that 'person' is not only a product of external influences but something we partly make for ourselves. Glover draws on Proust, psychology and Freudian theory, examines the roles of memory, tribalism and recognition by others, to provide intriguing evidence for his ideas; their implications are crucial for our attitude to society and politics.

'Fascinating ... the ideas which Glover pours forth in profusion deserve more detailed consideration' – Anthony Storr in the *Sunday Times*

'This book is exceptional in that it is written by a philosopher who makes few mistakes about neurological and psychiatric facts, and also addresses concerns which are of immediate and practical interest' – *British Journal of Psychiatry*

E-learning in Nursing

Edited by

Sally Glen

and

Pam Moule

First published in 2006 by
PALGRAVE MACMILLAN
Houndmills, Basingstoke, Hampshire RG21 6XS and
175 Fifth Avenue, New York, N.Y. 10010
Companies and representatives throughout the world.

PALGRAVE MACMILLAN is the global academic imprint of the Palgrave Macmillan division of St. Martin's Press, LLC and of Palgrave Macmillan Ltd. Macmillan® is a registered trademark in the United States, United Kingdom and other countries. Palgrave is a registered trademark in the European Union and other countries.

ISBN-13: 978–1–4039–4559–4
ISBN-10: 1–4039–4559–4

This book is printed on paper suitable for recycling and made from fully managed and sustained forest sources.

10 9 8 7 6 5 4 3 2 1
15 14 13 12 11 10 09 08 07 06

Printed and bound in China

Contents

List of Figures

List of Tables

List of Contributors

Helen Cox, senior lecturer, Faculty of Health and Social Care, University of the West of England, Bristol, UK

Nicola Eaton, principal lecturer, Faculty of Health and Social Care, University of the West of England, Bristol, UK

Mollie Gilchrist, principal lecturer in statistics allied to health, School of Health and Social Sciences, Coventry University, UK

Sally Glen, dean of St. Bartholomew School of Nursing and Midwifery, City University, UK

Stephen Gomez, principal lecturer, Faculty of Applied Sciences, University of the West of England, Bristol, UK

Shalni Gulati, doctoral student, Department of Continuing Education, City University, UK

Pamela R. Jeffries, associate professor, Indiana University School of Nursing/Purdue University, Indianapolis, USA

David Lush, principal lecturer, Faculty of Applied Sciences, University of the West of England, Bristol, UK

Pam Moule, reader in nursing and learning technologies, Faculty of Health and Social Care, University of the West of England, Bristol, UK

Rod Ward, senior lecturer, Faculty of Health and Social Care, University of the West of England, Bristol, UK

Foreword

For many of us, these are times of significant change in our professional and personal lives; never before have healthcare professionals had so many demands placed on them. Pre- and post-registration education is therefore being reshaped as educationalists strive to provide learning opportunities that are truly flexible and accessible for busy healthcare students and practitioners. New and exciting possibilities are opening up for the design and delivery of flexible education, making it imperative for anyone who cares passionately about lifelong learning to explore the potential afforded by recent developments in information and communication technology (ICT) to enhance the learning experience of increasingly diverse populations of learners who come with high expectations. However, it is not the technology *per se* that brings enriched learning experiences, but rather it is the effective use to which the technology is put that is all important, and which is the focus of this edited collection.

In this climate of change and opportunity in professional education, this book offers advice and guidance relating to the use of e-learning, underpinned by the crucial assumption that pedagogy rather than technology must always be the key driver of education innovation. For those new to e-learning this text takes a pragmatic look at the main issues that need to be addressed when developing and delivering any technology-enhanced programme of learning, with appropriate emphasis throughout on sound educational principles and design. And for those educators more familiar with e-learning, the book opens up potentially fruitful areas of debate about the impact of technology on the student experience.

As for any education development, initial enthusiasm can so easily create false hopes and expectations. However, in the case of online learning, the burst of the dot.com bubble and the closure of the UK e-University in 2004 have been timely reminders of the importance of taking a balanced view of the likely educational benefits, highlighting that we should be thinking in terms of the evolution of e-learning rather than the revolution that was perhaps initially envisaged. Carefully used, technology certainly has the potential to enhance the learning support for a range of healthcare students and practitioners. Those working unsocial hours, or who cannot be released to attend lectures at specific times on set days, students on clinical placements and work-based learning programmes, and those who have to juggle the demands of a full-time job, family commitments and part-time study – we owe it to them all to find more effective ways of supporting their lifelong learning journeys.

I very much hope that everyone who reads this book or dips into specific chapters will pause to reflect critically on their e-learning activities and be motivated to evaluate systematically their innovative attempts to embed online learning in mainstream professional education. In this way we can begin to build up a sound knowledge base about the effective use of technology that can be used to inform future developments. Such increased knowledge and understanding should benefit future generations of students and, ultimately, the quality of healthcare services.

Elisabeth Clark
Head of Distance Learning
Royal College of Nursing, London
January 2006

Preface

The pedagogy of professional education has developed in recent years to include e-learning. This book aims to support and guide lecturers and practitioners in the development, delivery and use of e-learning in healthcare and education contexts. The eight chapters discuss various key aspects considering the policy context, pedagogy, development issues, assessment and evaluation.

Chapter 1 contextualises e-learning within the current socio-political context and outlines a brief historical overview of the evolution of e-learning. It considers the position of e-learning within government and institutional policies that are encouraging lifelong learning and widening participation (UKCC 1995, DH 2002, DFEE 2003).

Chapter 2 discusses the employment of constructivist approaches in the development of e-learning for healthcare and nursing education. It questions the notion that applications such as learning online at work, e-portfolios and discursive online learning are embedded in constructivist paradigms. The challenges of enabling practitioners to engage in online learning whilst in practice are reviewed. These include lack of e-literacy skills and the importance of considering power discourses between facilitators and learners. It highlights the importance of pedagogy being seen as the driver for e-learning developments in nursing education and practice.

Chapter 3 reviews the development of 'virtual communities' or 'e-communities'. It considers whether healthcare students learning online could develop elements of a Community of Practice (CoP) (Wenger 1998). Wenger's (1998) framework was developed through research with physically located communities, with a minimal evidence base suggesting CoP might have relevance for virtually located communities. Recent research conducted with nursing, radiotherapy and radiography students completing an interprofessional module online is presented, prior to highlighting key principles for developing collaborative online communities in nursing and healthcare.

Chapter 4 presents an approach to developing online learning materials known as the 'Hyperlearning Model' (Jeffries 2000). Developed from 'Principles of Best Practices in Undergraduate Education' (Chickering and Gamson 1987), it provides an instruction model that can be applied to designing e-learning courses, such as the critical care nursing programme presented. The chapter also highlights the role of the facilitator in the e-learning environment and the need for course evaluation.

Chapter 5 focuses on the historical development, interpretations and the employment of work-based learning (WBL). Centred on a case study project (Profile.ac.uk), it considers the harnessing of Internet technologies to produce systems that facilitate the tracking, monitoring and assessment of WBL students. It is hypothesised that such a system can enable contributions to the assessment process for students, lectures and practice facilitators, overcoming many of the issues associated with managing WBL.

Chapter 6 reviews the many barriers to accessing e-learning apparent within society. Discussions particularly highlight issues for different age groups, genders and those with disabilities. Current legislation is presented and examples of best practice are provided. Difficulties associated with the development of e-learning materials are explored, including ownership, intellectual property rights (IPR) and copyright.

Chapter 7 considers the development of online assessment and evaluation. The use of online Objective Structured Clinical Examinations (OSCEs) within a radiography programme is reviewed and applications to nursing are considered. It is postulated that computer mediated assessments might offer the potential for the assessment of knowledge, skills and attitude development in a variety of ways. An approach to evaluating web resources is presented, providing a list of questions to consider when evaluating such resources. Finally a review of different programme evaluation methods employed in online healthcare education is presented, offering examples of the types of evaluation approaches that might be employed.

Chapter 8 suggests that whatever the emerging shape of the nursing education system, it will be profoundly affected by changes in educational technology, such as interactive video, the Internet, CD Rom and virtual reality technology. However, the new technology's impact may be more incremental than the pioneers expected . E-learning is not an all or nothing activity and – technology trends should be a learning vision pull, rather than a technology push. The emphasis may be placed on sound pedagogical design rather than the technology itself. There is also a need to generate a knowledge-base about e-learning that can inform the development of e-learning programmes.

Professor Sally Glen and Dr Pam Moule

1

E-learning in Nursing: The Context

Sally Glen and Helen Cox

Introduction

The aim of this chapter is to examine e-learning within a policy context. Professional education is inevitably developed within a socio-political context, currently in particular, by government and institutional policies encouraging lifelong learning and widening participation (DFEE, 2003; DH, 2002; UKCC, 1995). These policy documents have identified information technology and learning as key drivers for socio-economic progress and professional development. They assume that the introduction of information technology in education will make learning more flexible and accessible.

Health professionals will need to develop the skills to use this technology in their clinical practice. Evidence suggests that consumers now have access to large amounts of unfiltered material via the Internet. Not only does this impact on the professional boundaries with consumers (Timmons, 2001), but adds further responsibility to the practitioner's role. Drucker (1994) argues that in the future anyone who wishes to be considered educated will be someone who has embraced the notion of lifelong learning. Nurses in the United Kingdom (UK) have a requirement to undertake educational activities to support their practice as part of the registration system. The ability to use a computer and effectively find and use the wealth of information that it enables access to, is a very useful tool in maintaining this lifelong commitment to education (cf. Chapter 6). Information and Technology (IT) skills being needed is becoming a universal truth for nurses working in many countries.

1

The National Health Service (NHS) was slow to develop IT as a strategic asset in the delivery of healthcare. However, national strategies have been developed since 1998 to address this situation. 'Information for Health' (DH, 1998) defined the strategic NHS approach when an information strategy was launched to improve use of information technology and provide staff with modern tools to improve treatment and care. It aims to improve management and delivery of services by provision of good quality data; support staff through effective electronic communications and support delivery of services designed around patients to be quicker, more convenient and seamless.

Many examples from the literature discuss the e-revolution and the impact computers have had or will have within educational and institutional environments and the continued response of policy development from government and educational institutions (Dearing, 1997; DEE, 1998; DEE, 2003), (cf. Chapter 5). Whatever the emerging shape of the nursing education system, it will be profoundly affected by changes in educational technology such as interactive video, the Internet, CD Rom and virtual reality technology. However, the word 'revolution' should be replaced by 'evolution', as the seeds have been sown as far back as the 1700s when the first correspondence course was developed. The following section outlines a brief historical overview of the evolution of e-learning.

Historical overview

Historically, the courses that have long been available were either open or distance learning courses. With the introduction of telecommunications the move was made to distance education, linking live educational broadcasts and correspondence between lecturer and student. These methods were criticised for poor standards and lack of quality control methods (Forman *et al.*, 2001). Early computer-based (CB) education programmes relied almost exclusively on the learner's ability to read information and to use that information to answer questions. The advantages of early computer-based instruction were self-pacing and instant feedback. While a textbook offered the same degree of self-pacing with the advantage of portability and usually much better visual presentation, a computer could tell students immediately whether they had answered a question correctly or not. A computer could also branch students to different parts of a programme, allowing them to skip sections of the programme that they had already mastered. Unsurprisingly, students who performed well using these programmes were those with good reading skills and advanced educational levels. The ability to provide training to staff with low literacy levels is of critical concern. Whether computer-based training is an effective and feasible format for training workers who have a poor education background is a critical question (Walker and Harrington, 2004. cf. Chapter 6).

The Open University in the United Kingdom established in the 1960s has made high standard distance learning accessible to all. This was followed by the first web-based course being developed in the United States of America in 1995 (Bates, 2001). Thomas Edison surmised that with the invention of film, schooling would be revolutionalised (Simpson, 2003). The same may have been thought of e-learning, however in fact the application of information technology has started slowly. Initially this technology has been incorporated into classroom lectures with PowerPoint presentations and illustrations obtained from the World Wide Web and has therefore been used to supplement rather than replace either the classroom or the lecturer (Bates, 2001). In the late 1980s and 1990s many nurse lecturers set out to develop their own programs and started to market them. Since then there has been a proliferation of teaching material and information to students in a format that requires the use of a computer to access it (cf. Chapter 7). The new technologies impact may be more incremental than the pioneers expected, but its critics forget the difference it has already made to student and academic life. E-learning is however differentially defined.

Towards a definition of e-learning

When conducting a literature search the terminology in respect of web-based or e-learning education is not standard. Other key words include Internet education, distance education, IT learning, web-based education, web-based instruction and advanced distributed learning (Kahn, 2001).

There is an active debate around what is being aimed for when teaching nursing students IT skills. It is variously described as computer literacy (Saranto and Leipo-Kilpi, 1997; Patrikas, 1999); information literacy (Shorten *et al.*, 2001); electronic literacy (Topping and McKenna, 1999) and even technical literacy (Charp, 1999). All of these terms are used as different descriptions for a very similar concept, that of having the skills to use information and technology to support professional practice. This is brought together by Johnson and Eisenberg (1996) who discuss the need to combine concepts of computer literacy and information literacy. Johnson and Eisenberg (1996) identify that teaching and learning programmes designed to develop both should focus on computer skills for information problem solving.

Bates (2001) has posed a continuum of e-learning applications. Commencing with face-to-face teaching, advancing along the continuum to technologically advanced face-to-face teaching in the classroom using PowerPoint and web sites to aid interactive learning. Applications continue through to a mixed mode delivery whereby a mixture of classroom and online learning at a distance is used with the aid of e-mail discussion boards (distributed learning). Kahn (2001) also sees e-learning as synonymous with web-based learning (UBL), Internet-based training (IBT), advanced distributed learning (ADL), web-based instruction (WBI), online learning (OL) and open/flexible learning (OFL).

This volume has no desire to become mired in discussing the terminology. Many of the chapters will discuss various definitions and terminology.

Societal changes

We are living in an era of profound and widespread social and cultural change:

- Changes in social, political and cultural institutions (for example, family, politics, consumption)
- Restructuring of work, employment and industry
- Shifts in personal and group identities and aspirations.
- A growing tendency for 'choice'
- The knowledge revolution
- Changing technologies
- Globalisation.
- Social fragmentation and discussion
- New forms and expressions of citizenship

Social commentators note the shift from an industrial to a knowledge economy and the growth of a self-reflexive culture in an uncertain society (Giddens, 1991). A massive communications evolution (paradigm shift) is underway, one that will have profound effects upon the art and science of nursing.

In industrialised countries the demand for education arises from two drivers. The first being the combination of the expansion of the workforce and technological advances within the workplace, and secondly structural unemployment which has increased the demand for retraining and re-skilling to meet occupational demands (Harry, 1999). It is anticipated that, by the end of the decade, 1.7 million jobs will require graduate employees and this requirement has a direct impact on the structure and process of higher education and how education is delivered (DFEE, 2003), including nursing education.

The Government has an agenda that the nation will prosper in a knowledge-based global economy (Whitsted, 2003). Within industry where high-tech areas such as biotechnology, computing, science, engineering and increasingly healthcare have a rapidly changing environment there is an expectation of both employees and education institutions to keep flexible and adaptable to current trends and developments and needs of society. The change has involved a shift from a focus on land, capital and markets to individual development (King, 2004). To create a wealthy and healthy economy the future will depend on the creativity and the innovation deployed by the workforce. This has a direct impact on education and it could be argued that universities should be given the freedom and resources to compete globally (DFEE, 2003). In order to respond to this agenda, traditional models of education may no longer be relevant (Whitsted, 2003). The percentage of school leavers who are accessing higher education is 2.5 per cent of the population. The other 97.5 per cent of the population are potentials learners in society. These individuals may well have full time jobs, a family life and a hectic social and personal life. To meet their educational needs and that of the workforce and business expectations, the delivery of education must be flexible enough to suit their particular circumstances (Bates, 2001).

In today's free market where the government encourages the power of market forces, there are individuals who may well have disposable income or are involved in industries willing to develop their staff, and thus the opportunities are there both within the private and public educational sectors to be exploited (Bates, 2001). This appropriately includes the healthcare employee population; many are mature individuals who now have an expectation from their employers to keep up to date with knowledge, skills and technology (2004).

Higher education context

A major impetus of policy and education reform was the Dearing report (1997). This strategy was a vision for the next 20 years of education, based on the philosophy of a lifelong-learning society to ensure the economical success of the nation. The expectation now is not only to strengthen international but also global links. The need is for higher education institutions to adapt to a changing world with the development of distance learning and the application and integration of modern technology to suit the needs of a changing economic market and labour workforce (DFEE, 2003). The strategy identifies the development of skills for the nation of communication, numeracy, information technology and learning; these skills should be developed throughout an individual's life, and have now been integrated into the curriculum from primary school through to higher education institutions. It is envisaged that to follow the philosophy of lifelong learning, educational institutions will collaborate on the 'production and transmission' of educational programmes and learning materials to reach a more global market.

The theme of collaboration was reiterated within the strategy for The Future of Higher Education (DFEE, 2003) with the need for universities to work together. The Higher Education Funding Council for England (HEFC) developed a UK e-universities project to encourage higher education institutions develop affordable e-learning materials to ensure that the e-learning market economy was viable taking into account the cost of development and the need to ensure a global availability. The idea was first put forward by the UK government in early 2000, which committed £6 million to the project between 2001 and 2004. The aim was to safeguard current overseas markets, and to exploit what is thought to be massive unmet demand for higher education that campus universities are unable to meet.

The UK e-university was an example of government support for a profit venture in a commercial environment; rather than learning institutions to fend for themselves. If was perhaps indicative of the seriousness with which the government views the threats and opportunities of borderless provision (Ryan, 2002). It was also envisaged that this would also ensure that the country's interest to expand education to meet the needs of the workforce and individuals would be flexible in the provision of courses ensuring widened participation, with individuals returning to education throughout the duration of their working and social life.

Ironically, the e-university at www.ukeuniversitiesworldwide.com had signed up only 900 students by the time HEFCE finally closed it down in June 2004, and it never attracted any private money. The Funding Council said that universities were more interested in 'blended' learning involving a mixture of IT, traditional, work-based and distance learning, to meet the diverse needs of students, rather than concentrating on wholly electronic learning (MacLeod, 2004).

Virtual networks of colleges and universities have however become a marker of the new economy. The term borderless developments applied to the education sector involves a number of components: students learning at a distance from the lecturer or tutorial support; students having access to Internet technology and the confidence to use it inter-actively and students from different pedagogical cultures and mother tongues studying the same material. There is no doubt that such global online education has a higher chance of success at the present time with provision of high levels of postgraduate and professional updating. Competition will come not only from within the United Kingdom, but in joining the European Union students will potentially have even greater access to e-learning and other educational institutions.

The government also has a strong agenda in the formation of a vir-tual university, the National Health Service University (NHSu) (DH, 2003). Traditionally, universities have had a single mode of delivery, for example, classroom and face to face instruction. With increased com-petition and a widening market, universities offering a dual mode of delivery incorporating e-learning may have an advantage. The imple-mentation of technology and e-learning will have cost implications in the recruitment of experts within this field and also the infrastructure to support it. If universities had dual modes of delivery a wider national if not international or global market might be captured (Harry, 1999; King, 2004). This possibility may have an impact within the health service which at present recruits students from overseas. There are undoubtedly some developments within e-learning such as a nursing registration that could be gained from an online programme. This may allow overseas students in the future to remain in their country of origin.

Healthcare context

As previously suggested, initially the NHS was slow to develop IT as a strategic asset in the delivery of healthcare. However, since 1996 strategies have been developed to address this situation. 'Information for Health' (DH, 1996) defined the strategic NHS approach when an information strategy was launched to improve use of information technology and provide staff with modern tools to improve treatment and care in the context of the government's modernisation programme. The UK-NHS has identified the ability to work effectively with information as a high priority for all staff, including clinicians, having published its information strategy, 'Information for Health', in 1996 (NHS Executive, 1998). In 2001 the Department of Health published further advice on the implementation of the strategy to compliment their other plans for developing the NHS, in Building the Information Core (DH, 2001).

The NHS is aiming to promote working with information technologies to improve care for patients in several ways, including

- ensuring that professional staff have access to up to date information on which to base their practice,
- speeding up, and easing, access to services for patients,
- improving communication flows of essential patient information,
- ensuring that patients and carers are informed about the NHS and best practice in relation to their condition.

Nurses need to be able to understand the role of information within the organisations they work in, as well as its role in supporting their professional practice. Additionally, with more care taking place at locations other than hospitals, nurses need to be able to communicate electronically within their own organisation and across professional and organisational boundaries (NHS Executive, 1998).

Information for patients is as important as information management and communications. Historically nurses have had a role as information gatekeepers, with most detailed health information only available in journals and health libraries, limiting access to professionals. With the widening availability of the Internet much more information is available not only to nurses but also to their patients. Patients can now access this information within going to a professional gatekeeper; however, the quality of information available through the Internet is very variable (Impicciatore *et al.*, 1997). This has given nurses a new role; that of facilitator, helping patients to evaluate the information they have found.

Nursing education context

Traditionally, schools of Nursing and Midwifery have developed and delivered highly structured programmes of study with a lecturer-centred approach, which is extremely costly. One of the challenges nursing education now faces is to devise alternative ways to deliver the programmes which will reduce class contact time without reducing the quality of the programme.

The ability to use IT effectively is an increasingly important skill for nursing students. It is essential to support their student experience and also to give them the basis of the information skills that they will need in practice once they are qualified nurses (Bond, 2004). The Nursing and Midwifery Council (NMC), which registers all practicing nursing in the United Kingdom, requires all nurses entering the register to demonstrate the skills needed to record, store, retrieve and organise data essential for care delivery.

The Quality Assurance Agency for Higher Education in the United Kingdom (QAA) has introduced benchmarks, which

> Describe the attributes, skills and capabilities that a graduate with an honours degree in a specific subject might be expected to have. (QAA, 2003)

The benchmarks for nursing identify that not only should nurses be competent in using common software packages including word processing, email, spreadsheets and databases, but that they should be able to access healthcare research and literature database; use the Internet as an information source; and use computerised patient information systems. They should also understand the associated issues of data integrity and security and patient confidentiality.

There has also been rapid growth in the provision of distance-learning courses worldwide across a range of disciplines (Ayer and Smith, 1998; Bradford, 1999; Cody, 1999; Evans and Smith, 1999; Ryan, 1998; Potempa, 2001; Stommel and Simmons, 2001). In nurse education in the United Kingdom, a number of factors have helped generate the emphasis that is currently placed on distance-learning courses as a key form of education, in particular post-qualifying education. These include a national shortage of qualified nursing staff, which has made it difficult for employers to release nurses from their work for study, a recognition of the value of developing knowledge through facilitated work-based learning

(Boud *et al.*, 2001; Chalmers *et al.*, 2001; Rolfe, 1998) and the need for continual learning to enable professionals to maintain and develop their knowledge and skills to function effectively (Wallace, 1999).

The former United Kingdom Council for Nursing and Midwifery (UKCC) (1999) and the Department of Health (1999, 2000) have promoted diversification of teaching methodologies, particularly those methods requiring less teacher contact and less classroom activity without compromising the quality of the educational experience (Burt, 1998). As a result NHS trusts and higher education institutions in the United Kingdom turned to distance learning as a cost effective solution to the increasing demand for flexible post-qualifying nursing programmes (Ayer and Smith, 1998; Kenworthy and Dearnley, 2001). Growth in media and technologies, such as live chats, video and audio-conferencing, asynchronous discussion boards, and email have broadened the scope for supporting both distance and face-to-face learning opportunities. However, to engage practitioners in their real work contexts work-based e-learning must do more than provide accessible content (Chapter 6). Information Technology could be one tool to facilitate active negotiation of students' needs in the context of their practice (cf. Chapter 2).

Rapid developments in Information and Communication Technology (ICT) over the last few years has led to an increasing demand for healthcare students to access net-based support mechanisms whilst away from university campuses on clinical placements. This demand appears to be a national trend. The former UKCC 'Fitness for Practice' (1999) document (recommendation 18.4.48–4.52 and recommendation 19.5.53–4.58) highlights the need for ICT facilities in practice settings. Such a move would however require rethinking the whole concept of 'infrastructure' to support learning in practice (Smørdal and Gregory, 2003).

The lecturer

Initially the technology has been incorporated into classroom lectures with PowerPoint presentations and illustrations obtained from the World Wide Web. The technology has therefore, as previously suggested, been used to supplement rather than replace either the classroom or the lecturer (Bates, 2001). However, the transition from classroom-based delivery to a facilitator of e-learning requires lecturers to adapt to different working practices. Williams (1998) and Campbell (2001) asserted that this is a major role change for lecturers and they may need to engage in an active process of rethinking their teaching and reordering their academic priorities. The key challenges that lecturers confront include alteration to their workloads, coping with new technologies, online course management, online student support and the development of skills to function effectively (Stark and Warne, 1999 and Cravener, 1999). Whilst e-learning cannot replace a lecturer it can change the role (Washer, 2001).

Historically the lecturer may have had a pedagogical approach to their teaching which included working alone, preparing and presenting lectures; a shift must come with the introduction of e-learning. This will require new skills to be developed with the collaboration of other partnerships to develop suitable materials for students. Bates (2001) discusses not only having a technological structure to support e-learning but also a human infrastructure with individuals ranging from technicians, web administrators to lecturers who will support a virtual-learning environment. Whereas the educator may previously have worked in isolation now they will work across continents with other universities to develop e-learning materials, with the prospect of developing a worldwide e-learning electronic library.

Some lecturers are deeply rooted in their specialist subject and see little satisfaction in merely guiding students through material which may have been designed by other colleagues, or even by commercial learning resource producers (Johnson, 1997). This will also challenge universities within the context of intellectual property and programme ownership, especially when some universities are now choosing to put all their curricula online and accessible to all.

At a pedagogic level, online course designers and educators also advocate the use of communication technologies to promote flexible, learner-controlled, yet interactive collaboration and constructivist learning (Salmon, 2002, cf. chapter 2). In a typical online-learning scenario, educators design online tasks that often require participation in online discussions, with ready instructions and learning material, followed by instructions for online discussion. Interaction is encouraged by expecting students to reply to others' messages. Salmon (2002) identifies this as an important strategy to promote collaboration and problem solving. Online facilitators perceive this structured approach to online learning as enabling reflection and building a learning community (Conrad, 2002).

Incorporating such a constructivist approach to e-learning requires a greater level of preparation in both material and format. Indeed the greater the level of interaction online, the greater the preparation required (Harry, 1999). Traditional methods of teaching cannot be just transplanted online and be called e-learning (Washer, 2001 cf. chapter 2).

To develop an e-learning environment will not only increase academic workload but also require IT skills and time. One survey of university teachers' use of web-based technology found that the most significant barrier to use of web-based technology, was time needed to use the technology (Pajo and Wallace, 2001). But, another study of attrition from a course on online teaching found that the lowest ranked reason for leaving by lecturers was the technology (highest were personal issues and time), (Gold, 2001). Furthermore, whereas the use of e-learning may initially be seen as an opportunity to cut costs it is anticipated that this process will actually require an increase in universities' teaching budgets (Bates, 2001). Unless the costs of supporting students through the process are accounted for, and courses are adequately staffed, the increase in student numbers can increase the lecturer's workload. Cravener (1999) suggested that the tension between institutional pressures to cut costs whilst aiming to provide a high quality educational experience was a source of frustration for lecturers.

The student

With advances in communication technology and proliferation of distance-learning mediums, such as CD ROM, video-conferencing, computer-aided instruction, the Internet, virtual-learning platforms as well as the traditional paper-based courses, students have the opportunity to select the educational approach that best suits their learning style. They can learn at their own pace and at any time of the day, from anywhere in the world (Billings *et al.*, 2001). Educational technologists and online educators also advocate the use of the Internet as a learning interface that allows increased access and informality in education (Twigg, 2000).

Many students leaving further education are equipped with IT and computer skills. The aim is now for nurses on registration to have obtained a European Computer Driving Licence. However, many students may not be using the Internet to any great extent prior to starting a course and their ability to carry out a range of basic tasks is equally low. Pertinently, given the high numbers of mature applicants to nursing, Bond (2004) questions a popular belief that older people have poorer computer skills than younger people.

As the UK government is seeking to increase the number of students entering nursing, changing the recruitment policy to only take students who already have good IT skills is not an option available as might be with some other university courses (cf. Chapter 7). The inclusion of a programme that develops students' skills and knowledge in the use of IT therefore needs to be an integral part of a pre-registration nursing programme.

It is important that student nurses learn not only how to keyboard, participate in virtual communities (cf. Chapter 7), or use important software applications appropriate to nursing knowledge, but that they also understand the underlying assumptions behind the technology. Students will need to learn how to be analytical of the wealth of knowledge available on the Internet, which at times can be overwhelming (Washer, 2001).

With student nurses spending 50 per cent of their time in practice and these placements often being at a distance from the university, it would seem that Internet-based communications have the potential for making life easier for students, or at least reducing the amount of travelling that they have to do. The use of computer conferencing however has not always been found to be a positive experience. Hammond (2000) found that the style of interaction did not always reflect the students' preferred learning style.

Computer conferencing is becoming a popular way to augment the learning experience and thus to seek to improve learning outcomes; with the flexibility offered by the asynchronous nature of the system allowing the student choices over when and how to participate, rather than needing to be online at the same time as colleagues (Barnes, 2000).

Email has been found to be a successful tool by Shaw and Polouina (1999) with students liking the convenience of mailing lists, especially as for the students in the study email was a frequently used tool, requiring no additional software, or programmes for students to have to use over and above their normal computer behaviour. Tansley and Bryson (2000) found that when they studied a virtual seminar system set up via email, staff made use of the system to discuss work in progress; however it was almost unused by students, as was a more information cyber café – styled area.

With students responsible for their own learning, less time will be spent face to face with lecturers and their student colleagues. This will require a range of support mechanisms for the student to access (Jarvis, 1998). This may require the lecturer to be online, with some universities joining together to run online modules and provide a 24-hour student support by a visual learning environment (VLE) or managed learning environment (MLE).

It may be argued that students from within the healthcare profession will have access to a computer within practice, with the drive for IT within the NHS. However in practice there may be one computer which would be needed for ward agendas not allowing the student to remain online for long periods of time to access e-learning material. Compatibility of machines and programmes may also be an issue. With such rapid changes in technology, and computers and their programmes commonly being updated, the student or the university programmes may not be able to compete with the technology demands or in fact with each other.

With the students responsible for their own learning, less time will be spent face to face with academics and their student colleagues, rather it can be accessed online anytime anywhere. To have such a strong pedagogic focus will require a range of support mechanisms for the student to access (Jarvis, 1998). This may require the lecturer to be online, with some universities joining together to run online modules and provide a 24-hour student support or by VLE or MLE.

The online-earning environment needs to be managed to allow isolated students to participate in group discussion forums. However it must be acknowledged that not many students to date have been comfortable with education solely online and prefer a hybrid of 'bricks and clicks' (King, 2004).

A constructivist approach to education may be seen as the best way forward utilising a range of teaching methods including face-to-face teaching to develop individual curricula (DH, 2003; cf. Chapter 2). It is important that the needs of the student come first rather than the novelty of technology (Jarvis, 1998). Information Technology alone will not create an effective learning environment; however by utilising a variety of teaching methods deeper learning can be achieved and 75 per cent more knowledge is retained if the student can see, hear and participate in their own learning (Richards, 2001). This may be especially true of student nurses who may well develop cognitive skills from an online-learning environment, but will also need to develop psychomotor skills which may be hard to achieve purely online. By using a virtual environment with the use of simulations the psychomotor experience could be practised and reviewed over and over again (Simpson, 2003).

Conclusion

In recent years government's educational and social policies have had a huge impact on the provision of higher education within the United Kingdom (DFEE, 2003). The key words identified from the available literature are 'creating a knowledge economy', 'life long learning', 'widening access' and 'flexibility'. Where once the educational population had been confined to the vicinity of the university, the aim now is global education. This will require new partnerships to be developed and changes within traditional structures of the university to enable participation in a global society.

The NHS is aiming to promote working with IT to improve care for patients. Nurses need to be able to understand the role of information within the organisations they work in, as well as its role in supporting their professional practice.

Student nurses also need to develop IT literacy to work in an increasingly computerised health service (Bond, 2004). They will need to learn how to be analytical of the wealth of knowledge available on the Internet, which at times can be overwhelming. Nursing students' experience suggests that using computerised support systems could have benefits, especially while the students are on placement away from the University. Growth in media and technologies, such as live chats, video- and audio-conferencing, asynchronous discussion boards and email have broadened the scope for supporting distance and face-to-face learning opportunities. However, not many students to date have been comfortable with education solely online and prefer a hybrid of 'bricks and clicks'.

Finally, millions of words have been written about the technology and its potential, but not much about what the lecturers and learners actually do online. We are catching up on what technology is offering, but not challenging it (Salmon, 2002). Those in nursing education need to ensure that innovations are led by sound educational principles and not techno-wizardry or the agendas of educational publishers (Ribbons, 1998. cf. chapter 8). The following chapters will identify strong guiding principles and case exemplars which illustrate their application.

References

Ayer, S. and Smith, C. (1998) Planning Flexible Learning to Match the Needs of Consumers: A National Survey. *Journal of Advanced Nursing*. 27(5), 1034–47.

Barnes, S (2000) What Does Electronic Conferencing Afford Distance Education? *Distance Education*. 21(2), 236–47.

Bates, T. (2001) *National Strategies for E-learning in Post-Secondary Education and Training*. France. United Nations Scientific and Cultural Organisation. Imprimerie Alenconnaise.

Billings, D., Connors, H. and Skida, D. (2001) Benchmarking Best Practices in Web-Based Nursing Courses. *Advances in Nursing Science*. 23(3), 41–52.

Bond, C. (2004) Surfing or Drowning? Student Nurses' Internet Skills. *Nurse Education Today*. 24, 169–73.

Boud, D., Solomon, N. and Symes, C. (2001) New Practice for New Times. In Boud, D. and Solomon, N. (eds), *Work-Based Learning – A New Higher Education?* Buckinghamshire, Open University Press.

Bradford, D. (1999) Distance Education Issues, Challenges and Leadership Implications for Educational Technology Professionals. *Journal of Educational Review and Library Sciences*. 36(4), 393–408.

Burt, G. (1998) Debates and Tradeoffs: Face-to-Face Versus Distance Education. *Learning Resources Journal*. 14(2), 32–5.

Campbell, C. A. (2001) Distance Learning in the Health Professions: On the Verge of Collapse or Poised to Soar? *Journal of Allied Health*. 30(1), 30–4.

Chalmers, H., Swallow, V. and Miller, J. (2001) Accrediting Work Based Learning (AWBL): An Approach for Collaboration between Higher Education and Practice. *Nurse Education Today*. 8, 597–606.

Charp, S. (1999) Technical Literacy – Where Are We? *The Journal*. 27(3), 6–8.

Cody, W. K. (1999) Theoretical Concerns Distance-Learning and the Extent Paradigm. *Nursing Science Quarterly*. 12(3), 190.

Cravener, P. A. (1999) Faculty Experience with Providing Online Courses: Thorns amongst the Roses. *Computers in Nursing*. 17(1), 42–7.

Dearing, R. (1997) Higher Education in the Learning Society. Report of the National Committee of Inquiry into Higher Education. LONDON. HMSO.

Department for Education and Employment (1998) Preparing for the Information Age. London . HMSO.

Department for Education and Employment (2003) The Future of Higher Education. London . HMSO.

Department of Health (DH) (1996) Information for Health. London. HMSO.

Department of Health (DH) (1997) The New NHS: Modern and Dependable. London. HMSO.

Department of Health (DH) (1998) Our Healthier Nation. London. HMSO.

Department of Health (DH) (1999) Working Together With Health Information. London. HMSO.

Department of Health (DH) (2000) The NHS Plan. London. HMSO.

Department of Health (DH) (2001) Working Together – Learning Together. A Framework for Lifelong Learning for the NHS. London. HMSO.

Department of Health (DH) (2001) Building the Information Core Implementing the NHS Plan. London. HMSO.

Department of Health (DH) (2001) The NHS University. London. HMSO.

Department of Health (DH) (2002) Delivering 21st Century IT Support for the NHS: National Strategic Programme. London. HMSO.

Department of Health (DH) (2003) Delivering 21st Century IT for the NHS: National Patient Record Analysis Service: Strategic Outline Case. London. HMSO.

Department of Health (DH) (2004) Making IT Happen: Information about the National Programme for IT. London. HMSO.

Drucker, P. (1994) The Age of Social Transformation. *The Atlantic Monthly.* (Nov), 53–80.

Evans, T. D. and Smith, P. (1999) Flexible Delivery in Australia: Origins and Conceptualisations. *FID Review.* 1(2/3), 116–20.

Forman, D. Nyatanga, L. and Rich, T. (2002) E-learning and Educational Diversity. *Nurse Education Today.* 22, 76–82.

Giddens, A (1991) *Modernity and Self-Identity: Self and Society in the Late Modern Age.* Cambridge. Policy Press.

Gold, S. (2001) A Constructionist Approach to Online Training for Online Teachers. *Journal of Asynchronous Learning Networks.* 5(1), 22–6.

Hammond, M. (2000) Communication with On-Line Forums: The Opportunities, the Constraints and the Value of a Communicative Approach. *Computers and Education.* 35, 251–62.

Harry, K. (1999) *Higher Education through Open and Distance Learning.* London. Routledge.

Impicciatore, P., Pandolfins, C., Casella, N. and Bonati, M. (1997) Reliability of Health Information for the Public on the World Wide Web: Systematic Survey of advice on managing fever in the children at home. *British Medical Journal.* 314 (7098), 1875–9.

Institute of IT Training (2001) Accreditation programme and code of practice for E-learning providers. http://www.iitt.org.uk/public/accreditation/elearn-prov.asp/

Jarvis, P. (1998) *Adult and Continuing Education. Theory and Practice*, second edition. London. Routledge.

Johnson, D. and Ersenberg, M. (1996) Computer Literacy and Information Literacy: A Natural Combination. *Emergency Librarian.* 23(5), 12–23.

Johnson, R. (1997) Distance-learning: Medium or message? *Journal of Further and Higher Education.* 21(1), 107–22.

Kahn, B. (2001) *A Framework for Web Based Learning.* Engelcliffs, NJ. Educational Technology Publications.

Kenny, A. (2000) Untangling the Web: Barriers and benefits for nurse education an australian perspective. *Nurse Education Today.* 20, 381–8.

Kenworth, D. and Dearnley, C. (2001) Achieving Lifelong Learning in Nursing. *Professional Nurse.* 16(6), 1162–4.

King, R . (2004) The University in the Global Age. Hampshire. Palgrave Macmillan.

Macleod, D. (2004) The Online Revolution, Mark II. *Guardian* 13.04.04.

NHS Executive (1998) *Information for Health.* London. Department of Health.

National Health Service-University; www.nhsu.nhs.uk accessed 3.3.2004.

Pajo, H. and Wallace, C. (2001) Barriers to the Uptake of Web-Based Technology by University Teachers. *Journal of Distance Education,* 16(1), 34–9.

Patrikas, E. (1999) Computer Literacy. *The Journal.* 27(5), 60–5.

Potempa, K. (2001) *Where Winds the Road of Distance Education* (Guest Editorial). *Journal of Nursing Education.* 40(7), 291–2.

Quality Assurance Agency for Higher Education Understanding Courses: Benchmark statements and programme specifications. http://www/qua.ac.ul/cratwork/students/understandcourses.htms

Quality Assurance Agency for Higher Education (1996) Code of practice for the assurance of academic quality and standards in higher education. London.

Quality Assurance Agency for Higher Education (2001) Information on quality and standards of teaching and learning. London.

Ribbons, R. (1998) The Use of Computers as Cognitive Tools to Facilitate Higher Order Thinking Skills in Nurse Education. *Computers in Nursing,* 16(4), 223–8.

Richards, J. A. (2001) Nursing in a Digital Age. *Dermatology Nursing,* October 2001, 3(5), 365–70.

Rolfe, G. (1998) Advanced Practice and the Reflective Nurse: Developing Knowledge Out of Practice. In Rolfe, G., Fulbrook, P. (eds), *Advanced Nursing Practice.* Oxford. Butterworth Heinmann. 219–28.

Ryan, J. H. (1998) Measuring Costs and Benefit of Distance-Learning. *Journal of Library Administration.* 26(1/2), 235–46.

Ryan, Y. (2002) Emerging Indicators of Success and Failure in Borderless Higher Education. *The Observatory on Borderless Higher Education.* London. www.obke.ac.uk

Salmon, G. (2002) *E-Moderating: The Key to Teaching and Learning On-line.* London. Kogan Page.

Saranto, K. and Leino-Kilpi, H. (1997) Computer Literacy in Nursing: Developing the Information Technology Syllabus in Nursing Education. *Journal of Advanced Nursing.* 25, 377–85.

Shaw, S. and Polovina, S (1999) Practical Experiences and Lessons Learnt from Internet Technologies in Higher Education. *Educational Technology and Society.* 2(3), 16–24.

Shorten, A., Wallace, M. and Crookes, P. (2001) Developing Information Literacy: A Key to Evidence-based Nursing. *International Nursing Review.* 48, 86–92.

Simpson, R. (2003) Welcome to the Virtual Classroom. How technology is transforming Nursing Education in the 21st century. *Nursing Administration Quarterly.* 12–18.

Smørdal, O. and Gregory, J. (2003) Personal Digital Assistants in Medical Education and Practice. *Journal of Computer Assisted Learning.* (2003) 19, 320–9.

Stark, S. and Warne, T. (1999) "Connecting" the Distance Relational Issues for Participants in a Distance-Learning Programme. *Journal of Further and Higher Education.* 23(3), 391–402.

Stommel, C. E. and Simmons, M. (2001) Implementing a Completely Web-Based Nursing Research Course: Instructional Design, Process and Evaluation Considerations. *Journal of Nursing Education.* 40(8), 359–62.

Tansley, C., Bryson, C. (2000) Virtual Seminars – a Viable Substitute of Traditional Approaches? *Innovations in Education and Training International.* 37(4), 335–45.

Timmons, S. (2001) Use of Internet by Patients: Not a Threat But an Opportunity? *Nurse Education Today.* 21(2), 104–9.

Topping, K. and McKenna, M. (1999) Introduction to Electronic Literacy Part 1. *Reading and Writing Quarterly.* 15(2), 107–11.

United Kingdom Central Council (1995) *PREPP and You: Maintaining Your Registration, Standard for Education Following Registration.* London. UKCC.

United Kingdom Central Council (1999) Fitness for Practice. The UKCC Commission for Nursing and Midwifery Education, Chaired by Sir Leonard Peach. London. UKCC.

Walker, B. L. and Harrington, S. S. (2004) Can Nursing Facility Staff With Minimal Education by Successfully Trained With Computer-Based Training? *Nurse Education Today.* 24, 301–9.

Washer, P. (2001) Barriers to the Use of Web-based Learning in Nurse Education. *Nurse Education Today.* 21(6), 455–60.

Whitsted, N. (2003) Learning and Teaching. *Health Information and Libraries Journal.* 20, 189–91.

Williams, J. (1998) Education from Face-to-Face to Distance: Experience of a Midwife Teacher. *British Journal of Midwifery.* 6(4), 230–3.

2

Application of New Technologies: Nurse Education

Shalni Gulati

Growth in Information and Communication Technology (ICT) is a challenge for nurse educators, who aim to provide learner-centred, flexible and accessible learning opportunities for professionals engaged in diverse roles. This chapter is a review of pedagogical applications of the emerging information technologies in healthcare and nurse education. The pedagogical applications of new technologies are reviewed in light of the different interpretations of the constructivist view in nurse education.

The chapter begins with an introduction to the constructivist view, followed by the problematisation of educational practices that employ information technology, to question if these practices are rooted in the constructivist view. The practices considered include learning online at work, e-portfolios for reflective learning, online access and application of evidence in practice, and discursive online learning. This discussion intends to highlight educational and contextual issues that often remain hidden in formal education, yet may be central to the constructivist philosophy. The latter discussion proposes new roles for nurse educators as nurse education encounters new technologies in the future. The overall discussion calls for educators to promote pedagogy as the driver for future applications of technologies in nurse education and practice. The chapter ends with a conclusive summary.

Constructivism in education

Pedagogy is a science of teaching and learning. It involves the complexities of knowing the effects of different learning strategies, and becoming aware of how, for whom, and when to apply those strategies (Bruner, 1999).

The objectivist view of knowledge has focused on the use of didactic pedagogic methods that perceive learners as passive recipients of knowledge. According to this view, knowledge and reality are objective and universal (Cohen *et al.*, 2000). Pedagogy emerging from this view may give little consideration to learner diversity in the process and context for understanding, when identifying learning strategies and defining the curriculum.

In contrast, constructivism is a philosophy that offers an appreciation of many ways of knowing and understanding the world. Constructivism is not new, and certainly not new to the nursing profession. In nursing, when we ask questions such as 'what is health?' and then extend our exploration to 'what is health for different people?' we are acknowledging the constructivist view. Constructivism challenges the traditional objectivist view that sees 'knowledge as a large accumulation of facts'.

According to Kelly (1955) the constructivist alternativism philosophy contends that our constructions and views of the world are not stable, but are undergoing ongoing change as we build on past experiences. This ongoing construing of *change* signifies learning. This understanding perceives human beings as never inert in their learning (Kelly 1955). Constructivism is a shift from 'a world of facts, to a world of symbols and models which take account not only of the cognitive and deliberative experiences of doers and creators but also of their social relationships' (Larochelle and Bednarz, 1998, 7).

There are various interpretations of constructivism with two extreme versions being 'radical individual' and 'radical social' constructivism (Phillips, 2000). The other interpretations take varying or combined accounts of the two extreme versions. Multiple interpretations of the view are accepted, as the philosophy itself acknowledges diversity in how we experience and understand the world. There are also many critiques of the different versions of constructivism (Phillips, 2000) that are rarely discussed in formal educational discourses (McCarty and Schwandt, 2000). Critiques of the different constructivist positions may enable nurse educators to recognise how nurse learners in different clinical and non-clinical contexts engage in different experiences, resulting in varying constructions of nursing.

Constructivism is not a method or a teaching model, but it is a philosophy that can contribute to the problematising of existing and emerging educational practices (Larochelle and Bednarz, 1998). This chapter intends to facilitate such problematisation of the emerging e-learning practices in nurse education. Contemporary nurse education has embraced various constructivist views often citing the writers in the following list:

- Nurses as active participants in learning (Dewey, 1966)
- Learning based in real clinical contexts (Kolb, 1984, Knowles *et al.*, 1998 and Brookfield, 1986)
- Take account of nurses' interests and specialities (Dewey, 1966, Knowles *et al.*, 1998)
- Seek out and value practitioners' experiences (Dewey, 1966, Freire, 1972, Knowles, 1998)
- Enable learning through collaboration in safe and trustworthy environments where learners feel confident (Vygotsky, 1962, Maslow, 1972)

Nurse educators who support these views need to recognise the importance of understanding their own and others learning processes, while being involved in active critique of the pedagogy they support. The following discussion provides this opportunity. It critically examines examples of contemporary online learning practices in the United Kingdom (UK) and the United States of America (USA); healthcare education that aims to promote educational technologies, applying various interpretations of constructivism.

Problematising information technology use in nurse education

Online pedagogy is emerging under a range of influences (cf Chapter 1). These include the policy initiatives promoting e-learning for widening participation and accessible lifelong learning, as explored in Chapter 1. There are pressures on universities to recruit more students from diverse backgrounds and contexts. It is suggested that e-learning will enable flexible access to learning, while providing a pedagogically sound space for the learner to engage in dialogue with peers and teachers (Laurillard, 2000).

Rhetoric calls for the increase in provision and expectation for nurses to participate in learning opportunities, to demonstrate accountability and to influence patient care. However in the climate of staffing and resource shortages, the critical questions for nurse educators are,

- Do e-learning applications allow nurses easier access to learning opportunities, collaboration and practice development? (cf. Chapter 7)
- Does the incorporation of educational technologies consider differences in nurses' contexts, information technology skills and learning preferences?

These issues are considered in the following sections.

Learning online at work

Practice is the core of nursing. The nature of nursing practice allows minimal opportunities to access information technology, and find resources for collaborative or individual learning. Nurse educators are familiar with the problems of linking theory to practice that is constantly changing (Spouse, 1998). Yet there is limited research to understand how nurses learn in busy, critical and demanding environments.

Garrick (2001) has written extensively on the tacit and informal nature of learning in professions. For nurses this may include observation, informal chats during and after shifts, and learning by doing. In an ongoing UK study comparing learning during the first three years after qualification of engineers, accountants and nurses, Eraut *et al.* (2004) describe learning for newly qualified nurses as 'learning in a pressure cooker'. The complexities, pressures and demands in healthcare settings make it an environment where rigid learning structures do not always work. This results in newly qualified nurses learning from being 'hit hard with responsibility', and gradually picking up what to look for, how to prioritise, and getting to know people, systems and equipment (Eraut *et al.*, 2004). Is there a place for learning supported by information technology in such complex contexts for nurses, and could its use enable a constructivist view of learning?

There are a growing number of e-learning packages available for self-directed learning in healthcare. North Glamorgan NHS Trust (Wales) has introduced self-learning online package for induction of locum and new junior doctors (Williams, 2004). Heriot-Watt University (Scotland) has developed an interdisciplinary 'Workplace Health' course, incorporating online and face-to-face discussions (Williams, 2004). University of Wales College of Medicine is running a web-based diploma in dermatology for GPs that includes text-based modules, multiple choice questions and weekly online tutorials (Brindley, 2004). Chapter 6 considers additional examples of workplace learning.

These practices advocate a flexible means of learning. However, from a constructivist perspective one may question if these learning opportunities consider the professional demands on healthcare professionals. Does delivering text online reflect learner-centred pedagogy? Do the learning design and content consider the diversity of practice, learning needs, access, information technology skills, and diverse range of work environments?

As in traditional class-based and distance courses, the emerging e-learning course-designs continue to assume that all learners will benefit from the same material and structure. Some courses may require or encourage participation in online discussions, to promote collaborative learning, from a social constructivist perspective. Nonetheless, for busy professionals this element of learning comes with its own restrictions, as discussed later.

This criticism does not mean to imply that e-learning cannot extend learning opportunities at work. Learning at work is a major aspect of developing as a nurse. In his personal construct theory, Kelly (1955) has described experience and reflection as implicit and explicit units of how we come to make meaning from the world around us. We construe and anticipate future events based on our past experiences and constructions of similar situations. The experience itself would then help us confirm or dis-confirm our understandings, leading to reconstruction and newer constructions (Watts, 1988).

Learning experiences built on constructivist epistemology would actively enable practitioner reflection on ongoing constructions of experiences and endorse practitioner theories (Fransella and Bell, 2003). Hence, to engage practitioners in their real work contexts, work-based e-learning must do more than provide accessible content. Information technology could be one tool to facilitate active negotiation of learners' needs in context of their practice (cf. Chapter 6).

At the George Washington University (USA), the online environment is used to enable practice-based learning projects for interdisciplinary healthcare professional education. The project brings together students from six different healthcare disciplines to identify health promotion projects while working with identified community organisations (Gulati, 2004). Academics work closely with these organisations to develop community preceptor roles and identify projects that will benefit the organisations. Information technology is employed as a facilitative tool rather than the driver of the work-based pedagogy. The main drivers of the pedagogy are the community organisations and interdisciplinary student teams, while academics have a guidance and organisational role.

Online pedagogy in this form could be used to support learners to identify, create and share different work projects, with assessment that allows presentation using different media and tools. This is explored further in Chapter 6. This approach also requires a challenge for educators, who need to engage and involve clinical mentors throughout the learning process. It also requires clinical managers to develop time and practice management strategies so that nurse employees can *situate* their learning in practice, to benefit patient care.

Using e-portfolios for reflective learning

Learning through reflection, reflective journals and professional portfolios is actively encouraged in contemporary nurse education in the UK (O'Connor *et al.*, 2003). Growth in online technologies and focus on building a knowledge-based economy, has led to a renewed enthusiasm for using e-portfolios in education (Besley, 2003). The European Institute for E-learning, EuroPortfolio's aim is for 'every citizen in Europe to have an ePortfolio by 2010' (Ravet, 2004), (cf. Chapter 6).

Traditional focus of reflective portfolios for nurses has been on building evidence of prior and ongoing learning experiences. This has largely been done either for formal course assessment or professional registration renewal. Hence, it may be compartmentalised, and seen as something that is 'taught, done and ticked off' (O'Connor *et al.*, 2003, 110). In these contexts, evidence requirements are often pre-defined and focus on measurable learning outcomes. This approach to reflective learning moves it outside the constructivist epistemology, concentrating solely on the visible and often superficial results of the reflection activity.

Shift from paper-based to e-portfolios may continue these limitations, if the purpose and essence of reflections continue to be defined and judged by an external authority. This perspective may not take account of large amounts of tacit knowledge in nursing, which may not be easily evidenced. These strategies may not always consider that deep reflection in constructivist epistemology demands time, experience, support, challenge, wholeheartedness, questioning, negotiation and reconstruction. Reflection in the constructivist view requires safe, trusting environments, where the practitioner can develop insights into their feelings and values, and are able to problematise their own knowledge, opening up to other potentialities (Desautels, 1998; cf. Chapter 4). Educators have a role in facilitating reflection, however the events involving defining criteria and judging the reflections may discourage open and deep questioning of one's actions. Reflection is something of the learning experience that belongs to the learner, who decides when and how to use it.

There is a potential for learners to use e-portfolios to reflect and express personal and professional diversity, while identifying relevance for their future learning. At LaGuardia Community College School of Nursing (New York, USA), each learner is allocated web-space in the form of a portfolio template. This space can be individualised to include a range of materials such as photographs, visits, course- and work-related projects, demonstration of professional skills, and reflective journal accounts (Gulati, 2004). Learners have the freedom and support to choose, create and design all their e-portfolio content from the time they start the course, and continue after qualification. It allows learners to express in their own way, how they have progressed from novice to expert in their respective fields. E-portfolios at LaGuardia have also helped educators to learn about their learners' diverse abilities and learning needs (Gulati, 2004).

The constructivist perspective would use e-portfolios as *learning* tools, rather than *assessment* tools. They could be tools for reflection, expression and sharing. Nurse educators encouraging learners to share their expressions, need to be aware of the power differences from using e-portfolios as tools of surveillance of professionals' lives, abilities, and developmental needs.

Learning for evidence-based practice

The Past 10–15 years have seen a growth in online provision of academic health and nursing databases to enable easier access to research evidence. These provisions are commanded by the premise that practicing and student nurses will engage in self-directed inquiry and evidence-based practice. In reality, practitioners may not always use these resources to develop practice, (cf. Chapter 7). One of the key issues related to access and use of these resources is information skills or e-literacy.

E-literacy includes the ability to access, retrieve, critically appraise and use information from e-resources.

Studies by Wilson (2003) and Anthony (2003) report lack of information technology skills among nurses as the main obstacle for accessing research for learning and practice. Wilson (2003) recommends the primary need for investment in information technology skills education for nurses, and other healthcare professionals, before assuming that provision of online resources will enable development of research-driven practitioners.

Information skills also include literature search and critical appraisal skills, in relation to practitioners' work contexts. Foundation of Nursing Studies (UK) is funding the development of an interactive openly accessible online education package at De Montfort University. The aim of the package is to help nurses build skills in locating, interpreting and implementing guidelines locally. However, findings of a study at University College London suggests learners perception of access and critical use of online resources, may be more complex than simply acquiring access and appraisal skills (Smith and Oliver, 2004). The findings suggest that although learners were aware of the academic databases, they frequently used the www.google.com search engine due to simplicity, versus the complex search specifications of academic databases. Smith and Oliver (2004) also suggest that there may be tacit learning elements related to critical application of information literacy, which some learners may pick up on more easily than others. They recommend that information skills can be best developed when embedded in the learners' contexts and discipline.

In this context, the constructivist view calls for the need to begin by exploring inequalities in skills, access and critical use of new research, as explored in Chapter 7. There is a need for educators and managers to aim for an implicit and explicit acculturation of regularly accessing, sharing and critically evaluating evidence to influence individual and team practice (Stevens, 1997). This approach also favours the use of information technology as a facilitative tool in developing self-directed, evidence-based learning culture, rather than using technology as the driving force for learning and practice development.

Discursive learning

Discursive pedagogy is encouraged in the social constructivist view, which sees learning as socially constructed through discourse (Vygotsky, 1962), collaboration and negotiation. In nursing, discursive learning in class-based discussions, discussions during clinical meetings and informal discussions with colleagues and patients during and after shifts, are common strategies.

Developments in communication technologies have seen the promotion of synchronous and asynchronous tools for online discursive learning, allowing flexible participation in collaborative learning (Wiecha *et al.*, 2003). Many online programmes (Kennedy and Duffy, 2000; Sandars, 2004) are using these tools to increase learner interaction to facilitate discussion of pre-given learning materials. The discussion element is seen as social constructivist.

The participatory rhetoric in online discussions assumes that all learners will be motivated and engaged in the required learning process. Educators, who identify participation as an important element, view lack of participation as a problem. The justification for online discussions may have ignored the complex issues of control and power central to constructivism.

This is evident in an evaluative study of a nurse management module at the University of West of England. Hughes and Daykin (2002, 222), who were the facilitators and reporting researchers, conclude 'knowledge construction debate was limited'. Although nurses actively discussed topics identified by their peers such as 'use of ICT in nurse education and practice' and 'stresses of online assignments and group work requirements', there was limited participation in tutor-defined topics (Hughes and Daykin, 2002). The researchers considered learner-initiated discussions, as irrelevant to knowledge construction. The study discussion refers to Salmon's (2000) five-stage model of online collaborative learning to conclude that constructivist learning would have been possible if learners participated in discussions on tutor-defined topics (Hughes and Daykin, 2002).

Phillips (2000, (89)) draws from Dewey's work and states,

> individuals learn by being a part of the sociocultural nexus and socially constructed public bodies of knowledge and discipline.

Nurses in the above study saw their social nexus in practice, and shared what they saw as common issues among practitioners trying to meet the course learning outcomes. Here, learners' ability to radicalise these issues as necessary for their learning, was promoted by their need to feel in control of their learning. A research study by Sims (2003) using open-ended questionnaires with 68 multimedia learning undergraduates in Australia, concluded that the learners want to have control over the discussion topics, and freedom to choose learning directions depending on their particular requirements. Sims (2003) acknowledges the inconsistency of this finding with the current teacher-centred model, which considers set sequences or fixed discussion threads as the best way to achieve discursive learning.

This is not to suggest that online learning should be devoid of structure. Alternatively, there is a need for an appreciation of how learning structures may influence control and learning. Constructivist view calls for educators to guide the negotiation of learning outcomes and discussion topics between learners, their practice contexts and the curriculum. This can help to integrate online discussion topics with what is relevant and motivating for learners.

Some online educators have responded to lack of participation in online discussions, by requiring participation as a compulsory element of assessment (cf. Chapter 8). This strategy views articulation of ideas to a formal authority as a critical element of learning (Beaudoin, 2002). Making participation compulsory is another way of making learners conform to the defined learning pathway, thus normalising learning experiences, driven by dominant formal education discourses and interpretations of constructivism. However, enforced or coerced participation may not result in deeper learning, as is evident in a study of formalised participation in asynchronous discussion for a Podiatry Medicine Degree in California (USA), where most participants were simply 'playing the game' of assessment (Oliver and Shaw, 2003).

Online collaborations may and often do form an important part of one's learning. Nevertheless, emphasis on contributions to online discussion may create power differences by rewarding active participation, while punishing online silence through deduction of marks. Power discourses in an online learning system are also evident in the increased ability of the teacher to pre-define learning requirements and monitor the learning process (Maza and Dimitrova, 2004). Awareness of teacher presence may be the awareness that one is being watched. Foucault (1979) has written extensively on institutional hierarchical relationships where the one is watched by another, while the watched needs to comply with the disciplines laid down by the watcher, giving rise to disciplinary power. The surveillance and disciplinary power of the teacher, who has normalised judgement for compulsory participation, may cause learners to feel pressured and powerless to continue silent learning.

Power differences in online spaces are also evident among learners who may feel less confident to share what they may be unsure about. In an in-depth study Nonnecke and Preece (2001) found one of the reasons for online 'lurking' was partially related to remaining anonymous and feeling safe. Feelings of 'lack of connection with individuals' and 'feeling like an intruder' were also cited as reasons for silent participation (Nonnecke and Preece, 2001).

Safety is not only central to participation in discussions, it is central to all learning (Maslow, 1972). In an online discussion some learners may continue to maintain their safe learning zone by reading, and choosing the silent course of learning. Educators who require compulsory participation (Epling *et al.*, 2003) need to consider the impact on learning, if the choice of silent learning is removed. The fear of loosing marks may deter learner confidence to be able to 'reach out to the environment in wonder, interest, and express whatever skills she [sic] has' (Maslow, 1972, 50). Within this unequal power distribution some learners' safe learning zone may be displaced by fear, lack of choice and lack of control. However, others may either conform or view participation as a positive challenge.

Differences in participation may also lead to power differences among learners, where some learners contribute more or display a greater depth of knowledge than others. If the online educator fails to facilitate this knowledge display constructively, the interaction may result in a feeling of inadequacy and disempowerment for some group members. 'A process that is empowering for someone may then be disempowering for others and will be resisted by them' (Leach *et al.*, 2001, 294).

Group online learning can be an enriching and empowering experience, but constructivism calls for acknowledgement of the overall learning context, subject and learner group. As nurse educators we need to begin by acknowledging the power discourses in formal education and healthcare workspaces that may affect nurses' engagement with pre-defined activities. The power discourses may further impact learning due to differences in nurses' information technology skills, access, time for learning, employer support, learning preferences, past learning experiences and personal life responsibilities.

Pedagogy or technology driving nurse education

The above discussion has explored how technological developments are being used to enable work-based, evidence-driven, reflective and discursive learning for nurses. Although these theoretical perspectives are derived from the constructivist view of learning, discussion in previous sections suggests that many practices may actually be based on assumptions that technological applications will improve learning opportunities for nurses. Educational practices that fail to consider differences in nurses' personal and work contexts, disregard the pressures of shift work and need for safe spaces for reflection, and demonstrate a limited understanding of constructivism.

The assumption that information technologies will enhance learning, with limited consideration of the learners' contexts suggests that technology rather than pedagogy has so far been driving the new developments. Some 'early adopter' academics have taken risks to explore new technologies to improve learning opportunities, leading to the first generation of e-learning pedagogy discussed in the previous sections. These developments may be labelled as constructivist, but continue to be defined in terms of what contemporary technology tools can do, rather than accounting for the different learning needs.

The widely used Virtual Learning Environments (VLEs, such as Blackboard and WebCT) currently offer limited interoperatibility to enable learner and practitioner involvement to define and negotiate their learning (Britain and Liber, 2004). In a recent pedagogical evaluation of VLEs, Britain and Liber (2004) confirm that these technology-driven developments continue to place emphasis on content creation and material delivery, with limited considerations for learner diversity and pedagogical innovation.

Recent educational technologies in the market include learning objects for educator and learners to reuse for new courses (Downes, 2003), and personal digital assistants (also called handheld computers) for mobile access to research and communication links for learners in practice (Smørdal and Gregory, 2003). 'Pushing' these technologies into healthcare education cannot consequentially lead to constructivist learning opportunities. New technologies need to be considered in light of nurses' socio-historical culture and networks in healthcare contexts. A pertinent question that needs to be asked is: why and how a particular technology could benefit nursing practice. Further to this, implementation needs to be supported with strategies that align technology use within the complex practice infrastructures (Smørdal and Gregory, 2003).

The information technologists involved in developing educational applications, have acknowledged the need for hypermedia that can be adapted to meet the needs of users with different learning styles (Stash *et al.*, 2004), to create context specific learning pathways. As new technologies emerge and offer exciting opportunities, nurse educators have an active and critical role in exploring the technology potential for nurses' learning. As critical practitioners, nurse educators need to interrogate the drivers behind new applications. There is an ongoing need to question whether technology or pedagogy is the driving factor.

This requires nurse educators to develop up-to-date awareness of how practice environments are changing and how these changes may be used to promote learning opportunities. A constructivist pedagogy needs to be challenging, motivating. and sensitive to learner diversity. It needs to be embedded in everyday practice, with active learner engagement, and learner control over learning pathway and processes. A constructivist view needs to place learners in the driving seat, and use technology as a facilitative tool to enhance pedagogy.

In the professional education context there is a need to further unravel complexities of tacit learning in clinical practice, and understand how nurses learn. Work-based learning designs need to enable explicit and tacit learning opportunities both engaging and challenging for different learners. This is a difficult task. It calls for a cultural shift in practice areas, to encourage nurses to learn to negotiate learning pathways, and actively integrate their learning into practice.

Technology will be facilitative in exploring and developing individual and group learning pathways. Nurse educators need to have greater influence on piloting the new technologies that facilitate construction of diverse and adaptive learning pathways. Flexibility enabled through such personalisation of learning should also consider non-traditional learners, for example, parent, single parent, part-timer, and night-shift learner. Online courses are not flexible unless the pedagogy and learning pathways are flexible.

Information technology will continue to play a growing role in nurse education. Nevertheless, face-to-face learning in different contexts will always remain an important aspect of nurses' learning. If constructivist nurse education acknowledges learner-centred and learner-driven pedagogy as the 'pull' for future learning developments, there is also a need for extensive institutional support. Institutional infrastructures need to provide more than just structural support for technology integration. Educators and practitioners need encouragement to try out new learning strategies, by taking risks and being receptive to new and adaptable learning pathways during formal validation events.

Conclusion

This chapter has considered new technology applications to nurse education to promote enquiry-driven, evidence-based, situated in clinical practice, discursive, and self-reflective learning. The discussion shows that these initial applications are being practiced on the assumption that information technology embedded in these theoretical perspectives is unproblematic. It is also assumed that new technologies will have a positive influence on pedagogy through more accessible, self-directed and collaborative learning for nurses. However, the problematisation of the emerging applications has highlighted many contextual and pedagogical issues in nurse education that remain unconsidered.

These issues include the emerging e-learning packages that do not consider the difficulties in learning online while in clinical practice. There is also a lack of integration of formal courses into what is really happening in practice. An example of interdisciplinary course is used to suggest how online technology could be used to embed learning in individual clinical practice. Limited time and depth that nurses spend on assessed reflections for e-portfolio development, also highlights limitations of formal reflective learning. The discussion appeals for educators to re-examine the meaning of reflection as a learning process, and not as a means for assessment and professional surveillance.

Another emerging issue for nurse e-learning is the nurses' lack of e-literacy skills to use 'accessible' evidence. It is concluded that if nurses are expected to access and use online research evidence, it is pertinent to support information technology access and skill development embedded in learners' contexts and speciality. The popularity of discursive online learning and emphasis on participation in online discussions is challenged as having a normalising influence on learning. Issues of control, safety, power differences. and individual learning preferences are identified as key aspects of participation in discursive learning, which may be ignored by course designs that require compulsory participation.

The discussion demonstrates the underlying assumptions about how nurse learners construe, learn and make sense of practice. The new technologies have not been used to involve clinicians in learning developments or to develop evidence to understand the implicit and tacit elements of learning in practice. The failure to consider power discourses affecting engagement in learning also demonstrates a shallow interpretation of constructivism. The discussion points call for a reflexive ongoing reconsideration of the constructivist view to question the application of technologies and educational perspectives that may appear unproblematic at first.

The last section of the chapter argues that thus far technology has been the main driver for e-learning in nurse education. Initial technology push has resulted in a pedagogy that is content-led and lacks the consideration of learner and context differences, pertinent to constructivism. The main conclusion is that as technology develops, educators and learners need to take greater control over how new e-learning applications are used to benefit nursing practice. It is suggested that pedagogical developments need to start with the learner and their practice through a reflexive understanding of the constructivist view. The argument is made for technology to function as an augment *not* the key driver of learning strategies. The suggestion is for greater learner and practitioner involvement in curriculum development, so nurses feel supported to construct their personal learning pathways, during a formal course and for their lifelong learning.

References

Anthony, D. (2003) Online Courses in Nursing and Midwifery: Comparisons with Allied Healthcare Professions. *British Journal of Healthcare Computer Information Management*. (February), 20(1), 28–30.

Beaudoin, M. (2002), Learning or Lurking? Tracking the 'Invisible' Online Student, *The Internet and Higher Education*, 5, 147–55.

Besley, S. (2003) *Towards a Unified E-learning Strategy*. Policy Briefing 2003/30. July. London. Qualifications Ltd. Edexcel.

Brindley, M. (2004) Virtual Medical School for GPs. *The Western Mail*. April 21st. Available online. http://www.icwales.co.uk (accessed 23.04.2004).

Britain, S. and Liber, O. (2004) A Framework for the Pedagogical Evaluation of eLearning Environments. Project Based at Bolton Institute, Funded by JISC. Available online. http://www.jisc.ac.uk/uploaded_documents/jtap-41.doc. (accessed 29.04.2004).

Brookfield, S. D. (1986) *Understanding and Facilitating Adult Learning*. Milton Keynes. Open University Press.

Bruner, J. (1999) Folk Pedagogies. Chapter 1. In Leach, J. and Moon, B. (1999) *Learners and Pedagogy*. The Open University and London. Paul Chapman Publishing.

Cohen, M., Manion, L. and Morrison, K. (2000) *Research Method in Education.* 5th edition. London. Routledge Falmer.

Desautels, J. (1998) Constructivism-in-Action: Students Examine Their Idea of Science. Chapter 8. In Larochelle, M. Bednarz, N. and Garrison, J. (1998) *Constructivism and Education.* Cambridge. Cambridge University Press.

Dewey, J. (1966) *John Dewey Selected Educational Writings.* Ed. Garforth, F. A. London. Heinemann Educational Books.

Downes, S. (2003) Design and Reusability of Learning Objects in an Academic Context: A New Economy of Education? USDLA: *Journal of the United States Distance Learning Association.* 17, 1.

Epling, M., Timmons, S. and Wharrad, H. J. (2003) An Educational Panoptican? New Technology, Nurse Education and Surveillance. *Nurse Education Today.* 23, 412–18.

Eraut, M., Steadman, S., Furner, J., Maillardet, F., Ali, A., Miller, C. and Blackman, C. (2004) Learning During the First Three Years of Postgraduate Employment: Nursing Interim Report. Project LiNEA- Learning in Nursing, Engineering and Accountancy. An ESRC TLRP funded project. Details online. http://www.sussex.ac.uk/usie/linea/publications.html. (accessed 24.04.2004).

Foucault, M. (1979) *Discipline and Punish: The Birth of the Prison.* London. Penguin Books.

Fransella, F. and Bell, R. (2003) *A Manual for Repertory Grid Technique.* Second edition. West Sussex. John Wiley and Sons Ltd.

Freire, P. (1972) *Pedagogy of the Oppressed.* Harmondsworth. Penguin.

Garrick, J. and Jakupec, V. (eds) (2001) *Flexible Learning, Human Resource and Organisational Development: Putting Theory into Practice.* London. Routledge.

Gulati, S. (2004) Online Learning Developments in Healthcare Education in the USA. Winston Churchill Travel Fellowship Report. Funded by Winston Churchill Memorial Trust, London. Available online. http://www.yourlearning. com/churchillreport.html. (accessed 23.09.2004).

Hughes, M. and Daykin, N. (2002) Towards Constructivism: Investigating Students' Perceptions and Learning as a Result of Using an Online Environment. *Innovations in Education and Teaching International.* 39(3), 217–23.

Kelly, G. (1955) *The Psychology of Personal Constructs. Volume 1: Theory of Personality.* New York. Norton.

Kennedy, D. and Duffy, T. (2000) Understanding the Effort: BSc Health Studies at University of Paisley Case Study. Available online. http:// otis.scotcit.ac.uk/casestudy/alphacs02.htm. (accessed 24.04.2004).

Knowles, M. S., Holton, E. F. and Swanson, R. A. (1998) *The Adult Learner: The Definitive Classic in Adult Education and Human Resource Development.* Fifth edition. Boston, MA. Butterwirth-Heinemann.

Kolb, D. A. (1984) *Experiential Learning: Experience as the Source of Learning and Development.* New Jersey. Prentice Hall.

Larochelle, M. and Bednarz, N. (1998) Constructivism and Education: Beyond Epistemological Correctness. Chapter 1. In Larochelle, M., Bednarz, N. and Garrison, J., *Constructivism and Education*. Cambridge. Cambridge University Press.

Laurillard, D. (2000) Mainstreaming Learning Technologies. Keynote address at ALT-C conference, UMIST. September. http://www.umist.ac.uk/alt-c2000/programme/keynote.htm. (accessed 30.11.2001).

Leach, L., Neutze, G. and Zepke, N. (2001) Assessment and Empowerment: Some Critical Questions. *Assessment and Evaluation in Higher Education*. 26(4), 293–305.

Maslow, A. H. (1972) Defence and Growth. pp. 43–51. In Silberman, M. L. (ed.) *The Psychology of Open Teaching and Learning*. Boston. Little Brown.

Mazza, R. and Dimitrova, V. (2004) Visualising Student Tracking Data to Support Instructors in Web-Based Distance Education. *Proceedings of the 13th International WWW Conference*, May, New York.

McCarty, L. P. and Schwandt, T. A. (2000) Seductive Illusions: Von Glaserfeld and Gergen on Epistemology and Education. Chapter 3. In Phillips, D. C. (ed.) (2000) *Constructivism in Education: Opinions and Second Opinions on Controversial Issues*: 99th Yearbook of the National Society for the Study of Education. Part 1. Chicago, IL. The University of Chicago Press.

Nonnecke, B. and Preece, J. (2001) Why Lurkers Lurk. *Proceedings of the Americas Conference on Information Systems*. Available online. http://www.cis.uoguelph.ca/~nonnecke/research.htm. (accessed: 24.09.2004).

O'Connor, A. Hyde, A. and Treacy, M. (2003) Nurse Teachers Constructions of Reflection and Reflective Practice. *Reflective Practice*. 4(2), 107–19.

Oliver, M. and Shaw (2003) Asynchronous Discussion in Support of Medical Education. *Journal of Asynchronous Learning*. February. 7(1), 56–67. Available Online. http://www.aln.org/publications/jaln/v7n1/pdf/v7n1_oliver.pdf. (accessed 08.09.2004).

Phillips, D. C. (ed.) (2000) *Constructivism in Education: Opinions and Second Opinions on Controversial Issues*: 99th Yearbook of the National Society for the Study of Education. Part 1. Chicago, IL. The University of Chicago Press.

Ravet, S. (2004) ePortfolio: Transforming Education and Training in Europe. Keynote Speech at *E-portfolio London 2004 Conference* at Cass Business School, City University London. 29th March.

Salmon, G. (2000) *E-moderating: The Key to Teaching and Learning Online*. London. Kogan Page.

Sandars, J. (2004) Presentation on E-learning for Prospective Students and Demonstration of a Unit. University of Manchester School of Epidemiology and Health Sciences. Available online. http://www.mphe.man.ac.uk/Prospectus/Default.htm. (accessed 24.04.2004).

Sims, R. (2003) Promises of Interactivity: Aligning Learner Perceptions and Expectations with Strategies for Flexible and Online Learning. *Distance Education*. 24(1), 87–103.

Smith, J. and Oliver, M. (2004) Exploring Behaviour in the Online Environment: Student Perceptions of Information Literacy. *Asynchronous Learning Technologies Journal*. 4. (Paper in press.)

Smordal, O. and Gregory, J. (2003) Personal Digital Assistants in Medical Education and Practice. *Journal of Computer Assisted Learning*. 19, 320–9.

Spouse, J. (1998) Learning to Nurse through Legitimate Peripheral Participation. *Nurse Education Times*. 18, 345–51.

Stash, N Cristea, A. and De Bra, P. (2004) Authoring of Learning Styles in Adaptive Hypermedia Problems and Solutions. Proceedings of the *13th International World Wide Web Conference*, New York. 17–24 May.

Stevens, J. (1997) Improving Integration between Research and Practice as a Means of Developing Evidence-Based Healthcare. *NT Research*. January/February. 2(1), 7–15.

Vygotsky, L.V. (1962) *Thought and Language*. trans. Hamfnann, E. and Vakar, G. Cambridge, Massachusetts. MIT Press and Wiley.

Watts, M. (1988) *Shared Learning*. RCN Research Series. London. RCN.

Wiecha, J. M., Gramling, R., Joachim, P. and Vanderschmidt, H. (2003) Collaborative E-learning Using Streaming Video and Asynchronous Discussion Boards to Teach the Cognitive Foundation of Medical Interviewing: A Case Study. *Journal of Medical Internet Research*. 5(2). Available online. http://www.jmir.org.org/2003/2/e13. (accessed 30.01.2004).

Williams, P. (ed.) (2004) News. *Public Sector Learning*: An E-learning Age Supplement. London.

Wilson, S. (2003) Delivering 21st century IT: How will Healthcare Informatics Education and Training be Provided? *British Journal of healthcare Computer Information Management*. *ASSIST column*. June. Available online. http://www.bjhc.co.uk/journal/1/2003/5001.html. (accessed 08.03.2004).

3

E-communities

Pam Moule

Introduction

The development of online 'virtual communities' or 'e-communities' is the subject of some debate and forms the centre of discussions in this chapter. Kirkup (2002) presents Brown and Duguid (2002) as critics of Internet-based learning systems, suggesting web-based learning groups fail to provide meaningful communities. It is also suggested that Dreyfus (1999), who feels the presentation of copious amounts of web-based information hinder learning online, shares this position. Additionally, Rheingold (2000) who previously described online groups as 'virtual communities' takes a revised position, using a description of 'online social networks' (p. 359) to refer to virtual groups, suggesting they share little more than common interests.

In order to consider whether communities of learning can be developed in an online environment, the 'Communities of Practice (CoP)' framework developed by Wenger (1998) is discussed. Wenger's (1998) framework was based on research with communities that had a physical rather than a virtual presence (see Lave and Wenger, 1991), yet Wenger (1998) provides an example of a web-based CoP using the computer to support community functioning, postulating the development of online communities of learners. Within the chapter there is an appraisal of the limited body of literature that has considered the application of the CoP framework to online environments. Elements of research that reviewed whether healthcare students could develop a virtual community of practice whilst completing an online interprofessional learning module are also presented. Finally, a discussion of the way forward for collaborative learning communities in nursing and healthcare is offered.

Communities of Practice framework

Wenger's (1998) framework has been developed from earlier work (Lave and Wenger, 1991) that viewed learning as a situated activity in the workplace. It was centred on a form of apprenticeship, where learners participated in a community of practitioners, gaining knowledge and skills through working with Masters and others within the community. Wenger (1998) developed this thinking into the Communities of Practice model of social learning where the role of the teacher or mentor is emphasised in supporting practice-derived learning. This said, the model has a focus on learning through being part of the community, which shapes the identity of the individual, where all members of the community are likely to be involved in learner development. It also has links to situated learning theory as it includes descriptions of learning in the socially and situated arena of the workplace, where learning is gained through the practice experience of working (Fowler and Mayes, 1999; Fox, 2000) (see Chapter 2).

The model includes four components of a social learning theory; identity, meaning, practice and community (Wenger, 1998):

1. Identity – learning as becoming. It is constructed and formed through learning as a member of a community.
2. Meaning – learning as experience. Meaning, which is historically and contextually bound, is derived from negotiated experience and participation in the community.
3. Practice – learning as doing. Practice is the engagement of the learner in the community setting, which may be the workplace, with the aim of achieving shared goals.
4. Community/communities – learning as belonging. Communities provide the context of learning that is achieved through belonging to the community and includes three essential dimensions; mutual engagement, joint enterprise and shared repertoire.

Dimensions of community

Three dimensions are described as being essential to a community; mutual engagement, joint enterprise and shared repertoire (Wenger, 1998).

Mutual engagement

This is based on the members of the group working together, building relationships and developing a negotiated meaning of practice within the community. The group interaction can be formally or informally constituted, involving work practice and social activities. Such interaction acts to maintain the community. An e-community will rely on the computer system and use of e-mail, discussion boards, virtual classrooms as vehicles for online communication and ongoing maintenance of community relationships. Relationships are built through working together, with individuals influencing the working of others in the community whilst creating their own identities in the community.

Wenger (1998) stresses the need for diversity within the community, not all members need to be same, yet there are concerns that the communities might tend to favour commonality and limit the effect of any diverse views, reducing conflict and maintaining a degree of harmony (Eraut, 2003). The notion that identity is developed through knowledge gained whilst engaging in the community suggests that members of the community hold others in trust, believing in them (Kirkup, 2002). Developing such a trusting environment online is not without problems. Tomes (2001) and Kirkup (2002) discuss the presentation of false identity on the Web. Turkle (1997) also comments on individuals who exploit the potential to create false identities online and the harm this can cause to those who trust the deceiver. If e-communities are populated by members who present false histories and persona it could call into question the authenticity of identities developed online (Kirkup, 2002).

Joint enterprise

This dimension is the process that maintains the existence of the CoP. It is about more than shared goals, but concerns negotiating joint enterprise that will involve the community agreeing endeavours and pursuing them jointly, taking some accountability for ways of working towards agreed goals. Joint enterprise will require those communities working virtually to negotiate ways of working towards communally agreed goals within the constraints of online environments. It may be that negotiating endeavours might result in a degree of disagreement amongst community members; this would require the community to jointly negotiate the way forward, which members then engage in with a sense of responsibility. This can be formally recorded in learning situations using ground rules devised by the community members and, in online environments, would require a conscious engagement with online learning.

Shared repertoire

The routines, language, ways of working and stories that are part of the community form the shared repertoire. It is shaped by the history of mutual engagement of the community and changes to create new meanings as new community members introduce their histories, stories, actions and ways of working. Wenger (1998) sees the dynamic nature of shared repertoire as being creative to the community, though warns that differences in interpretation and understanding that interfere with mutual engagement in the CoP would need addressing. This aspect of communities does suggest that they are sustainable over periods of time, which as Fowler and Mayes (1999) comment, might restrict their use in transient online environments.

Online Communities of Practice

Given the above concern regarding the possible use of communities of practice in transitory online settings, it is interesting to note the work of Rogers (2000). In the United States (US) Rogers (2000) used a case study methodology to review a three-week online workshop, 'Teachers of English as a Second or Other Language'. He considered whether a small sample of 26 teachers and administrators were able to develop a CoP through analysis of online discussions. Rogers fails to offer independent verification of his conclusions, though he identifies elements of the theory in his analysis and confirms that the group were able to develop a CoP, demonstrating aspects of mutual engagement, joint enterprise and shared repertoire.

In contrast, research by Orey *et al.* (2003), also in the United States, found that participants of an online learning course in network administration described limited interactions with community colleagues. The participants preferred to communicate with course coaches. The findings are centred on interviews with a sample of only two males and one female, but suggest that not all groups will develop a community of learners.

Further literature in the United States has considered the existence of CoP in blended environments, where information technology (IT) provided part of the learning in the community setting. Spitler and Gallivan (1999) completing an ethnographic study in a firm of management consultants reviewed how knowledge workers learnt their job. Thirty interviews were conducted and observations completed revealing that the CoP had significant influence, though the impact of IT within this is unclear. Further research with designers and journalists where knowledge sharing occurred in virtual and physical environments, postulated the importance of discussion-group moderators and webmasters in supporting an online CoP (Millen and Muller, 2001).

The aforementioned papers all reflect a review of small-scale studies, where online working has either been the main vehicle of delivery or has featured as part of the learning community. In contrast, Somekh and Pearson (2000) used the CoP framework (Wenger, 1998) to analyse participation in a European research project linked by electronic communication, with occasional face-to-face meetings. The findings identified difficulties in the functioning of the CoP that were linked to the reliance on electronic communication. Working in geographically spread locations had a negative effect on the development of joint enterprise. Agreed deadlines were often being forgotten as the lack of physical contact resulted in an absence of physical reminders found in a co-located community. Differing repertoires and histories also led to tensions in negotiating a shared understanding of the action research methodology used, with it being interpreted and employed in various ways across the research sites. As the community failed to negotiate meanings, mutual engagement was ultimately undermined.

More recent work by Murray (2003) discusses the possibilities of developing online communities using formal and informal e-learning environments. Murray (2003) suggests that there are potential advantages for nursing, where virtual communities might be used to explore practice, support information exchange and practice development.

Development of online Communities of Practice in healthcare students

Ethically approved research that reviewed whether nursing, radiotherapy and radiography students were able to develop online CoP was undertaken as part of a doctoral study (Moule, 2004, unpublished Thesis). A case study approach (see Yin, 1994) was employed and included a number of strands of data collection across a six-week Interprofessional module delivered online. Five students were asked to complete an online diary that was based on specific prompt questions that reflected Wenger's framework (1998). A discussion board of one group of seven students was collected and three interviews were conducted following completion of the course. The students involved represented the different nursing professions, radiotherapy and radiography. The interpretations of the data are discussed here in relation to the three elements of a CoP; mutual engagement, joint enterprise and shared repertoire.

The online Interprofessional learning module is based on a constructivist learning approach (Hughes *et al.*, 2004). It is delivered in the final year of the pre-registration curriculum and is completed online, following an initial introduction to the module and virtual learning environment (VLE) used to provide information, support discussion boards and virtual classroom. Groups of approximately seven students from different professions and differing sites of course delivery are facilitated in online working. The course structure sets a trigger question to start group discussions and requires students to use the discussion board and virtual classroom for communication and enquiry. As the course continues students submit work developed through their enquiry, which is peer reviewed and supports the development of a final assessment submitted online.

Mutual engagement

Mutual engagement necessitates members of the community working together in a common negotiated activity, something that the course structure supported. It required students to contribute to interprofessionally based discussions, prompted by an initial trigger and guided by the production of elements of academic work submitted on a regular basis.

Online introductions started the initial social chat that developed with references to working interprofessionally, so recognising the different professional groups engaged in the course and presenting different professional identities. Salmon's (2000) model of teaching and learning online stresses the importance of socialisation for the participant, which seems to have occurred to some degree amongst the groups. Students were working together online and starting to build relationships that transcended social chat and tried to understand working practices and policies of the different professional groups. Their contributions to discussions were often based on their professional backgrounds and interests. One radiography student for example, gave details of how the radiography course was structured and how they worked in practice, discussing a radiographer's role and responsibilities.

To support collaborative engagement, students explored the range of tools available for communication online, trying the discussion boards, virtual classroom and file exchange to post completed work. Communication was predominantly asynchronous, with the students inputting to the discussion board at different times. The groups tended to use the virtual classroom for synchronous chat, with the students talking online at the same time to assist with decision-making, an example being when they needed to agree on a framework for critical appraisal. The use of the virtual classroom at these times suggested that asynchronous online working held limitations for the groups and negotiation did on occasion require the use of the virtual classroom. The time lag involved in asynchronous communication hampered joint decision-making, which some students noted as far easier in a face-to-face forum. The use of the virtual classroom provided a space for synchronous discussion, though this was not always viewed positively, requiring organisation to initiate communication and establish rules for online chat, such as identifying who questions were to be answered by, that enabled meaningful conversation.

The use of the classroom raised issues for certain group members as it was not always possible for students to organise availability at particular times to 'meet' virtually, therefore not all members of the community were able to engage at all times. Other research suggests participants of online learning can require more time than is available (Conole *et al.*, 2002; Gillis *et al.*, 2000; Steele *et al.*, 2002). Gillis *et al.* (2000) found Canadian nurses had limited time to learn both new content and master technology and therefore tended to concentrate on learning to use the computer. Engagement was also hampered for some students by technical or VLE issues (cf. Chapter 6). Some required help in developing their IT skills and generally there were differing approaches to engagement, with some visiting the discussion board daily and others with less regularity. The lack of computer skills amongst nurses and other e-learners has been the subject of a number of research projects with Atack (2003) reviewing nurses in Canada. She found technical issues dominated focus group discussions during the first eight weeks of an online course.

There was evidence of relationships forming amongst members of the community, where others influenced the thinking and understanding in members of the group. Students reported that they had learnt from others and had their understanding of other professions and interprofessional working developed. The relationships were not always harmonious; there was a feeling that they found it easier to disagree online than in a face-to-face setting. This suggests that students were able to present diverse views, which it had been thought might be restricted (Eraut, 2003), though as stated in later discussions resolution was difficult at times, requiring facilitator input.

Group members also demonstrated the development of relationships, as they looked to each other for support, though on occasions addressed needs specifically to the group facilitator. Support was sought from group members in relation to technical issues, when difficulties arose with accessing the virtual classroom or posting work on the file exchange. Atack (2003) found there was reluctance amongst nurses to obtain help from technical staff, tending to look to other group members for support and help. Students also shared resources, information and experiences. A number of students stated they felt sad at saying goodbye to group members at the end of the course and had maintained a social dialogue as well as professional discussions throughout the six weeks.

There were however exceptions to this, suggesting that the development on relationships varied across the groups. A number of students delayed their introduction to the group and student input to the groups was not uniform. At certain stages students were working independently, concentrating on the tasks they needed to complete. Some students in the study relied on professional relationships outside the group, not really engaging in the online community, which obviously affected mutual engagement and joint enterprise. Ragoonden and Bordeleau (2000) researched a 15-week Internet-based introductory psychology course in Canada, attracting international students. They found some students preferred autonomous working, though this was particularly evident when collaborative working was not focused on assessments, though in the course presented here collaborative working tended to relate to assessment tasks. Fisher *et al.* (2000) also found group working issues emergent from a US-based study limited to a sample of five females. Group identity was slow to emerge, with initial participation being poor and communication problems were seen as resultant from a lack of visual contact and face-to-face meetings.

Joint enterprise

Negotiating joint enterprise involves the community agreeing to endeavour and jointly pursuing it, with members of the community taking accountability for ways of working towards the agreed goals. The enterprise of the group was to some extent detailed by the ongoing submission of elements of work and final assessment requirements of the course. However, the achievement of these outcomes did require the group members to negotiate and move forward with some degree of agreement and joint working.

To achieve their goals they initially clarified their understanding of the assessment requirements for the course. Students often elected a leader to co-ordinate the submission of particular aspects of work and they provided peer appraisal of submitted pieces, contributing to the ongoing development of fellow student's work.

Despite these positive findings, there were recorded disagreements amongst some community members and reconciliation of conflict through negotiation proved difficult for some. The development of online group relationships has been reported as problematic amongst American physician students (Kamin *et al.*, 2001), who found the development of relationships amongst web-based members difficult. Some students in the Interprofessional groups looked to the facilitator of the group to resolve issues. The sense of taking responsibility for self and others in the group was not uniform. There was evidence of some students submitting work late and others failing to participate in discussion boards and virtual classroom chat. It might be postulated that the lack of physical contact amongst the community members might have impacted on the development of joint enterprise as suggested by Somekh and Pearson (2000). Additionally, Salmon (2000) discusses the need for early motivation of participants to the use of the computer for learning, an issue considered in the design of the course, with face-to-face and online introductions featuring.

Shared repertoire

The shared repertoire of the community evolves as members contribute to and share histories, stories and ways of working that create new meanings. The development of shared repertoire was evidenced by a number of students who had been able to share understandings of aspects of their professions, their interpretations of histories and stories. It was also evident that students had shared knowledge and understandings to such an extent that those interviewed claimed they had been able to derive a new meaning of interprofessional working, which had been used in the assignment and subsequently in practice environments.

The development of new meaning was again not uniformly seen. Other students reported being unsure of what was required of the groups and felt they had been unable to give sufficient time to their group. There was also a sense from some that they were reluctant to invest in a group that was so short lived, whereas others found the communication and sharing in an online environment problematic and kept communication brief and stilted.

Effectiveness of online group working has been linked to the development of trust amongst members. Creating new meaning requires trust amongst the community members. Hidden identities online have led to harassment of women in particular (Mechanic, 1998) and can affect the development of trust which is seen as important to online group success (Hughes *et al.*, 2002). Strategies used to support responsibility taking amongst communities of learners have included the use of learning contracts (Murphy *et al.*, 2000). Social team development is also important, with teams where members know each other prior to online working being seen as more effective (Andrews and Schwarz, 2002).

Discussion

Though the research is limited by its concentration on one case study, an overview of the findings suggest that elements of Wenger's (1998) concepts of mutual engagement, joint enterprise and shared repertoire were present, though this was not uniformly so. During the six-week course students varied in their engagement and level of trust, affecting relationship building. Negotiation proved difficult online with some groups resorting to the virtual classroom for support in decision-making, though this was not always a panacea for their difficulties, remaining problematic for some. There was also evidence of some students failing to take responsibility for their actions and the effect of this was seen on the other group members. Repertoire was shared in some aspects. These centred around professional stories, which had some impact on the learning of the community, reported to have transferred to both academic and practice communities.

Ways forward

Despite the inconclusive findings regarding the development of online Communities of Practice, it is possible to extract principles to guide the development of learning communities in online environments using Wenger's (1998) concepts of community.

Skill requirements

To support the development of mutual engagement, students learning online as part of a community of practice must be enabled to access all components of the learning environment. This will require them having the necessary IT skills to engage online, being able to access and use the discussion board and the virtual classroom (cf. Chapter 6). If the level of ability and IT skill is unknown, it may be feasible to consider assessing IT development needs and ensuring development prior to commencing online learning.

Online communities

The composition of groups working in online communities has been seen to affect the performance and outcomes of groups (Andrews and Schwarz, 2002). Consideration should therefore be given to the initial group composition. If the facilitator generates groups from students with existing knowledge of each other where possible, this can enhance group working. It is also suggested that groups composed of students with differing levels of IT knowledge and confidence, may aid group performance. More able members are likely to support those who are less computer literate.

A group operating as an online community of practice will need to agree to joint enterprise, in the endeavours of the group. This requires negotiation and decision-making. It was seen that the virtual classroom proved a useful tool to enable the synchronous (real time) discussions needed. The emergence of a group co-ordinator was also important to agreeing on endeavour. To support this activity a facilitator should be in place for each group. The facilitator will be able to guide appropriate role adoption, perhaps identifying individuals to co-ordinate particular activities. They can additionally guide goal setting and trajectories within the group.

The facilitator will also have a key role in supporting the development of underpinning social processes amongst community members through initial face-to-face or online contact. This will allow some social (net)iquette between participants. Initial group socialisation is important to ongoing communication and working (Salmon, 2002). This is particularly crucial in online communities where sharing past histories and understandings is key to developing shared repertoire. This is also important to limiting the presentation of different personas (Kirkup, 2002) and supporting the development of trust amongst members. This might be enhanced through enabling the presentation of student profiles online, giving some individual history and context. Group working will be further enhanced through establishing ground rules and learning contracts following the early socialisation phase. Group development of rules and contracts of working are thought to not only support the development of shared repertoire but also joint enterprise. By agreeing on ways of working the members are making a commitment to the group and developing shared practices.

Designing for online communities

Those participating in online learning have suggested that more time is required to support this form of learning than is available, claiming it to be 'time poor' (Conole *et al.*, 2002). Course developers can make recommendations as to how much time learners might be expected to spend using particular learning resources online or spend engaged as part of a learning community. Building in expectations of the time needed to support online learning communities should enable learners to plan their commitment to the community.

To support the development of mutual engagement and joint enterprise, course developers need to consider a structure that requires and supports community negotiation of activity. Developing activities that require group members to agree on endeavour will be important. These might be centred around the group agreeing upon outcomes to be achieved and negotiating the ways to work towards this, including ground rules. Roles may be allocated to different group members throughout the period of engagement, perhaps with individuals taking responsibility for different activities being completed. This should help support the development of accountability amongst members, if each has a role and purpose that contributes towards the group achieving its negotiated outcomes. The composition of the group may also assist the degree of commitment achieved and the longevity of the course can impact on engagement seen. Those groups functioning for longer periods might foster greater investment. Salmon (2000) discusses the need to link activity to assessment processes to ensure online engagement is meaningful and has a purpose. This it is suggested, will encourage participation, though as seen in the research is no guarantee of engagement.

Whilst the longevity of the community can support the development of shared repertoire, it will be important to ensure that the course provides scope to explore professional working roles, identities, policies and values. Sharing histories and stories allows the negotiation of new meaning and dynamic development within the community. Early socialising within the community provides a forum for initial exploration of community members. This can be developed through the use of activities that centre on exploring professional roles, histories and current issues.

Involvement in a community of practice shapes identity, which is a produce of community membership, negotiated experience and is a product of learning (Wenger, 1998). In order to support reflection on relationships within the community and identity development, course outcomes can be designed to that which will consider growth of the community. An assessment of online presentations that encourage reflection on personal development, growth and learning can be employed.

Conclusion

The existence of e-communities has been debated in the literature. Currently there is a dearth of research that has considered the specific development of online communities of practice, though the work of Rogers (2000) and Moule (2004, unpublished) has identified elements of Wenger's (1998) theory in the analysis of online groups. Aspects of mutual engagement, joint enterprise and shared repertoire were present in both communities of learners studied. Both studies concentrated on courses with short delivery times and were limited to single cases and therefore further research is required. That said, tentative recommendations for educationalists relate to considering principles around community composition, preparation, facilitator support, social engagement and developing course structures that support community negotiation and reflection that is linked to course outcome.

References

Andrews, T. and Schwarz, G. (2002) Preparing Students for Virtual Organisation: An Evaluation of Learning with Virtual Learning Technologies. *Educational Technology & Society*. 5(3), 54–65. Available at http://ifets.ieee.org/periodical/vol_5_2002/andrews.htm. (accessed 11.03.2003).

Atack, L. (2003) Becoming A Web-Based Learner: Registered Nurses' Experiences. *Journal of Advanced Nursing.* 44(3), 289–97.

Brown, J. S. and Duguid, P. (2002) *The Social Life of Information.* Boston: Harvard Business School Press.

Conole, G., Hall, M. and Smith, S. (2002) An Evaluation of an Online Course for Medical Practitioners. *Educational Technology & Society.* 5(3), 66–75. Available at http://ifets.ieee.org/periodical/vol_3_2002/conole.html. (accessed 11.03.2003).

Dreyfus, H. L. (1999) Anonymity versus Commitment: The Dangers of Education on the Internet. *Ethics and Information Technology.* 1, 15–21.

Eraut, M. (2003) Editorial. *Learning in Health and Social Care.* 2(3), 117–22.

Fisher, K., Phelps, R. and Ellis, A. (2000) Group Processes Online: Teaching Collaboration through Collaborative Processes. *Educational Technology & Society.* 3(3), 484–95. Available at http://ifets.ieee.org/periodical/vol_3_2000/fisher.htm. (accessed 11.03.2003).

Fowler, C. and Mayes, J. (1999) Learning Relationships from Theory to Design. *Association of Learning Technology Journal.* 7(3), 6–16.

Fox, S. (2000) Communities of Practice, Foucault and Actor-Network Theory. *Journal of Management Studies.* 37(6), 853–67.

Gillis, A., Jackson, W., Braid, A., MacDonald, P. and MacQuarrie, M. (2000) The Learning Needs and Experiences of Women Using Print-Based and Cd-Rom Technology in Nursing Distance Education. *Journal of Distance Education.* 15(1), 1–20.

Hughes, M., Ventura, S. and Dando, M. (2004) On-line Interprofessional Learning: Introducing Constructivism through Enquiry-based Learning and peer review. *Journal of Interprofessional Care.* 18(3), 263–8.

Hughes, S., Wickersham, L., Ryan-Jones, D. and Smith, S. (2002) Overcoming Social and Psychological Barriers to Effective On-line Collaboration. *Educational Technology & Society.* 5(1), 1–9. Available at http://ifets.ieee.org/periodical/vol_1_2002/hughes.html. (accessed 11.03.2003).

Kamin, C., Glicken, A., Hall, M., Quarantillo, B. and Merenstein, G. (2001) Evaluation of Electronic Discussion Groups as a Teaching/Learning Strategy in Evidence Based Medicine Course: A Pilot Study. *Education for Health.* 14(1), 21–32.

Kirkup, G. (2002) Identity, Community and Distributed Learning. In Lea, M. and Nicoll, K. (eds) (2002) *Distributed Learning: Social, Cultural Approaches to Practice.* London: Routledge/Falmer, Chapter 11.

Lave, J. and Wenger, E. (1991) *Situated Learning: Legitimate Peripheral Participation.* Cambridge: Cambridge University Press.

Mechanic, M. (1998) *Gender and Power Issues in On-line Learning Environments.* Proceedings *1st International Conference on the Social Impacts of Technology,* Canada.

Millen, D. and Muller, M. (2001) Computer-Supported Communities of Practice. Available at http://www.staff.it.uts.edu.au/~lueg/pospapers/millenmuller.pdf. (accessed 11.11.2003).

Moule, P. (2004) E-learning for Healthcare Students: Developing the Communities of Practice Framework. Bristol: University of the West of England, Bristol. Unpublished EdD thesis.

Murphy, K., Mahoney, S. and Harvey, T. (2000) Role of Contracts in Enhancing Community Building in Web Courses. *Educational Technology & Society*. 3(3), 409–21. Available at http://ifets.ieee.org/periodical/vol_3_2000/murphy.htm. (accessed 11.03.2003).

Murray, P. (2003) E-learning and its Benefits for Developing Nursing Practice. Paper presented at the *IV International Congress of Medical Informatics*, Havana, Cuba, 17–22 March, 2003. *Information Technology in Nursing*. 15(2) 18–24. Available at http://www.bcsng.org.uk/itin15/VOL15–2res.pdf. (accessed 13.02.2004).

Orey, M., Koenecke, L. and Crozier, J. (2003) Learning Communities via the Internet à la Epic Learning: You Can Lead the Horses to Water, but You Cannot Get Them to Drink. *Innovations in Education and Teaching International*. 40(30), 260–7.

Ragoonden, K. and Bordeleau, P. (2000) Collaborative Learning via the Internet. *Educational Technology & Society*. 3(3), 1–15. Available at http://ieee.org/periodical/vol_3_2000/dll.html. (accessed 11.03.2003).

Rheingold, H. (2000) *The Virtual Community: Homesteading on the Electronic Frontier*. Reading, MA: Addison-Wesley.

Rogers, J. (2000) Communities of Practice: A Framework for Fostering Coherence in Virtual Learning Communities. *Educational Technology & Society*. 3(3). Available at http://ifets.ieee.org/periodical/vol_3_2000/eo1.html (accessed 11.03.2003).

Salmon, G. (2000) *E-moderating: The Key to Teaching and Learning On-line*. London: Kogan Page.

Somekh, B. and Pearson, M. (2000) Inter-Cultural Learning Arising from Pan-European Collaboration Using Electronic Communications: Sub-Text or Substance? Paper Presented at *BERA Conference*, Cardiff, September.

Spitler, V. and Gallivan, M. (1999) *The Role of Information Technology in the Learning of Knowledge Work*. New Information Technologies in Organizational Processes: Field Studies and Theoretical Reflections on the Future of Work IFIP-TC8-WG8.2 *International Working Conference*. 257–75.

Steele, D., Johnson Palensky, J., Lynch, T., Lacy, N. and Duffy, S. (2002) Learning Preferences, Computer Attitudes, and Student Evaluation of Computerised Instruction. *Medical Education*. 36, 225–32.

Tomes, N. (2001) Technology-Supported Collaborative Learning. In Falchicov, N (2001) *Learning Together- Peer Tutoring in Higher Education*. London: Falmer, Chapter 9.

Turkle, S. (1997) *Life On The Screen: Identity in the Age of the Internet.* New York: Touchstone Press.

Wenger, E. (1998) *Communities of Practice. Learning, Meaning and Identity.* Cambridge: Cambridge University Press.

Yin, R. (1994) *Case Study Research. Design and Methods.* Second edition. London: Sage.

4

Developing E-learning Materials

Pamela R. Jeffries

Introduction

Many colleges and universities across the world are discovering innovative and exciting ways of using information and communication technology (ICT) to promote the process of teaching and learning and to extend education to new populations of students (Twigg, 2003). Nurse educators in academic and service settings are developing interactive e-learning programs or courses to meet this need and to enhance practice concepts or skills or to orient new practitioners to the clinical setting. Student nurses or healthcare professionals are expecting more flexibility and convenience in education to meet personal goals and academic endeavors concurrently, and consumer demand is increasing for this mode of instruction (cf. Chapter 1). The challenge is to prepare comprehensive, high-quality, yet cost-effective e-learning programs so educational standards and competencies can be met. To address this challenge, the author has developed an instructional design approach known as the Hyperlearning Model (Jeffries, 2000) based on Chickering and Gamson's (1987) 'Principle of Best Practices in Undergraduate Education' to guide the development of online courses. The purpose of this chapter is to describe the instruction model as applied to designing an online course to teach critical care nursing, discuss the teacher's role in an e-learning environment and discuss the importance of the online evaluation process.

What is E-learning?

E-learning is the use of Internet learning tools such as online discussion forums, chat rooms and e-mail to support teaching and learning in an online community (cf. Chapter 3). Included in the online community can be teachers, students and experts. The critical feature of e-learning is the opportunity for learning to take place 'anytime, anywhere' in a rich and collaborative environment. E-learning is also known as online learning, Web-based learning, and Internet-based learning, and the learning environment as the online learning community or asynchronous learning network (Billings, 2002).

The separation of teacher and student in time and space makes e-learning a form of distance learning. The Internet is the main platform for e-learning in the same way as the communication delivery system of audio-conferencing uses the telephone to connect learners and teachers and video-conferencing uses interactive video equipment and closed circuit or satellite communications systems. With the evolution of instructional technology, communication tools of traditional distance learning are merging into the e-learning environment of the Internet and will perhaps offer the best audio, video and text.

Background and significance

Traditionally, nursing course content and skills have been taught in a lecture and laboratory format in which there is one teacher and a group of students. However, teaching this methodology cannot ensure an individualised approach to teaching skills, accommodate different schedules or take into account different student experiences and expertise. The linear approach assumes that everyone proceeds at the same pace, regardless of student experience, interests, background and time demands. Furthermore, students all have to attend lectures on particular days during a specific time period. Today, however, students expect control over when, where, how and how fast they learn, and they are motivating teachers to change their modalities of instruction and interaction (Barone, 2003). With new technological advances, e-learning is ideally suited to take into account individuals and their particular strengths, talents and demands, and to offer flexibility to learning.

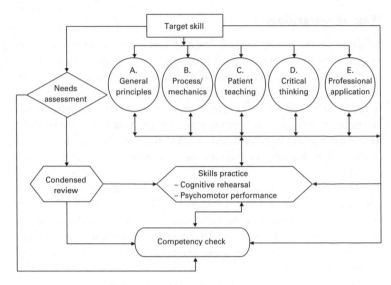

Figure 4.1 Hyperlearning framework for the instructional design
(Jeffries, 2000)

Using the model

In response to students' expectations and desire for more flexibility and individualised course structure, one approach to developing e-learning materials is Jeffries (2000) Hyperlearning model (Figure 4.1). An example of developing an online critical care course in nursing based on this framework will be discussed. This model incorporates the 'Principles of Best Practices in Undergraduate Education' proposed by Chickering and Gamson (1987) and can be very useful as an instructional design model for developing and testing online courses in nursing. The model can guide three general developmental steps: (1) identifying desired learning outcomes; (2) designing the course and (3) testing the program.

The model was successfully used as the basis for the structure of a basic life support CD-ROM developed as part of the INTaL project (Moule *et al.*, 2001), within the United Kingdom. The CD-ROM offered a highly interactive and flexible resource, that was positively received by students and staff (Moule and Gilchrist, 2001; Moule, 2002). It included a diagnostic pre-test, 'What How Why' of resuscitation, four problem-based Critical Thinking scenarios and final summative post-test.

Identifying learning outcomes

The first step when designing an online course or e-learning materials is to define what learning outcomes or performance behaviors are expected after the instruction has been received by the learner. In this critical care course example, expected learning outcomes included (1) didactic knowledge obtained in the online course and (2) basic skill acquisition, that is, whether the learner can perform the skills presented in the modules. Other outcomes expected for the course include (3) positive student perceptions of the embedded educational strategies and (4) satisfaction with the overall instructional method.

Designing the course

Once outcomes are decided upon, the design of the course can begin. One approach to this process, which will be used in this example, is using Jeffries (2000) Hyperlearning Model framework. The critical design elements used along with this framework include (1) incorporation of the 'Principles of Best Practices in Undergraduate Education', (2) a modular format and (3) the use of appropriate design features, including layout, fonts and interactive learning activities.

When developing content for an online course, a detailed framework assists the author to present content in some organised, consistent fashion. The final program should be intuitive and easy to navigate and should allow for easy access or escape. Order, flow and important content areas should be taken into consideration when developing lecture content for a nursing course. Furthermore, the online course should be designed to be logical and interesting.

The Principles of Best Practice in Undergraduate Education

The Principles of Best Practice in Undergraduate Education listed in Table 4.1 (Chickering and Gamson, 1987) were used to guide the framework, screen design, text, and pedagogical approach of the online course.

Current research and practice in instructional design and instructional psychology should be used to guide the pedagogical approach. To achieve good student performance levels as well as student satisfaction with the learning methodology, decisions must be made in this stage about how best to incorporate the Principles of Best Practice in Undergraduate Education.

Table 4.1   Principles of best practices in undergraduate education
(Chickering and Gamson, 1987)

Active learning	Students learn content and basic skills as active participants in the learning process
Prompt feedback	Information is given about the learner's response, the process by which the response is derived, or the learning strategy used to respond
Time on task	Time is used wisely to learn content and basic skills
Diverse talents and ways of to learning	Many different ways are offered meet students' different learning needs
Collaborative learning	Students learn with others
High expectations	Good outcomes are anticipated from the student
Faculty/student interaction	There is contact between student and instructor during the learning process

The effectiveness of the Principles of Best Practice in Undergraduate Education has been supported by numerous nursing studies of clinical teaching behaviours (Bergman and Gaitskill, 1990; Morgan and Knox, 1987; Thompson and Scheckly, 1997), studies related to classroom teaching (Gandy and Jensen, 1992; Hughes, 1993) and studies using multimedia platforms (Jeffries, 2000; Jeffries, 2001; Jeffries *et al.*, 2003). Table 4.2 describes how each principle of best practice was incorporated into the online critical care course.

Another strategy to consider when using Jeffries's (2000) Hyperlearning model is to break the course into selected dimensions or modules. The modular format allows the learner easy access and flexible learning segments for just-in-time learning or a review of material that perhaps was learned in the past. If a learner comes with specific experience and expertise, for example, a strong cardiovascular background from working in a cardiac catherisation lab, then perhaps less time needs to be spent on the cardiovascular module than on the other critical care modules.

Table 4.2 Principles of best practices as incorporated into the instructional activities

Principle of best practice	Online instructional design or activity
Active learning	Discussion questions are posted for the student to reflect on and discuss in addition to various other activities (e.g., case studies, gaming-type activities)
Prompt feedback	Pre-test questions, activities, or critical thinking vignettes are presented with rationale for why the students' answers or decisions are correct or incorrect. Formative feedback through email, discussion forums, and/or chat rooms, is given throughout the course to guide the learner. Email is best for individual feedback to students
Time on task	Content is offered in modules with subsections so students can select the content desired or skip over content already known to use their time wisely
Diverse styles of learning	Different learning styles are addressed by the instructional design, including visual learning with graphics, charts, images and other items. Strategies aimed at auditory learning are included where appropriate, and kinesthetic learning can be obtained in the clinical practice with hands-on experience with the preceptor in addition to simulation activities involving the use of hands and skills
High Expectations	Expectation levels are carefully programmed into the online course, for example, dialogue between the instructor and student in the discussion forums and establishing competency outcomes for the module exams and skills acquisition with a minimal passing score for the cognitive knowledge
Teacher/student interaction	Teachers get to know the student individually through email and discussion postings. The instructor provides specific questions for the students to answer, evaluates the answers and, again, gives individualized as well as group feedback

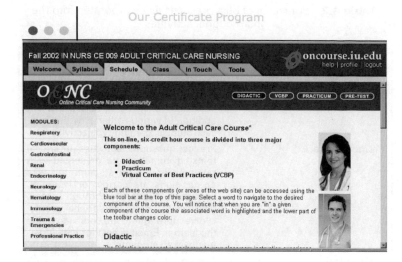

Figure 4.2   An example of module sections as seen on the left of the online screen (for example, respiratory, cardiovascular, gastrointestinal, renal, endocrinology, neurology, hematology, immunology, trauma and emergencies, and professional practice)

Once the modules are defined, smaller subsections need to be organized and incorporated into the course framework before content is inserted as in the Figure 4.2 example. The smaller subsections allow for more specific content to be delineated in the course.

Online critical care course framework

In the online critical care course used here as the example, the course design involves three major areas: (1) a core didactic or traditional lecture component, (2) a clinical practicum and (3) the Virtual Centre of Best Practices (VCBP). Each of these components is divided into smaller modules or sections.

The core didactic component of the Web-based course provides the participant with background knowledge, general principles and opportunities for critical thinking regarding selected critical care health disruptions. Within the core didactic section, for each module, specific content areas are covered using online/interactive mini-lectures, activities, and Web-links to provide the participant with a comprehensive overview of

Table 4.3 Content areas for the didactic portion of the specific critical care modules

Content area	Content outline
General principles	• Anatomy/physiology (review) • Pathophysiology • Patient Assessment (risk factors, history-taking questions and physical assessment findings) • Diagnostic Assessments (laboratory and radiology findings and special procedure findings associated with the particular health disruption)
Management process	• Nursing Management (includes symptom management, patient education and community resources) • Medical Management (pharmacological treatment, nutritional guidelines and special concerns/treatments)
Critical thinking	Application of content within the core didactic section includes a critical thinking section where small vignettes of realistic patient scenarios are provided. The participant can apply the knowledge learned from the content within the module to answer questions about the vignettes. This provides a mechanism of self-evaluation, and therefore the score is not included in the course grade.

the selected health disruption. Specific modules delineated are based on organ systems, for example, cardiovascular, respiratory, renal and others generally found as an organising framework in critical care textbooks. For each specific module, content was then designed using the outline shown in Table 4.3.

Student evaluation in relation to the core content includes scores on nine multiple-choice module exams, one comprehensive final, class participation points and discussion of an ethical/cultural/legal dilemma experienced in the clinical practicum during the semester. All evaluations are conducted online.

The second part of the course design is the 'Clinical Practicum', which provides the participant an opportunity to apply course concepts in a clinical setting caring for critical care patients. The practical occurs throughout the semester-long course as the participant applies the concepts of each online module to an identified group of clinical patients. The practicum consists of 112 clinical hours working on a specific clinical unit.

The clinical practicum uses the preceptor model for the clinical experience (Rowles and Stone, 2002). This model involves a relationship between the learner, preceptor/clinician and course facilitator or teacher. The role of the preceptor is to serve as the clinical expert and to assist the learner with problem solving, critical thinking, skills supervision and evaluation in the practice setting. Within the clinical practicum, the learner reviews and practices a selected set of skills, with the preceptor/clinician ultimately evaluating the student's skill sets using a standardised skill checklist.

The third major area in the content design of the critical care course is the 'Virtual Centre of Best Practices (VCBP)', which serves as a learning resource centre. The participant can visit this online site to retrieve resources such as clinical standards for specific skills, information on the range of available practices within the professional community and the standard protocols of the professional nursing organisations for specific procedures. Additionally, empirical research findings and opportunities to dialogue with nationally recognised nurse experts are contained within the VCBP. Several nurse experts can be asked to participate in an asynchronous consulting session during a selected time period within the course so the participant can ask questions. Within this VCBP, the aim is to build an online community of professional practice in which not only can the student and instructor interact, but the student has opportunities to interact with other experts in the professional community of nursing. This online community of professional practice (OCPP) is designed to connect experts and learners and provide a mechanism for nurses, nursing students and educators to acquire professional knowledge and skills (Billings, 2001; Norris *et al.*, 2003).

Throughout the course, the participant is referred to the VCBP to obtain research-based articles on particular critical care topics, for critique or perhaps use in other assignments. Additionally, the participants are able to have asynchronous discussions with some of the top critical care educators, clinicians and researchers through the discussion forums that are posted within the course. The VCBP provides a rich learning resource centre, with the participant usually able to access the site at any time, although sometimes the learner must go to the VCBP during a particular time frame for a specific assignment. There is no student evaluation component related to the VCBP, but for particular assignments the site must be visited to obtain needed materials.

Adding design features: modules, font/graphics and learning activities

Once the framework is established and the content written, there are design features important for making any online course interesting, inviting and stimulating to the students. These features help the student to navigate easily, promote richness and realism to the content, and provide graphics or animation that can help to explain concepts more clearly.

Lay-out, fonts, colours and graphics

The term lay-out refers to how elements such as text, graphics, images and tables fit on a screen page (Hollingsworth, 2002). The most difficult part of constructing the lay-out is identifying what is important and only putting this information on the screen in an easily understood, creative way. The style and shape of the letters are defined by the fonts used in the program. Arial and Verdana fonts at a size 10–12 level are typically used in the Web-based environment. In Web development white space is the open area, gray space is the area composed of text and black space is the space used by images. White, black and grey spaces are considered part of the page lay-out since they define the type of element on a page or screen. There are two components of colours: background and foreground. Background is the wallpaper or paint on which all other page or screen elements will be placed. The text and image elements of the page or screen make up the foreground.

When designing a course, there is no ideal layout. It is important, however, to develop a layout that makes it easy for learners to locate any information they may need. For example, the use of white space and wise use of spacing will make it easier for the reader to scan information.

Several factors should be kept in mind when selecting font type and style from the computer program. First, fonts reside on individual computers. This means that if a font is used in a program that is not on the user's computer, then the font will appear differently from what is anticipated. Also, the number of fonts within a document should be restricted to no more than three. Ideally, there should be a single font for the text, including headings.

Graphics or images should be used to enhance the text and not simply to avoid having too many words. Furthermore, the approach should not be on looking for places to insert pictures but rather on making concepts clear and enhancing understanding by inserting tables, photos or visual representations.

Integrating learning activities into the course

Interactive activities and other features to enhance learning should be incorporated into an online course to promote quality and effective learning outcomes. Examples of interactive design features in the critical care course include

Pre-test: A multiple-choice pre-test was designed as a self-evaluation assessment for the learner. By taking the pre-test the learner can assess the learning environment and see the level of questions and expectations in the course. The test includes feedback, specifically, reasons why choices are correct or incorrect.

Interactive exercises: Online modules should have activities or exercises embedded in the content to enhance and promote student learning of the course concepts. Examples from the critical care course include discussion questions for learners to post answers and critique each other, completion of case studies and one-minute papers, which can provide interaction for the learner.

One-minute paper: Within the course, the learner is required to post brief discussion comments on a concept being taught that requires critical thinking about the responsibilities, ethical decision-making and problem solving issues related to that concept. Students can respond to comments, issues or others.

Multiple choice tests: Multiple-choice exams are threaded throughout the course to assess the learner's knowledge of the material discussed in each specific course module. Small module exams (20–25 questions/module) provide a module goal and serve as a learning benchmark for the student.

Final comprehensive exam: A comprehensive exam at the end of the course evaluates overall knowledge of the course concepts and care learned throughout the course. The exam covers content from all course modules.

Class participation: Class participation is expected throughout the Web course, including interacting with peers and being active in the learning process. Points are awarded at the end of the semester for satisfactory class participation. Specific criteria for participation are provided in the course to the student.

Reflective journals: The learner submits a diary of reflections about the learning experience, socialisation to the clinical environment, and/or the overall clinical experience. The learner is encouraged to think critically about the critical care concepts and incorporate these into the reflections. The comments are posted in the reflective journal in the discussion forum for the instructor to see and, as appropriate, respond to.

Facilitating learning in an online environment

Student responsibilities

Students are responsible for active and timely participation in the online community of learning. For an online community and development to be successful, student interaction with teachers and other constituents of the community are essential. Students are also responsible for demonstrating the values and ethics of professional networking in the online learning community. These values are often illustrated through the public nature of the discussion boards and/or forum postings to the entire community.

Differences in online versus traditional teaching

The environmental setting is the most obvious difference between online and traditional instruction methods. In the classroom, the physical presence of other learners creates a sense of belonging to a community. The educator's presence can create a sense of security, even authority. Most educators have been oriented to teach in the traditional setting that allows face-to-face interaction with the students. Verbal and non-verbal cues are assessed in the classroom, providing feedback to the educator about whether the students understand the content. Within the online environment, facilitators will need to provide cues to the students to direct them in their learning and assess their responses to the content being delivered.

Online learning is very student-centreed and it is a unique environment lacking consistent physical structure, personal motivation and self-discipline that is needed by the student. The positive side of a less structured environment is that participants can learn anytime, anywhere. For most students and many instructors, the home is the learning environment. The online atmosphere, although lacking with face-to-face interactions, is a comfortable and convenient environment. The online environment also provides and allows for unlimited resources. Although many classrooms have their PowerPoint slides incorporated into the lecture, the Web instruction offers many rich opportunities to both instructors and students that enhance exploration of ideas and concepts within the discipline. Resources are only a link away.

In the classroom, the instructor attempts to motivate students to interact and answer questions provided in class. However, in the typical classroom situation, not all students participate and a few dominate the discussion. A hallmark of online learning is participation. All participants must enter the virtual classroom ready to answer questions and dialogue with the teacher and other students. Participation is required in these courses, making every student become an active learner in the educational process. Online learning thus becomes relatively more valid in relation to student preparation, depth and quality of assignments.

Teaching strategies for e-learning

Educators can provide a variety of teaching strategies, including synchronous and asynchronous communication, to promote a sense of community (cf. Chapter 3). Typically the course should begin with student and teacher introductions providing an opportunity for all to learn who is in the class with them. Warm-up activities give all participants a chance to interact and 'get started.'

As the students begin to feel more comfortable with the online environment other activities can be added such as games, case scenario discussions, critical-thinking vignettes, nurse expert discussions about a related topic in the course, debates and other interactive exercises. The online community continues to form as everyone contributes and has a sense that their participation is valued and contributes to the goals.

To maintain engagement in the online course different strategies can be used. Participation points can be assigned with the rubric for these points given at the beginning of the course. Posted questions by the instructor help to engage students in the topic and learning process. Questions providing decision-making and problem-solving should be posted to develop these skills of the learner. Sometimes the instructor may need to send an individual email or make a phone call to motivate a student who has been inactive for a certain time period.

Innovative activities are encouraged in the online setting to make the course interesting and enjoyable. Different teaching strategies can be tried out in the course to see if the students enjoy the content, activities and interaction. Streaming a video of the latest intervention for a specific health disruption may be incorporated into learning. Assignments requiring active engagement from other disciplines, professionals and the community can be incorporated to enhance the online community of learning.

Evaluation of e-learning

Usability testing

As Web courses or other e-learning materials go online, usability testing needs to be conducted. The goal of this testing is to uncover any serious problems with the Web environment (such as navigation, clarity of instructions) that might present difficulties to students when they are enrolled in the course.

Pilot-testing the program

Before using an online course in the curriculum, pilot-testing needs to be conducted to evaluate the ease of navigation, flow of content, and comprehensiveness of the material. Final testing is then performed after the pilot to evaluate student outcomes for learning course concepts and satisfaction with the instructional method.

Instruments for testing the course

Instructor-made module tests and post-tests, skills competency check lists and surveys can be used in the usability test and final testing to assure that all components of the course's instructional model are effective. Types of instruments that can be used to measure outcomes of an online course or e-learning activity follow.

Knowledge can be measured by using multiple-choice module exams. The tests should be included in the online course to be accessed electronically when the learner is prepared to take them.

Skills acquisition can be measured using skills competency checklists based on procedural points from the students' textbooks. The checklist can be designed to evaluate the performance of the actual skill after the learner has observed, practised and implemented the skill with his/her preceptor on the clinical unit. The skills competency evaluations should be done when the learner feels prepared and ready to demonstrate the skill to the selected preceptor on the clinical unit.

Inclusion of the best practices in undergraduate education in the process model can be measured by using the Evaluating Educational Uses of the Web in Nursing (EEUWIN) instrument (Billings *et al.*, 2001). The 15-item instrument using a response scale of 1–5 determines the effectiveness of the education practices and outcomes of the course.

Student satisfaction with e-learning materials or an online course can be measured with standardised satisfaction scales that have appropriate validity and reliability measures established (cf. Chapter 7).

Conclusion

When developing e-learning materials or an online course, the non-linear, Hyperlearning model approach (Jeffries, 2000) to the design can help students be more self-directed and independent in their learning. The inclusion of the 'Principles of Best Practices in Undergraduate Education' within the course should help to ensure good student performance and student satisfaction. Preliminary pilot-testing on a small group will show that the course concepts and skills can be learned through e-learning. Online courses allow educators to design and deliver complex content in a manner that supports the development of critical thinking and lifelong learning skills. Ongoing assessment and research need to be conducted as new technological advances and pedagogical approaches are developed to ensure that these new developments do not compromise the quality of education and clinical practice (cf. Chapter 8). The Hyperlearning model offers an initial framework for developing an online course and other types of e-learning clinical nursing experiences and is proposed for further empirical testing and revision. As teachers shift to an e-learning platform, the educator becomes a facilitator and needs to use different teaching strategies.

Because e-learning is very student-centred, teachers need to make sure students are self-disciplined and motivated to complete their assignments and course requirements. As with any programme of instruction, evaluation is a necessary component of the online teaching process and it is important to measure the learning outcomes and student achievement.

References

Barone, C. A. (2003) The Changing Landscape and the New Academy. *Educause Review*, September/October 2003, 41–47.

Bergman, K. and Gaitskill, T. (1990) Faculty and Student Perceptions of Effective Clinical Teachers. An Extension Study. *Journal of Professional Nursing*. 6(1), 33.

Billings, D. (2001) Teaching and Learning in On-line Communities of Professional Practice in Nursing. In Chaska, N. (ed.), *The Nursing Profession*. Thousand Oaks, CA. Sage Publishing, 177–88.

Billings, D. (2002) *Conversations in E-Learning*. Pensacola, FA. Pohl Publishing, Inc.

Billings, D., Connors, H. and Skiba, D. (2001) Benchmarking Best Practices in Web-based Nursing Courses. *Advances in Nursing Science*. 23(3), 41–52 http://tltgroup.org/services/EEUWIN/Home.htm (accessed 7.10.2004).

Billings, D. M. (2000) Framework for Assessing Outcomes and Practices in Web-based Courses in Nursing. *Journal of Nursing Education*. 38(7), 60–7.

Chickering, A. and Gamson, Z. (1987) Seven Principles of Good Practice in Undergraduate Education. *American Association of Higher Education (AAHE) Bulletin*. March.

Gandy, J. and Jensen, G. (1992) Group Work and Reflective Practicums in Physical Therapy Education: Models for Professional Behavior Development. *Journal of Physical Therapy Education*. 6(1), 6–10.

Hollingsworth, C. (2002) Lay-Outs, Colors, Fonts, and Graphics. In Billings, D. (ed.), *Conversations in E-Learning*. Pensacola, FA. Pohl Publishing, 141–51.

Hughes, L. (1993) Peer Group Interactions and the Student Perceived Climate for Caring. *Journal of Nursing Education*. 32(2), 78–83.

Jeffries, P. (2000) Development and Test of a Model for Designing Interactive Cd Roms for Teaching Nursing Skills. *Computers in Nursing*. 18(3), 118–24.

Jeffries, P. R. (2001) Computer Versus Lecture: A Comparison of Two Methods of Teaching Oral Medication Administration in a Nursing Skills Laboratory. *Journal of Nursing Education*. 40(7), 323–9.

Jeffries, P. R., Wolf, S. and Linde, B. (2003) Technology-Based vs. Traditional: A Comparison of Two Instructional Methods to Teach the Skill of Performing a 12- lead ECG. *Nursing Education Perspectives*. 24(2), 70–4

Morgan, J. and Knox, J. (1987) Characteristics of 'Best' and 'Worst' Clinical Teachers as Perceived by University Faculty and Students. *Journal of Advanced Nursing*. 12, 331–7.

Moule, P. (2002) Evaluation of a Basic Life Support CD-ROM: Its Effectiveness and User Experiences. *Educational Technology and Society*. Special Education. Evaluation of Learning Technologies in Higher Education. 5(3), 163–74. http://ifets.ieee.org/periodical/vol_3_2002/v_3_2002 (accessed 7.10.2004).

Moule, P., Gilbert, P. and Chalk, V. (2001) A Multimedia Approach to Teaching Basic Life Support – The development of a CD-ROM. *Nurse Education in Practice*. 1, 73–9.

Moule, P. and Gilchrist, M. (2001) An Evaluation of a Basic Life Support CD-ROM. *Health Informatics Journal*. 7, 29–36.

Norris, D., Mason, J. and Lefrere, P. (2003) *Transforming E-Knowledge*. Ann Arbor, MI. Society for College and University Planning.

Rowles, C and Stone, C (2002) Developing an Online Community of Professional Practice in Critical Care. National League for Nursing Summit, San Diego, CA. September.

Thompson, C. and Sheckly, J. (1997) Differences in Classroom Teaching Preferences between Traditional and Adult BSN Students. *Journal of Nursing Education*. 36(4), 163–9.

Twigg, C. (2003) Improving Learning and Reducing Costs: New Models for On-line Learning. *Educause Review*. September/October, 2003, 28–38.

5

Facilitating Work-Based Learning Online

Stephen Gomez and David Lush

Facilitating work-based learning online: An established pedagogy

Mark Twain (1835–1910) famously said, 'I have never let my schooling interfere with my education.' This profound statement alludes to the fact that education is much more than what you are told, it is what you experience and what you actually do, and the truism, 'learning by doing' is perhaps the most effective way to learn. For nurses, these truths are self-evident. Nurses are practitioners and while in academic and background knowledge lay the foundation for a nurse's education, practical skills are most effectively gained in the work-place. Arguably, it is work-place learning that best prepares student nurses for their profession. This chapter explores the history, meaning and practice of work-based learning (WBL) and its place within the present higher education (HE) agenda. The focus is on the generic aspects of WBL though some reference will be made to nursing education. The second half of the chapter will present a case study of a project, called Profile.ac.uk, that exploits new Internet technologies to produce a system that tracks, monitors and assesses students on WBL.

Work-based learning in many ways is a basic pedagogy and is arguably the oldest means by which humans learnt from one another. Well before formal academic learning, knowledge and skills were handed down through the generations from 'tutor' to 'apprentice' by the former showing the latter how to perform a task, then watching how the task was performed and perfecting the action by repetition and coaching.

Historically, this combination of passive (observing) and active (doing) learning has been one of the most dominant, and the transfer of manual skills that it permits is responsible for much of our success as a species; as Jacob Bronowski said in *The Ascent of Man* (1973), Man 'is not a figure in the landscape – but a shaper of the landscape' (p. 19).

Boud and Solomon (2001) describe WBL as programmes that meet the needs of learners, contribute to the longer-term development of the organisation and are formally accredited as university courses. The description highlights the tripartite nature of WBL, a key element of which is negotiation. Gray (2001) stresses that WBL is not a subject for study, it is a mechanism for learning. Boud and Symes (2000) believe that the term WBL is used to describe accredited university courses in which a significant proportion of study, if not all, is undertaken in the workplace whose issues and challenges form the principal focus of the study.

Brennan and Little (1996) refer to Seagraves *et al.* (1996) who, when linking learning to work, identified three strands; learning *for* work, learning *at* work and learning *through* work. All three strands arguably relate to WBL, however, traditional teaching relates specifically to learning *for* work. Traditional practice-based units tend to emphasise clinical competence. The competency to be achieved and the level of attainment are prescribed within the programme or unit. The relationship in this case is generally between the student and the practice-based mentor or assessor. Although arguably a tripartite arrangement with university staff reviewing the work might be in place, the level of negotiation is generally restricted to the student and mentor.

In recent years, WBL has gained increasing prominence within the agenda of HE. Two high profile policy reviews of HE provision in the United Kingdom (UK), the Dearing review of Higher Education (National Committee of Inquiry into Higher Education, 1997) and the UK Government's White Paper on HE (Department for Education and Employment (DfEE), 2003), both stress that industry needs to be involved in the education of graduates. The National Committee of Inquiry into Higher Education (1997) advocated that universities provide students with the opportunity to undertake WBL, whilst the White Paper stressed the contribution HE can make to the economic and social well-being of the nation both by working with business and by powering the economy by educating a graduate workforce with appropriate and relevant skills. Although some purists within HE may question the role that university education is expected to play in producing a workforce (Boud and Solomon, 2001), graduate employability is high on the Government's agenda and is likely to become an increasingly important factor for students deciding upon undergraduate courses who will later be required to re-pay loans taken out to finance their studies.

Inefficiency of WBL as a teaching method

Regardless of its potential contribution to graduate employability and national wealth, there are aspects of the delivery of WBL that may undermine its efficiency. The learner often comes to a work situation knowing very little about the workplace, the workplace tutors, or the learning opportunities. The workplace may also seem a daunting environment to the learner; in the more familiar setting of academia, students are generally part of a larger, more autonomous group that all start at the same time and within which learning activities proceed at an even pace set by the tutors. In the work setting, the learner will be joining an experienced and established, largely non-transitory workforce and the teaching will be on a more one-to-one basis. Also, the training experienced by the trainee can be more variable and subjective, depending on the competence and experience of the tutor and the personal and working relationship between tutor and student. On the other hand, it could be argued that all these factors have the potential to enrich the learning experience and resemble the real world.

Academic suspicion of WBL

In our experience, many academics, especially those involved with non-vocational subjects, view WBL as the poor relation to formal academic study at a HE institution. This may be associated with the fact that WBL occurs outside the academic institution and, by extension, beyond the involvement of and the control by academics. One consequence of this geographical separation can be a similar separation between the assessment and qualification framework of WBL and HE-based components; the tacit criticism is how can you ensure appropriate academic rigour for students in the workplace? A good example of this would be the typical Sandwich degree (where the third year of a four-year degree is spent in industry) in which successful completion of a period of WBL contributes to the title of the conferred degree rather than its classification.

In most cases, this mindset is a consequence of the inability of HE institutions to incorporate WBL into existing academic frameworks, rather than any fundamental objection to the intrinsic merits of WBL *per se* (Boud and Solomon, 2001). The diverse nature of placements and their geographical separation from the HE institution makes it difficult to support, track and assess students taking WBL to the same extent as those studying within the institution itself; in other words, it is a problem arising from practicalities more than principles. But the explosive growth in Information and Communication Technology (ICT) offers opportunities to develop cost-effective solutions to many of these practical problems, as is discussed later.

Definitions and key features of work-based learning

Part of the reticence of academics to embrace WBL stems from ignorance of its meaning (Symes and McIntyre, 2000). Although a whole chapter could be devoted to exploring the meaning of terms such as work-based learning, work-related learning, and experience-based learning, only the salient points will be touched upon briefly here. For a more pedagogical review of WBL see Boud and Solomon (2001).

Work-based learning has been defined as 'that learning which is derived from (and whose purposes are located in) utilising opportunities, resources and experiences in the workplace. It will, in general, have outcomes relevant to the nature and purposes of the workplace' (Margham, 1997, p. 2). Seagraves *et al.* (1996, cited in Brennan and Little, 1996, p. 5) produced one of the most succinct and memorable definitions, 'learning for work, learning at work and learning through work.' In many programmes WBL is 'negotiated, defined and understood by all parties, adequate opportunities and support are provided for learning to occur, and the achievement of the intended outcomes are demonstrated and assessed' (Laycock, 2003, p. 1). The Quality Assurance Agency for Higher Education (QAA, 2001) in its Code of Practice for Placement Learning lays out a set of precepts and guidance for learning that is part of an academic programme but which occurs outside the institution with the cooperation of a placement provider. The Code considers an effective placement learning opportunity as 'one in which the aims and intended learning outcomes are clearly defined and understood by all parties and where the responsibilities of the higher education institution, placement provider and student are made explicit' (QAA, 2001, p. 2).

The Code recognises and tries to address the *ad hoc* nature of WBL that can occur, for example, within Sandwich degrees and sets it on a firmer basis with benchmarked expectations to be gained from the experience.

Beyond the nuances of the definition of WBL, there will be a number of key features of WBL that will depend on the context of the actual placement. Foster (1996) has proposed some ideal characteristics of WBL:

- It is performance-related, focusing on tasks arising in the workplace.
- It is problem-based, focusing on tackling complex work-based problems in management or care.
- It is autonomously managed, with learners taking a large measure of responsibility for ensuring that they learn from their work activities.
- It is team-based, tackling problems requiring effective cooperation between people with different roles and expertise.
- It is concerned with performance enhancement, and the updating and upgrading of experience, which is now a normal feature of most people's work experience.
- It is innovative, focusing on new techniques or approaches, which create opportunities for learning and provide experience of managing change.

It may not be possible for all these characteristics to feature within a single work placement but the above provides some valuable benchmarks for deciding on a suitable work environment for learning.

The place of WBL within a formal academic course of study

Universities that address WBL and employability issues use a variety of approaches. The oldest, most established way to prepare graduates for the workplace is through industrial placements. Many UK universities offer four-year Sandwich degrees in which one of the years, most often the third year, is spent gaining work experience related to their degree subject. Students opting for Sandwich degrees are better placed for employment when they graduate compared with students who lack this experience (Bowes and Harvey, 2000), reflecting the conclusion that 'placements are seen by employers and graduate employees as the single most significant missing element of the majority of degree programmes' (Harvey *et al.*, 1997). Part of this benefit to graduate employability might be linked to a beneficial effect of the placement year on academic performance in the final year of study. In fact, experience of our own Bioscience students at the University of the West of England (UWE), Bristol suggests an independent effect of taking the Sandwich year on final year performance that equates to about one quarter of a degree classification, although Daniel and Pugh (1975) suggested that the academic benefits of the placement experience were largely unrealised. From our own experience, laboratory-based placements also benefit students performing laboratory-based research projects; moreover, returning placement students also report improved study techniques and time-management skills (Croker *et al.*, 2004) in addition to any improvement in their working knowledge of the subject matter. Although improvement in academic performance is not one of the intended outcomes of going on placement (Duignan, 2003), such effects are certainly to be welcomed.

For pre-registration students enrolled on a Diploma or Honours degree in nursing, placements constitute 50 per cent of the course and are interspersed throughout the three-year programme. Each placement period length may vary though typically is for 13–14 weeks, and often occurs in areas such as surgery, medicine, community, elderly and high dependency care. Placement learning is assessed by a trained mentor. The student keeps a portfolio of their learning, including the clinical placement documentation based on the professional governing body's competences for practice, formally the UKCC (United Kingdom Central Council) and now the Nursing and Midwifery Council (see English National Board, 2000 and UKCC, 1999). Typically, the mentor works with the student in practice for two days a week and, through continuous assessment using performance indicators, reviews evidence provided by the student of achievement of the competences. Every skill within a competency must be achieved before it can be 'signed off'. The role of the professional practitioner is central to the assessment of practice, and is supported by Practice Education Facilitators employed by the Strategic Health Authority. Work-based learning also features as part of the pre-registration student experience, where university lecturers in exploring practice, facilitate students' exploration of practice issues and learning.

Within post-registration nursing programmes the development and attainment of specialist clinical skills is often a feature. A tripartite system between the student, mentor and university lecturer, supports competency development. This tends to focus on what Seagraves *et al.* (1996)

term, learning *for* work, where the student and mentor prioritise learning around the achievement of key competencies for specialist practice. Work-based learning is also emerging as a component of such programmes of study.

The Department of Health (DH) document, 'Working Together – Learning Together' (2001) places emphasis on lifelong learning and the need to continually update knowledge and existing skills (p. 37) (cf. Chapter 1). They also stress the importance of the relationship between the individual and their immediate world of work and of the primary obligation of staff, that of caring, should be expressed through the organisation in which they work. In order to achieve this, the DH actively promotes the skills escalator model and WBL. Indeed, WBL is adopted as one of the approaches to learning within the newly formed NHS university (NHSu), that seeks to support learning for all NHS staff.

Supporting students across a diversity of work-placement experience

Work-placements, particularly those within Sandwich degrees and interspersed within a formal programme of study, such as nursing, tend to offer highly diverse and individual experiences. Each student comes to the workplace with a unique set of skills, attitudes, previous experiences and motivation, as do the work supervisors or mentors who will instruct the student. In order fully to support such a variety of students in a diversity of work situations, a flexible system is required that can accommodate differences yet not prove an administrative burden. However, HE is organised for the mass transfer of knowledge whereby large groups of students are exposed to a similar learning experience in terms of facilities and staff; consequently, systems tailored for the individual are costly to support. A typical model by which the individual needs of students in the workplace are partially addressed assigns a 'visiting' academic tutor to the student in addition to the work supervisor or mentor. Unlike the extensive contact between the work mentor and the student, the academic generally has only irregular contact with the student and mentor and therefore, by necessity, little influence on the academic progression of the placement. Within nursing the role of the 'visiting' academic has been the subject of change in many institutions. Though academics are expected to engage in practice, this can take different guises, through the facilitation of research and professional development. Academic staff engagement in student support is through WBL, with the focus of ongoing work-place support being provided through mentors and other roles such as Practice Education Facilitators. However, it is proposed that online technologies can be of assistance in redressing this imbalance.

Since the introduction of Project 2000, pre-registration nursing students have worked as learners within healthcare, rather than as employees. Students experience a range of placements in a number of community and institution-based areas, mainly within the NHS, though the use of private and voluntary sector placements is apparent. A programme of learning outcomes guide the experiences, supported by locally based mentors, with assessment of achievement against the learning outcomes being documented between the mentor and student throughout the placement period. Lecturers facilitating WBL during the placement offer an opportunity for students to explore aspects of the practice learning experience that will often explore aspects of the assessment. Lecturer input is therefore facilitative to learning rather than assuming any active role in assessment, which is the domain of the mentor. Yet, the lecturer might also be involved in reviewing and commenting on the assessment process following its completion. In post-qualifying practice-based modules, the tripartite system can be more evident; however, the lecturer input is likely to be subdued.

It is postulated that Internet or Web-based systems might support a more coherent tripartite system, enabling lecturer involvement and supporting easier management of assessment processes and documentation.

Fundamental character of the Web

The terms 'Internet' and 'World Wide Web' are often used synonymously but, strictly speaking, the Internet is the global network of inter-connected computers whereas the World Wide Web, or just 'Web', describes one means by which information is exchanged between those computers (http://www.w3.org/). The Web represents the latest example of the benefits of advances in the Human Computer Interface that have shifted the relationship between the computer and the user to one in which the computer behaves in ways to which humans can relate more easily (such as putting an unwanted file in the Recycle or Waste Bin). Because the

Web has a friendly interface, with links, animations, sounds and downloads, it is ideally suited to online learning.

Links or hyperlinks allow simple navigation through a complex array of information and allow the user some autonomy in deciding what is viewed and in what order. For instance, traditional word-processed documents are stand-alone entities and the information contained within the documents should be viewed sequentially. The same information, but now presented as Web-pages containing links to each other, allows the user to jump from one Web-page to another determining their own agenda for learning.

More recently, however, Web-pages allows the user to do more than just click links; users can interact with the page by completing forms, play online games and view multimedia files such as audio and video. There are other characteristics that make the Web ideal for the support of WBL:

Egalitarian potential

An endearing feature of the Web is the relative ease with which information can be made available to a global audience. A plethora of books, guides and software applications facilitate publication on the Web. With relatively little computer knowledge, almost anyone can have a global Web-presence. The low cost of software, computer server and Web-hosting charges allow more people than ever to exploit the reach and power of the Internet.

Internet standards

Hypertext mark-up language (html) defines the way in which information is encoded and displayed in the Web. A large number of software packages (for example, MacroMedia Dreamweaver and Microsoft FrontPage) can help produce sophisticated Web-pages that incorporate Web-forms, graphics and audio information in addition to text.

Sophistication of users

More people are becoming Internet savvy. However, even though the Internet is becoming increasingly ubiquitous (with approximately 5 per cent of UK homes now having Internet access (Office of Telecommunications, Oftel, 2003)), there remains an important group of users without the key skills that develop from repeated exposure to the Internet whose needs must not be ignored.

Organisation and access to material

Inclusion of more than one hyperlink within a document gives rise to 'hypertext', a term first coined in 1965 by Ted Nelson to indicate non-sequential writing; hypertext provides a potentially large number of different routes by which users can negotiate learning-support material. In addition, adjacent links on a Web-page can point to different sources located in different countries. All that is needed is the Internet 'address' of that particular resource, and search engines such as Google are extremely useful in tracking down such material. By allowing information to become independent of geographical location, the Web can help solve one of the fundamental problems associated with the support of WBL – that of providing effective remote access to information.

Other benefits of Web-based support

Access

IT-based learning, especially online learning, provides temporal as well as geographical independence for the learner. The student is able to study material at any time (so called 24/7 access), as well as at his or her own pace. These features are ideal for a diverse range of students and are discussed in Chapter 6.

Communication

To promote interaction with tutors or other students, communication tools in the form of bulletin boards, chat rooms or email are readily available. Some systems seek to provide 'virtual classrooms' that permit real-time inter-actions to take place even though the participants may be widely distributed.

Automation and interactivity

Web-sites can – and many would argue, should – be more than just passive repositories of information, and this is achieved through the development and application of programs that mediate interaction between the client/user and the server. Originally termed Computer Gateway Interface (CGI) applications, these have rapidly developed into very powerful software environments that permit advanced functionality such as the Multiple-Choice Question-like (MCQ-like) testing seen within many virtual learning environments (VLEs) to deliver formative and summative assessment, mainly though multiple choice tests. These provide reinforcement and feedback to the student on the strengths and weaknesses of their learning, as well as providing authors with feedback on student learning that can be used to inform further development of the learning environment. The 'anonymity' engendered by this type of online assessment is often favoured by students; more so perhaps for students engaged in WBL where group sizes may be small. This type of raw potential can be harnessed to provide support for more than just direct learning activities; for example, page access can be logged and reports based on this data used to identify key areas that can be targeted for additional support. In fact, it is the creation of additional, tailor-made functions on Web-servers that can help solve the other fundamental problem associated with the support of WBL, that of providing effective record-keeping.

Cost-effectiveness

Delivery of online learning can be perceived as costly in time and resources, particularly in relation to the development of learning support material. In contrast, server costs are reducing, especially in relation to their hardware specifications. However, as a corpus of learning support material is developed and, importantly, improved through experience and feedback, the overall value of such a system may ultimately be viewed as greater than the sum of its parts.

When considered from the point of view of WBL, the suitability of Web-based solutions is sharply focused. Provision of theory underpinning practice typically takes place away from the place of work, in an 'academic' environment such as that found in a college or university. For professional disciplines with a high practical component (for example, that of a biological scientist or nurse) the practical aspects are usually provided either within the artificial constraints of a teaching laboratory, or through the provision of separate placement experiences. The latter has the advantage of providing face-to-face experiences closer to that found in the profession itself, but has the disadvantage of being outside the supportive academic framework (including assessment) found within the teaching institution itself. By transcending geographical barriers, online learning offers the potential to bring the academic framework into the work environment. This can give the learner the best of both worlds by providing both the professional context and experience of the workplace in addition to a structured academic framework to support that experience, with the overall effect promising to be synergistic.

The profile project case study: Where we were

The setting for the Profile case study is the Bioscience discipline area of the Faculty of Applied Sciences (FAS) at the University of the West of England (UWE), Bristol, UK. As part of a former polytechnic, our Faculty has a long tradition of offering four-year Sandwich degrees in which the student goes on a one-year placement in the third year. Students work in industry (for example, chemical and pharmaceutical companies), research groups in university departments and government organisations, or in hospital laboratories. The relevance of such an industrial placement on professional practice training for nurses may not be initially apparent, but within the Profile project we have approached the monitoring of students' WBL in a generic fashion.

Credit value of the Sandwich year

Like many HE institutions, UWE operates a modular degree scheme in which degree programmes are defined in terms of a number of individual, stand-alone modules. The scheme allows flexibility of module choice so students can follow a variety of routes to achieve specific degrees in a number of bioscience subject areas; for example, human physiology and pharmacology. The Sandwich year occurs in the third year and is valued at 120 'p' credits; these are notional credits which do not contribute to credit accumulation for the degree but do confer the title 'Sandwich' to the degree.

Assessment of the Sandwich year

The difficulties associated with the management of the diversity of placements (both in terms of student experience and geographical location) have prevented the assessment of WBL in a manner suitable for the award of 'real' credit. As a consequence, the assessment has been rather basic, involving four elements that need to be assessed on a pass/fail basis: a 40-week placement period, a visiting tutor's report based on an on-site visit, an employer's report, and a 5000-word report submitted by the student at the end of the placement. It should be stressed that this simple approach reflected the management problems mentioned above rather than any lack of appreciation of the value of the Sandwich year.

Trend against Sandwich degrees

Student debt
Although students enrol on the Sandwich route by default, the bioscience degrees are non-professional programmes and, therefore, the placement year is optional (however, the degrees are advertised predominantly as Sandwich degrees). With so many benefits it is surprising that the numbers of students opting for the Sandwich route has declined considerably over recent years. A number of factors were thought by us to contribute to this trend including perceived value and peer-group considerations.

Since many of our students pay university fees and obtain loans, the 'extra' year of a placement can increase their debt. Fees for the placement year are half that for other years, and this can be a hardship for students on low-paid placement. Taking a placement can also be seen by students as deferring their entry into the job market and, potentially, the opportunity for higher earnings. Lack of appreciation of the value of the placement year is only reinforced by the fact that it only attracts notional credit; if the institution appears not to value the placement experience, then why should we expect the students? Overall, the year may seem to provide very little return for their half-fees and increased debt burden.

Peer pressure
University students, though treated as rational adults, are still subject to the influence of peer-pressure. Many students who opt out of the placement year cite the fact that 'none of their friends are going on placement', suggesting that they do not wish to take their final year with another peer group.

Accommodation
Another important consideration is accommodation. Many of our students state they need a placement in Bristol because if they left for a year they would have problems finding a place for their final year and would need to share accommodation with a different group of students.

Our response

Raising awareness
In response to the declining interest in the Sandwich year, a number of approaches were taken to make it more attractive to students; these

included raising awareness of the benefits of placements in induction programmes, counselling students seeking exemption from the Sandwich year, raising the quality of the placement experience to prevent students being used as a 'cheap pair of hands', and increasing the mean salary paid to placement students. Another area we addressed was the credit-rating of the placement year as a way of recognising the learning that occurred in the workplace and increasing its perceived value.

The Professional Practice Module
As the majority of our placements offer an excellent learning experience, with many of our students effectively working at postgraduate level, we decided to offer a Professional Practice Module to students during the placement year (worth the equivalent of one taught module in the final year). One potentially attractive consequence to students of this approach was that one less taught module would need to be taken in the final year. To satisfy ourselves and colleagues that there was evidence for level three (L3) learning activities, a system was needed to monitor, support and assess students' learning on work placement. Given the diversity of the placement learning experience and the logistical problems associated with creating a sufficiently rigorous paper-based system, we decided to develop a Web-based tracking system that would permit the detailed 'profiling' of individual placements in terms of their specific learning activities; details of the eventual Web-based Profile system are given. In parallel with designing the tracking system we also needed a mechanism to translate learning activities on placement into a form suited to the award of academic credit.

Criteria for Academic Credit
The scheme we produced was a simple one in concept; we would look at how academic learning was credited within existing academic programmes and apply it to the work situation. Our degrees are composed of modules, and these modules have the following five characteristics: Credit value; Notional learning time (where 1 credit is equivalent to ten hours learning time); Levels of learning (such as those described in the Southern England Consortium for Credit Accumulation and Transfer (SEEC, 2003) guidelines); Learning outcomes; Assessment. Just as a specific degree is made up of discrete smaller units (for example, modules) we took the view that at least part of the placement year could be deconstructed

into smaller units (which we call 'tasks' or 'activities') that, individually, could assume the characteristics of modules first listed and so be used for the purpose of awarding credit.

Funding opportunity

Around this time a funding opportunity in the form of the Fund for the Development of Teaching and Learning (FDTL) was announced, and we put in an application based on our plans to profile placements and develop a Web-based system to manage this approach. The project was appropriately called 'Profile' since we wanted to use the word in its forensic sense. Effectively we wanted to look for evidence of learning. We were successful in our bid and the project started in 2002; the Profile system under development is intended to provide a generic framework for describing a placement (or other WBL experience) in terms of these 'tasks' or 'activities' – in our case they are assessed and contribute towards the Professional Practice Module (PPM).

The profile project case study: Where we are

Profiling placement learning

When a student first starts a placement, an early decision is whether or not to enrol on the PPM. If the student wishes to take the module, he or she then liaises closely with the work supervisor to produce a Learning Agreement which identifies in 'task' form a series of activities to be taken during the year which will contribute to the PPM. The nature of many placements, particularly those in a research environment, is such that the Learning Agreement is regarded as a fairly dynamic document that may change during the year. Once the Learning Agreement is approved by the Placement Tutor, who checks that the proposals meet L3 standard, the student can start working through the tasks, describing them in terms of the following attributes: *Title of task*; *Nature of task* (a brief, one paragraph description written so that a non-expert can understand); *Learning outcomes* (what the student expects to learn from this task); *Generic skills* (all tasks involve the use of generic or transferable skills; students select the most appropriate skills for that task from a list of suggestions); *Specific skills* (an example might be the theory and practice of a particular type of assay); *Assessment* (the student is required to provide evidence of meeting the learning outcomes for the task); *Justification of level* (students are provided with the L3 criteria and justify why they consider the L3 standard has been met); *Reflection on the task* (students are encouraged to reflect on their learning within the task).

Signing-off

Once a task is completed the work supervisor 'signs off' the task to confirm that the student has performed the work to a satisfactory standard. Similarly, the academic tutor 'signs off' the task using the evidence gathered as stated earlier. During the year the student effectively builds up a portfolio of signed-off tasks and the supporting evidence; this portfolio is used to meet the assessment requirements of the PPM.

Communicating through the Web

The introduction of the PPM obviously increases the level of communication, co-ordination and detailed tracking required between the various stakeholders during the placement year, and the diversity of placement types and geographical location only serve to increase the complexity. Central to the introduction of the PPM, therefore, was the development and introduction of a Web-based system to mediate the communication and administrative aspects of the module. The current version of the Web-site (http://www.profile.ac.uk) represents the interim stage in the development of the Profile project and contains two main areas.

Open access area

The first is an 'open access' area containing generic information about the Profile project as well as information for students currently on placement (some of which specifically concerns the operation of the PPM; for example, word templates and examples for the Learning Agreement).

Controlled access area

The second is a 'controlled access' area of the Web-site that requires users to logon in order to use its facilities. Once a user's identity is authenticated in this way, all further interaction with the site is subject to an authorisation check and can also be recorded for audit purposes. In the present system, users designated as administrators can create new user accounts and 'link' these together to represent placements (such as the association of a student, work supervisor and academic tutor). Each placement student can logon to the Profile Web-site using Internet Explorer and upload any computer files they create on their local machine to a secure file storage area on the Web-server set aside for their personal use. The student is expected to upload files contributing to the PPM; for example, the Learning Agreement and the sets of evidence supporting each of the tasks defined in that agreement. The appropriate work supervisor and academic tutor have view-only access to the student's storage area for the purposes of assessment and feedback, and are automatically informed by email whenever the student uploads files contributing to this 'electronic portfolio'. Furthermore, each placement has a simple but effective communication tool in which the student, work supervisor and academic tutor can 'post' comments to a continuously, accumulating 'diary', similar to an online forum. Since each entry is electronically stamped with the authenticated user's credentials, this communication tool forms a means of 'signing off' the various tasks as the placement progresses as well as providing an audit trail of activity during the year and evidence of reflection.

The profile project case study: Where we want to be

Interim stage

The operational system as described above represents our interim, staged solution to the problem of the integration of WBL within the academic framework. It addresses problems associated with the diversity of place-ments by defining aspects of the placement experience in terms of 'tasks' or 'activities' that can contribute to the PPM, and also addresses problems asso-ciated with communication and record-keeping through a controlled-access Web-site providing storage and communication functions.

Shared electronic library

Extending the earlier analogy of the structure of modular degree schemes, then just as specific degrees are defined in terms of a sub-set of individual, autonomous modules taken from a catalogue of available modules, we argue that it would be possible to describe aspects of placement learning in terms of a set of similarly autonomous tasks that could be selected from a pre-existing library. Such an 'electronic library' approach promises to be cost-effective, for in the same way that a new modular degree can be rapidly and efficiently developed and deployed by defining at least part of its specification in terms of existing modules, so it will be possible to 'profile' a proportion of the activities within a new placement in terms of existing activities drawn from the 'library'. This is most apparent for activities covering generic skills (for example, giving an oral presentation), but there is sufficient overlap in the types of specific activities that take place within our biosciences placements to suggest that even specific activities (for example, the use of particular laboratory techniques such as polymerase chain reaction, PCR) can be 'recycled' in this way.

Structured storage

The adoption of a consistent, structured approach to defining placements in terms of activities, and those activities in terms of learning outcomes, assessment, and so on. makes a database-driven, Web-based solution the ideal vehicle for the creation, storage, access and deployment of these activities within individual placements. At present, activities are created, stored and evidenced within the *ad hoc* structure of the individual placement's file storage area. In the next version of the Profile Web-site, Web-forms will be used to channel the creation, storage and use of activities to and from the back-end database 'library'. It will also be possible, of course, to extend this primarily administrative framework for the monitoring and recording of WBL to include learning support material, so enhancing the quality of the learning experience in addition to simply recording it.

Critical mass

There will be an initial period of time when the majority of activities within a given placement will need to be developed in full, but eventually a 'critical mass' of activities will exist in the library so that the amount of effort required to profile a new placement will be reduced dramatically.

Generic solution

The Profile system is being designed to provide as generic a solution as possible: for example, the current system associates a placement with three users – a student, a work supervisor and an academic tutor, whereas the next version will allow completely flexible associations of users to be made. We are also seeking to keep the design generic so that the system can provide a service to the UK HE sector in general. By adopting free, anonymous access to a common activities library as a feature of the new system, we hope to shorten the time for the library to reach the 'critical mass' that will make it a cost-effective and flexible tool to promote closer integration of theory and practice.

Roll out

At present we are in the development and evaluation phase, using the system as a proof-of-concept with science placement students at UWE. The initial indications are highly positive and we have tracked learning of about 70 placement students throughout the world. From the academic year 2005–06 the system will be rolled out to other HE institutions and will be available for all disciplines where WBL is an integral feature.

Skinner said rather sardonically that 'education is what survives when what has been learned has been forgotten' (1964), alluding to the serial nature of academic education and the subsequent contextualisation of knowledge through experience and the workplace. However, the integration of WBL with traditional academic structures provides an opportunity for synergism between these two facets of learning, and the Profile project can provide one mechanism by which this can be managed.

The profile project: Ways forward for nursing education

As pre-registration nurses spend 50 per cent of their pre-qualifying programme in placement areas, there is an obvious need to ensure learning and assessment is supported in disparate locations. Additionally, post-registration learners require ongoing support when undertaking practice modules, that require the completion of assessments, often in geographically spread locations. It is suggested that aspects of the Profile Project might help address the complexity of supporting practice located learners within nursing, through applying some components of the project to nurse education. The ways forward might include

- information provision through the use of a database detailing placement areas
- profiling of individual placements, including an outline of the learning opportunities and how these link to support achievement of the learning outcomes of different practice modules

- providing key practice documentation online, such as module handbooks and assessment documents
- development of e-portfolios for completion throughout the period of the programme or course
- providing access to online learning materials and learning resources
- providing support for students on placement through discussion boards that might be linked to personal or academic tutor groups, cohort groups or could provide a forum for interprofessional discussion amongst students

Obviously the scope is vast, though successful implementation will require access to technology and e-learning, overcoming the barriers prevailing within the NHS and student population at present, as discussed in Chapter 6. It is anticipated however, that online educational provision is likely to increase and nurse education must ensure that it capitalises on its pedagogic potential within the work-based environment.

References

Boud, D. and Solomon, N. (2001) Work-Based Learning. A New Higher Education? Buckingham: SRHE and Open University Press.

Boud, D. and Symes, C. (2000) Learning for Real: Work-Based Education in Universities. pp. 14–29. In Symes, C. and McIntyre (eds), *Working Knowledge. The New Vocationalism and Higher Education*, Buckingham: Society for Research into Higher Education and Open University Press.

Bowes, L. and Harvey, L. (2000) *The Impact of Sandwich Education on the Activities of Graduates Six Months Post-Graduation*. London: The National Centre for Work Experience and CRQ.

Brennan, J. and Little, B. (1996) *A Review of Work-based Learning in Higher Education*. London: Quality Support Centre/Department for Education and Employment.

Bronowski, J. (1973) *The Ascent of Man*. London: British Broadcasting Corporation.

Croker, K., Gomez, S. and Lush, D. (2004) The Effect of Work Placements on the Perceived Skills-Set of Science Students. Proceedings of the Association of Sandwich, Education and Training (ASET) 2004 Conference: *Integrating Work and Learning: Partnerships for Placement*, 7–9 September 2004, Cambridge.

Daniel, W. W. and Pugh, H. (1975) Sandwich Courses in Higher Education. PEP Report on CNAA Degrees in Business Education. Volume XLI Broadsheet No. 557, September.

Department for Education and Employment (DfEE) (2003) *The Future of Higher Education*. Norwich: HMSO.

Department of Health (2001) *Working Together – Learning Together: A Framework for Lifelong Learning for the NHS*. London: DH.

Duignan J (2003) Placement and Adding Value to the Academic Performance of Undergraduates: Reconfiguring the Architecture – An Empirical Investigation. Presentation at the *Journal of Vocational Education and Training* Fifth International Conference, 16–18 July 2003, University of Greenwich. http://www.triangle.co.uk/jvet/Resources/Duignan.pdf (accessed 11.05.2004).

English National Board for Nursing and Midwifery (ENB) (2000) Education in Focus: Strengthening Pre-Registration Nursing and Midwifery Education. London: ENB.

Foster, E. (1996) *Comparable but Different: Work-based Learning for a Learning Society*. Leeds: University of Leeds.

Gray, D. (2001) *A Briefing on Work-Based Learning*. Assessment Series No. 11. York, UK: Learning and Teaching Support Network Generic Centre.

Gray, D. and Symes, C. (2000) Learning for Real: Work-based education in universities. pp. 14–29. In Symes, C. and McIntyre, J. (eds), *Working Knowledge. The New Vocationalism and Higher Education*. Buckingham: Society for Research into Higher Education and Open University Press.

Harvey, L., Moon, S., Geall, V. with Bower, R. (1997) *Graduates' Work: Organisational Change and Students' Attributes*. http://www.uce.ac.uk/crq/publications/gw/gwch8f.html (accessed 18.06.04).

Laycock, M. (2003) Notes for Guidance on Work-Related Learning. SEEC (Southern England Consortium for Credit Accumulation and Transfer) Paper, London: Cravitz.

Margham, J. P. (1997) *A Green Paper on Work-based Learning*. Liverpool: John Moores University.

National Committee of Inquiry into Higher Education (1997) *Higher Education in the Learning Society* (The Dearing Report). Norwich: HMSO.

Office of Telecommunications (Oftel) (2003) Oftel's Internet and Broadband Brief – July 2003 http://www.oftel.gov.uk (accessed 18.06.2004).

Quality Assurance Association (2001) *Code of Practice for Placement Learning*. http://www.qaa.ac.uk/public/cop/copplacementfinal/PlacementLearning.pdf (accessed 12.05.2004).

Seagraves, L., Osbourne, M., Neal, P., Dockerell, R., Hartshorn, C. and Boyd, A. (1996) *Learning in Smaller Companies (LISC) Final Report*. Stirling: University of Stirling: Educational Policy and Development.

Skinner, B. F. (1964) New Methods and New Aims in Teaching. *New Scientist*. 122, 483–84.

Southern England consortium for Credit Accumulation and Transfer, SEEC (2003) Credit Level Descriptors for Future and Higher Education. http://www.seec/20 FE-HECLDS-mar 03 des-1.doc

Symes, C. and McIntyre, J. (2000) Working Knowledge: An Introduction to the New Business of Learning. In Symes, C. and McIntyre, J. (eds) *Working Knowledge: The New Vocationalism and Higher Education*. Buckingham: SHRE/Open University Press.

United Kingdom Central Council for Nursing, Midwifery and Health Visiting (1999) Fitness for Practice. The UKCC Commissioning for Education (Peach Report). London: UKCC.

6

Facilitating Access to Online Learning

Mollie Gilchrist and Rod Ward

Introduction

Easy access to e-learning material is vital to engaging students in modern healthcare education because of its increasing use and flexibility, and to reduce the possible 'digital divide' and improve equity. Some of the fundamental access issues to be considered include; technology, gender, age and disability awareness, and associated concerns of cost, availability, confidence and competence. This chapter will provide an overview of some of the technological issues, which may produce barriers to access in e-learning. These will be related to the current nursing community and levels of Information Technology (IT) skills, amongst qualified staff and students entering via the wide entry gate for nursing education. Specific consideration is given to the use of e-learning for relevant and potentially disadvantaged sections of society including those with disabilities, learners from all age groups, and both genders including examples of legislation and best practice. The difficult areas of ownership, intellectual property rights (IPR) and copyright are also considered with guidance for current and future management.

Access to technology and e-learning

To facilitate effective e-learning, students must have access to the appropriate Information and Communications Technology (ICT) hardware and software and, where appropriate, network connections. Although access to IT and the Internet is increasing rapidly in the

United Kingdom (UK) there are still difficulties for many, which may inhibit or reduce the use of e-learning opportunities in the home, in healthcare settings and in educational institutions.

All universities provide networked IT access for their staff and students. Some are not open 24 hours a day and 7 days a week, due to security and supervision worries. For nursing students who spend 50 per cent of their course in clinical environments, both in the National Health Service (NHS) and other settings, access to ICT and network connections can be limited, in terms of both time and place. Alternative sites of access may include public libraries or cyber cafés, although opening hours may still cause access difficulties.

Access to the Internet from home is possible for many students who have their own computers. However, for others the cost of equipment or line rental can be prohibitive. Even for those who do have computers at home, the limitations of using a modem rather than broadband connections cause problems when large files are a part of the e-learning resource, for example, video or sound files. In some cases attempts have been made to overcome these issues by providing video, audio and other large files on Compact Disc (CD), and using online tools for the interactive discussion and support components of the course. Further difficulties may be caused for staff and students using different hardware, for example, Personal Computers (PCs) and Macintosh computers, or those with different software such as word-processing with Microsoft® Word or Works, which may mean that they are unable to open files created with different software.

Students placed in clinical environments have widely varying levels of access to IT and network facilities. In some nursing homes and similar placements there is still no IT access, let alone network capabilities. Even within the NHS wide variation exists between acute hospital settings, community areas, and mental health and learning disability areas, with the equipment that is available being restricted to particular groups of staff, often excluding students.

During June 2001 and May 2003 the Community Practitioners' and Health Visitors' Association (CPHVA, 2003) carried out a campaign to increase IT access. This included two surveys showing 80 per cent of staff had access to computers at work. However, they were resorting to using their own equipment because the vast majority have to share computers at work, often with more than four other colleagues and sometimes up to 20.

A study by Latchford (2003) surveyed UK midwives and found that, over 10 per cent of midwives had no access to a computer at all. The majority (around 60 per cent) had shared access to a computer, with the vast majority sharing with at least three people. There is evidence that mature, more experienced staff (particularly those in management positions) are likely to have better access, but less favourable attitudes to their use (Latchford, 2003).

Current IT skills varied between different areas, with most midwives more confident in using common software such as e-mail and word processing, but much less skilled in other areas, such as using computerised patient records and critical appraisal of information on best practice. The quality of training undertaken seemed to vary greatly, and many commented on the difficulty of becoming confident in using IT when they had poor access, leading to some disillusionment. (Latchford, 2003, p. 4)

In addition to shortages of equipment there have been other access issues. In some NHS trusts there are restrictions that reduce access to materials outside the NHS network, primarily because of worries about staff accessing pornography and using the Internet for non-work activities. This may mean that students and staff have to leave their work area and visit a library to gain access. An additional hurdle has been imposed by problems with the reliability of IT equipment and network systems in some parts of the NHS, which have included network crashes and bandwidth limitations.

The NHS has recognized and identified the need for improvements to enable access to e-learning to improve access for e-learning.

The national vision for e-learning in the NHS is to enable staff to access learning opportunities at times and places that best fit in with their lifestyle. This means 24-hour access to knowledge and learning resources, 365 days per year, from places that are most convenient for individuals and groups, with the technical support structure to ensure this happens. (Department of Health (DH), 2001 para. 72, p. 70)

As a result of the access limitations, e-learning materials need to be available in generic formats, rather than utilising proprietary software. In addition e-learning activities should not require long periods of continuous access.

IT Skills

E-learning requires students to have some basic IT skills, such as knowing their way around the desktop, mouse-use and file management. However, as long as learners can log onto the Internet, with a modicum of common sense, they can soon access vast sources of information. A related skill is that of evaluating the information as reliable evidence. At the start of a course in higher education (HE), some students may not have the ability to critique information from a variety of sources including journals, media and the Internet. They tend to accept what they find at face value and, according to Washer (2001), they may never develop good evaluative skills. A useful tool to guide students in the acquisition of these vital skills is the 'Internet for Nursing, Midwifery and Health Visiting Tutorial' (Ward, 2002).

Currently, all NHS employees have the opportunity to gain the European Computer Driving Licence (ECDL) qualification offered by the British Computer Society (BCS), managed by the NHS Information Authority (www.ecdl.nhs.uk). A recent survey has shown that this course improves computer literacy and saves time for NHS staff (National Health Service Information Authority (NHSIA), 2004). It is therefore imperative that all pre-registration healthcare students are encouraged to gain this, or at least an equivalent or introductory qualification. Indeed students should be encouraged to acquire relevant IT skills, usefully the ECDL, before embarking on a higher education course of study. The BCS has recently introduced the 'Equalskills' introductory scheme to help complete novices (www.ecdl.co.uk). This could perhaps be a useful starting point for new students. Other relevant qualifications, which may be included in General Certificate of Secondary Education (GCSE) IT, include the Oxford, Cambridge and Royal Society of Arts (RSA) (OCR, 2004) Computer Literacy And Information Technology (CLAIT), National Open College Network (NOCN, 2004) and the City and Guilds of London Institute certificates (City and Guilds, 2004). Students may also have the opportunity to gain IT Key Skills at levels 2 and 3, which can provide a good foundation (Qualification Curriculum Authority (QCA), 2004).

In a recent audit (academic year 2003/04) Gilchrist (2004) reported that, from a total of 444 responding nursing students, 18 had the ECDL qualification, that 57 had a RSA CLAIT certificate, with a further 3 having the follow-on qualification, Information Business Technology 2 (IBT2).

Eighty-one students had also achieved the GCSE IT and 58 had other relevant awards, including A1 and A2 levels in IT or Computer Studies and Key Skills at levels 2 and 3. Overall, 46 per cent of the students had some recognised IT qualification, or other qualifications, which are likely to include an IT component, such as business administration.

New students of nursing have a diverse range of IT skills, and hence 'core IT competence should be identified and all courses should have the clear objective of raising students' confidence in using computers' (Sinclair and Gardner, 1999, p. 1441). In our experience, if students receive adequate support when they first need it, the majority of users become more proficient in using computers, once the initial mechanisms become familiar. As e-learning becomes more prevalent in HE, and with more opportunities included in the nursing curriculum to demonstrate appropriate usage, it is to be hoped that students will acquire and maintain valuable IT skills (Adams, 2004).

Many nurses currently in practice in the UK have limited IT skills and see the provision of training in this areas as important. A Royal College of Nursing (RCN) survey (RCN, 2004) showed

> The vast majority (93 per cent) think that training is very important to the success of NHS IT developments. When asked how much training they had received in working time in the last six months, over 60 per cent had had none.

In addition to the IT skills required by students, those of tutors and lecturers may need to be examined as more academic staff begin to take on roles in the development of e-learning and student support. There is a range of courses both face to face and online, which can help to achieve improvements in IT skills and e-learning facilitation. This has been highlighted as an issue for many staff who will act as mentors to others (National Health Service university (NHSu), 2004).

Disabilities and IT use

One of the potential advantages of e-learning approaches is that those with disabilities such as physical, visual or auditory impairments or dyslexia can access and participate on an equal basis with the able-bodied. However, for this to be possible their needs must be taken into account at all stages in the design and implementation of e-learning activities.

In the UK all educational provision now needs to comply with the 1995 Disability Discrimination Act (DDA) (Her Majesties Stationery Office (HMSO), 1995) and the 2001 Special Educational Needs and Disability Act (SENDA) (HMSO, 2001). To show compliance with these acts educational technologists and designers must ensure that material can be accessed by those using a variety of software, in particular web browsers, and can be used by those employing screen magnifiers and text to speech software. The use of screens containing multiple frames should be avoided and a logical and consistent structure adopted (Techdis, 2004). This is ideally with reliance on cascading style sheets rather than hypertext mark-up language (html) coding for layout, separating the content from the layout features. Attention also needs to be given to the use of colour and contrast within pages. Any graphics used must include explanatory 'Association of Learning Technologists (ALT)' tags, and any audio or video clips used should include transcripts for those who may not be able to access them.

A variety of tools and validators are available to help ensure that design follows best practice guidelines, including Bobby (Watchfire Corporation, 2002) and the World Wide Web Consortium (W3C) validation tools (W3C, 1994) (cf. Chapter 7). However, these are no substitute for actually testing your own materials by accessing them using a variety of software, including screen magnifiers and text-to-speech tools. Further tools and advice can be obtained from Techdis, a service funded by Higher Education Funding Council for England (HEFCE) to help higher and further education institutions ensure that their electronic material is accessible to all and compliant with statutory and best practice guidelines.

Many institutions are using Virtual Learning Environments (VLEs) or Managed Learning Environment (MLEs) from commercial suppliers such as WebCT and Blackboard. Others are developing their own systems with similar functionality. These can be used to deliver content to students at a time and place that is convenient to them and provide mechanisms for interactive learning activities. The use of these systems should enable those developing and delivering the courses to focus on the content and student learning rather than technical aspects. However, staff may need to undertake a steep learning curve themselves to become familiar with the systems needed to put their course together online and manage them once students are enrolled. This may include courses, referring to those with previous experience and undertaking e-learning activities themselves.

A great deal of current work is moving towards the use of institutional or subject based portals, which have been defined as

> a network service that brings together content from diverse distributed resources using technologies such as cross searching, harvesting, and alerting, and collates this into an amalgamated form for presentation to the user. For users, a portal is a possibly personalised, single point of access where searching can be carried out across one or more than one resource and the amalgamated results viewed. (Joint Information Systems Committee (JISC) Portals (2004) FAQ)

Gender and age related to IT use

There is some suggestion that single sex computer education helps females (Sax, 2002). The majority of nursing students are women (typically, the ratio of female to male students is approximately 9:1 for Adult and Child nursing, and 2:1 for Mental Health and Learning Disabilities (Pollard *et al.*, 2004), potentially providing an environment sympathetic to female learning. However, provided careful consideration is given to the construction and use of online materials and activities, there is reason to believe that all students will participate in a valuable learning experience (Duffy *et al.*, 2002).

A further complication arises, as a third to half of nursing students are mature (over 21) (Pollard *et al.*, 2004). Many have completed their schooling before ICT was so readily taught in schools, and hence often do not have IT skills. It should be noted, however, that some of these mature students have worked in situations allowing them to have acquired enviable key-board skills, which soon increases their confidence, and ultimately general IT skills.

There is a traditional view that women are disadvantaged when it comes to using, and therefore learning from, a computer (Ordidge, 1997). This may result from a lack of opportunity to access personal computers and a lack of skills or confidence to gain access to information held on computers (Gunn *et al.*, 2002). Stereotypically, it is considered that boys are encouraged to use computers more than girls in schools (Hesse-Biber and Gilbert, 1994). There is also an assumption that boys are taught computer programming, and that they more naturally work with machinery than girls (Wajcman, 1991). Males often form the larger proportion of students on computer-related courses, and computers have been defined as 'male machines' (Eden and Hulbert, 1995). In school classrooms with limited IT resources, it has been the boys who dominate computer use. Many boys play computer games, which give some familiarity and confidence in computer use. Girls are less interested in such games. This is perhaps because they do not appear meaningful enough and do not relate to real problems (American Association of University Women Education Foundation, 2000). In general females seem to prefer communicative and collaborative activities (Gunn *et al.*, 2002; Hughes, 2002). Luchetta (2000) reports that male students describe a 'magnetic attraction between themselves and computers', whereas females link their computer interest to a larger societal framework, solving real world problems.

Gunn *et al.* (2002) may be suggesting that technology access and literacy are disappearing problems, in terms of gender, but even when girls do perform well while using IT, they express low levels of confidence in their ability (Eden and Hulbert, 1995). Indeed, when girls use computers in their education, they often succeed very well, especially when the boundaries are clearly set (Richardson and French, 2000). However, Hughes (2002) suggests that the gender gap is closing as a construct of social class and academic background, rather than as a result of access and achievement. Certainly, computers are more widespread in homes with ready access to the Internet. United Kingdom government figures indicate 49 per cent of households (12.1 million) had access to the Internet in the fourth quarter of 2003 (Office for National Statistics, 2004), compared with nine per cent (2.2 million) in the same quarter of 1998. Within HE there is evidence of increased home computer access amongst students of the healthcare professions. A recent (academic year 2003/04) audit of 444 nursing students indicated that 67 per cent of the students used a computer at home with Internet access (Gilchrist, 2004). There is perhaps an expectation that a computer would be a useful resource for learning in HE. This is in marked contrast to a similar audit carried out eight years ago, in which approximately a quarter (21 from 81) of students used a computer at home, and this was used mainly for word processing and playing games (Gilchrist, 1995 unpublished).

It may be that in HE, women are more comfortable with using computers, as they can realise the benefits to their learning and presentation of their assignments. Turkle and Papert (1990, cited in Barrett and Lally, 1999) suggest that many women prefer to learn through orderly routine in which they understand the reason for each step, whereas many men (and boys) have been encouraged to learn through experimentation and trial and error. This aspect certainly needs addressing when designing online materials.

The gender divide does not seem to be so evident in nursing students, with many of either gender not being proficient in IT skills and being uncomfortable in having to use computers. Maybe this also has something to do with the fact that both male and female nursing students have self-selected to come into a caring, hands-on, socially, not technically orientated environment, which does not match with expectations of using computers (Wishart and Ward, 2002). However, personal experience suggests that recent cohorts of students are much more 'tuned-into' the technological age and now expect to have to use computers in their work, even though often they would rather not!

One application of computers in education is the 'drill and practice' situation. An example of this is in the support of numeracy skills, where students can interact with support material, gain immediate feedback and repeat the content as often as wanted (Gilchrist, 2002). All students appear happy to use this type of learning material, but students of both genders have expressed mixed feelings, when using computer-mediated communication (CMC). In our experience of one level three (L3) module delivered online, many students reported that they particularly enjoyed the flexibility of access, and the reflective learners valued the thinking time available before replying. However, they also expressed feelings of isolation when 'talking to a computer', and missed the body language, tone of voice and visual cues present in face-to-face communication. There was a feeling that the communication was not as rich as it could have been in a classroom situation. Quite a lot of concern was articulated at first over technical issues, due in part to lack of skills and confidence, but once embarked on the course, there appeared to be an increase in confidence with the medium. However, there were those that never became comfortable with it. The majority, both male and female, found it a useful, albeit stressful, learning curve, with one student recently commenting

I do not like computer work at all, although this has improved for me as time goes by [mature student – that has had no computer experience at all]. E-learning is quite strange, although you can always refer back, a lot easier to control. This method of learning is very different, I know it has helped my computer skills.

Indeed, overall, students seemed to prefer face-to-face sessions rather than CMC opportunities, despite the flexibility, but that may be due to the fact that this was a new experience for them. It will be interesting to see if these feelings change at all, when the same online module is taken by later cohorts of students, who will be more familiar with, and hence less apprehensive of, this mode of delivery.

Current literature suggests that there is a difference in the way that males and females interact in CMC (Gunn *et al.*, 2002). Data from a study on a small group of post-graduate (MEd) distance learners at a university in the UK suggested that, although the learning content of online seminar contributions was the same for men and women, their social and interactive behaviour was different. It was also noted that five students (four women and one man) were unable to 'get online', despite support, which raises issues of equality in terms of access to the learning environment. Women's contributions were more task-orientated, and they posted shorter messages (Barrett and Lally, 1999). It was also noted that men contributed twice as much social exchange as the women, and that the women acknowledged contributions of others more, supporting previous findings by Herring (1993). Yates (1997) suggests that it may be the absence of non-verbal cues in online communication, which disadvantages women.

In a study of 156 undergraduates (35 male and 121 female), following education programs in a Korean University, Lee (2002, p. 108) confirmed differences in motivational and behavioural learning strategies, in particular finding 'highly significant gender differences in the category of textual encoding strategies', encompassing presenting written information either in daily life or online. Lee (2002, p. 109) suggests alternative 'dialogue-like interaction modes such as real-time chatting, audio-learning resources, and verbal interactions should be used more extensively' to provide informal and social interaction opportunities. McSporran and Young (2001, p. 3) found that their first-year online learning course in Internet and Web Design favoured women and older students. These students seemed 'more motivated, better at communicating online and at scheduling their learning'. Such studies have implications for learning technology design.

Working online requires high 'learner regulation' (Bonk and Dennen, 1999, cited in Lee, 2002), including strategies such as sincere effort, diligence and persistence, which were evident in the fact that the females submitted significantly more assignments consistent with the instructor's directions and on time. This is perhaps an indication of the better self-regulated learning skills of female students. In our experience female and some male nursing students are often balancing home, family and frequently work commitments, as well as studying. Richardson and French (2000) also found that women on a computer degree course fitted their studying around their family, working late into the evening, whereas the males' main study time was between four and eight in the evening. The flexibility of online access, although maybe having to share access with other family members, proved popular, but both genders also liked the use of paper-based materials.

Lack of confidence and competence can be two of the biggest barriers to online access. Gilchrist (2004) found the mean confidence, on a scale of 1 (poor) to 6 (excellent), of nursing students at the beginning of their HE course in using computers was reported as 3.7, standard deviation (SD) = 1.2, for the female students, and statistically significantly higher for males at 4.3 (SD = 1.4) ($t = 3.0$, $p = 0.002$). Figure 6.1 shows the confidence scores for the 435 students who recorded their gender. Despite the significant difference, there is a clear indication that most students felt reasonably confident about using computers at the start of their course. There was no statistically significant difference in confidence

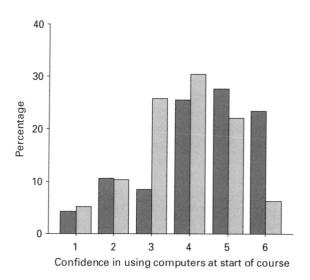

Figure 6.1 Confidence in using computers on a scale of 1 (poor) to 6 (excellent) of nursing students by gender (Gilchrist, 2004)

scores between the traditional age students (20 years or less), mean = 3.9 (SD = 1.1) and the mature (aged 21 years and over), mean = 3.7 (SD = 1.4). However, this confidence does not always translate into competence with IT uses, although students reported higher knowledge about word processing and ICT, than other applications. In terms of web searching, an earlier study by Bond (2002) on 334 new student nurses found no differences in abilities according to the age of students, but rather that the frequency of use determined their competence.

Individual and cultural differences

Several studies have been undertaken in the last few years to try to examine the experiences of students in e-learning courses and other technological innovations in nurse education (Hills, 2003). They try to identify charac-teristics, and personality types, which make the students more willing and motivated to participate in these learning opportunities, and have obvious implications for future planning and practice.

In Australia, Kenny (2002) used a qualitative focus group design with 21 students and identified four major themes that influenced student participation in online courses; computer confidence, flexibility, active learning and practicalities of teaching. This largely supported the findings in the UK of a quantitative study (Wishart and Ward, 2002) that compared individual differences between nursing and teacher training students in their attitude towards the use of information technology. A sense of being in control of the computer was found to be a significant factor in IT use.

Some students find the e-learning environment enabling, not just in terms of being able to study when and where they want and at their own pace, but also being able to contribute and question when they may have been unlikely to do this in the classroom environment. Other students find the converse and for them the challenges in learning to overcome technological hurdles and phobias inhibit their ability to learn via this medium. For the later group of students, initial training in using the IT and ongoing support are needed to enable them to contribute and learn from the experience.

Financial, copyright and IPR issues

The development of e-learning materials has significant costs in design and development, often higher than those for a face-to-face course.

Most of the costs are 'front loaded' so that major expenditure is needed before course can commence, although the costs in ongoing delivery may be lower. However, e-learning should definitely not be seen as a 'cheap option'. As a result, careful planning is needed to look at the initial and ongoing costs, likely student numbers taking the course, and 'shelf life' of the materials, before decisions are taken to develop an e-learning course. In addition to pure financial costs and technical costs there are other issues about ownership, plagiarism, copyright and intellectual property rights (IPR), which although they have always existed with traditional courses are seen as more problematic in e-learning courses. The development of e-learning courses and materials are often a team effort involving several staff from different departments and sometimes from different organisations, this means that the ownership of the materials, can be complex and lead to issues around the copyright and IPR.

There have been examples where people have been using handouts and images developed by others, sometimes with identifiable patient information, in their face-to-face teaching for years. It is only when these are being developed into e-learning materials that this abuse of copyright, IPR or patient confidentiality comes to light. The wider distribution and availability of electronic materials also means that it is more likely that the material will be spotted by the person who owns the IPR or the patient involved (Technical Advisory Service Images (TASI), 2004).

Models to manage IPR have been proposed that are similar to those in traditional academic book publishing. Here the material developed by the author is their own property, even if it is based on research or teaching they have undertaken within an educational setting. Materials are not seen as the property of the employer and here the author can sign over the copyright to the books publisher. Alternatively it can be argued that, as the e-learning course has been developed as part of an author's work, the institution for which they work holds the ownership, copyright and IPR. This question has led to many difficulties in the past and various universities are currently struggling to develop policies in this area, which are acceptable to all concerned. It is preferable that all parties agree on IPR issues prior to the development of the e-learning resources.

Plagiarism is another issue, which has been around for years, but has been made more obvious and explicit by the electronic delivery and technical ease of copying materials. Many students have submitted material copied from the Internet without appropriately citing their sources. Due to the massive volume of information available it may be less likely that this will be picked up than the passage copied from a well-known text book. As well as technology providing the means for easier copying, technological systems are being developed to help to overcome it, an example is the Joint Information Systems Committee (JISC) funded plagiarism advisory service (JISCPAS, 2003), which can check an electronic submission against thousands of web sites to identify possible plagiarism.

Some of the issues identified above have proved to be hurdles to institutional validation and accreditation of e-learning courses. In some institutions, validation or approval committees for modules or courses have been difficult to convince of the potential benefits of e-learning, requiring even stronger guarantees of academic rigour and assessment than with traditional courses.

One approach to the costly development of e-learning materials has been a move towards the creation of re-usable learning objects (RLOs), which could be an animation, image, video or sound file, which can then be reused in a variety of contexts or learning experiences. If this approach is to be adopted it is important that the resources are created and catalogued in a way which enables others to find the appropriate objects and incorporate them into their learning materials.

If RLOs are to be shared outside of the institution that creates them, then a method of payment may be required. Development could be by a consortium of organisations each contributing a set number of RLOs and then being able to use any, which have been created by other members of the consortium. Another method is micro charging, similar to the approach taken by some publishers to charge for an individual article rather than an annual subscription to a journal, which enables a small payment each time an RLO is used by another institution.

Recommendations

- Encourage prospective students to acquire IT skills prior to commencing a course, and where necessary provide IT skills development opportunities at the beginning of any course. This may include negotiation with education purchasers to deliver and assess the European Computer Driving License (ECDL).
- Build into the curriculum many relevant opportunities to practice IT skills, not just word processing of assignments and using bibliographic

databases, but also the use of a variety of other applications including statistical software and presentation packages to increase student's confidence and competence.

- Encourage placement opportunities for computer access, particularly in relation to the NHS National Programme for IT. This could include the use of electronic portfolios, as described in Chapter 5 and the development of e-communities in Chapter 3.
- Ensure adequate and accessible support and IT training for tutors including both online and face-to-face components.
- Ensure adequate and accessible support and IT training for students, which could include clear, unambiguous guidelines, a set of frequently asked questions (FAQs), and also opportunities to engage with online learning material, while technical support is available. Students will often be working in isolation, and they need to be confident that they will have the skills to be able to log into the system.
- Develop a culture of sharing e-learning experiences and resources to support lecturers in creating and using online learning materials, particularly paying attention to differences in male and female modes of use.
- Be aware of the necessity to create e-learning resources to accommodate the diversity of users' learning styles, cultures and disabilities and compliance with Special Education Needs and Disability Act (SENDA) and other relevant legislation and guidelines for best practice.
- Consider the hardware and software likely to be available to users when creating e-learning materials, but with a vision to future technological developments.
- Ensure online learning material is reusable in order to recoup costs.
- Ensure creative assessment opportunities are employed in an attempt to avoid plagiarism issues.

Conclusion

E-learning brings a variety of challenges, as well as opportunities to both educators and students. The varied skill levels and backgrounds of the students need to be taken into account throughout the planning and delivery stages, taking into account access and design considerations. The extra work involved in the utilisation of online approaches can provide great benefits including inclusivity and wider access to learning. However, these need to be balanced with financial and legal constraints. The widespread adoption of lifelong flexible learning strategies at the national level need to be adapted to the particular circumstances faced by students of nursing and the healthcare professions.

E-learning will not always be the best option and face-to-face delivery or a mix of various blended approaches need to be considered in the light of learning objectives and student needs.

References

Adams, A. M. (2004) Pedagogical Underpinnings of Computer-Based Learning. *Journal of Advanced Nursing.* 46(1), 5–12.

American Association of University Women (AAUW) Education Foundation Commission on Technology, Gender, and Teacher Education (2000) *Tech-Savvy Girls: Educating Girls in the Computer Age.* Washington: AAUW Education Foundation. Report available at http://www.aauw.org/search/index_action.cfml. (accessed 14.6.2004).

Association of Learning Technologies. http://www.alt.ac.uk. (accessed 11.01.2006)

Barrett, E. and Lally, V. (1999) Gender Differences in an On-line Learning Environment. *Journal of Computer Assisted Learning.* 15, 48–60.

Bond, C. (2002) Surfing or Drowning? Students' Internet Skills. Paper presented at *Information Technology in Regional Areas, Making IT happen.* Rockhampton, QLD, Australia. Available at http://www.leeds.ac.uk/educol/documents/00002387.doc. (accessed 11.4.2004).

Bonk, C. J. and Dennen, V. (1999) Learner Issues with WWW-Based Systems. *International Journal of Educational Telecommunications.* 5(4), 410–17, cited in Lee I-S (2002) Gender Differences in Self-regulated On-line Learning Strategies within Korea's University Context. *Educational Technology Research and Development International Review.* 50(1), 101–11.

British Computer Society (1996) www.ecdl.co.uk. (accessed 6.5.2004), last updated May 2004.

City and Guilds (2004) http://www.city-and-guilds.co.uk/ (accessed 21.5.2004).

Community Practitioners and Health Visitors Association (CPHVA)(2003) Make IT Happen Campaign. Available at http://www.amicus-cphva.org/campaigns/campaignshome.html#make. (accessed 18.2.2004).

Department of Health (DH) (2001) Working Together – Learning Together, A Framework for Lifelong Learning for the NHS. *Department of Health Publications Reference 25725.*

Duffy, T., Gilbert, I., Kennedy, D. and Kwong, P. W. (2002) Comparing Distance Education and Conventional Education: Observations from a comparative study of post registration nurses. *Association for Learning Technology Journal.* 10(1), 70–82.

Eden, C. and Hulbert, W. (1995) Gender and IT in the Primary Classroom: Building Confidence through Laptops. *Computer Education.* 81, 10–14.

European Computer Driving License (EDCL). http://www.ecdl.nhs.uk. (accessed 11.01.2006).

Gilchrist, M. (1995) New Students of Nursing: Their attitudes towards using computers. Unpublished dissertation for MA in IT in Education, Reading University, UK.

Gilchrist, M. (2002) Supporting Basic Maths Skills for Nursing Students. *Impact, WebCT 2002 Conference,* Boston, USA.

Gilchrist, M. (2004) Internal Faculty Report. Faculty of Health and Social Care, UWE, Bristol.

Gunn, C., French, S., McLeod, H., McSporran, M. and Conole, G. (2002) Gender Issues in Computer-Supported Learning. *Association for Learning Technology Journal.* 10(1), 32–44.

Her Majesties Stationery Office (1995) Disability Discrimination Act 1995 (DDA) http://www.hmso.gov.uk/acts/acts1995/1995050.htm. (accessed 7.1.2004).

Her Majesties Stationery Office (2001) Special Educational Needs and Disability Act 2001 (SENDA). http://www.hmso.gov.uk/acts/acts2001/20010010.htm. (accessed 7.1.2004).

Herring, S. C. (1993) Gender and Democracy in Computer-Mediated Communication. *Electronic Journal of Communication.* 3(2), 1–17.

Hesse-Biber, S. and Gilbert, M. K. (1994) Closing the Technological Gender Gap: Feminist pedagogy in the computer-assisted classroom. *Teaching Sociology.* 22(1), 19–31.

Hills, H. (2003) *Individual Preferences in E-learning.* London: Gower.

Hughes, G. (2002) Gender Issues in Computer-Supported Learning: What We Can Learn from the Gender, Science and Technology Literature. *Association for Learning Technology Journal.* 10(2), 77–9.

Joint Information Systems Committee Plagiarism Advisory Service (JISCPAS) (2003) *JISC Plagiarism Advisory Service.* Available at http://www.jiscpas.ac.uk. (accessed 21.5.2004).

Joint Information Systems Committee (JISC) Portals project (2004) http://www.portal.ac.uk/spp/. (accessed 18.2.2004).

Kenny, A. (2002) Online Learning: Enhancing Nurse Education? *Journal of Advanced Nursing.* 38(2), 127–35.

Latchford, G. (2003) Computers and Midwives: The experiences of Midwives in the UK. Available at http://www.informatics.nhs.uk/download/557/mid_surv_rep.pdf. (accessed 18.2.2004).

Lee, I.-S. (2002) Gender Differences in Self-regulated On-line Learning Strategies within Korea's University Context. *Educational Technology Research and Development International Review.* 50(1), 101–11.

Luchetta, T. (2000) Gender Differences and Similarities among Children, Youth, and College Students Concerning Computer Attitudes and Use. Paper presented at *spring 2000 Wisconsin Association of Academic Librarians Conference.* Available at http://www.uwgb.edu/luchettt/waaltalk.htm. (accessed 1.6.2004).

McSporran, M. and Young, S. (2001) Does Gender Matter in Online Learning? *Association for Learning Technology Journal.* 9(2), 3–15.

National Health Service Information Authority (NHSIA) (2004) The impact of the European Computer Driving Licence (ECDL®) in the NHS. Available at http://www.ecdl.nhs.uk/pages/ECDL_highlights_booklet_v4.pdf. (accessed 1.6.2004).

National Health Service university (NHSu) (2004) E-learning discussion paper. Available at http://www.nhsu.nhs.uk/learning/elearning/getinvolved.html. (accessed 21.5.2004).

National Open College Network (NOCN) (2004) http://www.nocn.org.uk/ (accessed 21.5.2004).

Office for National Statistics (2004) www.statistics.org.uk. (accessed 6.5.2004), last updated April 2004.

Ordidge, I. (1997) IT's for Girls – or Is It? *Education and Training.* 39(1), 30–5.

Oxford, Cambridge and Royal Society of Arts (OCR) (2004) http://www.ocr.org.uk/OCR/WebSite/docroot/campaigns.jsp?oid=8591. (accessed 21.5.2004).

Pollard, K., Miers, M. and Gilchrist, M. (2004) Collaborative Learning for Collaborative Working? Initial Findings from a Longitudinal Study of Health and Social Care Students. *Health and Social Care in the Community.* 12(4), 346–58.

Qualification Curriculum Authority (QCA) (2004) ICT Key Skills. Available at http://www.qca.org.uk/qualifications/types/2791.html. (accessed 1.6.2004).

Richardson, H. and French, S. (2000) Education On-line: What's in It for Women?' *Women, Work and Computerization: Charting a Course to the Future.* Vancover BC: Kluwer Academic Publishers.

Royal College of Nursing (RCN) (2004) Royal College of Nursing Survey Shows Nurses Keen to Get Involved in Implementation of New Electronic Systems. Available at http://www.rcn.org.uk/news/display.php?ID=1093. (accessed 21.5.2004).

Sax, L. (2002) Science, Computers, and Gender Equity: Is there a Role for Single-Sex Education? Available at www.singlesexschools.org/computers.html. (accessed 6.05.2004).

Sinclair, M. and Gardner, J. (1999) Planning for Information Technology Key Skills in Nurse Education. *Journal of Advanced Nursing.* 30(6), 1441–50.

Techdis (2004) http://www.techdis.ac.uk/ (accessed 21.05.2004).

Technical Advisory Service for Images (TASI) 2004 Bristol Biomedical Image Archive Case Study. Available at http://www.tasi.ac.uk/resources/biomed.html. (accessed 21.5.2004).

Wajcman, J. (1991) *Feminism Confronts Technology.* UK: Polity Press.

Ward, R. (2002) Internet for Nursing, Midwifery and Health Visiting Tutorial – Virtual Training Suite. Available at http://www.vts.rdn.ac.uk/tutorial/nurse. (accessed 12.5.2004).

Washer, P. (2001) Barriers to the Use of Web-Based Learning in Nurse Education. *Nurse Education Today* 21, 455–60.

Watchfire Corporation (2002) Bobby. Available at http://bobby.watchfire.com/bobby/html/en/index.jsp. (accessed 12.5.2004).

Wishart, J. and Ward, R. (2002) Individual Differences in Nurse and Teacher Training Students' Attitudes Toward and Use of Information Technology. *Nurse Education Today*. 22, 231–40.

World Wide Web Consortium (W3C) (1994) Markup Validation Service. Available at http://validator.w3.org/ (accessed 12.5.2004).

Yates, S. J. (1997) Gender, Identity and CMC. *Journal of Computer Assisted Learning.* 13(4), 281–90.

7

Assessment and Evaluation

Nicola Eaton and Pam Moule

Introduction

It has been the vision of some educationalists since computer-aided learning (CAL) was first recognised that the computer could deliver much of their teaching material. In the late 1980s and 1990s many nurse lecturers set out to develop their own programs and started to market them (cf. Chapter 1). The early programs, for example by Open Software Learning, were limited by the authoring tools and the programming expertise available. Since then there has been a proliferation of teaching material and information available to students in a format that requires the use of a computer to access it. However, as in more traditional forms of teaching material delivery, the quality of the content needs to be evaluated before it is presented to students. This leads to the need for methods of evaluating teaching resources made available on the World Wide Web.

It is also necessary to assess or measure the student learning that has taken place after using the technology-mediated courseware. Assessment is said to shape learning and this is true of e-learning too. The usual theories of learning and teaching apply to e-learning and assessments in e-learning, as in classroom learning, need to reflect the goals of the course. When it comes to assessment of e-learning, the use of technology adds a few extra factors, to be considered at the design stage. Computers can be programmed to provide formative feedback at strategic stages in the learning process and can also deliver summative assessments at the end of a course. These assessments may involve the individual student attending an assessment centre or may be conducted online. One of the main problems with distance assessment is that it may be difficult to authenticate the person taking the assessment. Many e-learning courses involve assessing cognitive skills but programs to assess practical skills are limited. However, computer programs are increasingly being designed to carry out the assessment of more practical skills.

This chapter looks at the use of online Objective Structured Clinical Examinations (OSCEs) to assess students. The example reported draws on a radiography programme, however the technique is equally applicable to nursing courses. The evaluation of Web resources is discussed and a list of questions to ask when evaluating them is included. Examples of the different program evaluation methods are presented with reference to published studies in the field of online healthcare education.

Student assessment using OSCEs

Objective Structured Clinical Examinations have provided a vehicle for the assessment of practical clinical skills in health care professionals, giving a valid and reliable measure of knowledge and skill competency (Harden and Gleeson, 1979; Ali *et al.*, 1996). With their origins in medical education, OSCEs have been used as a method of measuring competence in clinical skills within contrived clinical settings, such as laboratories and clinical skills suites (Fahy and Lumby, 1988; Rose *et al.*, 1988). They facilitate the evaluation of a range of clinical skills, as well as giving scope to measure knowledge, attitudes, problem-solving and decision-making skills. Generated scenarios are presented at workstations, with visual presentation of realistic situations being paramount. Tests of clinical competence are divided into measurable components. In a nursing OSCE, the steps involved in carrying out a nursing assessment of a newly admitted patient might involve the observation and recording of blood pressure and pulse rate. This can be achieved by the use of role-play with real or simulated patients. An observer will usually employ a predetermined checklist to rate performance, although some workstations can be unmanned and students are required to record written answers.

The obvious benefits of OSCEs come from the assessment of clinical skills in a safe environment and the possibilities of developing a range of scoring tools that can measure a range of skills. The drawbacks of use within professions such as nursing relate to logistical issues seen in attempting to manage the testing of large groups of students in a short assessment timeframe. Their resource intensive nature has proven problematic for a range of health professions, prompting radiography staff in a west of England university to develop electronic or e-OSCEs.

The development of e-OSCEs

The OSCE is used extensively in the assessment of undergraduate and postgraduate radiography students, such as trauma radiography, testing the student's ability to assess and report on medical images. Previous use of OSCEs in diagnostic imaging was limited to reported accounts from Robert Gordon University (1998), although wider use is confirmed on other University web-sites. These reports however, refer to OSCEs rather than e-OSCEs, which are in their infancy, with publication evidence limited to this development (see Parlarm *et al.*, 2003).

The use of e-OSCEs was developed as part of a six-month action research project involving three lecturers and 33 students studying either diagnostic radiography or medical ultrasound as a post-qualifying programme. Following ethical research principles, data collection drew on a range of data including diaries, observations, interviews and student evaluation forms.

The design of the software was cognisant of the University's information technology (IT) hardware and software provision and aimed to maintain security in delivery, using Web-authoring software recognised for its flexible and real-time use (Griffiths and Guffogg, 2002). The text software interface used was hypertext mark-up language (html). Both images and text were presented at the same time in paper format, allowing students to see all the information concurrently. The Web environment also allowed students, who were familiar with the Web-browser used, to navigate easily through the assessment, moving between questions and images. The images were anonymised and presented in electronic format on a CD-ROM to prevent the problems of online use, where server downtime can be an issue, especially with increased usage (Bradley and Oliver, 2002).

Students were positioned in the examination room, a multimedia suite, to comply with examination conditions, which included consideration of the distancing of students to avoid possible collusion. Lighting and monitor settings were standardised and students were able to adjust their local environment for maximum comfort. A mouse was employed for navigation, again reducing the risk of collusion. Students were introduced to the assessment environment with a familiarisation session prior to the commencement of the e-OSCE. Answers were collated in paper format during the research project.

Student feedback

Despite initial reported anxiety, students' comments were favourable. They found navigation easy, helped by the initial introduction and they suggested that typed answers might be considered in the future. The quality of presentation of some images needed further development, though it was interesting that the group were seen to spend less time viewing images than those students using a paper-based approach. Some found the lighting was poor, a problem remedied by issuing desk lamps. The integration of a visual display unit (VDU) break conformed to computer user regulations (Health and Safety Executive, 1992), giving 10 minutes break each hour when the room lights were switched on. The overall conclusions recommended the use of e-OSCEs as an effective approach to assessment of certain clinical skills within radiography programmes.

Further development of e-OSCEs

Given the positive evaluation of the e-OSCEs received from radiotherapy students, there is potential to develop this mode of assessment for a range of healthcare students and professionals. Particular consideration is given to nursing students, where the pre-registration curriculum demands competency in a range of skills both on completion of the first year and on completion of the programmes (UKCC, 1999). There is also scope to develop e-OSCEs in testing the development of a number of skills present in post-qualifying programmes.

The facilitation of e-OSCEs will require access to appropriate testing environments, such as computer centres, organised to meet local examination regulations and conditions. Given the student feedback received regarding the provision of adequate lighting, the supply of desk lamps might be given consideration. The employment of mouse navigation should reduce possible collusion. Additionally, any changes to assessment formats will need acceptance through local examination committees and may require external examiner approval.

Possible areas for e-OSCE development are vast. Examples within nursing might include the assessment of drug calculations, infection control measures and electrocardiogram interpretations.

The developers of assessment materials will need to consider both technical and presentation as well as user issues:

Technical and presentation issues

- Technical specifications required for the development
- Colour presentation within the screens
- Amount of material presented on each screen
- How to manage the presentation of text and images on one screen
- Quality of images presented
- The development of a bank of questions that could be randomly accessed
- Security of provision of the examination papers and recorded results
- Development of online marking

User issues

- Introducing students to the e-OSCE environment
- Ease of navigation on the site
- Enabling students to see a clock on or off screen
- Mobility around the test, allowing students to move forwards and backwards through the test
- Building in VDU breaks to the examination

Evaluation

For the purposes of this chapter evaluation is seen as judging the value of a programme against a set of criteria. It can measure how it meets those criteria, of satisfaction with the programme, as well as student perceptions of learning.

Evaluation of educational programmes is an essential part of the teaching-learning process. There is a need to identify effective and efficient ways of evaluating programmes (Nestel, 2002), although it is recommended that the evaluation methods of each programme depend upon its stated purpose. Somekh (2001) argues that evaluation is an essential and integral part of all innovative programmes. Communications and information technology programmes are particularly difficult to evaluate but unless we do this we cannot learn from the mistakes or successes of each.

Evaluation involves judging the value of what has been achieved. Somekh (2001) suggests that there are four reasons for evaluation, the main one being for educative reasons which can be summative or formative. Evaluations are conducted to establish what has gone well and what has not, in order to learn from this. Summative evaluations focus on the future, drawing conclusions from the use of a programme to facilitate the development of further programmes. Formative educative evaluations may be carried out whilst a programme is current. Their primary focus then is on improving the programme whilst it is in use.

There are broadly two types of questions which may be the focus of evaluation. First, questions that seek factual information and ask questions of how much, how many, how quickly, are called quantitative or hard data. Second, qualitative questions may be asked, either simultaneously or as an alternative. These seek reasons and explanations and ask how and why, and are usually labelled soft data. Evaluators prefer to use a mixture of these two types of data, so called mixed methods, to provide reliable information and robust explanatory theories.

Evaluating programmes on the Web

The World Wide Web includes many examples of teaching/learning materials. Levesque and Kelly (2002) when discussing the value of using e-learning for radiologists and technologists for CPD recommended that an online course site should consider the design elements, such as friendly format that facilitates easy navigation. They list other helpful features as bookmarking to allow the student to return to the last page studied, visualisation (of x-rays) technologies and feedback. Presented below is a list of suggested questions to ask when ascertaining the value of these programmes.

1. Is the author identified? It should be evident who is the author of Web-based material. If they are identified are they qualified/experienced in this field? It is possible to do an Internet search on the name to check on expertise. Is contact information supplied? If an address or phone number is supplied a prospective user can easily get further information.

2. Who is the publishing body or server – this can help determine the authenticity of the information? Is it produced by a charitable body, a government agency or a profit-making (commercial) company?

A university or institution Web-site is likely to be a more reliable objective source than a commercial company web-site.

3. Who is sponsoring the site? Is the site approved by the organisation to which it is linked? It is possible to have a page on the parent site which is not officially sponsored by that organisation, for instance, as university. A personal home page at a university's server does not automatically confer reliability.

4. How up to date or recent is the program? It should be possible to identify when it was created and whether it has been updated and maintained. Outdated information and broken links may indicate that the page is not being maintained.

5. What is the scope of the program? Does it present information in a creative, useful way or just rehash information presented elsewhere?

6. How accurate and objective is the program? Can the facts presented be substantiated elsewhere to guard against bias? Web-sites may have an agenda or point of view they are portraying, which may affect the way the information is presented.

7. Are there footnotes and bibliographies? These can support a document's credibility, the depth of scholarship and authority.

8. Is there evidence of outside review? Has the site been rated by one of the Internet rating groups? Sites awarded ratings are quick to display them. A potential user should be aware of the criteria used by Internet ratings groups.

9. Consider the design. Is the site well organised and easy to navigate around? Look for an overall design that makes it easy to find information or search the site.

(Adapted from Columbia University Web-site)

Evaluation of e-learning

Within the literature there are many reports on the use of e-learning and how programs are evaluated and student learning assessed. Examples presented below are drawn from the health sciences looking at the issues involved in evaluating software and assessing student learning.

Course evaluation tools are usually developed by the course designers to reflect the purpose, design and subject content of each program and often cannot be compared as they are developed for different reasons. Milstead and Nelson (1998) describe the issues around the development and management of the first completely online doctoral programme in nursing. Learning was evaluated by traditional methods using qualitative and quantitative tools, with the stated aim of making administrative decisions about the course.

In the published literature reporting the use and evaluation of e-learning, some researchers compare traditional teaching/learning method of face-to-face classroom learning delivery with computer delivery of the same or similar material (Roesch *et al.*, 2003; Rose *et al.*, 2000). Some use a mixture of both face-to-face and online methods (Kowlowski, 2002). Rose *et al.* (2000) reported on the comparison of two methods of course delivery. They implemented and evaluated an online epidemiology course for graduate nursing students and compared it with a classroom-taught module which ran concurrently. Evaluation approaches compared the results of the two methods of delivery through the use of objective measures such as exam scores and subjective ratings by students.

Roesch *et al.* (2003) also designed their own evaluation questionnaires. They reported on the evaluation of a dermatology CAL programme designed for medical students. The program, called 'Dermatology 2000,' and was an interactive multimedia program, developed and integrated into the medical education program at five German medical schools. The evaluation used two online questionnaires, which showed high learner acceptance of the program's instructional design, the ergonomics and the didactic presentation style. Looking at the learning objective, users outperformed non-users of the program and also showed a ten per cent lower rate of errors in a conventional knowledge test. Case studies demonstrated the increased ability of the participating students to apply the acquired knowledge to diagnostic problems. The authors conclude that the use of CAL can contribute to a medical education programme, and is well accepted and suitable to provide both theoretical biomedical knowledge and clinical skills. An additional benefit noted in the evaluation suggested that after completion of the programme the students demonstrated an increased interest in medical education software.

In the use of distance learning programmes evaluation issues may be even more difficult. Watt *et al.* (2002) describe an electronic course survey system designed to evaluate a distance learning programme in management. Distance education makes conventional evaluation slow and expensive. To overcome such difficulties they designed an automated process based on a Web survey system, which allowed performance indicators and complex analyses to be embedded in high quality word-processed reports generated quickly after each module was run.

Most researchers in the field of e-learning rely heavily on student satisfaction questionnaires. Devlin and James (2003) report that the most common form of student evaluation of technology-mediated learning projects in Australia in the mid-1990s was the student satisfaction questionnaire (Alexander and McKenzie, 1998). That was still the case in 2003 when satisfaction ratings were still high (Devlin and James, 2003). But student satisfaction surveys may not tell us whether the student learning has changed or improved due to the teaching being mediated through the computer. There is also an element of confusion between student learning and student satisfaction. To this end Devlin and James (2003) developed an attitude and experience questionnaire. This considered the student's perception of their expectation and the reality of their learning experience. They used a quasi-experimental methodology and compared students who had had high and normal levels of exposure to technology-mediated learning. Over 70 per cent of students encountered multimedia learning at some point in their first undergraduate year. The targeted group rated the usefulness of the learning tool (the technology used to teach) as high. This group also reported a more positive attitude to multimedia and related technologies. The responses of the targeted group highlight the impact on student learning of well-designed and well-integrated applications. They suggest that more exposure to technology leads to a greater feeling of belonging to a learning community and a stronger belief that courses are intellectually stimulating.

The evaluation methods described above are mainly quantitative using questionnaires to elicit knowledge gains or satisfaction. Other evaluation approaches include more qualitative methods. Black *et al.* (2003) describe the design, development and evaluation of an online module for health promotion developed for use with community pharmacists. They used a qualitative phenomenological approach to explore learners' experiences of a new module, their perceptions of the delivery system and its usability. They also considered their experiences of studying and learning using asynchronous computer-mediated communication. The results indicated that the use of online modules does improve the quality of student learning.

Kowlowski (2002) reports on a conversion from registered nurse to Bachelor of Nursing course, which uses both face-to-face and online modes. Evaluation of the course used a computer administered qualitative questionnaire, a focus group and a Likert style course evaluation.

Nestel (2002) also used a focus group approach to evaluation and compared it to a written evaluation format in relation to time, quality and nature of feedback from participants. The focus group needed less time from students and staff and yielded useful and specific information about the module development. However, Nestel (2002) also reports that the students' evaluations of the modules were more positive when in written format.

The literature presented has considered the different methods of programme evaluation and student assessment of e-learning using both qualitative subjective and quantitative objective measures. Examples of the different methods used include focus groups (Kowlowski, 2002; Nestel, 2002), student satisfaction questionnaires (Alexander and McKenzie, 1998), examination scores (Rose *et al.*, 2000), a qualitative phenomenological approach (Black *et al.*, 2003), a computer generated qualitative questionnaire (Kowlowski, 2002), and a Likert scale course evaluation (Kowlowski, 2002).

A further issue reported in the literature is that of peer support and communication with peers and tutors when learning online. Spallek *et al.* (2002) looking at online dental education reported on participants' experiences. Results showed that online courses partly met the student's knowledge needs but suggested that students missed face-to-face communication with peers and instructors. Interestingly, Kowlowski (2002), presents contrasting findings when describing her course, which used both face-to-face and online modes. Her students commented on the sense of community and peer support they received, which might well have developed as a result of the face-to-face component.

Sims *et al.* (2002) argue that the main outcome of any teaching programme, achievement on the part of the student, is still the main priority when using online teaching. This may be done using one or a number of different evaluation methods. They suggest evaluation is usually performed at the end of the development process citing two reasons for this. First, to assess whether the creative effort achieved the original product goals and second, to measure whether learning outcomes are realised. However, Sims *et al.* (2002) propose an addition to the post development evaluation, a proactive evaluation framework. This identifies critical online learning factors, and influences, for example, content, learning design, interface design, interactivity, assessment, student support, content utility and outcomes, which will support the planning, design and development of learning resources. This framework includes the same stages used in formative assessment.

Conclusion

This chapter has given a brief overview of the potential for the use of evaluation and assessment in online learning for healthcare professionals. The use of computer-mediated assessments means that in the future examinations may become less rigid in terms of development and presentation, and different skills, attitude and behaviours could be assessed in a variety of ways. The necessity to evaluate e-learning programmes increases as they become more sophisticated and diverse. However, the research literature seems to suggest that there are many ways of evaluating programmes, which are related to the objectives of the programmes and that demonstrate learning on the part of the students using them. In the future it may be that students will be able to take all their courses and assessments online at a time and place suitable to them, get immediate feedback and accreditation all through the medium of the World Wide Web.

References

The authors acknowledge the intellectual contributions of Marc Griffiths, former Senior Lecturer in Radiography, University of the West of England, in the early development of this chapter.

Alexander, S. and McKenzie, J. (1998) *An Evaluation of Information Technology Projects for University Learning.* Canberra, Australian Government Publishing Service (Cited in Devlin and James op cit).

Ali, J., Cohen, R. and Adam, R. (1996) Teaching Effectiveness of the ATLS Program as Demonstrated by Objective Structured Clinical Examination for Practising Physicians. *World Journal of Surgery.* 20, 1121–6.

Black, P. E., Misson, J. and Bracegirdle, L. (2003) The Formative Developmental Evaluation of an Online Module in Health Promotion Using Asynchronous Computer-Mediated Communication. *Pharmacy Education.* 3(3), 195–204.

Bradley, C. and Oliver, M. (2002) E-Learning Courses for Work-Based Learning. Presented at World Wide Web Conference. Available at http://www.2002.org/CDROM/alternate/703 (accessed 14.12.2002).

Columbia University. www.columbia.edu/cu/lweb/indiv/under/eval.html (accessed 04.03.2004).

Devlin, M. and James, R. (2003) The Potential of a Methodology for University-Wide Multimedia and Educational Technology Evaluation. *Assessment and Evaluation in Higher Education.* 28(1), 47–58.

Fahy, K. and Lumby, J. (1988) Critical Assessment In A College Program. *The Australian Journal of Advanced Nursing.* 5(4), 5–9.

Griffiths, M. and Guffogg, J. (2002) Continuing Professional Development: Giving Electronic Presentations. *Synergy*. April, 10–13.

Harden, R. and Gleeson, F. (1979) Assessment of Clinical Competence Using Objective Structured Clinical Examination (OSCE). *Medical Education*. 13, 41–9.

Health and Safety Executive (1992) *The Health and Safety (Display Screen Equipment) Regulations*. London: Health and Safety Executive. Available http://www.hse.gov.uk/pubns/index.htm (accessed 11.04.2004).

Kozlowski, D. (2002) Using Online Learning in a Traditional Face-To-Face Environment. *Computers in Nursing*. 20(1), 23–30.

Levesque, D. R. and Kelly, G. (2002) Meeting the Challenge of Continuing Education with E-Learning. *Radiology Management*. 24(2), 40–3.

Milstead, J. A. and Nelson, R. (1998) Preparation for an Online Asynchronous University Doctoral Course: Lessons Learned. *Computers in Nursing*. 16(5), 247–58.

Nestel, D. (2002) Development of an Evaluation Model for an Introductory Module on Social Medicine. *Assessment and Evaluation in Higher Education*. 27(4), 301–8.

Parlarm, T., Griffiths, M. and Phillips, R. (2003) The Design, Implementation and Evaluation of Electronic Objective Structured Clinical Examinations in Diagnostic Imaging: An 'Action Research' Strategy. *Journal of Diagnostic Radiography and Imaging*. 5, 1–9.

Robert Gordon University Anon (1998) Postgraduate Certificate, Diploma and MSc in Medical Ultrasound Assessment Procedures. Available at http://w3.abdn.ac.uk/pgultrasound/info/assessme/procedu.htm (accessed 11.04.2004).

Roesch, A., Gruber, H., Hawelka, B., Hamm, H., Arnold, N., Popal, H., Segerer, J., Landthaler, M. and Stolz, W. (2003) Computer Assisted Learning in Medicine: A Long Term Evaluation of the 'Practical Training Programme Dermatology 2000'. *Medical Informatics and the Internet in Medicine*, 28, 147–59.

Rose, M., Carroll, G., Knight, J., Chamberlain, M., Fothergill-Bourbonnais, F. and Linton, J. (1988) Using the OSCE to Measure Clinical Skills Performance in Nursing. *Journal of Advanced Nursing*. 13(1), 45–46.

Rose, M., Frisby, A. J. Hamlin, M. D. and Jones, S. S. (2000) Evaluation of the Effectiveness of a Web-Based Graduate Epidemiology Course. *Computers in Nursing*. 18(4), 162–7.

Sims, R., Dobbs, G. and Hand, T. (2002) Enhancing Quality in Online Learning: Scaffolding Planning and Design Through Proactive Evaluation. *Distance Education*. 23(2), 135–48.

Somekh, B. (2001) The Role of Evaluation in Ensuring Excellence in Communications and Information Technology Initiatives. *Education, Communication and Information*, 1, 75–101.

Spallek, H., Pilcher, E., Lee, J. Y. and Schleyer, T. (2002) Evaluation of a Web-Based Dental CE Courses. *Journal of Dental Education*. 66(3), 393–404.

United Kingdom Central Council (1999) *Fitness for Practice: The UKCC Commission for Education (Peach Report)*. London: UKCC.

Watt, S., Simpson, C., McKillop, C. and Nunn, V. (2002) Electronic Course Surveys: Does Automating Feedback and Reporting Give Better Results? *Assessment and Evaluation in Higher Education*. 27(4), 325–33.

8

E-learning in Nursing Education: Incremental Not Revolutionary Change?

Sally Glen

Revolutionary change: Incremental development?

Whatever the emerging shape of the nursing education system, it will be profoundly affected by changes in educational technology such as interactive video, the internet, CD ROM and virtual reality technology.

Many of today's computer-based educational programmes employ all of the features of video games. They are colourful and fast paced, they include animation and sound. The designer's goal is to catch the students' attention and keep it focused. These programmes continue to require reading but do not rely exclusively on the learner's reading skills (cf. Chapters 1 and 6). Narrators read the text presented on a screen that includes a variety of visuals – graphs, animation, video demonstrations or photographs. However, the new technology's impact may be more incremental than the pioneers expected. E-learning is not an all or nothing activity.

Stylistically vibrant: Educationally shallow?

Subjects have thus been brought to life by distance learning and research methods have been transformed. Even the more mundane process of communication between lecturer and students has improved. Indeed, millions of words have been written about the technology and its potential, but not much about what the lecturers and learners do online (cf. Chapter 2). The tendency is for computer interactives to be stylistically vibrant but educationally shallow. Web pages may be crammed with text, visual images, links and interactives which may be visually stimulating, but not necessarily educational. E-learning should offer interactive education but this must go deeper than just clicking from one link to another, and it does not necessarily follow that teaching computer skills includes teaching thinking skills.

Billings *et al.* (2001) considered the technology/pedagogy divide in their discussion of best practices in web-based nursing programmes. These authors warned against letting technology over-ride pedagogical goals and emphasised that even the most futuristic and exciting technology does not automatically improve the learning process (cf. Chapter 2). They argued that technology trends should be a learning vision pull, rather than a technology push. Fetherston (2001) clarified this technology/pedagogy debate in proposing that pedagogical challenges are not unique to the web-based learning environment and have been discussed in higher education for a long time. Downing (2001) argued that emphasis must be placed on sound pedagogical design rather than the technology itself. He identified the challenges as building on existing practices rather than replacing them, and using the new technologies to best effect.

The enormous commercial influence in the field of online teaching and learning also means that large e-learning corporations tend to be the driving force in the development of this new educational methodology. But the technology should not transform teachers into technical trainers and technical support staff. Instead, it should help lecturers to create teaching and learning environments, to mediate between knowledge and the student and to become open and critical professionals (Trench, 2001). There is evidence from nursing research that research on online teaching reveals a lack of theoretical focus (De Castell *et al.*, 2002; Thurmond, 2002; Phipps and Merisotis, 1999). Phipps and Merisotis (1999) commented that theoretical frameworks are rarely referred to in research on distance learning in higher education.

> The consequences of educators' (in particular educational theorists) failures to seriously engage with educational questions about technology have had a

devastating impact on both research and practice in the domain of education technology. (De Castell *et al.*, 2002)

Thurmond (2002) proposed that theoretic frameworks are necessary to assess the quality of Web-based courses. One pattern was an extensive discussion of a theoretical framework, without commenting on how the theory was tested in research. The other pattern involved reporting on research conducted on, without explaining the theoretical discussions that exist in distance teaching, online teaching and nurse education literature that may seem to omit or neglect traditional framework and curriculum discussions. Constructivism provides a solid theoretical framework from which to expand the internet-based pedagogical approach among those whose interest is the promotion of learning (Twomey, 2004). There are many examples of traditional education theory which can inform the development of internet-based education. Constructivism seems to be accepted as a suitable theoretical framework for designing and delivering Web-based courses. Gold (2001) wrote about constructivist instruction in online education and particularly outlined the shift from objectivist to constructivist theories of education (cf. Chapter 2).

Constructivism, is a theory of learning, which in its purest form, assumes that the learner builds up their meanings and understanding of a topic and that they discover the basic principles for themselves (Shunk, 2000). The teacher, rather than being the expert, becomes a facilitator of the learning. The teaching and learning experience is structured so that it supports and develops the process of learning. The teaching and learning experience is structured so that it supports and develops the process of learning. Constructivism can be an appropriate theory to promote an understanding of the educational needs of registered nurses. The extent of their nursing experiences enables them to construct meanings from new knowledge that they are exposed to (Twomey, 2004).

Hopper and Harman (2000) expected to find constructivist teaching philosophies in their analysis of exemplary Internet programmes but they found more evidence of positivism. These systems seemed to be designed to facilitate traditional instructive pedagogies rather than encouraging constructivist learning and instruction. Two learning management systems that they identified were 'Web CT' and 'Blackboard'. However, it must be acknowledged that they selected a very small sample of Internet programmes from discussion made by participants in online discussion fora.

Miller and Miller (1999) in their in-depth theoretical analysis, present cognitive processing and cognitive constructivist paradigms as well as relevant teaching and communicative strategies for each in the web-based learning environment. They proposed a constructivist, collaborative, problem-solving, learner-centred approach where learners articulate, discuss, reflect and revise their thinking to ensure accuracy and knowledge construction. Downing (2001) also believed that constructivist learning should be the base for internet-based teaching in healthcare to promote access to learning opportunities. A constructivist approach to education may be seen as the best way forward utilising a range of teaching methods including face-to-face teaching to develop individual curricula (DH, 2003, cf. Chapter 2). Information Technology alone will not create an effective learning environment; however, by utilising a variety of teaching methods deeper learning can be achieved and 75 per cent more knowledge is retained if the student can see, hear and participate in their own learning (Richards, 2001). This may be especially true to student nurses who may well develop cognitive skills from an online learning environment, but will also need to develop psychomotor skills which may be hard to achieve purely online. However, by using a virtual environment with the use of simulation the psychomotor experience could be practised and reviewed over and over again (Simpson, 2003).

Self-paced learning or increased surveillance?

Concerns have been raised about the use of new technology in nurse education. It is possible that new forms of computer-based learning and teaching carry with them the possibility of new kinds of 'panoptic' surveillance and control of students. Within education settings, as in society generally, electronic surveillance of students is increasing. Electronic systems of recording attendance are being used in schools and colleges in response to the problem of absenteeism (Barwuah and Walkley, 1997). Electronic searches of the websites accessed by student users are routinely carried out by system administrators in order to identify whether any 'inappropriate' sites have been accessed. Tracking and monitoring tools are built into electronic course management packages. For example, the 'Tract Students' option in the course management package, WebCT, provides detailed information including: the first time the student accessed the course, the last time the student accessed the course, the number of times the student accessed a home page, tool page and content module page, and the number of articles the student accessed and posted in the discussions. This electronic tracking data provides important feedback for formative evaluation and course development.

The 'acceptable' level of electronic surveillance is difficult to define and will depend on the underpinning philosophy of a course and course team members, but crucial questions are: who is benefiting from the surveillance and with who is the primary locus of control? How are students who deviate from the required standard dealt with – a concept that Boshier and Wilson (1998) describe as 'surveillance and discipline', and from an ethical stand point, are the students fully informed and aware of the level of monitoring that they are being subjected to? (Epliny *et al.*, 2003). Therefore, the 'surveillance-capable' nature of these technologies may mean that they are used in ways which are inimical to the underpinning philosophies of education in general and nurse education in particular. It may be that their use can, in certain circumstances, be justified. However, what perhaps is more concerning is that they will slip into use, unnoticed and undebated.

Private sector partnerships

Universities may need to join together to run online modules and provide a 24-hour student support (cf. Chapter 1). A number of the major American research led universities such as V. C. Berkely, Michigan and Columbia have linked up with major 'knowledge providers' in the private sector, such as 'Time Warner', 'Disney Corporation' and 'Microsoft', to form partnerships which develop the appropriate course work and the support needed to attach the global market in higher education in the twenty-first century. More globally, publishing houses are assuming an increasingly dominant role in delivering borderless higher education.

At a conference entitled 'The Future of Higher Education', Alan Nelson (2002), former Chief Executive Officer of Thompson Learning UK/Europe, asked the question – what is the role of universities in borderless education? While the universities provide most of the academic expertise – and crucially the 'branding' necessary for market credibility – the partners provide production facilities, distribution and marketing, as well as much of the underlying technology in order for the operation to proceed on a truly global basis. The universities have access to the necessary large amounts of funding needed to invest in the development and maintenance of course work; while the private sector partners having access to the quality control procedures, accreditation and status to some of the most prestigious universities (see http://www.gua.com) continuously strive to maintain a high quality service by

- assisting students in selecting their programmes
- guaranteeing a secure and reliable access to chosen programmes of study
- assuming up to date and most effective technology for the delivery of programmes
- guaranteeing technical support throughout the duration of the programme

Educational research

The incorporation of computer-based technologies into educational practices has increased tremendously in the past decade. Not surprisingly, research into the uses of new technologies has failed to keep pace. Research carried out by educators involved in Web-based teaching for nurses, is mostly based in Canada, Australia and America. The research on Internet-based teaching is quite diverse and generally in the form of case studies, descriptive research and evaluation research. Some examples from nurse education literature included the comparison of online teaching to face-to-face teaching (Cravener, 1999), the use of benchmark for best practice (Billings *et al.*, 2001), preferences for Distance Education delivery methods (Cragg *et al.*, 2003) peer review of teaching (Cobb *et al.*, 2001) and evaluation of distance education delivery methods (Androsysyn *et al.*, 1999). Delivery of distance education was one of the only clear themes that was evident in the literature in Internet-based teaching for nurses.

Fortunately, much of what we are learning from research that is not specifically interested in computer-based applications can also inform their use. Specific questions to start asking include the following: How does the use of tools such as objectives and self-check questions relate to students beliefs about learning and self-discipline skills? How is participation in an online discussion impacted? How does the choice of paths through the content relate to students' beliefs and skills? For example, are students with self-discipline skills likely to progress through the content in a more systematic fashion? As e-learning becomes commonplace in the nursing education system, an understanding of these relationships becomes increasingly vital (Hartley and Bendixen, 2001).

Conclusion

The concept of education is changing as we move from the paradigm of lectures as communicator of information to students learning through discovery and the new media. Traditional approaches to learning are linear, and computers potentially can free people from this linear way of thinking (Tapscott, 1998). Information technology facilitates access to information which is more interactive and nonsequential and has been portrayed as a means of enabling practitioners and lecturers to meet the need for lifelong learning and professional updating without taking time out of their busy working schedules. Consequently, there has been a surge of activity to provide this type of education. Often the development has occurred at a rapid pace and with little attention paid to the nature of e-learning and its implications for nursing education.

The lecturer's role is still critical, but changing to structure the learning experience, motivate, provide context and integrate disciplines (Dertouzos, 1997; Johnson, 1997; Tapscott, 1998). There is a shift away from traditional pedagogy to the creation of learning partnerships and learning cultures. Pedagogy has to do with optimising the transmission of information (Johnson, 1997; Negroponte, 1995; Tapscott, 1998). However, not every student can benefit from e-learning programmes.

Finally, there is a need to generate a knowledge-base about e-learning that can inform the development of e-learning programmes. There is a need for more research into learner characteristics and their implications for the use of computer-based technologies such as the Web. Such a knowledge-base will also facilitate a greater understanding of the process of adjustment that lecturers and students experience in e-learning. There is no doubt lecturers are catching up on what technology offers, but not challenging it (Salmon, 2001).

References

Anderson, T., Rourke, K., Garrison, D. R. and Archer, W. (2001) Assessing Teaching Presence in a Computer Conferencing Context. *Journal of Asynchronous Learning Networks.* 5(2): 9–14.

Andrusyszyn, M. A., van Soeren, M., Laschinger, H. K. S., Goldenberg, D. and DiCrnso, A. (1999) Evaluation of Distance Delivery Methods for a Primary Care Nurse Practitioner Program. *Journal of Distance Education.* 14(1), 14–33.

Barwuah, A. and Walkley, P. (1997) Monitoring Student Attendance. Further Education Development Agency Paper, FE Matters, 1, No. 6.

132 Sally Glen

Billings, D. M., Connors, H. R. and Skiba, D. J. (2001) Benchmarking Best Practice in Web-Based Nursing Courses. *Advances in Nursing Science.* 23(3), 41–2.

Boshier, R. and Wilson, M. (1998) Panoptic Variations: Surveillance and Discipline in Web Courses. In Proceedings of *The Adult Education Research Conference.* University of British Columbia, Vancouver available at http://www.edst.educ.ubc.ca/aerc/1998/98boshier.htm

Cobb, K. J., Billings, D. M., Mays, R. M. and Canty-Mitchell, J. (2001) Peer Review of Teaching in Web-Based Courses in Nursing. *Nurse Educator.* 26(6), 274–9.

Cragg, C. E., Edwards, N., Zhao, Y. Song, L. X. and Zou, D. H. (1999) Integrating Web-Based Technologyu into Distance Education for Nurses in China. *Computers, Informatics, Nursing.* 21(3), 265–74.

Cravener, P. A. (1999) Faculty Experiences With Providing Online Courses: Thorns Among Roses. *Computers in Nursing.* 17(1), 42–7.

De Castell, S., Bryson, M. and Jenson, J. (2002) Object Lessons: Towards an Educational Theory of Technology. *First Monday.* 7(1), 2–5.

Department of Health (2003) *Delivering 21st Century IT for the NHS: National Patient Record Analysis Service. Strategic Outline Case.* London: HMSO.

Dertouzos, M. (1997) *What Will Be: How The New World of Information Will Change our Lives.* San Francisco: Harper Collins.

Downing, K. (2001) Information Technology Education and Healthcare Constructivism in the 21st Century. *Education Studies.* 27(3), 19–23.

Epling, M., Timmus, S. and Wharrad, H. (2003) An Educational Panopticon? New Technology, Nurse Education and Surveillance. *Nurse Education Today* (2003) 23, 412–18.

Fetherston. T. (2001) Pedagogical Challenges for The World Wide Web. *Education Technology Review.* 9(1), 6–10.

Gold, S., (2001) A Constuctivist Approach to Online Training for Online Teachers. *Journal of Asynchrononouos Learning Networks.* 5(1), 12–16.

Hartley, K. and Bendixen, L. (2001) Educational Research in the Internet Age. *Educational Researcher,* December 2001, 22–6.

Hopper, K. B. and Harman, S. W. (2000) A Multiple Case Study of Exemplary Internet Courses. *Education at a Distance.* 14(9), 22–8.

Johnson, R. (1997) Distance-learning: Medium or Message? *Journal of Further and Higher Education.* 21(1), 107–22.

Miller, S. M. and Miller, K. L. (1999) Using Instructional Theory to Facilitate Communication in Web-Based Courses. *Educational Technology and Society.* 4(3), 18–24.

Negroponte, N. (1995) *Being Digital.* New York: Random House.

Nelson, A. (2002) The Roles of Publishing Houses in Borderless Higher Education. Unpublished paper presented at *The Future of Higher Education Conference,* QEII Conference Centre, London, 14 June 2002.

Phipps, R. and Merisotis, J. (1999) *What's The Difference? A Review of Contemporary Research on The Effectiveness of Distance Learning in Higher Education.* Washington DC: The Institute for Higher Education Policy.

Richards, J. A. (2001) Nursing in a Digital Age. *Dermatology Nursing,* October 2001, 3, (5) 365–70.

Shunk, D. H. (2000) *Learning Theories: An Educational Perspective,* Third edition, New Jersey: Merrill.

Simpson, R. (2003) Welcome to the Virtual Classroom. How Technology is Transforming Nursing Education in the 21st Century. *Nursing Administration Quarterly.*

Tapscott, D. (1998) *Growing up Digital.* New York: McGraw-Hill.

Thurmond, V. A. (2002) Considering Theory in Assessing the Quality of Web-Based Courses. *Nurse Educator,* 27(1), 6–10.

Trench, B. (2001) Computers in Schools: A Level Playing Field. In O'Fathaigh. M (ed.), *Education and the Information of Age: Current Progress and Future Strategies.* Conference Papers, Cork: Bradshaw Books.

Twomey, A. (2004) Web-Based Teaching in Nursing: Lessons from the Literature. *Nurse Education.* 24, 452–8.

Index